The Rough (

Tokyo

written and researched by

Jan Dodd and Simon Richmond

with additional contributions by

Mark Sariban

ROUGH GUIDES

NEW YORK • LONDON • DELHI

www.roughguides.com

△ Neon signs, Shinjuku

Introduction to
Tokyo

Perplexing and beguiling, Tokyo is a city that confounds simple translation. Gaudily hung about with eyeball-searing neon and messy overhead cables, plagued by seemingly incessant noise and often clogged with bumper-to-bumper traffic, this concrete-and-steel sardine can is home to at least eight million people and can often seem like the stereotypical urban nightmare.

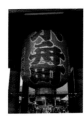

Yet step back from the frenetic main roads and chances are you'll find yourself in a world of tranquil backstreets, where wooden houses are fronted by neatly clipped bonsai trees; wander beyond the high-tech emporia, and you'll discover temples and shrines where the trappings of contemporary Japan dissolve in wisps of smoking incense. Although Tokyo has been frequently razed to the ground during its six-hundred-year history and much of what you see has been rebuilt, often several times over, this is still a city which is fiercely proud of its traditions and heritage. Lively neighbourhood festivals are held virtually every day of the year, people regularly visit their local shrine or temple and scrupulously observe the passing seasons. And at the centre of it all lies the mysterious Imperial Palace – the inviolate home of the emperor and a tangible link to the past.

The paradoxes don't stop there. Tokyo's centuries-long experience of organizing itself to cope with the daily demands of millions of inhabitants has made it something of a modern-day utopia. Trains run on time and to practically every corner of the city, crime is hardly worth worrying about, and shops and vending machines provide everything you could need (and many things you never thought you did) 24 hours a day. This is impressive enough, but, as if to constantly challenge itself, like some cartoon creature from a manga, Tokyo keeps on changing. Buildings go up one day, only to

Pachinko

Could one in four Japanese be wrong? Throughout the country a staggering ¥26.3 trillion is spent each year on pachinko, a pinball game that is one of Japan's top pastimes – and also one of its major industries. Tokyo has thousands of pachinko parlours – they're easy to spot since they look like mini Las Vegas casinos on steroids, all flashing lights and big neon signs. Inside, the atmosphere is no less in-your-face. The noise of thousands of steel balls clattering through the upright electronic bagatelles is deafening, and rows of players sit mesmerized as they control the speed with which balls fall through the machine – though the game requires only limited skill and a fair amount of luck. The aim is to make the balls drop into the right holes so that more balls can be won. These are traded in for prizes such as cigarette lighters and calculators, and although it's illegal for the parlours to pay out cash, there's always a cubbyhole close by where prizes can be exchanged for money, a charade that the authorities have long turned a blind eye to. The initial cost of indulging in this mechanized mayhem can be as little as ¥100 for 25 ball bearings; just remember to take your earplugs too.

△ Rowing boat and cherry blossom

be torn down the next, and whole neighbourhoods are now being re-imagined, the darling of Tokyo's recent rash of mega-developments being Roppongi Hills.

With so much going on, first-time visitors should be prepared for a massive assault on the senses – just walking the streets of this hyperactive city can be an energizing experience. It need not be an expensive one, either. Despite Tokyo's reputation as one of the world's costliest places, you'll be surprised by how affordable many things are. Cheap-and-cheerful *izakaya* (bars that serve food) and casual cafés serving noodles and rice dishes are plentiful, while tickets for a sumo tournament or a Kabuki play can be bought for the price of a few drinks. Browsing the shops and marvelling at the passing parade can be great fun – the next best thing to having a ringside seat at the hippest of fashion shows. Likewise, in *über*-chic bars, restaurants and clubs you can experience today what the rest of the world will get tomorrow.

Underscoring – and adding a certain *frisson* to – Tokyo's cutting-edge modernity and effervescent trends is its incredibly volatile geographical position. Legend says that a giant catfish sleeps beneath Tokyo Bay, and its wriggling can be felt in the hundreds of small tremors that rumble the capital each year. Around every seventy years, the catfish awakes, resulting in the kind of major earthquake seen in 1995 in the Japanese city of Kōbe. Yet, despite the fact that the city is well overdue for the Big One, talk of relocating the capital remains just talk. Now, more than ever before, Tokyo is the centre of Japan, and nobody wants to leave and miss any of the action.

What to see

One way to ease yourself into the city is by taking a relatively crowd-free turn around the **Imperial Palace** – although most of the grounds remain tantalizingly off limits. From here it's a quick hop to Tokyo's most famous high-class shopping and entertainment district, **Ginza**, where you'll also find the **Kabuki-za**, the best theatre in which to watch this quintessential Japanese performing art form. Ginza's elite shops have faced stiff competition recently from the new boutiques of Roppongi Hills and Omotesandō, but the area is fighting back with new urban developments in **Marunouchi** and **Shiodome**,

△ Sake barrels, Asakusa

▽ Shinjuku at dusk

both dominated by shiny commercial towers, as well as the **Tokyo International Forum**, a great example of contemporary architecture.

More obviously Oriental scenes can be found in the evocative **Shitamachi** (low city) area, covering Asakusa, Ueno, Nezu and Yanaka, where the spirit and infrastructure of old Tokyo remain. **Asakusa**'s primary focus is the major Buddhist temple of **Sensō-ji**, surrounded by a plethora of traditional craft shops. **Ueno Kōen**'s leafy precincts contain several major museums, including the **Tokyo National Museum**. From here it's an easy stroll to the charming and tranquil districts of **Nezu** and **Yanaka**, packed with small temples, shrines and shops. The spirit of Edo also lives on in **Kanda**, where you'll find the **Kanda Myojin**, one of Tokyo's oldest shrines and home to one of the city's top three festivals, and across the Sumida-gawa in **Ryōgoku**, home to the colossal **Edo-Tokyo Museum** and the **National Sumo Stadium**.

Roppongi used to be all about nightlife, but the opening of the **Roppongi Hills** complex, with its many high-class boutiques and the excellent Mori Arts Centre atop the lofty Mori Tower has made it a must-see day-time destination, too. Fashionistas should head towards the teenage shopping meccas of **Shibuya** and **Harajuku** and the super-chic, bou-tique-lined boulevards of **Aoyama**. When you've reached consumer satu-ration point, retreat to the wooded grounds of nearby **Meiji-jingū**, the city's most venerable Shinto shrine, or peruse the delicate woodblock prints and crafts and art works in the **Ōta Memorial Museum of Art**, the **Nezu Museum of Art** or the **Japan Folk Crafts Museum**.

West of the Imperial Palace lies the mini-city centre of **Shinjuku**, an archetypal Tokyo district bursting with towering skyscrapers, endless amounts of neon, TV screens several storeys tall, and the largest and most complicated railway station in the city. Main attractions include the monumental **Tokyo Metropolitan Government Building**, the beautiful gardens of **Shinjuku Gyoen**, many department stores, and the lively and raffish **Kabukichō** entertainment area. Similar to Shinjuku, though not so trendy or so full-on in scale, is **Ikebukuro**. This is also where you'll find the **Toden–Arakawa Line**, Tokyo's last tramline, and a couple of lovely Japanese-style gardens: **Rikugi-en** and the **Kyū Furukawa Gardens**.

It costs nothing (other than a few hours' sleep) to experience the frenetic early-morning fish market at **Tsukiji**, on the edge of **Tokyo Bay**, while **Hama Rikyū Teien**, one of the city's loveliest traditional gardens, lies close by. Across the bay from here, and linked to the main city by the impressive Rainbow Bridge, is **Odaiba**, a futuristic man-made island, where you'll find **MeSci**, Tokyo's most fascinating science museum, and a passable beach, also man-made.

Away from the usual tourist routes, the district of **Meguro** is home to the elaborate wedding hall of **Meguro Gajōen** and the serene **Happōen**, another wonderful Japanese garden where you can sip frothy green tea. Afterwards you can wind your way through the backstreets south to the **Hatakeyama Collection**, a small but exquisite museum showcasing tea-

The Big Sushi

Tokyo is a food lover's delight. Like all other areas of Japan it rejoices in its own food specialities, top of the list of which is sushi – mounds of vinegared rice topped with raw fish. Culinary legend has it that sushi was invented here in the early nineteenth century, and not for nothing is the city's nickname the "Big Sushi". Nowhere is the preference for fish more apparent than at the mammoth fish market at Tsukiji, and a dawn visit here, followed up with the freshest of sushi and sashimi (raw fish) breakfasts is practically an obligatory part of any visit to the city. Other essential Tokyo dining experiences include scoffing *yakitori* (grilled, skewered chunks of meat) under the railway arches at Yūrakuchō and Shimbashi; slurping soba noodles at one of the classic noodle houses in Kanda such as *Yabu Soba* (p.159); and getting your chopsticks around the slippy *mon-jayaki*, a kind of scrambled egg batter fry-up that's an original Tokyo concoction.

ceremony implements. Southeast of Meguro, the **Hara Museum of Contemporary Art** hosts quirky exhibitions in an atmospheric family house dating from the 1930s.

High-speed trains put several important sights within **day-trip** range of Tokyo, including the ancient temple and shrine towns of **Kamakura** to the south and **Nikkō** to the north. **Mount Fuji**, 100km southwest of the capital, can be climbed between June and September, while the adjoining national park area of **Hakone** offers relaxed hiking amid beautiful lakeland scenery and the chance to take a dip in an onsen – a Japanese mineral bath.

If you're looking for a quick and convenient trip to the countryside, sacred **Mount Takao**, just an hour west of the capital, provides a verdant escape. On the way there or back pause at **Mitaka** to meet up with the cute animated characters who call the **Ghibli Museum** home. Just 40km north of Tokyo is **Kawagoe**, a great place to wander through nineteenth-century streetscapes and indulge in some serious souvenir shopping. Pop pilgrims will also want to make their way to the **John Lennon Museum** at Saitama Shintoshin.

Last, but not least, there's **Yokohama**, a whole other city – Japan's second largest in fact – right on Tokyo's doorstep and well worth a look for its vibrant Chinatown and breezy waterfront districts.

Cosu-play-zoku

Harajuku is guaranteed to throw up a selection of pretty out-there fashion plates any day of the week, but visit on a Sunday if you really want to see the strangest clothes parade of all. This is when the "cosu-play-zoku", or "costume-play-tribe", hang out on the bridge over the railway tracks at Harajuku Station beside the entrance to Meiji-Jingū's inner garden. Most of the participants – mainly girls, but some boys – are Japanese teenagers, but you may also spot the odd *gaijin* getting in on the fun by dressing up in out-rageous outfits copied from and inspired by their favourite rock star from bands such as Psycho Le Lemu or Dir Engrey. Some of the costumes, incorporating Nazi regalia or the kind of garments more regu-larly seen in a porn video than on 13-year-olds, are confronting and not a little disturbing, but most will blow you away with their creativity and downright weirdness.

When to visit

One of the best times to visit Tokyo is in the **spring**, from April to early May. At the start of this period flurries of falling cherry blossom give the city a soft pink hue and by the end the temperatures are pleasant. October and November are also good months to come; this is when you'll catch the fireburst of **autumn** leaves in Tokyo's parks and gardens.

Avoid the steamy height of **summer** in August and early September, when the city's humidity sees its citizens scurrying from one air-conditioned haven to another. From January to March temperatures can dip to freezing, but the crisp blue **winter** skies are rarely disturbed by rain or snow showers. Carrying an umbrella in any season is a good idea but particularly so during *tsuyu*, the rainy season in June and July, and in September, when typhoons occasionally strike the coast.

Note that many attractions shut for several days around New Year when Tokyo becomes a ghost town as many people return to their family homes elsewhere in the country. In mid-February cheap accommodation can be be near impossible to secure as high school seniors from around Japan descend on the capital to sit college entrance exams.

Before deciding when to visit, check the city's calendar of **festivals** and special events, which range from grand sumo tournaments to the spectacular Sannō and Kanda *matsuri* (festivals) held in alternate years (see "Festivals", p.35, and "Sports and martial arts", p.191).

Average Tokyo monthly temperatures and rainfall

	Average daily temperature (°F)		Average daily temperature (°C)		Average monthly rainfall	
	Max	Min	Max	Min	Inches	mm
January	49	33	10	1	4.3	110
February	50	34	10	1	6.1	155
March	55	40	13	4	9	228
April	65	50	18	10	10	254
May	73	58	23	15	9.6	244
June	78	65	25	18	12	305
July	84	72	29	22	10	254
August	87	75	31	24	8	203
September	80	68	27	20	11	279
October	70	57	21	14	9	228
November	62	47	17	8	6.4	162
December	58	38	12	3	3.8	96

24

things not to miss

It's impossible to see everything that Tokyo has to offer in one trip – and we don't suggest you try. What follows is a selective and subjective taste of the city's highlights, from the most impressive museums and pieces of modern architecture to the tranquil tea gardens and the best day-trip destinations around the city – all arranged in colour-coded categories to help you find the best things to see, do and experience. All entries have a page reference to take you straight into the Guide where you can find out more.

01 **Shinjuku Gyoen** Page **103** • Japanese, English and French styles of landscape gardening combine in delightful Shinjuku Gyoen.

02 Yūrakuchō Page **155** • Join off-duty salarymen over a beer and a plate of *yakitori* (small meat kebabs) at the many raucous joints beneath the railway tracks.

03 Ghibli Museum Page **238** • This imaginative museum, a short journey west of Tokyo, is dedicated to the animated movies of Studio Ghibli.

05 Onsen bath Page **65** • Soak your stresses away in an old neighbourhood bathhouse such as the Azabu-Jūban Onsen or the resort-like spa complex of LaQua at Kōrakuen.

04 Asakusa Page **75** • The city's most colourful and evocative district, full of old craft shops, traditional inns, restaurants and the bustling Sensō-ji temple.

06 Meiji-jingū Page **105** • Enjoy one of the many annual festivals or regular wedding ceremonies held at Tokyo's most venerable Shinto shrine.

07 Harajuku

Page **75** • Pick through the Sunday flea market at Tōgō-jinja and trawl the funky boutiques and galleries in the backstreets of Harajuku.

08 Sumo

Page **192** • Witness the titanic clashes of sumo giants at the Ryōgoku National Stadium.

09 Rikugi-en

Page **95** • Quintessential Japanese-style garden designed to reflect scenes from ancient Japanese poetry.

10 Tokyo's fireworks Page **37** •
Spectacular displays are held every July and August over the Sumida-gawa in Asakusa and in Tokyo Bay.

11 Prada Building Page **110** • Set at the heart of fashionable Aoyama, the Prada Building is the newest addition to Tokyo's outstanding range of modern architecture.

12 Kabuki Page **185** • Enjoy the liveliest of Japan's traditional performing arts at the grand Kabuki-za theatre in Ginza.

13 Happōen Page **121** • Sip *matcha* (thick green tea) in one of Tokyo's loveliest traditional gardens.

14 Tsukiji Page **124** • Get up early to see the nation's top fish market in full flight and to enjoy a fresh sushi breakfast.

15 **Hanami parties** Page **36** • Unpack your bentō and sake in Ueno Kōen or around the Imperial Palace moat for a picnic under the falling blossoms.

17 **Roppongi Hills** Page **71** • Explore the city's hippest neighbourhood, home to the new Mori Art Museum and a plethora of restaurants and top-class boutiques.

16 **Yanaka** Page **88** • Charming old-fashioned district crammed with small temples and wooden houses on twisting byways.

18 Shibuya
Page 113 • Go shopping, go clubbing, go crazy in Tokyo's trendsetting, neon-festooned suburb.

20 Kamakura
Page 244 • Japan's ancient seaside capital offers great walks between temples and shrines, plus a giant bronze Buddha.

19 Nikkō
Page 217 • Dazzling Tōshōgu shrine is the star turn of this mountain town, which also boasts some of the most beautiful countryside in Japan.

21 River buses
Page 27 • Cruise down the Sumida-gawa or across Tokyo Bay on one of the city's river buses, including the manga-inspired *Himiko* sightseeing boat.

22 **MeSci** Page **128** • Get to grips with the latest in scientific advances at this hands-on high-tech museum in Odaiba.

23 **Drinking in Shinjuku** Page **174** • From the rariefied heights of the *Park Hyatt*'s New York Bar to the tiny drinking dens of Golden Gai and the gay district of Ni-chōme, Shinjuku has a bar for you.

24 **Rainbow Bridge** Page **130** • Walk across this elegant, 918-metre-long suspension bridge for fabulous views across Tokyo Harbour towards the futuristic mini-city of Odaiba.

Contents

Using this Rough Guide

We've tried to make this Rough Guide a good read and easy to use. The book is divided into eight main sections, and you should be able to find whatever you want in one of them.

Colour section

The front colour section offers a quick tour of Tokyo. The **introduction** aims to give you a feel for the place, with suggestions on where to go and information about the weather. Next, our authors round up their favourite aspects of Japan in the **things not to miss** section – whether it's amazing sights, great food or a special festival. Right after this comes a full **contents** list.

Basics

The Basics section covers all the **pre-departure** nitty-gritty to help you plan your trip. This is where to find out which airlines fly to Japan, what paperwork you'll need, what to do about money and insurance, Internet access, food, security, public transport, car rental – in fact just about every piece of **general practical information** you might need.

The City

This is the heart of the book, divided into user-friendly chapters, each of which covers a city district. Every chapter starts with an **introduction** to help you to decide where to go, followed by a tour of the sights.

Listings

This section offers critical reviews of the city's best hotels, restaurants, bars, shops and more.

Out of city

This section covers **day-trips** around the city, including details of transport, local accommodation and places to eat.

Contexts

Read Contexts to get a deeper understanding of what makes Tokyo tick. We include a brief **history** plus reviews of the best books about the city.

Language

The Language section gives useful guidance for speaking Japanese and pulls together all the vocabulary you might need on your trip, including a **menu reader**, plus a **glossary** of words and terms peculiar to the country.

small print + Index

As well as a **full index**, this section covers publishing information, credits and acknowledgements, and also has our contact details in case you want to send in updates and corrections to the book – or suggestions as to how we might improve it.

Colour maps

The back colour section contains **maps** of the city, with sights and attractions clearly marked, and a plan of the metro system to help you find your way around.

Map and chapter list

Contents

Out of city

Contexts

Language

small print + Index

Colour maps at back of book

1. Around Tokyo
2. Greater Tokyo

3. The Tokyo subway

Basics

Basics

Getting there

Tokyo is Japan's main international air gateway (although New Tokyo International Airport – better known as Narita – is actually 66km east of the city centre). Airfares always depend on the season, with the highest being around the Japanese holiday periods of Golden Week, at the beginning of May, and the Obon festival period in mid-August; as well as at Christmas and New Year, when seats are at a premium. Prices drop during the "shoulder" seasons (April–June, Sept & Oct), and you'll get the best deals in the low season (Jan–March & Nov–Dec, excluding Christmas and New Year when prices are hiked up).

You can often cut costs by going through a **specialist flight agent** – either a consolidator, who buys up blocks of tickets from the airlines and sells them at a discount, or a **discount agent**, who in addition to dealing with discounted flights may also offer special student and youth fares and a range of other travel-related services such as travel insurance, rail passes, car rentals, tours and the like. Another way to cut the cost of a flight – although you'll be limited on your luggage – is to apply for a **courier flight**, where in exchange for a lower fare you have to carry documents or parcels from airport to airport. In the UK, contact the **International Association of Air Travel Couriers** (☏0800/074 6481 or ☏01291/625 656, ⓦwww.aircourier.co.uk), who act as agents for lots of companies. North American courier flight operators are listed on p.13–14.

If you have time, you might think about breaking your journey with a **stopover** en route to Japan. Not all airlines charge extra for this option, and with some you'll have to stop over anyway while waiting for a connecting flight.

If Tokyo is just one stop on a longer journey, you might want to consider buying a **Round the World (RTW)** ticket. Some travel agents can sell you an "off-the-shelf" RTW ticket that will have you touching down in about half a dozen cities (Tokyo is on some itineraries); others will have to assemble one for you, which can be tailored to your needs but is apt to be more expensive. Count on £800/US$2500/A$3800 and upwards for an RTW ticket including Japan. It may also be worth checking out the **Circle Pacific** deals

offered by many of the major airlines; these allow four stopovers at no extra charge if tickets are bought fourteen to thirty days in advance of travel.

On airlines that serve more than one international airport in Japan, it's possible to buy **open-jaw tickets**, usually at no extra cost, making it possible, say, to fly into Tokyo and out of Ōsaka. These tickets are well worth considering as a way of saving the time and money involved in backtracking on a journey around the country. Both JAL and ANA offer open-jaw tickets for the same price as a simple return.

Japan isn't a difficult country for the independent traveller to negotiate, nor need it be horrendously expensive. However, if you're worried about the cost or potential language problems, a **package tour** is worth considering. Packages tend to come into their own if you want to stay in upmarket hotels – these usually offer cheaper rates for group bookings. All tours use scheduled airline flights, so it's usually no problem extending your stay beyond the basic package. If you want to venture off the beaten track, however, package tours will not be for you. For a return flight, five nights' accommodation at a three- to four-star hotel, airport transfers and a sightseeing tour, prices begin around £600, based on double occupancy. You'll pay more if you're on a package that combines Tokyo with other areas of Japan or a specialized tour. All the tour prices quoted include flights unless otherwise stated.

Booking flights online

Many airlines and discount travel websites

offer you the opportunity to book your tickets, hotels and holiday packages online, cutting out the costs of agents and middle-men; these are worth going for, as long as you don't mind the inflexibility of non-refund-able, non-changeable deals. There are some bargains to be had on auction sites too. Almost all airlines have their own websites, offering flight tickets that can sometimes be just as cheap, and are often more flexible.

Online booking agents and general travel sites

ⓦwww.cheapflights.co.uk (in the UK & Ireland), ⓦwww.cheapflights.com (in the US), ⓦwww.cheapflights.ca (in Canada), ⓦwww.cheapflights.com.au (in Australia). Flight deals, travel agents, plus links to other travel sites.
ⓦwww.cheaptickets.com Discount flight specialists (US only). Also ☎1-888/922-8849.
ⓦwww.ebookers.com Efficient, easy-to-use flight finder, with competitive fares.
ⓦwww.etn.nl/discount A hub of consolidator and discount agent links, maintained by the nonprofit European Travel Network.
ⓦwww.expedia.co.uk (in the UK), ⓦwww.expedia.com (in the US), ⓦwww.expedia.ca (in Canada). Discount airfares, all-airline search engine and daily deals.
ⓦwww.flyaow.com "Airlines of the Web" – online air travel info and reservations.
ⓦwww.gaytravel.com US gay travel agent, offering accommodation, cruises, tours and more. Also at ☎1-800/GAY-TRAVEL.
ⓦwww.geocities.com/thavery2000 An extensive list of airline websites and US toll-free numbers.
ⓦwww.hotwire.com Bookings from the US only. Last-minute savings of up to forty percent on regular published fares. Travellers must be at least 18 and there are no refunds, transfers or changes allowed. Log-in required.
ⓦwww.kelkoo.co.uk Useful UK-only price-comparison site, checking several sources of low-cost flights (and other goods and services) according to specific criteria.
ⓦwww.lastminute.com (in the UK), ⓦwww.lastminute.com.au (in Australia), ⓦwww.lastminute.co.nz (in New Zealand), ⓦwww.site59.com (in the US). Good last-minute holiday package and flight-only deals.
ⓦwww.opodo.co.uk Popular and reliable source of low UK airfares. Owned by, and run in conjunction with, nine major European airlines.

ⓦwww.orbitz.com Comprehensive Web travel resource, with the usual flight, car rental and hotel deals plus great follow-up customer service.
ⓦwww.priceline.co.uk (in the UK), ⓦwww.priceline.com (in the US). Name-your-own-price website that has deals at around forty percent off standard fares.
ⓦwww.skyauction.com Bookings from the US only. Auctions tickets and travel packages to destinations worldwide.
ⓦwww.travelocity.co.uk (in the UK), ⓦwww.travelocity.com (in the US), ⓦwww.travelocity.ca (in Canada), ⓦwww.zuji.com.au (in Australia). Destination guides, hot fares and great deals for car rental, accommodation and lodging.
ⓦwww.travelshop.com.au Australian site offering discounted flights, packages, insurance, and online bookings. Also on ☎1-800/108 108.
ⓦtravel.yahoo.com Incorporates some Rough Guides material in its coverage of destination countries and cities across the world, with information about places to eat and sleep.
ⓦwww.travelzoo.com Great resource for news on the latest airline sales, cruise discounts and hotel deals. Links take you directly to the carrier's site.

Flights from the UK and Ireland

Four airlines (All Nippon Airways, British Airways, Japan Airlines and Virgin) fly non-stop **from London** into New Tokyo International Airport (better known as Narita). There are plenty of airlines with indirect flights to Narita. Direct flights from London take around twelve hours.

There are no direct flights **from Ireland** – you'll need to stop over in Europe en route, with the cheapest deals usually being via London (Ryanair fly daily from Dublin to London for around €50).

To find out the best deals on **fares** to Japan, contact a flight agent – see the list on p.11–12 for a selection of dependable ones. You could also check the ads in the travel pages of the weekend newspapers, regional listings magazines, Teletext and Ceefax and the websites opposite. Whoever you buy your ticket through, check that the agency belongs to the travel industry bodies ABTA or IATA, so that you'll be covered if they go bust before you receive your ticket. **Students** and **under-26s** can often get discounts through specialist agents such as USIT in Ireland or STA (see box on below).

Seasons differ from airline to airline, but July, August and December are generally the costliest months to travel. If you're not tied to particular dates, check the changeover dates between seasons; you might make a substantial saving by travelling a few days earlier or later. **Fares** to Tokyo from London start from around £500. However, you can find occasional special deals from as low as £300, so it pays to shop around.

Airlines

Aeroflot ℡020/7355 2233, ⓦwww.aeroflot.co.uk. Direct flights from Heathrow to Tokyo twice a week, and via Moscow four times a week.

Air France ℡0845/084 5111, ⓦwww.airfrance.com. Flights from eight UK cities daily to Tokyo via Paris.

Alitalia ℡0870/544 8259, Republic of Ireland ℡01/677 5171, ⓦwww.alitalia.co.uk. Daily departures from Heathrow to Tokyo, all via Milan or Rome.

All Nippon Airways (ANA) ℡020/7224 8866, ⓦwww.anaskyweb.com. Daily direct services from Heathrow to Tokyo. You can also book discounted domestic flights when booking from abroad (restrictions apply).

British Airways ℡0870/850 9850, ⓦwww.britishairways.com. Direct flights from Heathrow to Tokyo daily.

Cathay Pacific ℡020/8834 8888, ⓦwww.cathaypacific.com/uk. Flights from Heathrow daily to Tokyo via Hong Kong.

Finnair ℡020/7408 1222, ⓦwww.finnair.com. From Heathrow twice weekly, and from Manchester weekly, to Tokyo via Helsinki.

Japan Airlines (JAL) ℡0845/774 7700, Republic of Ireland ℡01/408 3757, ⓦwww.jal-europe.com. Daily direct flights from Heathrow to Tokyo.

KLM Royal Dutch Airlines ℡0870/507 4074, ⓦwww.klm.com. Flights from fifteen UK cities via Amsterdam to Tokyo daily.

Korean Air International toll-free ℡00800/0656 2001, Republic of Ireland ℡01/799 7990, ⓦwww.koreanair.eu.com. Five flights weekly from Heathrow to Tokyo via Seoul.

Lufthansa German Airlines ℡0870/837 7747, ⓦwww.lufthansa.co.uk. Daily flights from Heathrow to Tokyo via Frankfurt.

Malaysia Airlines ℡0870/607 9090,

ⓦwww.malaysiaairlines.com. Daily flights from Heathrow to Tokyo via Kuala Lumpur.

Ryanair UK ℡0871/246 0000, Republic of Ireland ℡0818/30 30 30, ⓦwww.ryanair.com. Daily flights from Dublin to Gatwick, Stansted or Luton, for connecting flights to Tokyo.

SAS Scandinavian Airlines ℡0870/6072 7727, Republic of Ireland ℡01/844 5440, ⓦwww.scandanavian.net. Daily flights from Heathrow and Manchester to Tokyo via Copenhagen.

Singapore Airlines ℡0870/608 8886, Republic of Ireland ℡01/671 0722, ⓦwww.singaporeair.com. From Heathrow and Manchester daily to Tokyo via Singapore.

Swiss UK ℡0845/601 0956, Republic of Ireland ℡1890/200 515, ⓦwww.swiss.com. Daily from Heathrow to Tokyo via Zurich.

Thai Airways ℡0870/606 0911, ⓦwww.thaiair.com. From Heathrow daily to Tokyo via Bangkok.

Virgin Atlantic Airways ℡0870/574 7747, ⓦwww.virgin-atlantic.com. Daily from Heathrow to Tokyo.

Discount travel agents

Aran Travel First Choice Republic of Ireland ℡091/562595, ⓦwww.firstchoicetravel.ie. Worldwide flight agent offering deals to Japan.

AWL Travel UK ℡020/7222 1144, ⓦwww.awlt.com. Specialists in travel to Japan, offering bargain airfares and Japan Rail passes.

Bridge the World UK ℡0870/443 2399, ⓦwww.bridgetheworld.com. Specialists in long-haul travel, with good-value flight deals, RTW tickets and tailor-made packages, all aimed at the backpacker market.

Dial-a-Flight UK ℡0870/333 4488, ⓦwww.dialaflight.com. Telephone sales of scheduled flights; the website has some good bargains.

Emerald Travel UK ℡020/7312 1700, ⓦwww.etours-online.com. Discount flight agent.

North-South Travel UK ℡01245/608291, ⓦwww.northsouthtravel.co.uk. Friendly and competitive travel agency offering discount fares worldwide; profits are used to support projects in the developing world, especially the promotion of sustainable tourism.

Quest Travel UK ℡020/8481 4000, ⓦwww.questtravel.com. Specialists in RTW and discount fares to Asia.

STA Travel UK ℡0870/160 0599, ⓦwww.statravel.co.uk. Worldwide specialists in low-cost flights, overland and holiday deals. Good discounts for students and under-26s.

Trailfinders UK ☎020/7938 3939, ⓦwww.trailfinders.com; Republic of Ireland ☎01/677 7888, ⓦwww.trailfinders.ie. One of the best-informed and most efficient agents for independent travellers; they produce a very useful quarterly magazine worth scrutinizing for round-the-world routes (ring for a free copy).

USIT Northern Ireland ☎028/9032 7111, ⓦwww.usitnow.com; Republic of Ireland ☎0818/200 020, ⓦwww.usit.ie. Specialists in student, youth and independent travel – flights, trains, study tours, TEFL, visas and more.

Tour operators

Asia Fare ☎020/7038 3940, ⓦwww.asia-fare.co.uk. Customized itineraries.

Carrick Travel Ltd ☎01926/311 415. Flight agent and specialist tour operator offering tailor-made packages to Japan.

Explore Worldwide ☎01252/760 000, ⓦwww.exploreworldwide.com (in the Republic of Ireland contact Maxwells Travel ☎01/679 3948). Offers a "Shogun Trail" two-week guided tour of Japan, flying into Tokyo and out of Fukuoka. From £1899, including flights and accommodation.

Far East Gateways (The Cheshire Travel Centre) ☎0161/437 4371. Offers escorted sightseeing tours and accommodation packages, promoting multi-country trips. The "Classical Japan Escorted Tour" comprises a seven-day trip (including Tokyo) for £1329, including flights.

The Imaginative Traveller ☎01473/667337, ⓦwww.adventurebound.co.uk. This flight agent and tour operator offers two tours of Japan, including the fifteen-day "Empire of the Sun" tour which includes a night on Mount Fuji and time in Tokyo. Prices start at £1295 (not including international flights).

Jaltour ☎020/7462 5577, ⓦwww.jaltour.co.uk. Japanese specialists – they're the tour arm of Japan Airlines. Can arrange flights, tours, city breaks in Tokyo, rail passes and accommodation packages.

Japan Journeys ☎020/7437 5453, ⓦwww.japanjourneys.co.uk. New tour company offering nine-night tour of Japan, including Tokyo, for around £2200. Luxury tailor-made trips are also available on an individual basis.

Japan Travel Centre ☎020/7255 8283. Offers flights to Japan, accommodation packages, Japan Rail passes and guided tours of Japan. Four nights in Tokyo cost from £579, including flights and accommodation.

Flights from the US and Canada

A number of airlines serve Tokyo International Airport (Narita) nonstop from North America, with connections from virtually everywhere in Canada and the US. Many flights are offered at up to half-price, so keep an eye out for special offers. It's also possible to reach Japan via Europe, though this is likely to be a lot more expensive.

Barring special offers, the cheapest of the airlines' published fares is usually an **Apex** ticket, although this will carry certain restrictions: you have to book – and pay – at least 21 days before departure, spend at least seven days abroad (maximum stay three months), and you tend to get penalized if you change your schedule. Some airlines also issue **Special Apex** tickets to people under 24, often extending the maximum stay to a year. Many airlines offer youth or student fares to **under-26s**, though these tickets are subject to availability and can have eccentric booking conditions. It's worth remembering that most cheap return fares involve spending at least one Saturday night away and that many will only give a percentage refund if you need to cancel or alter your journey, so make sure you check the restrictions carefully before buying a ticket.

You can normally cut costs further by going through a **specialist flight agent** – either a consolidator or a discount agent. Bear in mind, though, that penalties for changing your plans can be stiff. Remember too that these companies make their money by dealing in bulk – don't expect them to answer a lot of questions. If you travel a lot, **discount travel clubs** are another option – the annual membership fee may be worth it for benefits such as cut-price air tickets and car rental. The **Internet** is also a useful resource; check the websites listed on p.10.

Airlines running **direct nonstop** flights from North America to Narita include All Nippon, American, Delta, Korean, Northwest and United. Flying time is fifteen hours from New York, thirteen hours from Chicago and ten hours from Los Angeles and Seattle. Returning to North America from Japan takes an hour less due to favourable wind currents. Many European and Asian airlines, such as Air France, Cathay Pacific and Malaysia Airlines, offer **indirect** flights (often with a stopover in their home city included in the price) to Narita.

Fares are highest in July and August, and at Christmas and New Year; prices drop April through June and September through October; you'll get the best deals in low season (Jan–March & Nov to mid-Dec). The fares quoted below give a rough idea of what you can expect to pay for a round-trip ticket to Tokyo bought direct from the airlines exclusive of airport tax, which is an extra $20. From Chicago tickets cost $930–1600 (midweek in low season to weekend in high season); from Los Angeles, $675–1600; from Vancouver, CAN$900–1400; from New York, $960–1800; from San Francisco, $675–1450; from Seattle, $830–1400; and from Toronto, CAN$1215–1650. However, unless you need to travel at very short notice, you are likely to get a much better deal through a specialist flight agent or consolidator (see below).

Airlines

Air Canada US & Canada ☏ 1-888/247-2262, ⓦ www.aircanada.ca. Daily nonstop to Tokyo's Narita airport from Toronto.

Air France US ☏ 1-800/237-2747, Canada ☏ 1-800/667-2747, ⓦ www.airfrance.com. Flights from several US cities, as well as Montreal and Toronto, to Narita via Paris.

All Nippon Airways (ANA) ☏ 1-800/235-9262, ⓦ www.anaskyweb.com. Daily nonstop flights to Narita from New York, Los Angeles and Washington DC.

American Airlines ☏ 1-800/433-7300, ⓦ www.americanairlines.com. Nonstop daily flights to Narita from New York, Los Angeles, Chicago, Dallas and San José.

Asiana Airlines ☏ 1-800/227-4262, ⓦ www.flyasiana.com. Flights via Seoul to Narita from New York, Los Angeles, San Francisco and Seattle.

British Airways US ☏ 1-800/247-9297, Canada ☏ 1-800/668-1059, ⓦ www.britishairways.com. The best value of the routes via Europe, with flights via London to Tokyo's Narita airport from several US and Canadian cities.

Cathay Pacific ☏ 1-800/233-2742, ⓦ www.cathay-usa.com. Daily flights from New York, Los Angeles, San Francisco, Vancouver and Toronto to Narita with stopovers. Also sells the good-value All Asia Pass ($999–1499, register online to get this fare), valid for a round-trip flight to any Asian city they serve from North America.

Continental Airlines ☏ 1-800/231-0856, ⓦ www.continental.com. Daily East and West Coast flights to Narita, some via Honolulu and Guam.

Delta Airlines ☏ 1-800/241-4141, ⓦ www.delta.com. Daily nonstop flights to Narita from Atlanta, with connections across the US.

Japan Airlines (JAL) ☏ 1-800/525-3663, ⓦ www.japanair.com. Daily nonstop flights to Narita from New York, Chicago, Los Angeles and San Francisco. Departures to Tokyo from Vancouver five times a week.

Korean Airlines ☏ 1-800/438-5000, ⓦ www.koreanair.com. Daily nonstop flights to Narita from Los Angeles. Flights to Narita via Seoul from New York (daily), from San Francisco, Atlanta and Chicago (5 weekly).

Malaysia Airlines ☏ 1-800/552-9264, ⓦ www.malaysia-airlines.com. Flights to Narita from Los Angeles via Kuala Lumpur five times weekly.

Northwest Airlines ☏ 1-800/447-4747, ⓦ www.nwa.com. Daily nonstop flights to Narita airport from Chicago, Los Angeles, San Francisco, Seattle and Honolulu, with extensive connections from other American cities.

Singapore Airlines ☏ 1-800/742-3333, Canada ☏ 1-800/387-8039 or 663-3046, ⓦ www.singaporeair.com. Daily nonstop flights to Narita from Los Angeles.

United Airlines ☏ 1-800/538-2929, ⓦ www.united.com. Daily nonstop flights to Narita from Los Angeles and San Francisco, with numerous connections from other American cities.

Discount flight agents

Air Brokers International ☏ 1-800/883-3273, ⓦ www.airbrokers.com. Consolidator and specialist in RTW and Circle Pacific tickets.

Air Courier Association ☏ 1-800/280-5973, ⓦ www.aircourier.org. Courier-flight broker. Membership ($35 for a year) also entitles you to twenty percent discount on travel insurance and name-your-own-price non-courier flights.

Cheap Tickets, Inc. ☏ 1-888/922-8849, ⓦ www.cheaptickets.com. Consolidator.

Discount Airfares Worldwide On-Line ⓦ www.etn.nl/discount.htm. A hub of consolidator and discount-agent Web links, maintained by the non-profit European Travel Network.

Dr Cheaps ☏ 1-800/731-5086, ⓦ www.drcheaps.com. Consolidator.

Education Travel Center ☏ 1-800/747-5551, ⓦ www.edtravel.com. Student/youth and consclidator fares.

High Adventure Travel ☏ 1-800/350-0612 or 1-415/977-7100, ⓦ www.highadv.com. Specialists in RTW and Circle Pacific tickets.

International Association of Air Travel
Couriers ☎308/632-3273, ⊛www.courier.org.
Courier flights; annual membership $45.

Now Voyager ☎212/459-1616,
⊛www.nowvoyagertravel.com. Gay- and lesbian-
run courier-flight broker and consolidator.

Skylink ☎1-800/AIR-ONLY or 212/573-8980.
Consolidator.

STA Travel US ☎1-800/781-4040, Canada
☎1-888/427-5639, ⊛www.statravel.com.
Worldwide discount travel firm specializing in
student/youth fares; also arranges student IDs, travel
insurance, car rental and so on.

Student Flights ☎1-800/255-8000 or
480/951-1177, ⊛www.isecard.com. Student/youth
fares and student IDs.

Travel Avenue ☎1-800/333-3335,
⊛www.travelavenue.com. Full-service travel agent
that offers discounts in the form of rebates.

Travel Cuts Canada ☎1-866/246-9762 or US
☎1-800/592-CUTS, ⊛www.travelcuts.com.
Student fares, IDs and other travel services.
Branches all over Canada.

Travelocity ⊛www.travelocity.com. Online
consolidator.

Tour operators

Abercrombie & Kent ☎1-800/554-7016 or
630/954-2944, ⊛www.abercrombiekent.com.
High-end tailor-made tours, including transfers and
sightseeing with private local guides.

Adventure Center ☎1-800/228-8747 or
510/654-1879, ⊛www.adventurecenter.com.
Fifteen-day tour starting in Tokyo, with visits to
temples and traditional villages, cities and hot
springs on the islands of Honshū and Kyūshū.

Asia Transpacific Journeys ☎1-800/642-
2742 or 303/443-6789,
⊛www.asiatranspacific.com. Upmarket tours of
the capital and customized trips.

Cross-Culture ☎1-800/491-1148 or 413/256-
6303, ⊛www.crosscultureinc.com. Cultural tours
of Tokyo and countryside.

General Tours ☎1-800/221-2216,
⊛www.generaltours.com. Wide selection of tours
and authorized Japan Rail pass agent.

Geographic Expeditions ☎1-800/777-8183 or
415/922-0448, ⊛www.geoex.com. City, village and
walking tours, plus one focusing on Japanese cuisine
and arts.

Japan Travel Bureau ☎1-800/235-3523 or
☎212/698-4900, ⊛www.jtbusa.com. Day-trips
across the country, including Tokyo, Tokyo
Disneyland, Kamakura, Nikkō and Mount Fuji.

Journeys East ☎1-800/527-2612 or 707/987-

4531, ⊛www.journeyseast.com. Tours focusing on
art and architecture.

Kintetsu International Express ☎212/259-
9600, ⊛www.kintetsu.com. Package and day-tour
operator.

Northwest World Vacation Northwest Airlines
☎1-800/800-1504, ⊛www.nwaworldvacations
.com. Standard package tours.

Orient Flexi-Pax Tours ☎1-800/223-7460,
⊛www.orientflexipax.com. Run a six-night tour of
Tokyo, Takayama and Kyoto. From $2585, including
flights and accommodation.

Pacific Holidays ☎1-800/355-8025 or 212/629-
3888, ⊛www.pacificholidaysinc.com. Solid
package-tour operator.

Pleasant Holidays ☎1-800/742-9244, ⊛www
.pleasantholidays.com. Several "modules" from which
to select and combine, including Tokyo, Mount Fuji and
Hakone, and a tea ceremony experience.

Tour East ☎1-800/667-3951 or 416/929-0888,
⊛www.toureast.ca. Cultural tours combining
modern and traditional Japan.

Vantage Travel ☎1-800/322-6677,
⊛www.vantagetravel.com. Tours of Asia, including
Japan, for over-55s.

Worldwide Adventures ☎1-800/387-1483,
⊛www.worldwidequest.com. Operator focusing on
mountain trekking, with a culture tour as well.

Flights from Australia and New Zealand

There are few **direct flights** to Tokyo from
Australia and New Zealand, although you
can also reach Japan from either country via
a whole range of other destinations in
Southeast Asia.

Fares for services from **eastern Australia**
(Sydney, Brisbane and Cairns) to Tokyo are
generally the cheapest, kicking off at around
A$1400 return. There are a few direct flights
each week to Tokyo from **Melbourne** with
prices around A$2100 return. From **western
Australia**, Qantas fly direct from Perth to
Tokyo for around A$1700. All the fares quot-
ed here are for travel during low or shoulder
seasons, and exclude airport taxes; flying at
peak times (primarily mid-Dec to mid-Jan)
can add substantially to these prices. Call
one of the **discount flight agents** listed on
opposite to find out about the latest fares
and any special offers. If you're a **student** or
under 26, you may be able to undercut
some of the prices given here; STA is a good
place to start. Return fares with Garuda,
Korean and Malaysia airlines can be as low

as A$1100, but these generally restrict stays to ninety days or less and involve longer flight times and stops en route. Tickets valid for stays of up to a year cost around A$2000, though special fares are sometimes available to holders of working-holiday visas, which can bring prices down nearer the A$1400 mark. For an **open-jaw ticket**, which enables you to fly into one Japanese city and out of another, count on around A$2000 out of Sydney, flying with JAL or Qantas.

From **New Zealand**, Air New Zealand, Garuda, Qantas and Singapore Airlines (among others) operate regular or code-share services to to Tokyo, with fares starting at NZ$1400, though the most direct routings will cost at least NZ$1600.

Five-night **packages** in Tokyo from eastern Australia start at around A$1700, including return airfare, transfers, twin-share accommodation and breakfast – a good deal considering the cost of airfares alone. A few **specialist tour operators**, such as Jalpak and Japan Experience (and others listed on opposite), offer more comprehensive tours; most can also arrange Japan Rail passes and book accommodation in regional Japan – either in business-style hotels or at more traditional minshuku and ryokan through consortia such as the Japanese Inn Group.

Airlines

Air New Zealand Australia ☎13 24 76, New Zealand ☎0800/737 000, ⓦwww.airnz.com.
Asiana Airlines Australia ☎1300/767 234, ⓦwww.flyasiana.com.
Cathay Pacific Airways Australia ☎13 17 47, New Zealand ☎09/379 0861, ⓦwww.cathaypacific.com.
Garuda Australia ☎02/9334 9944, New Zealand ☎09/366 1862, ⓦwww.garuda-indonesia.com.
JAL (Japan Airlines) Australia ☎02/9272 1111, New Zealand ☎09/379 9906, ⓦwww.jal.co.jp.
Korean Air Australia ☎02/9262 6000, New Zealand ☎09/307 3687, ⓦwww.koreanair.com.
Malaysia Airlines Australia ☎13 26 27, New Zealand ☎09/373 2741, ⓦwww.mas.com.my.
Philippine Airlines Australia ☎02/9279 2020, ⓦwww.philippineair.com.
Qantas Australia ☎13 13 13, New Zealand ☎09/661 901, ⓦwww.qantas.com.au.
Singapore Airlines Australia ☎13 10 11, New Zealand ☎09/303 2129, ⓦwww.singaporeair.com.

Discount flight agents

Anywhere Travel 345 Anzac Parade, Kingsford, Sydney ☎02/9663 0411, ⓔanywhere@ozemail.com.au. Bargain airfare retailer.
Budget Travel 16 Fort St, Auckland, plus branches around the city ☎09/366 0061 or ☎0800/808 040, ⓦwww.budgettravel.co.nz.
Destinations Unlimited 3 Milford Rd, Auckland ☎09/373 4033.
Flight Centres Australia ☎13 31 33, New Zealand ☎09/358 4310, ⓦwww.flightcentre.com.au.
Northern Gateway 22 Cavenagh St, Darwin ☎08/8941 1394, ⓦwww.northerngateway.com.au.
STA Travel Australia ☎1300/733 035, ⓦwww.statravel.com.au; New Zealand ☎0508/782 872, ⓦwww.statravel.co.nz.
Student Uni Travel 92 Pitt St, Sydney ☎02/9232 8444, ⓔaustralia@backpackers.net.
Trailfinders 8 Spring St, Sydney ☎02/9247 7666, ⓦwww.trailfinders.com.au.
Travel.Com.Au 76–80 Clarence St, Sydney ☎02/9249 5444, ⓦwww.travel.com.au.

Specialist tour operators

Active Travel 1st Floor, Garema Centre, Canberra ☎1800/634 157, ⓦwww.activetravel.com.au. Offers some unusual itineraries, including hiking trips and tours themed around food and Japanese gardens, including some time in Tokyo.
Adventure World ☎02/8913 0755, ⓦwww.adventureworld.com.au; New Zealand ☎09/524 5118, ⓦwww.adventureworld.co.nz. Agents for Explore Worldwide's Shogun Trail train tour from Tokyo to Fukuoka.
Jalpak Travel Sydney ☎02/9285 6600. Sells Jaltour packages and can put together personalized itineraries.
Japan Experience Tours Australia Square Tower, Sydney ☎02/9247 3086. Contact them to find out about Price Travel Service, who have 21 years' experience in running tours in Japan, including two-week language programmes.
Japan Travel Bureau Level 24, 1 Market St, Sydney ☎02/9510 0100. Head office for Jaltour packages, with a good range of hotel options and specialist tours of Tokyo.
Nippon Travel Agency Level 9, 135 King St, Sydney ☎02/9338 2333; 25/151 Queen St, Auckland ☎09/309 5750. The local offices of this giant Japanese travel agency, offering standard and bespoke tours.

Visas and red tape

All visitors to Japan must have a passport which is valid for the duration of their stay, but only residents of certain countries need apply for a visa in advance. Citizens of Ireland, the UK and certain other European countries can stay in Japan for up to ninety days without a visa provided they are visiting for tourism or business purposes. This stay can be extended for another three months (see below).

Citizens of Australia, Canada, New Zealand, and the US can also stay for up to ninety days without a visa, though this is unextendable and you are required to be in possession of a return airline ticket. Anyone wishing to stay longer will have to leave the country and then re-enter.

Citizens of certain other countries must apply for a visa in advance in their own country – if in doubt, check with your nearest embassy or consulate. These are usually free, though in certain circumstances you may be charged a fee of around ¥3000 for a single-entry visa. The rules on visas do change from time to time, so check first with your embassy or consulate, or on the Japanese Ministry of Foreign Affairs website (⊛www.mofa.go.jp/j_info/visit/visa/index.html), for the current situation.

To get a **visa extension** you'll need to fill in two copies of an "Application for Extension of Stay", available from the Tokyo immigration bureau (see Directory, p.211). These must be returned along with passport photos, a letter explaining your reasons for wanting to extend your stay, and a processing fee of ¥4000. In addition, you may be asked to show proof of sufficient funds, and a valid onward ticket out of the country. If you're not a national of one of the few countries with six-month reciprocal visa exemptions (these include Ireland and the UK), expect a thorough grilling from the immigration officials. An easier option – and the only alternative available to nationals of those countries who are not eligible for an extension – may be a short trip out of the country, say to South Korea or Hong Kong, though you'll still have to run the gauntlet of immigration officials on your return.

Citizens of Australia, Britain, Canada, and New Zealand aged between 18 and 30 can apply for a **working-holiday visa**, which grants a six-month stay and one possible six-month extension. This entitles the holder to work for a maximum of twenty hours a week. You need to apply at least three weeks before leaving your home country, and must be able to show evidence of sufficient funds, which effectively means a return ticket (or money to buy one) plus around US$2000 or the equivalent to live on while you look for work. Contact your local embassy or consulate to check the current details of the scheme.

British nationals are also eligible for the **volunteer visa** scheme, which allows holders to undertake voluntary work for charitable organizations in Japan for up to one year. Your application must include a letter from the host organization confirming details of the voluntary work to be undertaken and the treatment the volunteer will receive (pocket money and board and lodging is allowed, but more formal remuneration is not). You must also be able to show evidence of sufficient funds for your stay in Japan, such as a return ticket (or money to buy one) plus money to live on if you're not receiving full board and lodging from your host institution. Contact your local embassy or consulate to check the current details of the scheme.

If you enter Japan on a working-holiday or volunteer visa you must apply for an Alien Registration card (from your local government office), within ninety days of arrival. In addition, if you're on any sort of working visa and you leave Japan temporarily, you must get a **re-entry visa** before you leave, if you wish to return and continue working. Re-entry visas are available from local immigration bureaux.

The **duty-free allowance** for bringing goods into Japan is 400 cigarettes or 100 cigars or 500 grams of tobacco; three 760cc bottles of alcohol; two ounces of perfume; and gifts and souvenirs up to a value of ¥200,000. As well as firearms and drugs, Japanese customs officials are particularly strict about the import of pornographic material, which will be confiscated if your bags are searched.

On the plane you'll be given an immigration form and a **customs declaration** to fill out; if you're within the allowances outlined above, you can ignore the customs form. If you're arriving from a developing country you'll also have to fill out a yellow health form, detailing any illness you may have suffered in the previous fourteen days. If you've been well, you can ignore this form, too.

There is no limit on the amount of foreign or Japanese **currency** that you can bring into the country, but ¥5 million is the maximum that you can take out of Japan.

Japanese embassies and consulates

You'll find addresses for other embassies and consulates on the Ministry of Foreign Affairs website (ⓦwww.mofa.go.jp/j_info/visit/visa/index.html), and links to many of them from the UK Embassy site (ⓦwww.uk.emb-japan.go.jp/en/webjapan/links.html). Australia 112 Empire Circuit, Yarralumla, Canberra, ACT 2600 ☎02/6273 3244, ⓦwww.japan.org.au; 17th Floor, Comalco Place, 12 Creek St, Brisbane, Queensland 4000 ☎07/3221 5188; Level 15, Cairns Corporate Tower, 15 Lake St, Cairns, Queensland 4870, ☎07/4051 5177; 45th Floor, Melbourne Central Tower, 360 Elizabeth St, Melbourne, Victoria 3000 ☎03/9639 3244; 21st Floor, The Forrest Centre, 221 St George Terrace, Perth, WA 6000 ☎08/9321 7816; Level 34, Colonial Centre, 52 Martin Place, Sydney, NSW 2000 ☎02/9231 3455. Canada 255 Sussex Drive, Ottawa, ON K1N 9E6 ☎613/241-8541, ⓦwww.ca.emb-japan.go.jp; 2480 ManuLife Place, 10180-101 St, Edmonton, AB T5J 3S4 ☎780/422-3752; 600 Rue de la Gauchetière Ouest, Suite 2120, Montreal, PQ H3B 4L8 ☎514/866-3429; Suite 3300, Royal Trust Tower, 77 King St W, PO Box 10, Toronto-Dominion Centre, Toronto, ON M5K 1A1 ☎416/363-7038; 800-1177 West Hastings St, Vancouver, BC V6E 2K9 ☎604/684-5868.

China 7 Ri Tan Rd, Jian Guo Men Wai, Beijing ☎10/6532-2361, ⓦwww.cn.emb-japan.go.jp; 46–47th Floors, One Exchange Square, 8 Connaught Place, Central, Hong Kong ☎2522 1184, ⓦwww.hk.emb-japan.go.jp.

Ireland Nutley Building, Merrion Centre, Nutley Lane, Dublin 4 ☎01/202 8300, ⓦwww.ie.emb-japan.go.jp.

New Zealand Level 18, Majestic Centre, 100 Willis St, Wellington 1 ☎04/473 1540, ⓦwww.nz.emb-japan.go.jp; Level 12, ASB Bank Centre, 135 Albert St, Auckland 1 ☎09/303 4106; Level 5, Forsyth Barr House, 764 Colombo St, Christchurch 1 ☎03/366 5680.

Singapore 16 Nassim Rd, Singapore 258390 ☎6235-8855, ⓦwww.sg.emb-japan.go.jp.

South Korea 18-11 Jhoonghak-dong, Jhongro-gu, Seoul, Republic of Korea ☎02/2170 5200, ⓦwww.kr.emb-japan.go.jp.

Thailand 1674 New Petchaburi Rd, Bangkok 10320 ☎02/252-6151, ⓦwww.embjp-th.org.

UK 101–104 Piccadilly, London W1J 7JT ☎020/7465 6500, ⓦwww.uk.emb-japan.go.jp; 2 Melville Crescent, Edinburgh EH3 7HW ☎0131/225 4777, ⓦwww.edinburgh.uk.emb-japan.go.jp.

US 2520 Massachusetts Ave NW, Washington DC 20008-2869 ☎202/238-6700, ⓦwww.us.emb-japan.go.jp; Alliance Center Suite 1600, 3500 Lenox Rd, Atlanta, Georgia 30326 ☎404/240-4300; Federal Reserve Plaza, 14th Floor, 600 Atlantic Ave, Boston, MA 02210 ☎617/973-9772; Olympia Centre, Suite 1100, 737 North Michigan Ave, Chicago, IL 60611 ☎312/280-0400; 400 Renaissance Center, Suite 1600, Detroit, MI 48243 ☎313/567-0120; Wells Fargo Plaza Suite 2300, 1000 Louisiana St, Houston, TX 77002 ☎713/652-2977; 350 South Grand Ave, Suite 1700, Los Angeles, CA 90071 ☎213/617-6700; Brickell Bay View Centre, Suite 3200, 80 SW 8th St, Miami, FL 33130 ☎305/530-9090; Suite 2050, 639 Loyola Ave, New Orleans, LA 70113 ☎504/529-2101; 299 Park Ave, New York, NY 10171 ☎212/371-8222; 50 Fremont St, Suite 2300, San Francisco, CA 94105 ☎415/777-3533; 601 Union St, Suite 500, Seattle, WA 98101 ☎206/682-9107.

Insurance

It's essential to take out a good travel insurance policy, particularly one with comprehensive medical coverage, due to the high cost of hospital treatment in Japan. A typical travel insurance policy should also provide cover for the loss of baggage, tickets and – up to a certain limit – cash or cheques, as well as cancellation or curtailment of your journey. Most policies exclude so-called dangerous sports unless an extra premium is paid: in Japan this can mean scuba-diving, whitewater rafting and bungee jumping, skiing and mountaineering. Read the small print and benefits tables of prospective policies carefully, as coverage can vary wildly for roughly similar premiums.

With many policies you can exclude coverage you don't need, but for Japan you should definitely take **medical coverage** that includes both hospital treatment and medical evacuation; be sure to ask for the 24-hour medical emergency number. Keep all medical bills and, if possible, contact the insurance company before making any major outlay. Very few insurers will arrange on-the-spot payments in the event of a major expense – you'll usually be reimbursed only after going home.

When securing **baggage cover**, make sure that the per-article limit – typically under £500 equivalent – will cover your most valuable possession. If you have anything stolen, get a copy of the **police report**; otherwise you won't be able to claim. Always make a note of the policy details and leave them with someone at home in case you lose the original.

Before buying a policy, check that you're not already covered. Your **home insurance**

policy may cover your possessions against loss or theft even when overseas, or you can extend cover through your household contents insurer. Many **bank** and **charge accounts** include some form of travel cover, and insurance is also sometimes included if you pay for your trip with a **credit card** (though it usually only provides medical or accident cover).

In **North America**, Canadian provincial health plans usually provide some overseas medical coverage, although they are unlikely to pick up the full tab in the event of a mishap. Holders of official student/teacher /youth cards are entitled to meagre accident coverage and hospital in-patient benefits. Students will often find that their student health coverage extends during the vacations and for one term beyond the date of last enrolment.

Rough Guide travel insurance

Rough Guides Ltd offers a low-cost travel insurance policy, especially customized for our readers. There are five main Rough Guides insurance plans: **No Frills** for the bare minimum for secure travel; **Essential**, which provides decent all-round cover; **Premier** for comprehensive cover with a wide range of benefits; **Extended Stay** for cover lasting four months to a year; and **Annual Multi-Trip**, a cost-effective way of getting Premier cover if you travel more than once a year. Premier, Annual Multi-Trip and Extended Stay policies can be supplemented by a "Hazardous Pursuits Extension" if you plan to indulge in sports considered dangerous, such as scuba-diving or trekking. For a policy quote, call the Rough Guide Insurance Line: toll-free in the UK ☎0800/015 0906 or ☎+44 1392 314 665 from elsewhere. Alternatively, get an online quote at ⊛www.roughguides.com/insurance

Information, maps and websites

The Japan National Tourist Organization (JNTO) maintains a number of overseas offices (see below) which are stocked with a wealth of free maps and leaflets, covering everything from Japanese culture to detailed area guides, accommodation lists and practical information about local transport. You'll find a selection of the same material on the JNTO website; see the box on p.21 for details of this and other recommended information sources on the Internet.

In Tokyo itself, the Tokyo Convention and Visitors Bureau's new **TCVB Tourist Centre**, Tokyo Chamber of Commerce and Industry Building, 3-2-2 Marunouchi, Chiyoda-ku (Mon–Fri 10am–5pm, Sat & Sun 10am–4pm; ☎03/3287-7024, ⊛www.tcvb .or.jp; Yūrakuchō Station), opposite the Imperial Palace, is the first place to head for information, with a good stock of maps, pamphlets and printed guides in a range of languages, as well as free Internet access.

Also useful, if you're in the Shinjuku area, is the **Tokyo Tourist Information Centre**, 1st Floor, Tokyo Metropolitan Government No. 1 Building, 2-8-1 Nishi-Shinjuku (daily 9.30am–6.30pm; ☎03/5321-3077; Tochō-mae Station). There are also small branches at Haneda Airport (daily 9am–10pm; ☎03/5757-9345) and in the Kesei line station at Ueno (daily 9.30am–6.30pm; ☎03/3836-3471).

The Japan National Tourist Organization (JNTO) operate a couple of **Tourist Information Centres** (TIC) in Tokyo, both of which have English-speaking staff. There are small desks in the arrivals halls of both terminals at Narita airport, while JNTO's main office (Mon–Fri 9am–5pm, Sat 9am–noon; ☎03/3201-3331) is on the tenth floor of Tokyo Kotsu Kaikan, immediately east of Yūrakuchō Station in the heart of the city. There are multilingual staff here, a Welcome Inn booking desk for accommodation across Japan and a noticeboard with some information on upcoming events. A more comprehensive monthly list of festivals is available on request.

Another useful source of English-language information are the **Goodwill Guides**, groups of volunteer guides located in Tokyo and nearly thirty other cities, mostly in central and western Japan. The guides' services are free – although you're expected to pay for their transport, entry tickets and any meals you have together – and their language ability obviously varies. But they provide a great opportunity to learn more about Japanese culture and to visit local restaurants, shops and so forth with a Japanese-speaker. The TICs have a list of groups and their contact details, or the local information office should be able to help with arrangements; try and give at least two days' notice.

If you need to check travel information either domestically or internationally it may also be worth dropping by the **JTB Travel Library** (1F, Tekko Building No. 2, 1-8-2 Marunouchi, Chiyoda-ku Mon–Fri 10am –5.30pm; free; ☎03/3214-6051; Tokyo Station), a dedicated travel library with over 25,000 volumes.

JNTO offices overseas

Australia Level 18, Australia Square Tower, 264 George St, Sydney, NSW 2000 ☎02/9251 3024, ⓔjntosyd@tokyonet.com.au.
Canada 165 University Ave, Toronto, ON M5H 3B8 ☎416/366-7140, ⓔjnto@interlog.com.
China 6F, Chang Fu Gong Office Building, 26 Jianguomenwai Dajie, Chaoyang-qu, Beijing 100022 ☎010/6513-9023; Suite 3704-05, 37F, Dorset House, Taikoo Place, Quarry Bay, Hong Kong ☎2968-5688.
South Korea 10F, Press Centre Offices, 25 Taepyongno 1-ga, Chung-gu, Seoul ☎02/732-7525.
UK Heathcoat House, 20 Savile Row, London W1X 1AE ☎020/7734 9638, ⊛www.jnto.go.jp.
US One Rockefeller Plaza, Suite 1250, New York, NY 10020 ☎212/757-5640, ⓔinfo@jntonyc.org;

Tokyo addresses

Tokyo addresses are described by a hierarchy of areas, rather than numbers running consecutively along named roads. A typical address starts with the largest administrative district – in Tokyo's case its Tokyo-*to* (metropolis), but most commonly its the *ken* (prefecture) accompanied by a seven-digit postcode – for example, Saitama-ken 850-0072. Next comes the *ku* (ward; for example Shinjuku-ku), followed by *chō* (districts), then *chōme* (local neighbourhoods), blocks and, finally, individual buildings.

Japanese addresses are therefore written in reverse order from the Western system. However, when written in English, they usually follow the Western order; this is the system we adopt in the guide. For example, the address 2-12-7 Roppongi, Minato-ku identifies building number 7, somewhere on block 12 of number 2 *chōme* in Roppongi district, in the Minato ward of Tokyo. Most buildings bear a small metal tag with their number (eg 2-12-7, or just 12-7), while lampposts often have a bigger plaque with the district name in *kanji* and the block reference (eg 2-12). Note that the same address can also be written 12-7 Roppongi, 2-chōme, Minato-ku.

Though the system's not too difficult in theory, actually **locating an address** on the ground can be frustrating. The consolation is that even Japanese people find it tough. The best strategy is to have the address written down, preferably in Japanese, and then get to the nearest train or bus station. Once in the neighbourhood, start asking; local police boxes (*kōban*) are a good bet and have detailed maps of their own areas. If all else fails, don't be afraid to phone – often someone will come to meet you. In addition, technology may soon come to the rescue: hand-held personal navigation systems, much like those for cars, are already becoming common in Japan.

360 Post St, Suite 601, San Francisco, CA 94108 ℡415/989-7140, ✉sfjnto@webjapan.com; 515 Figueroa St, Suite 1470, Los Angeles, CA 90071 ℡213/623-1952, ✉info@jnto-lax.org.

Maps

You can pick up free **maps** of the city from any of the tourist centres; look out for the handy "Welcome to Tokyo" map of central Tokyo (within the Yamanote line), with detailed area maps on the back. If you plan to be in the city for more than just a few days or want to wander off the beaten track it's well worth investing in Kodansha's bilingual *Tokyo City Atlas* (¥2100), which gives more detail and, importantly, includes *chōme* and block numbers to help pin down addresses (see box above).

Specialist map suppliers

UK and Ireland

Blackwell's Map and Travel Shop 50 Broad St, Oxford OX1 3BQ ℡01865/793 550, ⓦwww.blackwell.bookshop.co.uk. Branches in

Bristol, Cambridge, Cardiff, Leeds, Liverpool, Newcastle, Reading and Sheffield.

Daunt Books 83 Marylebone High St, London W1U 4QW ℡020/7224 2295, ℻7224 6893; 193 Haverstock Hill, London NW3 4QL ℡020/7794 4006.

Easons Bookshop 40/42 Lower O'Connell St, Dublin 1 ℡01/873 3811.

Fred Hanna's Bookshop 27–29 Nassau St, Dublin 2 ℡01/677 1255, ⓦwww.hannas.ie.

John Smith and Sons Glasgow Caledonian University, 70 Cowcaddens Rd, Glasgow G4 0BA ℡0141/332 8177, ⓦwww.johnsmith.co.uk.

National Map Centre 22–24 Caxton St, London SW1H 0QU ℡020/7222 2466, ⓦwww.mapsnmc.co.uk.

Newcastle Map Centre 55 Grey St, Newcastle upon Tyne NE1 6EF ℡0191/261 5622, ⓦwww.newtraveller.com.

Stanfords 12–14 Long Acre, London WC2E 9LP ℡020/7836 1321, ⓦwww.stanfords.co.uk. Other branches at 39 Spring Gardens, Manchester ℡0161/831 0250, and 29 Corn St, Bristol ℡0117/929 9966. One of the best travel bookshops in the world. Offers a worldwide mail-order service.

The Travel Bookshop 13–15 Blenheim Crescent, London W11 2EE ☏020/7229 5260, Ⓦwww.thetravelbookshop.co.uk.
Waterstone's 91 Deansgate, Manchester M3 2BW ☏0161/837 3000, Ⓦwww.waterstonesbooks.co.uk.

North America

110 North Latitude US ☏336/369-4171, Ⓦwww.110nlatitude.com.
Book Passage 51 Tamal Vista Blvd, Corte Madera, CA 94925 and in the historic San Francisco Ferry Building ☏1-800/999-7909 or ☏415/927-0960, Ⓦwww.bookpassage.com.
Globe Corner Bookstore 28 Church St, Cambridge, MA 02138 ☏1-800/358-6013, Ⓦwww.globecorner.com.
Longitude Books 115 W 30th St 1206, New York, NY 10001 ☏1-800/342-2164, Ⓦwww.longitudebooks.com.
Travel Bug Bookstore 3065 W Broadway, Vancouver, BC V6K 2G9 ☏604/737-1122, Ⓦwww.travelbugbooks.ca.
World of Maps 1235 Wellington St, Ottawa, ON K1Y 3A3 ☏1-800/214-8524 or ☏613/724-6776, Ⓦwww.worldofmaps.com.

Australia and New Zealand

Mapland 372 Little Bourke St, Melbourne ☏03/9670 4383, Ⓦwww.mapland.com.au.
The Map Shop 6–10 Peel St, Adelaide ☏08/8231 2033, Ⓦwww.mapshop.net.au.
Mapworld 173 Gloucester St, Christchurch ☏0800/627 967 or ☏03/374 5399, Ⓦwww.mapworld.co.nz.
Perth Map Centre 1/884 Hay St, Perth ☏08/9322 5733.
Specialty Maps 46 Albert St, Auckland ☏09/307 2217.
Travel Bookshop Shop 3, 175 Liverpool St, Sydney ☏02/9261 8200.
Worldwide Maps and Guides 187 George St, Brisbane ☏07/3221 4330.

Websites

There's a massive number of **websites** in both English and Japanese on Japan and Tokyo. Yahoo's directory (Ⓦwww.yahoo.com) is a good jumping-off point for a general overview of Japan-related sites – a few of the more useful are detailed below. See p.33 for information about getting online while in Tokyo.
Being A Broad Ⓦwww.being-a-broad.com. Tons of useful info on life in Japan from a female perspective.

Big Daikon Ⓦwww.bigdaikon.com. Lets you find out what JETs past, present and future think about Japan.
Japan Rail (JR) Ⓦwww.japanrail.com and Ⓦwww.world.eki-net.com. Information on rail passes, train and ferry schedules and some fares. The World Eki-net site allows you to book Shinkansen tickets online.
Japan Reference Forum Ⓦwww.jref.com/forum. For anything Japanese you wish to chat or ask questions about.
Japan Travel Updates Ⓦwww.jnto.go.jp The best single place on the Web to start looking for general travel-related information. The databases are particularly useful, particularly the train and flight timetables, as well as links to accommodation resources.
Kabuki for Everyone Ⓦwww.fix.co.jp/kabuki/kabuki.html. Good introduction to Kabuki, with video and sound clips, play summaries and so forth.
Kids Web Japan Ⓦwww.jinjapan.org/kidsweb/index.html. Anyone travelling with children should take a look at this site. In addition to simple background information, folk legends and general cultural titbits, it offers an insight into what's currently cool at school in Japan.
Links Ⓦhttp://jguide.stanford.edu, Ⓦwww.jinjapan.org and Ⓦhttp://jin.jcic.or.jp/navi/index.html (Japan Web Navigator). Stanford University's *Jguide* has a vast, well-organized list of sites. The *Japan Information Network* comprises a number of useful and interesting sites, among them the *Japan Web Navigator*, with a more manageable array of links.
Metropolis Ⓦwww.metropolis.japantoday.com. You can read this weekly English-language freesheet online and trawl its back issues for everything from celebrity interviews to personal ads.
News Ⓦhttp://mdn.mainichi.co.jp, Ⓦwww.japantimes.co.jp and Ⓦwww.japantoday.com. Among the online English-language newspapers, the *Mainichi Daily News* is the pick of the bunch, while the digital *Japan Times* has the advantage of searchable archives. *Japan Today* features all the latest news in English from Japan and around the region, including business news, features and commentary.
Online Odakyu Ⓦwww.odakyu-group.co.jp/english. Details of Odakyū Railway Company's tours, discount tickets and service centre in Tokyo's Shinjuku Station. Also has information on sightseeing around the Odakyū network, which covers Hakone and Kamakura.
Outdoor Japan Ⓦwww.outdoorjapan.com. The best resource for information on all outdoor activities

across the country, plus lots of travel advice for off-the-beaten-track destinations.

Prices ⓦwww.pricechecktokyo.com. Lists prices for a whole range of items, from café latte to a tube of toothpaste. If it's not there, they'll find the price for you.

Superfuture ⓦwww.superfuture.com. Tells you where to head for the coolest shops and bars.

Tokyo Food Page ⓦwww.bento.com. Lists scores of restaurants, cafés and bars around the city.

Tokyo Q ⓦwww.club.nokia.co.jp/tokyoq/. Long-running online weekly magazine with a fun,

authoritative and quirky take on the city, including a good clubbing guide

Tokyo Toursim Info
ⓦwww.tourism.metro.tokyo.jp. The official site of the Tokyo Government, with details of events around the city, including local festivals, plus a wide range of self-guided walking tours.

Trends in Japan ⓦwww.jinjapan.org/trends. Covers arts and entertainment, as well as business, sports, fashion and much more.

Yes! Tokyo ⓦwww.tcvb.or.jp. Put together by the Tokyo Convention and Visitors Bureau, this is one of the most comprehensive guides around.

Arrival, orientation and city transport

If you're arriving in Tokyo from abroad, you'll almost certainly touch down at New Tokyo International Airport. If you're coming to the capital from elsewhere in Japan, you'll arrive at Haneda Airport on Tokyo Bay, one of the main train stations (Tokyo, Ueno, Shinagawa or Shinjuku), the ferry port at Ariake on Tokyo Bay, or the long-distance bus terminals, mainly at Tokyo and Shinjuku stations.

By plane

Some 66km east of the city centre, **New Tokyo International Airport** (better known as Narita) has two terminals, both with similar facilities. Flight arrival and departure information is available on ☎0476/34-5000 and ⓦwww.narita-airport.or.jp. Be prepared for immigration delays and baggage searches. There are **cash machines** which accept foreign credit and debit cards and a **bureau de change** at both terminals (Terminal One: 6.30am–11pm; Terminal Two: 7am–1pm), which offer the same rates as city banks. The main **tourist information centre** (daily 9am–8pm; ☎0476/34-6251) is at the newer Terminal Two; staff here can provide maps and leaflets for across Japan. The neighbouring Welcome Inn counter can make hotel bookings free of charge. Terminal One has a smaller information centre (daily 9am–8pm), providing much the same service. If you have a Japan Rail Pass exchange order, you can arrange your to use your pass

either immediately or at a later date at the JR travel agencies (not the ticket offices) in the basement; English signs indicate where these are.

Located on a spit of land jutting into Tokyo Bay 20km south of the Imperial Palace, **Haneda Airport** is where most domestic flights touch down (flight information ☎03/5757-8111; ⓦwww.tokyo-airport -bldg.co.jp). There's a small branch of the **Tokyo Tourist Information Centre** (daily 9am–10pm; ☎03/5757-9345), and the airport information desk can provide you with an English-language map of Tokyo. There are direct bus and train connections from Narita to Haneda; the bus (1hr 20min; ¥3000) is more frequent than the train (1hr 10min; ¥1580).

By train

If you're coming into Tokyo by Shinkansen **JR train** from Ōsaka, Kyoto and other points west, you'll pull in to **Tokyo Station**, close to

Transport between the city and airports

The fastest way into Tokyo **from Narita** is on one of the frequent JR or Keisei **trains** that depart from the basements of both terminals. Keisei, located on the left side of the basements, offers the cheapest connection into town in the form of the no-frills *tokkyū* (limited express) service, which costs ¥1000 to Ueno (every 30min; 1hr 10min). This service also stops at Nippori, a few minutes north of Ueno, where it's easy to transfer to the Yamanote or the Keihin Tōhoku lines. If you're staying around Ueno, or you're not carrying much luggage, this – or the slightly faster and fancier Skyliner (¥1920) – is the best option.

JR, who operate from the right-hand side of the basements, run the more luxurious red and silver **Narita Express** (N'EX) to several city stations. The cheapest fare is ¥2940 to Tokyo Station (every 30min; 1hr), and there are frequent direct N'EX services to Shinjuku (hourly; 1hr 20min) for ¥3110. The N'EX services to Ikebukuro (¥3110) and Yokohama (¥4180) are much less frequent – you're better off going to Shinjuku and changing onto the Yamanote line for Ikebukuro, while there are plenty of trains to Yokohama from Tokyo Station. Cheaper than the N'EX are JR's *kaisoku* (rapid) trains which, despite their name, chug slowly into Tokyo Station (hourly; 1hr 20min) for ¥1280.

Limousine buses are useful if you're weighed down by luggage, though they're prone to delays in traffic. Although the tickets are pricier than the train, once you factor in the cost of a taxi from one of the train stations to your hotel, these buses are probably a better deal. You buy tickets from the limousine bus counters in each of the arrival lobbies; the buses depart directly outside (check which platform you need) and stop at a wide range of places around the city, including all the major hotels and train stations. The journey to hotels in Shinjuku and Ikebukuro costs around ¥3000 and takes a minimum of ninety minutes. **Taxis** to the city centre can be caught from stand 9 outside the arrivals hall of Terminal One and stand 30 outside the arrivals hall of Terminal Two; the journey will set you back around ¥20,000, and is no faster than going by bus.

From **Haneda Airport** it's a twenty-minute monorail journey to Hamamatsuchō Station on the Yamanote line (daily 5.20am–11.15pm; every 5–10min; ¥460). A taxi from Haneda to central Tokyo costs ¥6000, while a limousine bus to Tokyo Station is ¥900.

If you're **leaving Tokyo** from Narita airport, it's important to set off around four hours before your flight, though you can skip the queues to some extent by checking in and completing immigration formalities (8am–6pm) at the Tokyo City Air Terminal (TCAT; ☎03/3665-7111), located above Suitengūmae Station at the end of the Hibiya line. Not all airlines have desks at TCAT, so check first. The onward journey is then by limousine bus – allow at least one hour – with departures every ten minutes (¥2900). If you went through immigration at TCAT, you'll have been given a special card that allows you to scoot through the "crew line" at passport control in Narita. Nevertheless, during peak holiday periods, queues at the baggage check-in and immigration desks at both Narita and TCAT are lengthy. **International departure tax** from Narita is included in the price of your ticket.

the Imperial Palace, or **Shinagawa Station**, around 6km southwest. Most Shinkansen services from the north (the Hokuriku line from Nagano, the Jōetsu line from Niigata and the Tōhoku lines from Akita, Hachinoe and Yamagata) arrive at Tokyo Station, though a few services only go as far as **Ueno**, some 4km northeast of the Imperial Palace. Tokyo, Shinagawa and Ueno stations are all on the Yamanote line and are connected to several subway lines, putting them within reach of most of the capital. Other long-distance JR train services stop at Tokyo and Ueno stations, Shinjuku Station on Tokyo's west side and Ikebukuro Station in the city's northwest corner.

23

Tokyo: arrival

Haneda Airport	*Haneda Kūkō*	羽田空港
New Tokyo International Airport (Narita)	*Shin-Tōkyō Kokusai Kūkō (Narita)*	新東京国際空港（成田）
Bus, ferry and train stations		
Ikebukuro	*Ikebukuro-eki*	池袋駅
Shibuya	*Shibuya-eki*	渋谷駅
Shinagawa	*Shinagawa-eki*	品川駅
Shinjuku	*Shinjuku-eki*	新宿駅
Tokyo	*Tōkyō-eki*	東京駅
Tokyo Ferry Port	*Tōkyō Ferii Noriba*	東京フェリー乗り場
Ueno	*Ueno-eki*	上野駅

Non-JR trains terminate at different stations: the Tōkyū Tōyoko line from Yokohama ends at Shibuya Station, southwest of the Imperial Palace; the Tōbu Nikkō line runs from Nikkō to Asakusa Station, east of Ueno; and the Odakyū line from Hakone finishes at Shinjuku Station, which is also the terminus for the Seibu Shinjuku line from Kawagoe. All these stations have subway connections and (apart from Asakusa) are on the Yamanote rail line.

By bus

Long-distance buses pull in at several major stations around the city, making transport connections straightforward. The main overnight services from Kyoto and Ōsaka arrive at the bus station beside the eastern Yaesu exit of Tokyo Station – other buses arrive at Ikebukuro, Shibuya, Shinagawa and Shinjuku.

By boat

The most memorable way to arrive in the capital is by long-distance ferry, sailing past the suspended roads and monorail on the Rainbow Bridge and the harbour wharves to dock at Tokyo Ferry Port at Ariake, on the man-made island of Odaiba (see p.146) in Tokyo Bay. There are ferry connections to Tokyo from Kita-Kyūshū in Kyūshū, Kōchi and Tokushima on Shikoku, and Naha on Okinawa-Hontō. Buses run from the port to Shin-Kiba Station which is both on the subway and the JR Keiyō line and ten minutes' ride from Tokyo Station. A taxi from the port to central Tokyo

shouldn't cost more than ¥2000.

Orientation

Think of Tokyo not as one city with a central heart but as several mini-cities, linked by the arteries of the railway and the veins of the subway system. It's a vast place, but as a visitor you're unlikely to stray beyond its most central wards. The most useful reference point is the **Yamanote line**, an elongated overland train loop that connects and encloses central Tokyo and virtually everything of interest to visitors. Sightseeing destinations that fall outside of the loop are mainly within what was once called Shitamachi, or the "low city", east of the Imperial Palace, including Asakusa and Ryōgoku, and on Tokyo Bay to the south, including the nascent 21st-century metropolis of Odaiba.

Get your bearings by tracing the Yamanote route on a map, starting at the mini-city of **Shinjuku**, on the west side of Tokyo, where a cluster of skyscrapers provides a permanent directional marker wherever you are in the city. From Shinjuku, the line heads north towards the mini-city of **Ikebukuro**, where the sixty-storey Sunshine Building, east of the station, is another landmark. The Yamanote then veers east towards **Ueno**, the jumping-off point for the park and national museums. Further east of Ueno, at Asakusa, is **Sensō-ji**, Tokyo's major Buddhist temple.

From Ueno the Yamanote runs south to **Akihabara**, the electronic discount shop district. From Akihabara Station, the **Sōbu** line heads directly westwards, providing – together with the **Chūō line** from Tokyo Station – the shortest rail route back to Shinjuku. Handy stations along these two lines include Suidōbashi for Tokyo Dome and Kōrakuen garden; Iidabashi for the Tokyo International Youth Hostel; and Sendagaya for the Metropolitan Gymnasium and the gardens of Shinjuku Gyoen. East of Akihabara, on the other hand, the Sōbu line runs across the Sumida-gawa to the sumo centre of Ryōgoku.

From Akihabara the Yamanote continues south through **Tokyo Station**, immediately east of the Imperial Palace and business districts of Ōtemachi and Marunouchi. Further south lie the entertainment districts of **Ginza** (closest stop Yūrakuchō) and **Shimbashi**, after which the line passes **Hamamatsuchō** (connected by monorail to Haneda airport), where you'll be able to see, to the east, the gardens of Hama Rikyū, next to the market at Tsukiji, on the edge of Tokyo Bay. On the west side is Tokyo Tower, just beyond which is the party district of **Roppongi**, marked by the colossal Mori Tower, heart of the new Roppongi Hills development.

The Rainbow Bridge across to the man-made island of **Odaiba** is clearly visible as the Yamanote veers down to **Shinagawa**, a hub of upmarket hotels, with rail connections through to Kawasaki, Yokohama and beyond. From here, the line turns sharply north and heads up towards fashionable **Shibuya**, another mini-city. On the western flank of **Harajuku**, the next stop after Shibuya, are the wooded grounds of Meiji-jingū, the city's most important shrine, and Yoyogi Park. **Yoyogi**, the station after Harajuku, is also on the Chūō line, and is just one stop from the start of your journey at Shinjuku.

City transport

The whole of Tokyo's public transport system is efficient, clean and safe, but as a visitor you'll probably find the **trains and subways** the best way of getting around. The lack of any signs in English makes the **bus system** a lot more challenging. However, once you've got a feel for the city, buses can be a good way of cutting across the few areas of Tokyo not served by a sub-

way or train line. For short, cross-town journeys, **taxis** are handy and, if shared by a group of people, not that expensive. **Cycling** (see p.211 for rental outlets) can also be a good way of zipping around if you stick to the quiet back streets. Given the excellent public transport facilities, the often appalling road traffic, the high cost of parking (if you're lucky enough to find a space) and Tokyo's confusing street layout, you'd need a very good reason to want to **rent a car** to get around the city, but we've listed some rental companies on p.211.

The subway

Its colourful map may look like a messy plate of noodles, but Tokyo's **subway** is relatively easy to negotiate: the simple colour-coding on trains and maps, as well as clear signposts (many in English), directional arrows, and new alpha-numeric codes for all central subway stations, make this by far the most *gaijin*-friendly form of transport. And while during rush hour (7.30–9am & 5.30–7.30pm) you may find yourself crushed between someone's armpit and another person's back, only rarely do the infamous white-gloved platform attendants shove commuters into carriages.

There are two systems, the nine-line **Tokyo Metro** (formerly called the Eidan; ⓦwww.tokyometro.jp/e/top.html) and the four-line **Toei** (ⓦwww.kotsu.metro.tokyo.jp), run by the city authority. The systems share some of the same stations, but unless you buy a special ticket from the vending machines that specifies your route from one system to the other, you cannot switch mid-journey between the two sets of lines without paying extra at the ticket barrier. Subways have connecting passageways to overland train lines, such as the Yamanote. See the colour section at the back of the book for a **map** of the subway system.

You'll generally pay for your **ticket** at the vending machines beside the electronic ticket gates – apart from major stations (marked with a triangle on the subway map), there are no ticket sales windows. If you're fazed by the wide range of price buttons, buy the cheapest ticket and sort out the difference with the gatekeeper at the other end. You must always

Sightseeing tours

For a quick overview of Tokyo, there are several **bus tours**, ranging from half-day jaunts around the central sights to visits out to Kamakura, Nikkō and Hakone. The tours are a hassle-free way of covering a lot of ground with English-speaking guides, though all the places they visit are easy enough to get to independently. If bus tours are not your cup of tea, but you still fancy having a guide on hand, there are also various **walking tours** of the city.

Hato Bus ℡03/3435-6081, ⑭www.hatobus.co.jp/english/index.html. Hato Bus's yellow coaches are a firm fixture on the Tokyo sightseeing circuit. The company runs a range of tours of the capital with English-speaking guides starting at ¥4000 for a half-day tour of the major central sights. Potentially the most interesting itinerary is its full-day Edo Tokyo tour (¥6000), including visits to Sengaku-ji, Zojo-ji, Tsukiji and the Edo Tokyo Museum.

Japan Gray Line ℡03/3433-5745, ⑭www.jgl.co.jp/inbound/traveler/traveler.htm. Offers one full-day and two half-day city tours and a one-day Fuji–Hakone excursion (¥12,000), with roughly the same itinerary and prices as Hato and Sunrise Tours.

Mr Oka's Walking Tours ℡0422/51-7673, ⑭www.homestead.com/mroka. Mr Oka has lived in the capital for over fifty years and offers a wide range of historically oriented walking tours starting from ¥2000. The main itineraries cover Yoyogi to Ginza and Jimbochō to Ueno.

Odakyū Q Tours ℡03/5321-7887, ⑭www.odakyu-group.co.jp/english. Located in Tokyo's Shinjuku Station, Odakyū Q offers unaccompanied excursions to Hakone including your train fare, lunch and an explanatory English-language guidebook (¥9500).

Sunrise Tours ℡03/5620-9500, ⑭www.jtb.co.jp/sunrisetour. Run by the Japan Travel Bureau (JTB), and offering several options. The cheapest is the half-day Cityrama Tokyo Morning (¥4000), covering Meiji-jingū, the Imperial Palace East Garden and Asakusa, while the full-day Dynamic Tokyo tour (¥12,000 including lunch) takes in Tokyo Tower, Asakusa, a tea ceremony, a river cruise and a drive through Ginza. Other options are Sukiyaki Night (¥6500), with a *sukiyaki* dinner and monorail ride over Tokyo Bay, and Kabuki Night (¥9800). One- and two-day excursions start at ¥11,000 for a day in Kamakura, ¥9500 by bus round Fuji and Hakone, and ¥11,500 for a trip to Nikkō. They also offer great deals on trips to Kyoto and Hiroshima by Shinkansen including one or more night's accommodation.

Taste of Culture ℡03/5716-5751, ⑭www.tasteofculture.com. Food writer Elizabeth Andoh runs cooking workshops and leads highly popular trips around Japanese markets, helping you to identify all those weird and wonderful Japanese products. You'll need to book well in advance for both.

---

buy separate tickets for subways and overland trains unless you're using an SF Metro or Pasunetto card (see opposite).

Trains run daily from around 5am to just after midnight, and during peak daytime hours as frequently as every five minutes (and at least every fifteen minutes at other times). Leaving a station can be complicated by the number of exits (sixty in Shinjuku, for example), but there are maps close to the ticket barriers and on the platforms indicating where the exits emerge, and strips of yellow tiles on the floor mark the routes to the ticket barriers.

The cheapest subway **ticket** is ¥160 and, since most journeys across central Tokyo cost no more than ¥190, few of the **travel passes** on offer are good value for short-stay visitors. However, if you're going to be travelling around a lot, it makes sense to buy **kaisūken**, carnet-type tickets where you get eleven tickets for the price of ten – look for the special buttons on the automated ticket machines at the stations. Off-peak tickets give you twelve tickets for the price of ten, but can only be used from 10am to 4pm on weekdays, while Saturday/Sunday and public holiday tickets give you fourteen tickets for the price of ten. Handiest of all is the **SF Metro Card**, or **Pasunetto Card**, which saves you no money, but can be used on both Tokyo Metro and Toei subways and all the private railways (but not JR) in the Tokyo area. As you go through a ticket barrier, the appropriate fare is deducted from the card's stored value (¥1000, ¥3000 or ¥5000); cards can be bought from ticket offices and machines, and also used in machines to pay for tickets. If you're here for a month or more and will be travelling the same route most days, you might buy a **teiki** season ticket, which runs for one, three or six months, and covers your specified route and stations in between.

Trains

Spend any length of time in Tokyo and you'll become very familiar with the JR **Yamanote train line** that loops around the city centre (see p.24 for a summary of its route). Other useful JR train routes include the **Chūō line** (shown in orange on subway maps; the trains are also painted orange), which starts at Tokyo Station and runs west to Shinjuku and the suburbs beyond to terminate beside the mountains at Takao – the rapid services (look for the red *kanji* characters on the side of the train) miss out on some stations. The yellow **Sōbu line** goes from Chiba in the east to Mitaka in the west, and runs parallel to the Chūō line in the centre of Tokyo, doubling as a local service, stopping at all stations. The blue **Keihin Tōhoku line** runs from Ōmiya in the north, through Tokyo Station, to Yokohama and beyond. It's fine to transfer between JR lines on the same ticket, but you'll have to buy a new ticket if you transfer to a subway line.

As on the subway, **tickets** are bought from vending machines. The lowest fare on JR lines is ¥130. Like the subways, JR offers pre-paid cards and *kaisūken* (carnet) deals on tickets. One of the handiest is the **Suica**, a stored-value card similar to the SF Metro Card (see above), which is available from ticket machines in all JR stations.

Buses

Although Tokyo's **buses** are handy for crossing the few areas without convenient subway and train stations, only a small number of the buses or routes are labelled in English, so you'll have to get used to recognizing the *kanji* names of places or memorizing the numbers of useful bus routes. The final destination is on the front of the bus, along with the route number. You pay on entry, by dropping the flat rate of ¥200 into the fare box by the driver (there's a machine in the box for changing notes). A recorded voice announces the next stop in advance, as well as issuing constant warnings about not forgetting your belongings when you get off the bus. If you're not sure when your stop is, ask your fellow passengers. The Transport Bureau of Tokyo Metropolitan Government issues a useful English pamphlet and map of all the bus routes; pick one up from one of the tourist information centres (see p.19).

Ferries

The Tokyo Cruise Ship Company (⊛ www.suijobus.co.jp) runs several **ferry** services, known as *suijū basu* (water buses), in and around Tokyo Bay. The most popular is the double-decker service plying the 35-minute route between the Sumida-gawa River Cruise stations at Asakusa, northeast of the city centre, and Hinode Sanbashi, on Tokyo Bay (daily every 40min until 6.15pm; ¥660). The large picture windows, which give a completely different view of the city from the one you'll get on the streets, are reason enough for hopping aboard, especially if you want to visit both Asakusa and the gardens at Hama Rikyū on the same day, and then walk into Ginza. The ferries stop at the gardens en route, and you can buy a combination ticket for the ferry and park entrance for around ¥720. For a few extra hundred yen you can travel on the space-age *Himiko* ferry (4 daily between Asakusa and Hinode), designed to resemble something out of a *manga*.

Hinode Sanbashi (close by Hinode Station on the Yurikamome monorail line or a ten-minute walk from Hamamatsuchō Station on the Yamanote line) is also the jumping-off point for several good daily **cruises** around Tokyo Bay and to various points around the island of Odaiba (one-way/return ¥500/900), or across to Kasai Rinkai-kōen (one-way/return ¥800/900) on the east side of the bay. In bad weather the ferries and cruises are best avoided, especially if you're prone to seasickness.

Taxis

For short hops around the centre of Tokyo, **taxis** are often the best option, though heavy traffic can slow them down. The basic rate is ¥660 for the first 2km, after which the meter racks up ¥80 every 274m, plus a time charge when the taxi is moving at less than 10km per hour. Between 11pm and 5am, rates are about twenty percent higher.

Taxis can be flagged down on most roads – a red light next to the driver means the cab is free; green means it's occupied. There are designated stands in the busiest parts of town, but after the trains stop at night, be prepared for long queues, especially in areas such as Roppongi and Shinjuku. There's a limit of four people in most taxis.

There's never any need to open or close the passenger doors since they are operated automatically by the taxi driver. It's also a good idea to have the name and address of your destination clearly written on a piece of paper to hand to the driver. Don't expect the driver to know where he's going, either; a stop at a local policebox may be necessary to locate the exact address.

The major taxi firms are Daiwa ☎03/3503-8421; Hinomaru Limousine ☎03/3212-0505, ⓦwww.hinomaru.co.jp; Kokusai ☎03/3452-5931; and Nippon Kōtsū ☎03/3799-9220 (24hr English answering service).

Costs, money and banks

Despite its reputation as an outrageously expensive city, with a little careful planning Tokyo is a manageable destination even for those on a fairly modest budget. The key is to do what the majority of Japanese do: eat in local restaurants, stay in Japanese-style inns and take advantage of any available discounts.

Currency

The **Japanese currency** is the yen (¥), of which there are no subdivisions. Notes are available in denominations of ¥1000, ¥2000, ¥5000 and ¥10,000, while coins come in values of ¥1, ¥5, ¥10, ¥50, ¥100 and ¥500. Apart from the ¥5 piece, a copper-coloured coin with a hole in the centre, all other notes and coins indicate their value in Western numerals. Note that not all ticket, change and vending machines have been upgraded to accept the new ¥2000 notes and ¥500 coins (although the older, more silvery ¥500 coins do work). At the time of writing the **exchange rate** was approximately ¥183 to £1, ¥108 to US$1, and ¥76 to A$1. Japan is currently experiencing negative inflation at a rate hovering between zero and minus one percent.

Costs

By staying in youth hostels and eating in the cheapest local restaurants, the absolute minimum **daily budget** for food and accommodation is ¥5000 (£27/US$46). By the time you've added in some transport costs, a few entry tickets, meals in better-class restaurants and one or two nights in a ryokan or business hotel, you'll be reaching a more realistic expenditure of at least ¥10,000 (approximately £54/US$92) per day.

Holders of **international student cards** are eligible for discounts on transport and some

Money and information

bank	*ginkō*	銀行
foreign exchange desk	*gaikoku kawase mado-guchi/ryōgae jo*	外国為替窓口／両替所
yen	*en*	円
tourist information office	*kankō annaijo*	観光案内所

admission fees, as are children. If you're planning to stay in hostels, it's worth buying a **Hostelling International card** in your home country; not only does the card qualify you for slight reductions at some hostels, but you can also take advantage of discount tour packages offered by the Japan Youth Hostel Association.

Before setting off, it's also worth checking JNTO's website for tips on how to save money – one recommendation is to buy the **GRUTT Pass**. This ¥2000 ticket is valid for two month after first being used and gains you entry to 44 public, national and private institutions, including all Tokyo's major museums, and also gives you discounts on special exhibitions at the museums. The ticket can be bought at the counters of most participating museums, or from Ticket PIA outlets (see Directory, p.211).

Changing money

Though credit cards are gaining in popularity, Japan is still very much a **cash society**. Thanks to the country's low crime levels and a surprisingly undeveloped banking system, most Japanese carry around relatively large amounts of yen, and it's fine for you to follow suit. That said, it's always safest to carry the bulk of your money in **travellers' cheques**, with the added advantage that in Japan they attract a slightly better exchange rate than

Consumption tax

A **consumption tax** (*shōhizei*) of five percent is levied on virtually all goods and services in Japan, including restaurant meals and accommodation. Sometimes this tax will be included in the advertised price, and sometimes not, so check first for large amounts.

notes. The most widely accepted cheques are American Express, Visa and Thomas Cook.

When exchanging either cash or travellers' cheques, **banks** usually offer the best rates, with little variation between them and no commission fees; look for banks announcing "Foreign Exchange Bank" in English outside the front door. Remember to take your passport along in case it's needed, and allow plenty of time, since even a simple transaction can take twenty minutes or more. Note that, while all authorized foreign exchange banks accept dollars and the vast majority will take sterling, other currencies can be a problem even in Tokyo; if you're stuck, Tokyo Mitsubishi Bank handles the widest range of currencies.

Main **post offices** often have an exchange counter where you can change cash or travellers' cheques in eight major currencies, including American, Canadian and Australian dollars, sterling and euros; their rates are usually close to the banks' and they have slightly longer opening hours (Mon–Fri 9am–4pm).

If you need to change money at any other time, big **department stores** often have an exchange desk, though most only handle dollars or a limited range of currencies and might charge a small fee. **Hotels** are only supposed to change money for their guests, but some might be persuaded to help in an emergency. Finally, when changing money, ask for a few ¥10,000 notes to be broken into lower denominations; these come in handy for ticket machines and small purchases.

Credit cards and wiring money

Credit and debit cards are far more widely accepted in Japan than they were a few years ago. The most useful cards to carry are

Banking hours

Banks open Monday to Friday 9am to 3pm, though some don't open their exchange desks until 10.30am or 11am. All Japanese banks close on Saturdays, Sundays and national holidays.

Visa and American Express, followed closely by MasterCard, then Diners Club, which you should be able to use in those hotels, restaurants, shops and travel agencies where they're used to serving foreigners. However, many retailers only accept locally issued cards, so it's never safe to assume you'll be able to use your foreign plastic.

Making **cash withdrawals** using plastic is becoming easier. Citibank and the post office operate ATMs which accept foreign-issued credit and debit cards; these can be found in many post offices and a few other handy locations such as Citibank offices, department stores and public buildings throughout the city. The machines are identified with a sticker saying "International ATM Service" and you can select instructions in English. They handle cards from nine networks, including Visa, PLUS, MasterCard, Cirrus, American Express and Diners Club; you'll need your PIN to make a withdrawal, which can be anywhere between ¥1000 and ¥999,000, depending on the issuer and your individual credit limit; if the machine doesn't allow you money in the first instance, try again with a smaller amount. The card must be inserted face up

and with the strip to the right. In major post offices the ATMs are accessible at weekends and after the counters have closed, though none is open 24 hours, and sometimes they just don't work for whatever reason, so it's best not to be totally reliant on your card.

In addition, Visa and MasterCard now have a fairly good spread of international ATMs, while Citibank operates a number of its own ATM corners in Tokyo. JNTO (see p.19) can provide lists of locations, or consult the relevant websites: Ⓦwww.visa.com, Ⓦwww.mastercard.com and Ⓦwww.citibank.co.jp. Most of these machines are accessible outside normal banking hours, and some are open 24 hours. The minimum withdrawal is normally ¥10,000. If you're having problems, pick up the phone beside the ATM and ask to speak to someone in English.

In an emergency, **wiring money** is the quickest option. You'll need to contact one of the major Japanese banks to check exactly how they handle these transfers and what charges they levy, then call on a reliable friend to make the arrangements at the other end. The whole process can take several days, and hefty charges are made at both ends (in Japan, typically around ¥2500 for yen transfers, while charges for other currencies are generally built into the exchange rate employed). Alternatively, you can use MoneyGram (Ⓦwww.moneygram.com), whereby you receive the transfer via a MoneyGram agent; charges vary according to the amount, but can be up to ten percent.

24-hour credit card emergency numbers

If you lose a credit or debit card, call the following toll-free numbers:
American Express ☏0120-020120 (general enquiries ☏0120-020666; Mon–Fri 9am–7pm).
MasterCard ☏00531/11-3886 (also handles general enquiries).
Visa International ☏0120-133173 (also handles general enquiries).

Post, phones and email

For a supposedly high-tech nation, Japan's communications infrastructure can at times seem rather old-fashioned – it's not unusual, for example, to see post office staff counting on an abacus. At the same time, everywhere you go in Tokyo you'll see people with mobile phones, and the Internet seems now to be equally ubiquitous, with connections in even humble business hotels and guesthouses, as well as at 24-hour manga and game-centre cafés.

Mail

Japan's **mail** service is highly efficient and fast, with post offices (*yūbin-kyoku*) easily identified by their red-and-white signs showing a T with a parallel bar across the top, the same symbol that you'll find on the red letter-boxes. All post can be addressed in Western script (*rūmaji*) provided it's clearly printed.

The Tokyo **Central Post Office** is on the west side of Tokyo Station (Mon–Fri 9am–7pm, Sat 9am–5pm, Sun 9am–12.30pm; 24hr service for stamps and parcels). The **International Post Office**, 2-3-3 Ōtemachi (same hours) is a bit less convenient, but usually quieter. For English-language information about postal services, call ☎03/5472-5851 (Mon–Fri 9.30am–4.30pm).

For **overseas post**, it costs ¥70 to send a postcard and ¥90 for an aerogram to anywhere in the world. Letters up to 25g cost ¥110 to North America, Australasia and Europe. Stamps are also sold at convenience stores, shops displaying the post office sign, and at larger hotels.

If you need to send bulkier items or **parcels** back home, all post offices sell reasonably priced special envelopes and boxes for packaging, with the maximum weight for an overseas parcel being 20kg. A good compromise between expensive air mail and lengthy sea mail is Surface Air Lifted (SAL) mail, which takes around three weeks to reach most destinations, and costs somewhere between the two.

Poste restante (*tomeoki* or *kyoku dome yūbin*) is available only at the Tokyo Central Post Office; mail is held for thirty days before being returned. To pick up post, go to the basement counter (Mon–Fri 8am–8pm, Sat 8am–5pm, Sun 9am–12.30pm) and take your passport. The postal address is 2-7-2 Marunouchi, Chiyoda-ku, Tokyo 100.

Phones

You're rarely far from a payphone in Tokyo, but only at certain ones – usually grey or metallic silver and bronze colour, with a sign in English – can you make **international calls**. It's sometimes difficult to find one of these phones – try a major hotel or international centre.

The vast majority of payphones take both coins (¥10 and ¥100) and **phonecards**

Mail and telephones

Post		
Post	*yūbin*	郵便
Post office	*yūbin-kyoku*	郵便局
Stamp	*kitte*	切手
Postcard	*hagaki*	はがき
Poste restante	*tomeoki/kyoku dome yūbin*	留置郵便/局留郵便

Telephones		
Telephone	*denwa*	電話
Mobile phone	*keitai-denwa*	携帯電話
Phonecard	*terefon kādo*	テレフォンカード

(*terefon kādo*). The latter come in ¥500 (50-unit) and ¥1000 (105-unit) versions and can be bought in department and convenience stores and at station kiosks. Virtually every tourist attraction sells specially decorated phonecards, which come in a vast range of designs, though you'll pay a premium for these, with a ¥1000 card only giving ¥500 worth of calls.

Payphones don't give change, but do return unused coins, so for local calls use ¥10 rather than ¥100 coins. For international calls, it's best to use a phonecard and to call between 7pm and 8am Monday to Friday, or at any time at weekends or holidays, when rates are cheaper. Alternatively, use a prepaid calling card, such as Brastel (advertised in all the Tokyo English-language media), to undercut the local rates altogether. All toll-free numbers begin with either ☎0120- or 0088-; for operator assistance for overseas calls, dial ☎0051.

Mobile phones

Nowadays, nearly everyone seems to have a **mobile phone** (*keitai-denwa*, sometimes just shortened to *keitai*). Most models take photos, video clips and can be used to surf the Net and send emails. The advanced technology systems that make all this possible also mean that, with a few high-tech exceptions, you cannot bring your mobile phone to Japan and expect it to work. The solution is to **rent** a Japan-compatible mobile phone or buy a prepaid one once you're in the country (go to any big electronics store where a phone plus calls should cost in the region of ¥10,000–15,000). Phones can be rented both abroad and in Tokyo. In the UK, Adam Phones rents phones for £1 a day; contact them on ☎0800/032 1200. In Japan, try Tokyobay Communication Co (✉www .tokyobay.co.jp/worldphone), who rent phones for ¥3500 for three days or ¥15,000 a month; you can pick up their phones at Narita when you fly into the country. For the latest info on Japan's cell phone system check the website of the biggest operator, NTT DoCoMo, ✉www.nttdocomo.com.

Phoning Japan from abroad

To **call Japan** from abroad, dial your interna-tional access code (UK and Ireland ☎00; US ☎011; Canada ☎011; Australia ☎0011; New Zealand ☎00), plus the country code (☎81), plus the area code minus the initial zero, plus the number.

Phoning abroad from Japan

The main companies in Japan offering **international phone calls** are KDDI (☎010), Japan Telecom (☎0041), Cable & Wireless IDC (☎0061) and NTT (☎0033). If you want to call abroad from Japan from any type of phone, choose a company (there's little difference between them all as far as rates are concerned) and dial the relevant number, then the country code (UK ☎44; US ☎1; Canada ☎1; Australia ☎61; New Zealand ☎64), plus the area code minus the initial zero, plus the number.

You can make **international operator-assisted calls** by using the Home Country Direct Call service to speak to an operator in your home country (UK ☎0039/441; US ☎005-39111; Canada ☎0039/161; Australia ☎0039/611; New Zealand ☎0039/641).

Alternatively, you could use a **charge card or calling card** (see below) which will automatically debit the cost of any calls from your domestic phone account or credit card. To use these, dial the relevant access code, followed by your account and PIN number, then the number you want to call. Discount calling cards in Japan, such as Brastel, can be bought at convenience stores.

Charge card operators

UK BT ☎00/3100 4410; Cable & Wireless Calling ☎00/665 5444 (☎0039/444 for calls to the UK).
US and Canada AT&T ☎0039/111; MCI ☎0039/121; Sprint ☎0039/131.
Australia and New Zealand Optus Calling Card ☎0039/612; New Zealand Telecom's Calling Card ☎0039/641; Telstra Telecard ☎00539/611.

Phoning within Japan

Everywhere in Japan has an **area code**, which must be dialled in full if you're making a long-distance call and is omitted if the call is a local one. Tokyo's area code is ☎03; the codes for places listed in this guide outside

Twenty-four-hour cybercafés

In all the main areas of the city you'll find 24-hour manga and computer-games parlours where you can also get online. The per-hour fees for these places can be quite steep during the day, but they come into their own in the wee small hours when they function as crash pads for kids waiting for the first train home in the morning after they've been partying.

One of the best of these cybercafés is **Gera Gera** (B1 Remina Bldg, 3-17-4 Shinjuku, Shinjuku-ku; ☎03/3350-5692). They charge ¥380 for one hour (then ¥50 for every extra 10min) and you can surf the Web, play video games, watch DVDs and leaf through over fifty thousand comics, as well as consuming all the soft drinks you want for an extra ¥180. **Bagus** (28-6 Udagawa-chō, Shibuya-ku ☎03/5428-3217), on the 6th floor of the same building as HMV Records (see p.209), also has English DVDs if you want to watch a movie. Internet access costs ¥510 for the first hour and then ¥75 for every extra ten minutes from Friday to Sunday (¥480 for the first hour at other times). From 11pm to 8am you can park yourself here for six hours for ¥1260, and drinks are free at all times.

the Tokyo metropolitan area are given in the review.

Faxes

Most hotels and youth hostels will allow you to send a **fax** for a small charge, while receiving a fax is usually free if you're a guest. Alternatively, most central post offices or convenience stores (often open 24hr) have public fax machines.

Email and the Internet

Cybercafés can be found across Tokyo – often as part of a 24-hour computer-game and manga (Japanese comic) centre. Free access is sometimes available; otherwise, expect to pay around ¥300–500 per hour. Cybercafés come and go fairly swiftly, although the copyshop Kinko's is pretty reliable and has branches throughout Tokyo; call their toll-free number (☎0120-001966)

to find the one nearest you. Otherwise, at the time of writing the following places were offering free or cheap (for the cost of a cup of coffee) Internet connections: Marunouchi Café (Mon–Fri 8am–8pm, Sat & Sun 10am–6pm), 1F, Shin Tokyo Building, 3-3-1 Marunouchi, Chiyoda-ku, where you can also plug in your own computer; Apple Ginza Store, 3-5-12 Ginza, Chūō-ku (daily 10am–9pm); Virgin record stores in Shinjuku and Ikebukuro (daily except Wed 11am–10pm). There's also free Internet access at the TCVB Tourist Centre (see p.19).Many hotels now have **broadband Internet** access in every room, often offered free or for a small daily fee (typically ¥1000 per day). For this you'll need to have a LAN (local area network) cable; if the hotel doesn't provide one, they can be bought in all electronic shops for around ¥500.

BASICS | Post, phones and email

The media

The most widely available English-language daily newspaper is the independent, but far from sparkling, Japan Times (¥160). It carries comprehensive coverage of national and international news, and a major situations vacant section every Monday, as well as occasionally interesting features, some culled from the world's media. A far better read and almost as widely available is The International Herald Tribune (¥150), published in conjunction with the English-language version of the Asahi Shimbun.

Doing a reasonable job on the features front is the *Daily Yomiuri* (¥120), with a decent arts and entertainment supplement on Thursdays. Also worth a look is the Japan edition of the *Financial Times*.

The best overall **English-language magazine** is the free weekly *Metropolis*, which is packed with ads, reviews, features and listings for film and music events. *Tokyo Notice Board* (Ⓦ www.tokyonoticeboard.co.jp) is another free weekly devoted almost entirely to classifieds. Also worth a look are a couple more freesheets: the irreverent national monthly magazine *Japanzine* (Ⓦ www.japan -zine.com), which has a Tokyo listings and review section; and *Tokyo Weekender* (Ⓦ www.weekender.co.jp), which caters to the expat and diplomatic scene. You might also find the quarterly *Tokyo Journal* (¥600; Ⓦ www.tokyo.to) of interest. You'll find all these at the Tokyo Tourist Information Centre, larger hotels, foreign-language bookstores and bars or restaurants frequented by *gaijin*. Bookstores such as Kinokuniya and Maruzen stock extensive (and expensive) ranges of imported and local magazines; Tower Records is the cheapest place to buy magazines.

Television and radio

Japanese **television**'s notorious reputation for silly game shows and *samurai* dramas is well earned. If you don't speak Japanese, you're likely to find all TV shows, bar the frequent weather forecasts, totally baffling – and only a little less so once you have picked up the lingo. However, watching some TV during your stay is recommended if only because of the fascinating insight it gives into Japanese society.

NHK, the main state broadcaster, has two channels (in Tokyo, NHK on channel one and NHK Educational on channel three), which are roughly equal to BBC1 and BBC2 in the UK, although much less adventurous. If you have access to a bilingual TV, it's possible to tune into the English-language commentary for NHK's nightly 7pm news. Films and imported TV shows on both NHK and the commercial channels are also sometimes broadcast with an alternative English soundtrack. In Tokyo, the other main channels are Nihon TV (four), TBS (six), Fuji TV (eight), TV Asahi (ten) and TV Tokyo (twelve), all flagship channels of the nationwide networks, with little to choose between them. **Satellite** and **cable** channels available in all top-end hotels include BBC World, CNN and MTV.

In Tokyo the main FM **radio** stations broadcasting bilingual programmes are J-WAVE (81.3MHz) and Inter FM (76.1MHz); both tend towards the bland end of the music spectrum. You can check out Inter FM on the Web at Ⓦ www.interfm.co.jp.

Opening hours, national holidays and festivals

Business hours are generally Monday to Friday 9am to 5pm, though private companies often close much later in the evening and may also open on Saturday mornings. Department stores and bigger shops tend to open around 10am and shut at 7pm or 8pm, with no break for lunch. Local shops, however, will generally stay open later, while many convenience stores stay open 24 hours. Most shops take one day off a week, not necessarily on a Sunday.

Banks open on weekdays from 9am to 3pm, and close on Saturdays, Sundays and national holidays. **Post offices** tend to work 9am to 5pm on weekdays, closing at weekends and also on national holidays, though a few open on Saturdays from 9am to 3pm. Central post offices, on the other hand, open till 7pm in the evening and on Saturdays from 9am to 5pm and Sundays and holidays from 9am to 12.30pm. Larger offices are also likely to operate an after-hours service for parcels and express mail, sometimes up to 24 hours at major post offices.

The majority of **museums** close on a Monday, but stay open on Sundays and national holidays; last entry is normally thirty minutes before closing. Most museums and department stores stay open on **national holidays**; they usually take the following day off instead. However, during the New Year festival (January 1–3), Golden Week (April 29–May 5) and Obon (the week around August 15), almost everything shuts down. Around these periods all transport and accommodation is booked out weeks in advance, and all major tourist spots get overrun.

Festivals and events

Whenever you visit Tokyo, chances are there'll be a **religious festival** (*matsuri*) taking place somewhere; the TICs (see p.19) publish a monthly round-up of festivals in and around the city and you can find details on the Web, too (see p.21).

Of the major events listed below, by far the most important is **New Year**, when most of the city closes down for a week (roughly Dec 28–Jan 3). Note that in some cases the

dates might change, so be sure to double-check before setting out. For a full list of public holidays, see below.

Tokyo also hosts three grand **sumo tournaments** each year (see p.192), as well as **film** and **theatre festivals**. Several non-Japanese festivals which have also caught on include **Valentine's Day** (February 14), when women give men gifts of chocolate, while on **White Day** (March 14) men get their turn with chocolates (white, of course), perfume or racy underwear. Another import

National holidays

If one of the holidays listed below falls on a Sunday, then the Monday is also a holiday.

Jan 1	New Year's Day
Second Mon in Jan	Adults' Day
Feb 11	National Foundation Day
March 20/21	Spring Equinox
April 29	Showa Day
May 3	Constitution Memorial Day
May 4	Greenery Day (a "bridge" day between the two holidays)
May 5	Children's Day
July 20	Marine Day
Sept 15	Respect-for-the-Aged Day
Sept 23/24	Autumn Equinox
Second Mon in Oct	Sports Day
Nov 3	Culture Day
Nov 23	Labour Thanksgiving Day
Dec 23	Emperor's Birthday

is **Christmas**, which is celebrated in Japan as an almost totally commercial event, with plastic holly and tinsel in profusion. **Christmas Eve**, in particular, is one of the most popular date nights of the year, when all the most expensive and trendiest restaurants are booked solid. By contrast, **New Year's Eve** is a fairly subdued, family-oriented event.

January

Ganjitsu (or Gantan) January 1. The first shrine-visit of the year (*hatsu-mōde*) draws the crowds to Meiji-jingū, Hie-jinja, Kanda Myōjin and other city shrines to pray for good fortune. Performances of traditional dance and music take place at Yasukuni-jinja.
Ippan Sanga January 2. Thousands of loyal Japanese – and a few curious foreigners – troop into the Imperial Palace grounds to greet the emperor. The royal family appear on the balcony several times during the day from 9.30am to 3pm.
Dezomeshiki January 6. Tokyo firemen in Edo-period costume pull off dazzling stunts atop long bamboo ladders. In Harumi, Tokyo Bay.
Seijin-no-hi (Adults' Day) Second Monday in January. National holiday. Colourful pageant of 20-year-old women, and a few men, in traditional dress visiting city shrines to celebrate their entry into adulthood. At Meiji-jingū various ancient rituals are observed, including a ceremonial archery contest.

February

Setsubun February 3 or 4. On the last day of winter by the lunar calendar, people scatter lucky beans around their homes and at shrines or temples to drive out evil and welcome in the year's good luck. The liveliest festivities take place at Sensō-ji, Kanda Myōjin, Zōjō-ji and Hie-jinja.

March

Hina Matsuri (Doll Festival) March 3. Families with young girls display beautiful dolls of the emperor, empress and their courtiers dressed in ancient costume. Department stores, hotels and museums often put on special displays at this time.
Hi Watari Second Sunday in March. Spectacular fire-walking ceremony held at the foot of Mount Takao.

April

Hana Matsuri April 8. The Buddha's birthday is celebrated in all Tokyo's temples, with either parades or quieter celebrations, during which a small statue of Buddha is sprinkled with sweet tea.
Kamakura Matsuri Mid-April. Kamakura's week-long festival includes traditional dances, costume parades and horseback archery.
Jibeta Matsuri Mid-April. In this celebration of fertility, an iron phallus is forged and giant wooden phalluses paraded around Kanayama-jinja in Kawasaki amidst dancing crowds, including a group of demure transvestites.
Design Festa Mid-April & November. Hundreds of young and aspiring artists converge on Tokyo Big Sight in Odaiba for this twice-yearly festival of design.

May

Kodomo-no-hi (Children's Day) May 5. National holiday. The original Boys' Day now includes all children as families fly carp banners, symbolizing strength, outside their homes.
Kanda Matsuri Mid-May. One of the city's top three festivals, taking place in odd-numbered years at Kanda Myōjin, during which people in Heian-period costume escort eighty gilded *mikoshi* (portable shrines) through the streets.

Hanami parties

With the arrival of spring in early April, a pink tide of **cherry blossom** washes north over Tokyo lasting little more than a week. The finest displays are along the moat around the Imperial Palace (particularly the section close by Yasukuni-jinja), in Ueno-kōen, Aoyama Cemetery, the riverside Sumida-kōen and on the banks of the Meguro-gawa west of Meguro Station, where every tree shelters a blossom-viewing party. The blossom is best seen at night, under the light of hanging paper lanterns, though this is also the rowdiest time as revellers, lubricated with quantities of sake, croon to competing karaoke machines.

Tōshō-gū Haru Matsuri May 17–18. Huge procession of one thousand armour-clad warriors and three *mikoshi*, commemorating the burial of Shogun Tokugawa Ieyasu in Nikkō in 1617.
Sanja Matsuri Third weekend in May. Tokyo's most boisterous festival, when over one hundred *mikoshi* are jostled through the streets of Asakusa, accompanied by lion dancers, geisha and musicians.

June

Sannō Matsuri June 13–20. The last of the big three festivals (after Kanda and Sanja) takes place in even-numbered years, focusing on colourful processions of *mikoshi* through Akasaka.

July

International Lesbian and Gay Film Festival Mid-July. One of the best Tokyo film festivals, dedicated to queer film and roundly supported by the international community. Films are screened at the Spiral Building in Aoyama.
Hanabi Taikai Late July and early August. The summer skies explode with thousands of fireworks, harking back to traditional "river-opening" ceremonies to mark the start of the summer boating season. The Sumida-gawa display is the most spectacular (view it from river-boats or Asakusa's Sumida-kōen on the last Sat in July), but those in Edogawa, Tamagawa, Arakawa and Harumi come close, or head out to Kamakura for their *hanabi taikai* on August 10.

August

Fukagawa Matsuri Mid-August. Every three years Tomioka Hachiman-gū hosts the city's wettest festival, when spectators throw buckets of water over 54 *mikoshi* being shouldered through the streets.
Obon Mid-August. Families gather around their ancestral graves, and much of Tokyo closes down, while many neighbourhoods stage dances in honour of the deceased.
Summer Sonic Mid-August. Two-day event held in Chiba, just across the Edo-gawa river from Tokyo, showcasing a good mix of local and overseas bands, and with both indoor and outdoor performances. The organizers like to compare it to the UK's Reading Music Festival. See ⓦ www.summersonic.com for more details.
Asakusa Samba Carnival Late August. Rio comes to the streets of Asakusa with this spectacular parade of besequinned and feathered

dancers. Teams compete and the crowds come out in force to support them.

September

Tsurugaoka Hachiman-gū Matsuri September 14–16. Annual shrine-festival of Tsurugaoka Hachiman-gū in Kamakura. The highlight is a demonstration of horseback archery (*yabasume*) on the final day.
Ningyō Kuyō September 25. A funeral service for unwanted dolls is held at Kiyomizu Kannon-dō in Ueno-kōen, after which they are cremated.

October

Tokyo Designer's Week Early October. Catch the best of contemporary Japanese design at this event held at a variety of venues around Aoyama and Odaiba. The funkier Tokyo Designer's Block and the nordic cool Swedish Style, held at the same time, showcase the work of more designers.
Kawagoe Grand Matsuri October 14–15. One of the liveliest festivals in the Tokyo area, involving some 25 ornate floats and hundreds of costumed revellers.
Tōshō-gū Aki Matsuri October 17. Repeat of Nikkō's fabulous procession held for the spring festival, minus the horseback archery displays.

November

Daimyō Gyōretsu November 3. Re-enactment of a feudal lord's procession along the Tōkaidō (the great road linking Tokyo and Kyoto), accompanied by his doctor, accountant, tea master and road sweepers. At Sōun-ji, near Hakone-Yumoto.
Tokyo International Film Festival Early November. Japan's largest film festival and one of the few opportunities to see foreign movies with English subtitles in Tokyo. Held mainly in the cinemas of Shibuya.
Tori-no-ichi Mid-November. Fairs selling *kumade*, bamboo rakes decorated with lucky charms, are held at shrines on "rooster days" according to the zodiacal calendar. The main fair is at Ōtori-jinja (Iriya Station).
Shichi-go-san-no-hi November 15. Children aged 7, 5 and 3 don traditional garb to visit the shrines, particularly Meiji-jingū, Hie-jinja and Yasukuni-jinja.

December

Gishi-sai December 14. Costume parade in Nihombashi re-enacting the famous vendetta of the 47 *rōnin* (see p.122), followed by a memorial service for them at Sengaku-ji.

Hagoita-ichi December 17–19. The build-up to New Year begins with a battledore fair outside Asakusa's Sensō-ji.

Ōmisoka December 31. Leading up to midnight, temple bells ring out 108 times (the number of human frailties according to Buddhist thinking), while thousands gather at Meiji-jingū, Hie-jinja and other major shrines to honour the gods with the first visit of the New Year. If you don't like crowds, head for a small local shrine.

Customs and etiquette

Japan is famous for its complex web of social conventions and rules of behaviour, which only someone who has grown up in the society could hope to master. Fortunately, allowances are made for befuddled foreigners, but it will be greatly appreciated – and even draw gasps of astonishment – if you show a grasp of the basic principles. The two main danger areas are shoes and bathing, which, if you get them wrong, can cause great offence.

The Japanese treat most foreigners with incredible, even embarrassing, kindness. There are endless stories of people going out of their way to help, or paying for drinks or even meals after the briefest of encounters. That said, foreigners will always remain "outsiders" (*gaijin*), no matter how long they've lived in Japan or how proficient they are in the language and social niceties. On the positive side this can be wonderfully liberating: you're expected to make mistakes, so don't get too hung up about it. The important thing is to be seen to be trying. As a general rule, when in doubt simply follow what everyone else is doing. For tips on dining and drinking etiquette see the boxes on p.150 and p.170.

Meetings and greetings

Some visitors to Japan complain that it's difficult to meet local people, and it's certainly true that many Japanese are shy of foreigners, mainly through a fear of being unable to communicate. A few words of Japanese will help enormously, and there are various opportunities for fairly formal contact, such as through the Home Visit System and Goodwill Guides (see p.19). Otherwise, youth hostels are great places to meet people of all ages, or try popping into a local bar, a *yakitori* joint or suchlike; emboldened by alcohol, the chances are someone will strike up a conversation.

Japanese people tend to **dress** smartly, especially in Tokyo. Though as a tourist you don't have to go overboard, you'll be better received if you look neat and tidy, and for anyone hoping to do business, a snappy suit is *de rigueur*. It's also important to be punctual for social and business **appointments**.

Whenever Japanese meet, express thanks or say goodbye, there's a flurry of **bowing**. The precise depth of the bow and the length of time it's held for depend on the relative status of the two individuals – receptionists are sent on courses to learn the precise angles required. Again, foreigners aren't expected to bow, but it's terribly infectious and you'll soon find yourself bobbing with the best of them. The usual compromise is a slight nod or a quick, half-bow. Japanese more familiar with Western customs might offer you a hand to shake, in which case treat it gently – they won't be expecting a firm grip.

Japanese **names** are traditionally written with the family name first, followed by a given name, which is the practice used throughout this book (except where the

Western version has become fa... such as Issey Miyake). When dealing with... ers, however, they may well write their... the other way round. Check if you're... sure because, when **addressing people**, it's normal to use the family name plus -san; for example, Suzuki-san. San is an honorific term used in the same way as Mr or Mrs, so remember not to use it when introducing yourself, or talking about your friends or family. As a foreigner, you can choose whichever of your names you feel comfortable with; inevitably they'll tack a -san on the end. You'll also often hear -chan as a form of address; this is a diminutive reserved for very good friends, young children and pets.

An essential part of any business meeting is the swapping of *meishi*, or **name cards**. Always carry a copious supply, since you'll be expected to exchange a card with everyone present. It's useful to have them printed in Japanese as well as English; if necessary, you can get this done at major hotels. *Meishi* are offered with both hands, facing so that the recipient can read the writing. It's polite to read the card and then place it on the table beside you, face up. Never write on a *meishi*, at least not in the owner's presence, and never shove it in a pocket – put it in your wallet or somewhere suitably respectful. Business meetings invariably go on much longer than you'd expect and rarely result in decisions. They are partly for building up the all-important feeling of trust between the two parties, as is the after-hours entertainment in a restaurant or karaoke bar.

Hospitality, gifts and tips

Entertaining, whether it's business or purely social, usually takes place in bars and restaurants. The host generally orders and, if it's a Japanese-style meal, will keep passing you different things to try. You'll also find your glass continually topped up. It's polite to return the gesture but if you don't drink, or don't want any more, leave it full.

It's a rare honour to be invited to someone's home in Japan and you should always take a small **gift**. Fruit, flowers, chocolates or alcohol (wine, whisky or brandy) are safe bets, as is anything from your home country, especially if it's a famous brand-name. The gift should always be wrapped, using plenty of fancy paper and ribbon if possible. If you buy something locally, most shops gift-wrap purchases automatically and anything swathed in paper from a big department ...re has extra cachet.

...anese people love giving gifts, and you shoul...ever refuse one if offered, though it's good ma...ners to protest at their generosity first. Again ...s polite to give and receive with both hands, a...d to belittle your humble donation while giving profuse thanks for the gift you receive. However, it's not the custom to open gifts in front of the donor, thus avoiding potential embarrassment.

If you're fortunate enough to be invited to a **wedding**, it's normal to give money to the happy couple. This helps defray the costs, including, somewhat bizarrely, the present you'll receive at the end of the meal. How much you give depends on your relationship with the couple, so ask a mutual friend what would be appropriate. Make sure to get crisp new notes and put them in a special red envelope available at stationers. Write your name clearly on the front and hand it over as you enter the reception.

Tipping is not expected in Japan, and if you press money on a taxi driver, porter or bellboy it can cause offence. If someone's been particularly helpful, the best approach is to give a small gift, or present the money discretely in an envelope.

Shoes and slippers

It's customary to change into **slippers** when entering a Japanese home or a ryokan, and not uncommon in traditional restaurants, temples or, occasionally, in museums and art galleries. In general, if you come across a slightly raised floor and a row of slippers, then use them; either leave your shoes on the lower floor (the *genkan*) or on the shelves (sometimes lockers) provided. Slip-on shoes are much easier to cope with than lace-ups and, tricky though it is, try not to step on the *genkan* with bare or stockinged feet.

Once inside, remove your slippers before stepping onto tatami, the rice-straw flooring, and remember to change into the special **toilet slippers** lurking inside the bathroom door when you go to the toilet. (See overleaf for more on toilet etiquette.)

Bathing

Taking a traditional Japanese **bath**, whether in a ryokan, hot spring (onsen), or public bathhouse (sentō), is a ritual that's definitely worth mastering. Nowadays most baths are segregated, so memorize the kanji for male and female (see the box opposite). It's customary to bathe in the evening, and in small ryokan or family homes there may well be only one bathroom. In this case you'll either be given a designated time or simply have to wait till it's vacant.

Key points to remember are that everyone uses the same water and the bathtub is only for soaking. It's therefore essential to wash and rinse the soap off thoroughly – showers and bowls are provided, as well as soap and shampoo in many cases – before stepping into the bath. Ryokan and the more upmarket public bathhouses provide small towels, though no one minds full nudity. Lastly, the bath in a ryokan and family home is filled once each evening, so never pull the plug out.

Toilets

Traditional Japanese **toilets** (toire or otearai) are of the Asian squat variety. Though these are still quite common in homes, old-style restaurants and many public buildings, Western toilets are gradually becoming the norm. Look out for nifty enhancements such as a heated seat – glorious in winter – and those that flush automatically as you walk away. Another handy device plays the sound of flushing water to cover embarrassing noises. These are either automatic or are activated with a button and were invented because so much water was wasted by constant flushing. In some places toilets are still communal, so don't be alarmed to see a urinal in what you thought was the women's room, and note that public toilets rarely provide paper. If you can't find a public lavatory on the street (there are lots of them around), then dive into the nearest department store or big shop, all of which have bathroom facilities for general use.

Increasingly, you'll be confronted by a high-tech Western model, known as a **Washlet**, with a control panel to one side.

T...	toire/ otearai	トイレ／お手洗い
Male	otoko	男
Female	onna	女

It's usually impossible to find the flush button, and instead you'll hit the temperature control, hot-air dryer or, worst of all, the bidet nozzle, resulting in a long metal arm extending out of the toilet bowl and spraying you with warm water.

Some general pointers

It's quite normal to see men urinating in the streets in Japan, but **blowing your nose** in public is considered extremely rude – just keep sniffing until you find somewhere private. In this very male, strictly hierarchical society, men always take precedence over women, so ladies shouldn't expect **doors** to be held open or **seats** vacated. Although meticulously polite within their own social group, the Japanese relish **pushing and shoving** on trains or buses. Never respond by getting angry or showing **aggression**, as this is considered a complete loss of face. By the same token, don't make your **opinions** too forcefully or contradict people outright; it's more polite to say "maybe" than a direct "no".

The meaning of "yes" and "no" can in themselves be a problem, particularly when **asking questions**. For example, if you say "Don't you like it?", a positive answer means "Yes, I agree with you, I don't like it", and "No" means "No, I don't agree with you, I do like it". To avoid confusion, try not to ask negative questions – stick to "Do you like it?" And if someone seems to be giving vague answers, don't push too hard unless it's important. There's a good chance they don't want to offend you by disagreeing or revealing a problem.

Finally, you'll be excused for not **sitting** on your knees, Japan-style, on the tatami mats. It's agony for people who aren't used to it, and many young Japanese now find it uncomfortable. If you're wearing trousers, sitting cross-legged is fine; otherwise, tuck your legs to one side.

Police and trouble

Tokyo boasts one of the lowest crime rates in the world, and personal safety is rarely a worry. On the whole, the Japanese are honest and law-abiding, there's little theft, and drug-related crimes are relatively rare. The main exception is bicycle theft, which is rife, so make sure yours is securely locked whenever you leave it. In addition, it always pays to be careful in crowded areas and to keep money and important documents stowed in an inside pocket or money belt, or in your hotel safe.

In theory, you should carry your **passport** or ID at all times; the police have the right to arrest anyone who fails to do so. In practice, however, they rarely stop foreigners, though car drivers are more likely to be checked. If you're found without your ID, the usual procedure is to escort you back to your hotel or apartment to collect it. Anyone found **taking drugs** will be treated less leniently; if you're lucky, you'll simply be fined and deported, rather than sent to prison.

The presence of **police boxes** (*kōban*) in every neighbourhood helps discourage petty crime, and the local police seem to spend the majority of their time dealing with stolen bikes and helping bemused visitors – Japanese and foreigners – find addresses. This benevolent image is misleading, however, as the Japanese police are notorious for forcing confessions and holding suspects for weeks without access to a lawyer, and recent Amnesty International reports have criticized Japan for its brutal treatment of illegal immigrants and other foreigners held in jail.

Racial discrimination can be a problem, especially for non-whites, though it is mainly directed at immigrant workers rather than tourists. **Sexual discrimination** is widespread, and foreign women working in Japan can find the predominantly male business culture hard going. The generally low status of women is reflected in the amount of groping that goes on in crowded commuter trains – there are even pornographic films and comics aimed at gropers. If you do have the misfortune to be groped, the best solution is to grab the offending hand, yank it high in the air and embarrass the guy as much as possible. Fortunately, more violent

sexual abuse is rare, though rape is seriously under-reported and may be up to ten times higher than the current statistics suggest (under 2000 cases per year). Women working in hostess clubs are particularly at risk, as the murder in Tokyo of Lucie Blackman in 2000 sadly goes to prove. In the wake of the publicity generated by that case, several other women came forward to make accusations of sexual abuse, including cases where the victims had been drugged.

If you need **emergency help**, phone ☏110 for the police or ☏119 for an ambulance or fire engine. You can call free from any public phone by pressing the red button before dialling, though with the old-style pink or red phones you need to put a coin in first to get the dialling tone. Better still, ask someone to call for you, since few police speak English. If you get really stuck, Tokyo Metropolitan Police operates an English-language hotline on ☏03/3501-0110 (Mon–Fri 8.30am–5.15pm).

Earthquakes

Earthquakes are a part of life in Japan, with at least one quake recorded every day somewhere in the country, though fortunately the vast majority consist of minor tremors which you probably won't even notice. The country is home to one-tenth of the world's active volcanoes and the site of one-tenth of its major earthquakes (over force 7 on the Richter scale).

The last really big quake to hit Tokyo was the **Great Kantō Earthquake**, which devastated the city in 1923, killing an estimated 140,000 people. There's a sequence of

Earthquake safety procedures

- Extinguish any fires and turn off electrical appliances (TV, air conditioners, kettles and so on).
- Open any doors leading out of the room, as they often get jammed shut, blocking your exit later.
- Stay away from windows because of splintering glass. If you have time, draw the curtains to contain the glass.
- Don't rush outside (many people are injured by falling masonry), but get under something solid, such as a ground-floor doorway, or a desk.
- If the earthquake occurs at night, make sure you've got a torch (all hotels and ryokan provide torches in the rooms).
- When the tremors have died down, go to the nearest park, playing field or open space, taking your documents and other valuables with you. It's also a good idea to take a cushion or pillow to protect your head against falling glass.
- Eventually, make your way to the designated neighbourhood emergency centre for information, food and shelter.
- Ultimately, get in touch with your embassy.

major quakes in Tokyo every seventy-odd years, and everyone's been talking about the next "Big One" for at least a decade. Whilst scientists argue about the likelihood of another serious earthquake, Tokyo is equipped with some of the world's most sophisticated sensors, which are monitored round the clock, and architects employ mind-boggling techniques to try to ensure the city's new high-rises remain upright.

Nevertheless, earthquakes are notoriously difficult to predict and it's worth taking note of a few basic **safety procedures** (see box above). You should beware of aftershocks, which may go on for a long time, and can topple structures that are already weakened, and note that most casualties are caused by fire and traffic accidents, rather than collapsing buildings. In the aftermath of a major earthquake, it may be impossible to contact friends and relatives for a while, since the phone lines are likely to be down or reserved for emergency services.

The City

The City

The Imperial Palace and around

Concealed in a green swathe of central Tokyo, wrapped round with moats and broad avenues, the enigmatic **Imperial Palace** lies at the city's geographical and spiritual heart. Home to the emperor and his family, the palace hides behind a wall of trees and is closed to the public, but the nearby parks are a natural place to start any exploration of Tokyo. The most attractive is **Higashi Gyoen**, the East Garden, where remnants of the old Edo Castle still stand amid formal gardens, while to its north **Kitanomaru-kōen** is a more natural park containing a motley collection of museums, the best of which is the **National Museum of Modern Art**.

Just outside the park's northern perimeter, the nation's war dead are remembered at the controversial shrine of **Yasukuni-jinja**, while life in Japan during World War II is portrayed at the equally contentious **Shōwa-kan**. A short walk west of Yasukuni-jinja towards Ichigaya a more peaceful world is evoked at the delightful **Takagi Bonsai Museum**. Southeast from here are the Chidoriga-fuchi and Hanzō-bori sections of the palace moat, Tokyo's top spots for springtime cherry-blossom-viewing parties, while continuing south brings you to the **National Theatre** and the **National Diet Building**, Japan's seat of government.

The Imperial Palace and around

Imperial Palace	Kōkyo	皇居
Budōkan	Budōkan	武道館
Crafts Gallery	Bijutsukan Kōgeikan	美術館工芸館
Higashi Gyoen	Higashi Gyoen	東御苑
Kitanomaru-kōen	Kitanomaru-kōen	北の丸公園
National Diet Building	Kokkai Gijidō	国会議事堂
National Museum of Modern Art	Kokuritsu Kindai Bijutsukan	国立近代美術館
Nijūbashi	Nijūbashi	二重橋
Science Museum	Kagaku Gijutsukan	科学技術館
Shōwa-kan	Shōwa-kan	昭和館
Takagi Bonsai Museum	Takagi Bonsai Bijutsukan	高木盆栽美術館
Yasukuni-jinja	Yasukuni-jinja	靖国神社

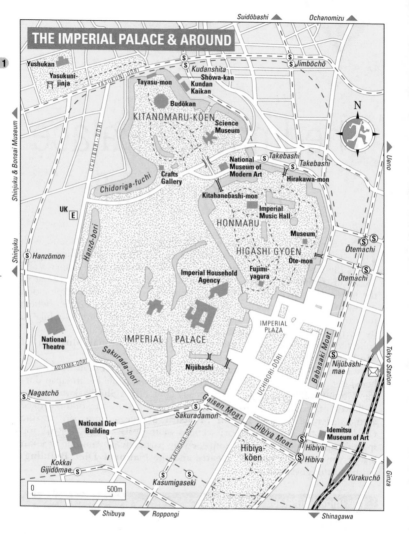

THE IMPERIAL PALACE & AROUND

Suidōbashi ▲   Ochanomizu ▲

Yushukan

Yasukuni-jinja

YASUKUNI-DŌRI

Tayasu-mon

Kudanshita
Shōwa-kan
Kundan
Kaikan

Jimbōchō

Budōkan

KITANOMARU-KŌEN

Science
Museum

N

Ueno ▶

National
Museum of
Modern Art

Takebashi

Takebashi

Chidoriga-fuchi

Crafts
Gallery

Hirakawa-mon

Kitahanebashi-mon

UK 🇬🇧

Imperial
Music Hall

HONMARU

Museum

Ōtemachi

Hanzō-bori

HIGASHI GYOEN

Ōtemachi

Hanzōmon

Imperial Household
Agency

Fujimi-
yagura

Ōte-mon

IMPERIAL PALACE

IMPERIAL
PLAZA

Babasaki Moat

Tokyo Station

National
Theatre

Sakurada-bori

Nijūbashi

UCHIBORI-DŌRI

Nijūbashi-
mae

ADYAMA-DŌRI

Gaisen Moat

Nagatchō

Sakuradamon

Hibiya Moat

Idemitsu
Museum of Art

National Diet
Building

Hibiya-
kōen

Hibiya

Hibiya

Ginza ▶

Kokkai
Gijidōmae

Kasumigaseki

Yūrakuchō

0   500m

Shinjuku & Bonsai Museum ◀

Shinjuku ◀

▼ Shibuya   ▼ Roppongi   ▼ Shinagawa

Some history

The site of the Imperial Palace is as old as Tokyo. A fortress was built here by
Ōta Dōkan (see History, p.271) in 1457 overlooking Tokyo Bay, which in
those times lapped up to where the district of Hibiya is today. After Ōta's
assassination in 1486 the castle was left to fall into ruin and it wasn't until the
1590s that its fortunes were revived under the patronage of Tokugawa Ieyasu,
the warlord whose family was destined to rule Japan for close on three hundred years. Little remains of the original Edo Castle save for three fortified
towers and some huge stone walls within the palace's 284-acre grounds.
When the Tokugawa shogunate collapsed in 1868, the Meiji emperor moved
his court here from Kyoto and Edo became Tokyo. His descendant Emperor
Akihito (see box, opposite) now lives in the Fukiage Palace built in the early

1990s in the western section of the palace grounds and reached via the Hanzōmon Gate.

The Imperial Palace

Huge and windswept, the **Imperial Plaza** forms a protective island in front of the modern royal palace. In earlier times the shogunate's most trusted followers were allowed to build their mansions here, but after 1899 these were razed to make way for today's austere expanse of spruce lawns and manicured pine trees. The primary reason to follow the groups of local tourists straggling across the broad avenues is to view one of the palace's most photogenic corners, **Nijūbashi**, where two bridges span the moat and a jaunty little watchtower perches on its grey stone pedestal beyond. Though this double bridge is a late nineteenth-century embellishment, the tower dates back to the seventeenth century and is one of the castle's few original structures. The present palace is a long, sleek, 1960s structure, built to replace the Meiji palace burnt down in the 1945 bombing raids. The imperial residences

Descendants of the Sun Goddess

Japan's **imperial family** is the world's longest-reigning dynasty – according to traditionalists, Emperor Akihito, the 125th incumbent of the Chrysanthemum Throne, traces his ancestry back to 660 BC and Emperor Jimmu, great-great-grandson of the Sun Goddess Amaterasu, a key Japanese mythological figure. Until the twentieth century, emperors were regarded as living deities whom ordinary folk were forbidden to set eyes on, or even hear. But on August 15, 1945, a stunned nation listened to the radio as Emperor Hirohito's quavering voice announced Japan's surrender to the Allies, and a few months later he declared that emperors no longer held divine status.

Today the emperor is a symbolic figure, a head of state with no governmental power, and the family is gradually abandoning its cloistered existence. Emperor Akihito was the first to benefit: as crown prince, he had an American tutor and studied at Tokyo's elite Gakushūin University, followed by a stint at Oxford University. In 1959 he broke further with tradition by marrying a commoner, Empress Michiko, whom he supposedly met on a tennis court.

His children have continued the modernizing trend without denting the public's deep respect for the imperial family, though polls reveal a growing indifference, and the more radical papers are becoming bolder in their criticism. Akihito's daughter in law, Crown Princess Masako (before her marriage a high-flying Harvard-educated diplomat) has been the subject of unusually severe censure for impudently walking in front of her husband Crown Prince Naruhito and for speaking too much at a press conference.

This stress has become even more apparent in the crown prince and princess's attempts to produce an heir. Following a miscarriage, Crown Princess Masako gave birth to a baby girl, Aiko, in December 2001. Rejoicing has turned to sadness as the crown princess has barely been seen in public since, suffering from fatigue and a variety of illnesses. Crown Prince Naruhito has gone so far as to suggest that his wife has been made ill by efforts to crush her personality – not just by the media but also by the powerful Imperial Household Agency, the government body that effectively runs the imperial institution.

Despite current laws forbidding female succession, there's growing support for the move to make Princess Aiko heir to the Chrysanthemum Throne – Crown Princess Masako is now 40 and the chances of her producing a male heir are becoming increasingly slim. With reforming Prime Minister Koizumi himself in favour of such a change, it may just come to pass that Japan one day has an empress as its head of state.

themselves are tucked away out of sight beyond another moat in the thickly wooded westernmost Fukiage Garden.

Twice a year (on December 23, the emperor's birthday, and on January 2) thousands of well-wishers file across Nijūbashi to greet the royal family, lined up behind bullet-proof glass, with a rousing cheer of "Banzai" ("May you live 10,000 years"). Apart from these two days, the general public is only admitted to the palace grounds on pre-arranged **official tours**, conducted in Japanese. The tours are a bit of a hassle to get on, but there is a certain fascination in taking a peek inside this secret world, and the pre-tour video shows tantalizing glimpses of vast function rooms and esoteric court rituals. Phone the Imperial Household Agency (℡03/3213-1111 ext 485; Mon–Fri 9am–4.30pm) several days in advance to make a reservation, then go to their office inside the palace grounds at least one day before the appointed date to collect a permit, taking along your passport. Tours take place twice daily on weekdays (10am & 1.30pm) and last about ninety minutes; there are no tours from July 21 to August 31.

Higashi Gyoen

The finest of Edo Castle's remaining watchtowers, three-tiered **Fujimi-yagura**, stands clear above the trees to the north of the Imperial Plaza. Built in 1659 to protect the main citadel's southern flank, these days it ornaments what is known as **Higashi Gyoen**, or the East Garden (Tues–Thurs, Sat & Sun 9am–4.30pm; closed occasionally for court functions; free). Hemmed round with moats, the garden was opened to the public in 1968 to commemorate the completion of the new Imperial Palace. It's a good place for a stroll, though there's little to evoke the former glory of the shogunate's castle beyond several formidable gates and the towering granite walls.

The main gate to the garden – and formerly to Edo Castle itself – is **Ōte-mon**; on entry you'll be given a numbered token to hand in again as you leave. The first building ahead on the right is a small **museum** (℡03/3213-1111, ⓦwww.kunaicho.go.jp; free), exhibiting a tiny fraction of the eight thousand artworks in the imperial collection, though it's still worth a quick look. Just beyond the museum is a shop where you can pick up a useful **map** of the garden (¥150).

From here a path winds gently up, beneath the walls of the main citadel, and then climbs more steeply towards **Shiomizaka**, the Tide-Viewing Slope, from where it was once possible to gaze out over Edo Bay rather than the concrete blocks of Ōtemachi. You emerge on a flat grassy area, empty apart from the stone foundations of **Honmaru** (the "inner citadel"), with fine views from the top, and a scattering of modern edifices, among them the bizarre, mosaic-clad **Imperial Music Hall**. Designed by Imai Kenji, the hall commemorates the sixtieth birthday of the (then) empress in 1963 and is used for occasional performances of court music.

Kitanomaru-kōen

The northern citadel of Edo Castle is now occupied by the park of **Kitanomaru-kōen**, home to a couple of interesting museums. The main one to head for, immediately to the right as you emerge from the Higashi Gyoen through the Kitahanebashi-mon gate, is the **National Museum of Modern Art** (Tues–Sun 10am–5pm, Fri until 8pm; ¥420; ℡03/5777-8600, ⓦwww.momat.go.jp), which reopened in 2002 following a ¥7.8 billion renovation. The museum's excellent collection features Japanese works, including Gyokudo Kawa's magnificent screen painting *Parting Spring* and works by Kishida Ryusei and Fujita Tsuguharu, as well as foreign artists such as Picasso, Juan Gris, Kandinsky and Francis Bacon. The renovation has also added a pleasant café with a terrace overlooking the Imperial Palace.

A short walk away on the west side of Kitanomaru-kōen, the **Crafts Gallery** (Tues–Sun 10am–5pm, Fri until 8pm; ¥420) exhibits a selection of top-quality traditional Japanese craft works, many of them by modern masters. Erected in 1910 as the headquarters of the Imperial Guards, this neo-Gothic red-brick pile is one of very few Tokyo buildings dating from before the Great Earthquake of 1923.

Back beside the entrance to Kitanomaru-kōen, a white concrete lattice-work building houses the **Science Museum** (daily 9.30am–4.50pm; ¥600; ℡03/5777-8600, ⓦwww.jsf.or.jp). Aimed at kids, it's often inundated with school parties, but some of the interactive displays are great fun. Start on the fifth floor and work your way down, stopping to step inside an Escher room, "listen" to the earth's magnetic field or get a bug's-eye view of life.

The park's last major building is the **Budōkan** martial arts hall, built in 1964 to host Olympic judo events. The design, with its graceful, curving roof and gold topknot, pays homage to a famous octagonal hall in Nara's Hōryū-ji temple, though the shape is also supposedly inspired by that of Mount Fuji. Today the huge arena is used for sports meetings, graduation ceremonies and, most famously, big-name rock concerts.

Yasukuni-jinja

Across the road from Kitanomaru-kōen an oversized grey steel *torii*, claiming to be Japan's tallest, marks the entrance to **Yasukuni-jinja**. This shrine, whose name means "for the repose of the country", was founded in 1869 to worship supporters of the emperor killed in the run-up to the Meiji Restoration. Since then it has expanded to include the legions sacrificed in subsequent wars, in total nearly 2.5 million souls, of whom some two million died in the Pacific War alone; the parting words of kamikaze pilots were said to be "see you at Yasukuni".

Despite its highly controversial nature (see box, below) every year some eight million Japanese visit Yasukuni to remember family and friends who died

The problem with Yasukuni

Ever since its foundation as part of a Shinto revival promoting the new emperor, Yasukuni-jinja has been a place of high controversy. In its early years the shrine became a natural focus for the increasingly aggressive nationalism that ultimately took Japan to war in 1941. Then, in 1978, General Tōjō, prime minister during World War II, and a number of other "Class A" war criminals were enshrined here, to be honoured along with all the other military dead. Japan's neighbours, still smarting from their treatment by the Japanese during the war, were outraged.

This has not stopped top politicians from visiting Yasukuni on the anniversary of Japan's defeat (August 15) in World War II. Because Japan's postwar constitution requires the separation of state and religion, ministers have usually maintained that they attend as private individuals, but in 1985 Nakasone, in typically uncompromising mood, caused an uproar when he signed the visitors' book as "Prime Minister". The current PM, Koizumi Junichiro, has visited every year since 2001, despite continued protests both at home and abroad.

in the last, troubled century. Its surprisingly unassuming Inner Shrine stands at the end of a long avenue lined with cherry and gingko trees, and through a simple wooden gate. The architecture is classic Shinto styling, solid and unadorned except for two gold imperial chrysanthemums embossed on the main doors.

To the right of the Inner Shrine you'll find the fascinating **Yushukan** (daily: 9am–4.30pm, March–Oct until 5pm; ¥800; ☎03/3261-8326, ⓦwww.yasukuni .or.jp), a military museum established in 1882 but recently fully renovated with the addition of a new gallery. Most exhibits consist of sad personal possessions: blood-stained uniforms, letters and faded photographs from conflicts stretching back to the Sino-Japanese war of 1894. The most disturbing displays concern the kamikaze pilots and other suicide squads active during the Pacific War. It's hard to miss them: the museum's central hall is dominated by a replica glider, its nose elongated to carry a 1200-kilo bomb, while a spine-chilling, black *kaiten* (manned torpedo) lours to one side.

As an antidote, take a walk through the little Japanese **garden** lying behind the shrine buildings. Just beyond, the sunken enclosure is the venue for a sumo tournament during the shrine's spring festival, when top wrestlers perform under trees laden with cherry blossom. It's also well worth visiting in early July during the shrine's lively summer *matsuri* when its precincts are illuminated by thousands of paper lanterns and there's nightly dancing, parades and music.

Shōwa-kan

There's scarcely a mention of bombs or destruction at the **Shōwa-kan** (Tues–Sun 10am–5.30pm; ¥300; ☎03/3222-2577, ⓦwww.showakan.go.jp) – a corrugated, windowless building east along Yasukuni-dōri from Yasukuni-jinja – which is odd, since this new museum is devoted to life in Japan during and after World War II. To be fair, the government originally wanted the museum to document the war's origins but ran into bitter opposition

Shrines and temples

Japan's main religions are the indigenous **Shinto**, combining ancient animism with ancestor-worship, and **Buddhism**, which was imported from Korea in the sixth century. They coexist happily, fulfilling distinct roles in society. Most Japanese will visit a Shinto shrine to pray for exam success or to get married, but will eventually be interred or cremated according to Buddhist rites.

Although Shinto's myriad gods (*kami*) inhabit all natural things, the focus of daily worship is the **shrine** (*-jinja* or *-jingū*). This stands in an area of sacred ground entered via one or more *torii*, symbolic gates made of two gently inclined uprights, topped with one or two crosspieces. Near the shrine itself, you'll find a large basin of water where worshippers purify themselves by rinsing their hands and mouth. Standing in front of the sanctuary, they then throw some coins into the large wooden box, shake the bell-rope to inform the deities of their presence, and pray: the standard practice is to bow deeply twice, clap twice, pray with eyes closed and finish with another low bow.

Buddhist temples (*-tera*, *-dera* or *-ji*) are usually much grander affairs, with an imposing entrance gate flanked by two guardian gods. Again, people often purify themselves with water before entering the main hall to pray before a statue of the Buddha. Of the several Buddhist sects in Japan, **Zen** is probably the most famous, a meditative form of the religion with a rigid moral code, which flourished in Kamakura during the thirteenth century.

from pacifists, insistent on tackling the hot-potato issue of responsibility, and a right-wing lobby opposed to any hint that Japan was an aggressor during the conflict. After twenty years of argument, they eventually decided on a compromise that pleases almost no one by sticking to a safe, sanitized portrayal of the hardships suffered by wives and children left behind. Nevertheless, there's some interesting material, most notably that concerning life during the occupation. For Japanese readers, they have also amassed a vast archive of war-related documents. The closest subway station is Kudanshita.

Takagi Bonsai Museum to the National Diet Building

Heading west along Yasukuni-dōri for around 500m from Yasukuni-jinja brings you to Ichigaya Station, close to which you'll find the serene **Takagi Bonsai Museum** (Tues–Sun 10am–5pm; ¥800; ☎03/3262-1611). Celebrating the art of creating bonsai (miniature trees), this small but delightful museum has a roof garden and regularly changes its displays of some five hundred bonsai and four thousand bonsai pots to reflect the season. Among the museum's prime specimens are dwarf pine trees, wild plum and mountain maples that are over a hundred years old. Admission includes a free drink which you can sip while watching an English video on how these miniature masterpieces of horticulture are crafted.

Retrace your steps to the northwest corner of the Imperial Palace and you'll hit **Chidoriga-fuchi**, an ancient pond that was incorporated into Edo Castle's moat. Rowing boats can be rented here and, with its ninety-odd cherry trees, it's a popular viewing spot come *hanami* time.

From here, following the moat south towards Hibiya, the main point of interest is the squat, three-storey **National Diet Building** (Mon–Fri 9.30am–4pm, unless the House of Councillors is in session; call ☎03/3581-3100 to check; free), dominated by a central tower block decorated with pillars and a pyramid-shaped roof. The Diet is supposedly based on the Senate Building in Washington DC, though Japan's style of government has more in common with the British parliamentary system. On the left stands the House of Representatives, the main body of government, while on the right, the House of Councillors, which is similar to Britain's House of Lords, is open for forty-minute **tours**. Some of the guides speak English and a taped English commentary is played in the actual chamber explaining what you can see.

There's an Edwardian-style grandeur to the Diet's interior, especially in the carved-wood debating chamber and the central reception hall, decorated with paintings reflecting the seasons and bronze statues of significant statesmen. You'll have to look at the room the emperor waits in when he visits the Diet through a glass panel: it's decorated in real gold. The tour finishes at the Diet's front garden, planted with native trees and plants from all of Japan's 47 prefectures. The nearest subway station is Kokkai Gijidomae.

2

Ginza and around

Walk east from the Imperial Palace, across Babasaki Moat, and you're plunged straight into the hurly-burly of downtown Tokyo, among grey-faced office blocks, swanky department stores and streets full of rush-hour crowds which are transformed at dusk into neon-lit canyons.

The heart of the area is **Ginza,** Tokyo's most exclusive shopping and dining district. There are no must-see sights here, but it's a compact area where you can happily spend an hour exploring a single high-rise stacked with boutiques and cafés, or rummaging in the backstreets. Even the most anonymous building can yield a speciality store or avant-garde gallery, while some wonderfully atmospheric eating and drinking places lurk under the train tracks that split the district from north to south.

West of the tracks **Yūrakuchō, Marunouchi** and **Hibiya** are theatre- and business-land, and also home to lots of airline offices, banks and corporate headquarters, as well as the dramatic modern architecture of the **Tokyo International Forum**. Marunouchi is enjoying a stylish reinvention with the recent opening of the 36-storey **Marunouchi Building** and the promotion of the area as a chi-chi shopping precinct. Hibiya's highlight is its Western-style **park**, a refreshing oasis of greenery.

On Ginza's southern flank is the new suburb of **Shiodome**, where a brace of sparkling skyscrapers harbour hotels, restaurants, and a few bona fide tourist sights, the best of which is **ADMT**, a museum dedicated to advertising. Head northwards from Ginza along Chūō-dōri, and you'll hit the high-finance district of **Nihombashi**, once the heart of boisterous, low-town Edo but now the preserve of blue-suited bankers. Here you'll find the original **Mitsukoshi** department store and the fine **Bridgestone Museum of Art**.

A **free bus** service (daily 10am–8pm; every 15min) runs in a loop from Hibiya to Tokyo Station up to Ōtemachi, across to the *Palace Hotel* and then back south along the Imperial Palace moat to Hibiya. For full details visit Ⓦ www.marunouchi.com.

Some history

Ginza, the "place where silver is minted", took its name after Shogun Tokugawa Ieyasu started making coins here in the early 1600s. It was a happy association – Ginza's Chūō-dōri grew to become Tokyo's most stylish shopping street. The unusually regular pattern of streets here is due to British architect Thomas Waters, who was given the task of creating a less combustible city after a fire in 1872 destroyed virtually all of old, wooden Ginza. His "Bricktown", as it soon became known, proved an instant local tourist attraction, with its rows of two-storey, brick houses, tree-lined avenues, gaslights and brick pave-

Ginza	Ginza	銀座
Kabuki-za	Kabuki-za	歌舞伎座
Sony Building	Sonii Biru	ソニービル
Wakō	Wakō	和光
Yūrakuchō	Yūrakuchō	有楽町
Tokyo International Forum	Tōkyō Kokusai Fōramu	東京国際フォーラム
Marunouchi	Marunouchi	丸の内
Hibiya	Hibiya	日比谷
Hibiya-kōen	Hibiya-kōen	日比谷公園
Idemitsu Museum of Arts	Idemitsu Bijutsukan	出光美術館
Shiodome	Shiodome	汐留
Nihombashi	Nihombashi	日本橋
Bridgestone Museum of Art	Burijisuton Bijutsukan	ブリヂストン美術館
Kite Museum	Tako no Hakubutsukan	凧の博物館
Mitsukoshi	Mitsukoshi	三越

ments. But since the airless buildings were totally unsuited to Tokyo's hot, humid climate, people were reluctant to settle until the government offered peppercorn rents. Most of the first businesses here dealt in foreign wares, and in no time Ginza had become the centre of all that was modern, Western and therefore fashionable – Western dress and hairstyles, watches, cafés and beer halls. Bricktown itself didn't survive the Great Earthquake, but Ginza's status was by then well established. The height of sophistication in the 1930s was simply to stroll around Ginza, and the practice still continues, particularly on Sunday afternoons, when Chūō-dōri is closed to traffic and everyone turns out for a spot of window-shopping.

Ginza

Though some of its shine has faded and cutting-edge fashion has moved elsewhere, **Ginza** still retains much of its elegance and its undoubted snob appeal. Here you'll find the greatest concentration of exclusive shops, art galleries and restaurants in the city, the most theatres and cinemas, and branches of most major department stores. The area is packed into a compact rectangular grid of streets completely enclosed by the Shuto Expressway. Three broad avenues run from north to south, Chūō-dōri being the main shopping street, while **Harumi-dōri** cuts across the centre from the east.

In the west, Ginza proper begins at the Sukiyabashi crossing, where Sotobori-dōri and Harumi-dōri intersect. The **Sony Building** (daily 11am–7pm; free; ☎03/3573-2371, ⓦwww.sonybuilding.jp), occupying the crossing's southeast corner, is a must for techno-freaks, with six of its eleven storeys showcasing the latest Sony gadgets. Continuing east along Harumi-dōri you'll reach the intersection with Chūō-dōri known as **Ginza Yon-chōme crossing**, which marks the heart of Ginza. Awesome at rush hour, this spot often features in films and documentaries as the epitome of this overcrowded yet totally efficient city. A number of venerable emporia cluster round the junction. **Wakō**, now an

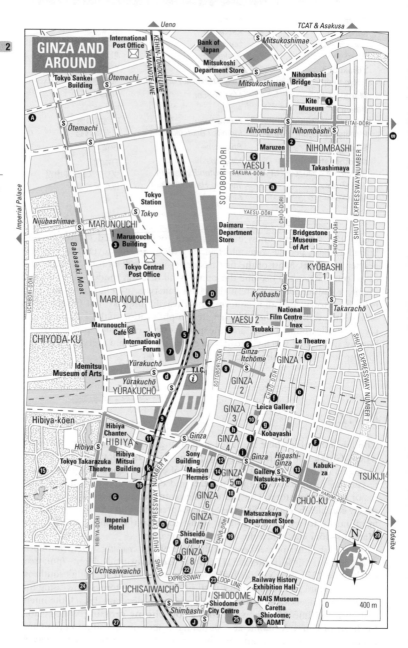

GINZA AND AROUND

Ueno ▲

TCAT & Asakusa ▲

International Post Office ✉

Bank of Japan ⓢ Mitsukoshimae

Tokyo Sankei Building

Mitsukoshi Department Store ⓢ

Ōtemachi

Mitsukoshimae

Nihombashi Bridge

Kite Museum ❶

ⒶⓈ Ōtemachi

ⓢ

Nihombashi ⓢ Nihombashi

EITAI-DŌRI

Maruzen ❷

Ⓒ YAESU 1

NIHOMBASHI

SAKURA-DŌRI

Takashimaya

ⓐ

Imperial Palace ▲

Nijūbashimae ⓢ

MARUNOUCHI

Tokyo Station ⓢ Tokyo

YAESU-DŌRI

Daimaru Department Store

SHUTO EXPRESSWAY NUMBER 1

Bridgestone Museum of Art

SHŌWA-DŌRI

KYŌBASHI 1

Babasaki Moat

Marunouchi Building ❸

Tokyo Central Post Office ✉

Ⓢ Kyōbashi

National Film Centre Inax

ⓈTakarachō

CHIYODA-KU

MARUNOUCHI 2

Ⓓ

❹

YAESU 2

Ⓔ Tsubaki

Marunouchi Café @

Tokyo International Forum

❼ ❺

ⓑ

Le Theatre

SHUTO EXPRESSWAY NUMBER 1

Idemitsu Museum of Arts

Yūrakuchō ⓢ

Yūrakuchō

T.I.C. ⓓ ①

❻ Ginza Itchōme ⓢ

GINZA 1 Ⓒ

SOTOBORI-DŌRI

YŪRAKUCHŌ

❽ GINZA 2

Ⓕ ⓔ

CHŪŌ-DŌRI

Hibiya-kōen

❾

GINZA 3 ❿

Leica Gallery

ⓕ

Hibiya Chanter HIBIYA

Hibiya ⓢ

GINZA 4

ⓗ ⓖ Kobayashi

ⓘ

Ⓕ

Tokyo Takarazuka Theatre

Hibiya Mitsui Building

⓫

ⓚ

Sony Building ⓬

Maison Hermès ⓮ GINZA 5 ⓜ

Ginza

Higashi-Ginza

Gallery ⓢ Natsuka+b.p ⓱

⓭ Kabuki-za

HIBIYA-DŌRI

⓯

⓰

Ⓖ

Imperial Hotel

GINZA 6 ⓝ ⓲

GINZA 7 ⓞ

Matsuzakaya Department Store

Ⓗ

CHŪŌ-KU

HARUMI-DŌRI

TSUKIJI

Odaiba ▲

N

Shiseidō Gallery ⓟ

⓳

Uchisaiwaichō ⓢ

GINZA 8 ⓠ ㉑

㉒ ⓡ

EXPRESSWAY

㉓ LOOP LINE

Railway History Exhibition Hall

❷⓪

UCHISAIWAICHŌ 1

SHIODOME

NAIS Museum

Shiodome City Centre

Shimbashi ⓈⒿⓢ

Caretta Shiodome; ⓵❷⓺ ADMT

㉔

㉗

0   400 m

54

exclusive department store, started life roughly a century ago as the stall of a young, enterprising watchmaker who developed a line called Seikō (meaning "precision"); its clock tower, built in 1894, is one of Ginza's most enduring landmarks. Immediately north of Wakō on Chūō-dōri, **Kimuraya bakery** was founded in 1874, while **Mikimoto Pearl** opened next door a couple of decades later. South of the crossing, just beyond the cylindrical, glass San'ai Building, **Kyūkyodō** has been selling traditional paper, calligraphy brushes and inkstones since 1800, and is filled with the dusty smell of *sumi-e* ink.

Further on east down Harumi-dōri, **Kabuki-za** has been the city's principal Kabuki theatre since its inauguration in 1889. Up until then Kabuki had belonged firmly to the lowbrow world of Edo's Shitamachi, but under Meiji it was cleaned up and relocated to this more respectable district. The original, European-style Kabuki-za made way in 1925 for a Japanese design, of which the present building is a 1950s replica. See p.185 for details of performances.

Yūrakuchō and Marunouchi

Immediately west of Ginza and east of the Imperial Palace is **Yūrakuchō**, home to the TIC (see p.19) and the **Tokyo International Forum** (ⓦwww.t-i-forum.co.jp), a stunning creation by American architect Rafael Viñoly which hosts concerts and conventions, plus the Ōedo Antique Fair (see p.198). The boat-shaped main hall consists of a sixty-metre-high atrium sheathed in 2600 sheets of earthquake-resistant glass, with a ceiling ribbed like a ship's hull – it looks magical at night.

Immediately north of the International Forum the business-focused **Marunouchi** district is currently being made more attractive to pedestrians and shoppers; check out the street sculptures and new shops along Marunouchi Naka-dōri as you stroll towards the glass tower of the **Marunouchi Building** (ⓦwww.marubiru.jp), the area's latest multi-storey development, combining offices and all manner of restaurants and cafés. There are great views from here of the handsome entrance to Tokyo Station.

Return to the south exit of the International Forum, then head west two blocks to reach the

ACCOMMODATION	
Four Seasons Hotel Tokyo at Marunouchi	D
Ginza Tōbu Hotel	H
Ginza Yoshimizu	F
Imperial Hotel	G
Palace Hotel	A
Park Hotel Tokyo	J
Royal Park Hotel	B
Royal Park Shiodome Tower	I
Yaesu Fujiya Hotel	E
Yaesu Terminal Hotel	C

RESTAURANTS, CAFÉS & BARS	
300 Bar	17
Afternoon Tea Baker and Diner	8
Aroina Tabeta	5
Atariya	10
Cha Ginza	14
Daidaiya	22
Edo-gin	20
En	25
Farm Grill	23
G-Zone	6
Kagaya	27
Lion	19
Little Okinawa	21
Mango Tree Tokyo & Soup Stock Tokyo	3
Matsumotoro	15
Nair's	13
Nataraj	18
Nylon	26
Old Imperial Bar	16
Paul	4
Robata Honten	11
Shin Hi No Moto	9
Taimeiken	1
Tenmaru	18
Takara	7
Torigin Honten	12
Town Cryer	24
Tsukiji Tama-zushi	18
Yamamotoyama	2

SHOPS	
Antiques Mall Ginza	c
Antiques Mall Tokyo	e
Apple Ginza Store	i
BIC Camera	d
Hakuhinkan Toy Park	r
Hayayashi Kimono	k
Itō-ya	f
Matsuya	g
Muji	b
Natsuno	n
Pokémon Centre	a
S Watanabe	q
Shimizu Camera	h
Shōeidō	o
Sofmap	b
Takumi	p
Wako	j
Washington	m

Ginza's modern art galleries

Ginza and its northern neighbours Kyōbashi and Nihombashi contain over two hundred **contemporary art galleries**, often just a single room rented out to amateur groups or aspiring individuals. It's all a bit of a lucky-dip, but as they're all free, it's worth popping in on the off chance. Selected exhibitions are listed in *Metropolis*; alternatively, try one of the galleries below, where you can pick up fliers for other galleries around town.

Inax 3–6–18 Kyōbashi, Chūō-ku ☎03/5250-6530, ⓦ www.inax.co.jp/Culture/gallery /1_tokyo.html (Mon–Sat 10am–6pm); Kyōbashi Station. This design plaza boasts two galleries on its second floor, showing contemporary art and art and design works. Located on Chūō-dōri, just under the northern Shuto Expressway.

Gallery Kobayashi B1, Yamato Building, 3-8-12 Ginza, Chūō-ku ☎03/3561-0515 (Mon–Sat 11.30am–7pm); Ginza Station. Profiles a wide range of up-and-coming local artists.

Leica Gallery 3F, 3-5-6 Ginza, Chūō-ku ☎03/3567-6706 (Tues–Sat 10.30am–5.30pm); Ginza Station. Great photo gallery with changing exhibitions. It's above the Matsushima Gallery on Chūō-dōri opposite Matsuya department store.

Maison Hermès 5-4-1 Ginza, Chūō-ku ☎03/3569-3611 (daily except Wed 11am–7pm); Ginza Station. On the eighth floor of the Renzo Piano-designed building, this gallery hosts shows that are usually themed and of both Japanese and international art.

Gallery Natsuka & b.p 8F, Ginza Plaza 58, 5–8–17 Ginza, Chūō-ku ☎03/3571-0130, ⓦ www.ginza.co.jp/natsuka (Mon–Sat 11am–6.30pm); Ginza Station. Well-respected gallery showcasing young artists. It's just down from the Ginza Yon-chōme crossing.

Shiseidō Gallery 8-8-3 Ginza, Chūō-ku ☎03/3572-3901, ⓦ www.shiseido.co.jp /gallery/html (Tues–Sat 11am–7pm, Sun 11am–6pm); Shimbashi Station. Located in the distinctive red headquarters of the Japanese cosmetics giant Shiseidō, this basement gallery hosts group and solo shows.

Tsubaki B1, 3–2–11 Kyōbashi, Chūō-ku ☎03/3181-7808 (Mon–Sat 10am–6pm); Ginza Station. Smart place in the basement opposite Inax. It's a little difficult to locate; take your bearings from the nearby Kyōbashi gallery.

Imperial Theatre, which hosts big-budget Western musicals. Above it, on the ninth floor, the **Idemitsu Museum of Arts** (Tues–Sun 10am–5pm; ¥800; ☎03/5777-8600, ⓦ www.idemitsu.co.jp) houses a magnificent collection of mostly Japanese art, though only a tiny proportion is on show at any one time. The collection includes many historically important pieces, ranging from fine examples of early Jōmon (10,000 BC–300 BC) pottery to Zen Buddhist calligraphy, handpainted scrolls, richly gilded folding screens and elegant, late seventeenth-century *ukiyo-e* paintings. The museum also owns valuable collections of Chinese and Korean ceramics, as well as slightly incongruous works by French painter Georges Rouault and American artist Sam Francis. The lounge area is a comfortable place for a break, with views over the Imperial Palace moats and gardens.

Hibiya

The area southwest of the museum (and immediately south of the castle) was occupied by the Tokugawa shogunate's less favoured *daimyō*. The land was cleared after 1868, but was too waterlogged to support modern buildings, so in

Tokyo's top parks and gardens

Look at any map of central Tokyo and you'll quickly realize that there isn't much in the way of parkland: just 5.3 square metres of park per resident compared to 29 square metres in New York and 26 square metres in Paris – and two of the biggest central patches of greenery (those immediately around the Imperial Palace and the Akasaka Detached Palace) are largely off limits to the general public. What's left is often covered by cemeteries, as in Aoyama and Yanaka), or public buildings, as in Ueno. If you need a quick escape from the concrete and neon here are our top ten suggestions.

Hama Rikyū Teien (p.125) Once the duck-hunting grounds of the shogun; now a beautiful bayside retreat.

Happōen (p.121) Harbours a gracious Japanese villa, bonsai trees and a tea house by a pretty pond.

Hibiya-kōen (see below) Spacious Western-style park with fountain and bandstand.

Higashi Gyoen (p.48) The tranquil east garden of the Imperial Palace.

Kyū Furukawa Gardens (p.95) An Italianate terrace with rose beds tumbles down to a traditional Japanese-style garden laid out around an ornamental pond.

Meiji-jingū Inner Garden (p.108) Peaceful grounds surrounding Tokyo's most important Shinto shrine.

National Park for Nature Study (p.120) Limited daily admissions help preserve this park's natural serenity; a haven for solitude seekers.

Rikugi-en (p.95) Tokyo's best example of an Edo-period stroll garden.

Shinjuku Gyoen (p.103) English, French and Japanese garden styles combine harmoniously at this spacious park.

Yoyogi-kōen (p.109) Modern park, next to Meiji-jingū shrine, and popular with families and couples.

1903 **Hibiya-kōen**, Tokyo's first European-style park, came into being. These days the tree-filled park is a popular lunchtime spot for office workers and courting couples, and makes a very pleasant escape from the bustle of nearby Ginza and Shimbashi.

Across the road is the celebrated **Imperial Hotel**, first opened in 1890, when it was Tokyo's first Western-style hotel. The original building was subsequently replaced by an Art Deco, Aztec-palace creation by American architect Frank Lloyd Wright, a stunning building which famously withstood both the Great Kantō Earthquake (which struck the city the day after the hotel's formal opening on August 31, 1923) and World War II. After all this, Wright's building finally fell victim to the 1960s property development boom, when it was replaced by the current looming tower. Today, just a hint of Wright's style exists in the *Old Imperial Bar* (see p.171), incorporating some old tiles and furniture.

Shiodome

Follow the railway tracks south from Ginza to reach the new commercial centre of **Shiodome**, a clutch of ultra-modern skyscrapers built on the site of Japan Railways' old freight terminal. The towers that have opened are already home to some of Japan's top companies, including ad agency Dentsu, Nippon TV and Kyodo News, and it's estimated that by 2005 some sixty thousand people will be living and working here.

The shortcomings of Shiodome are readily apparent when you compare it to the rival mega-development of Roppongi Hills, however. The way Shiodome fits into the existing streets and the connections between and around the various buildings are poorly thought out, creating an alienating concrete environment with none of the softening landscaping and street art that make Roppongi Hills so successful. There are a few attractions worth checking out, all the same, as well as many restaurants and four major hotels.

The most interesting sight is the high-tech Advertising Museum Tokyo, or **ADMT** (Tues–Fri 11am–6.30pm, Sat 11am–4.30pm; free; ℡03/6218-2500, ⓦwww.admt.jp), which can be found on the B1 and B2 floors of the **Caretta Shiodome** skyscraper, the sleek headquarters of the Dentsu ad agency. In the small permanent exhibition a montage of ads provides a fascinating flick through some of the twentieth century's most arresting commercial images, and it's fun to watch videos of past TV commercials; you can also peruse some 100,000 images on Dentsu's computerized database. Afterwards, zip up to the top of the Caretta Shiodome building in the glass-fronted lifts to the restaurants on the 46th and 47th floors for a free panoramic view across Tokyo Bay and the nearby Hama Rikyū Teien traditional garden.

Immediately west of Caretta Shiodome (and linked to it by a pedestrian deck) is Shiodome's second major tower complex, **Shiodome City Centre**. Back in 1872, this was the site of the original Shimbashi Station, the terminus of Japan's first railway line. A faithful reproduction of the station building, designed by American architect R. P. Bridgens, now rests incongruously at the foot of the tower and contains the passably interesting **Railway History Exhibition Hall** (Tues–Sun 11am–6pm; free; ℡03/3572-1872, ⓦwww.ejrcf.or.jp), as well as the fancy *Grand Café Shimbashi Mikuni*. Part of the foundations of the original building, uncovered during excavations on the site, have been preserved, and you can also see some fascinating woodblock prints and old photographs of how the area once looked.

Of even more minor interest is the **NAIS Museum** (Tues–Sun 10am–5.30pm; ¥500; ℡03/6218-0078, ⓦwww.shiodome.nais.jp), a small gallery with changing exhibitions alongside a permanent display of works by the French religious artist Georges Rouault. It's housed in the showroom of **Matsushita Electric Works**, where you can also see the latest in kitchen and bathroom technology, including the newest high-tech electronic toilets.

From Shiodome you can also pick up the monorail to **Odaiba**.

Nihombashi and around

North of Ginza, **Nihombashi** (Bridge of Japan) grew from a cluster of riverside markets in the early seventeenth century to become the city's chief financial district. Once the heart of Edo's teeming Shitamachi (see p.271), the earlier warehouses and moneylenders have evolved into the banks, brokers and trading companies that line the streets today.

Since 1603, the centre of Nihombashi, and effectively of all Japan, was an arched red-lacquer-coated **bridge** – a favourite of *ukiyo-e* artists – which marked the start of the Tōkaidō, the great road running between Edo and Kyoto. The original wooden structure has long gone, but distances from Tokyo are still measured from a bronze marker at the halfway point of the present stone bridge, erected in 1911. Although it's now smothered by the Shuto Expressway, it's still worth swinging by here to see the fabulous bronze statues of dragons and wrought-iron lamps that decorate the bridge.

A little further north on Chūō-dōri is the most traditional of Japan's department stores, **Mitsukoshi**. The shop traces its ancestry back to a dry-goods store opened in 1673 by Mitsui Takatoshi, who revolutionized retailing in Edo and went on to found the Mitsui empire. This was the first store in Japan to offer a delivery service, the first to sell imported goods, and the first with an escalator, though until 1923 customers were still required to take off their shoes and don Mitsukoshi slippers. The most interesting part of today's store is the north building, which dates from 1914 and whose main atrium is dominated by a weird and wonderful statue, carved from 500-year-old Japanese cypress, of Magokoro, the Goddess of Sincerity.

Crossing Nihombashi and heading south along Chūō-dōri, duck immediately to the left into the side steets to locate the cluttered little **Kite Museum** (Mon–Sat 11am–5pm; ¥200; ☎03/3275-2704, ⓦwww .tako.gr.jp/eng/index_e.html); there's no English sign, but it's on the fifth floor above *Taimeiken* restaurant. Since 1977 the restaurant's former owner has amassed over four hundred kites of every conceivable shape and size, from one no bigger than a postage stamp to a monster 8m square.

As you return to Chūō-dōri, a row of cheerful red awnings on the left-hand side announces another of Tokyo's grand old stores, **Takashimaya**, which started off as a kimono shop in the seventeenth century and is worth popping into for its fabulous old-fashioned lifts. Across the street, **Maruzen** bookstore is a relative upstart, founded in 1869 to import Western texts as part of Japan's drive to modernize and still a good source of foreign-language books.

Further south on Chūō-dōri, across Yaesu-dōri, is the **Bridgestone Museum of Art** (Tues–Sun 10am–6pm; entrance from Yaesu-dōri; ¥700; ☎03/3563-0241, ⓦwww.bridgestone-museum.gr.jp). This superb collection focuses on the Impressionists and continues through all the great names of early twentieth-century European art, plus a highly rated sampler of Meiji-era Japanese paintings in Western style. It's not an extensive display, but offers a rare opportunity to enjoy works by artists such as Renoir, Picasso and Van Gogh in an (often) almost deserted gallery.

In front of the museum, Yaesu-dōri heads west towards the east entrance to **Tokyo Station**, known as the Yaesu entrance. Here you'll find the main entrance to the Shinkansen tracks, as well as the desk for exchanging Japan Rail passes, the Express Bus ticket office and left-luggage room. Limousine buses for Narita and Haneda airports stop across the road outside Daiwa Bank.

3

Kanda, Ryōgoku and around

Kanda, the region immediately north and west of Nihombashi, straddles Tokyo's crowded eastern lowlands – the former Shitamachi (see History, p.271) – and the more expansive western hills. The area's scattered sights reflect these contrasting styles, kicking off at **Ochanomizu** with the lively Shinto shrine of Kanda Myōjin, and an austere monument to Confucius at Yushima Seidō. Below them lie the buzzing, neon-lit streets of **Akihabara**, Tokyo's "Electric City", dedicated to technological wizardry.

Heading west on the JR Sōbu line, **Suidōbashi** has a couple of minor attractions in the form of Tokyo's foremost baseball stadium, a top-class spa complex and funfair, and a classic seventeenth-century garden, while a studious hush prevails among the secondhand bookshops of **Jimbōchō**, to the south.

East from Akihabara, the Sōbu line crosses the Sumida-gawa to **Ryōgoku**, the heartland of sumo and home to the absorbing, ultra-modern **Edo–Tokyo Museum**. Further south, all within walking distance of each other, are **Kiyosumitei-en**, a pleasant Meiji-era garden; the delightful **Fukagawa Edo Museum**, an atmospheric re-creation of a mid-nineteenth-century Shitamachi neighbourhood; and the **Museum of Contemporary Art**, gathering together the best of post-1945 Japanese art in one spacious, top-class venue.

Ochanomizu

Kanda's two great shrines lie on the north bank of the Kanda-gawa river and are within easy reach of both **Ochanomizu**'s JR and Marunouchi line stations. If you're here in the afternoon, take a quick detour south along Hongō-dōri, to visit the Russian Orthodox **Nikolai Cathedral** (Tues–Fri 1–3pm; free). It's not a large building but its Byzantine flourishes stand out well against the characterless surrounding blocks, and the refurbished altarpiece positively glows in the soft light. Founded by Archbishop Nikolai Kasatkin, who came to Japan in 1861 as chaplain to the Russian consulate in Hokkaidō, the cathedral took seven years to complete (1884–91); the plans were sent from Russia but the British architect Josiah Conder (see box on p.63) supervised the project and gets most of the credit.

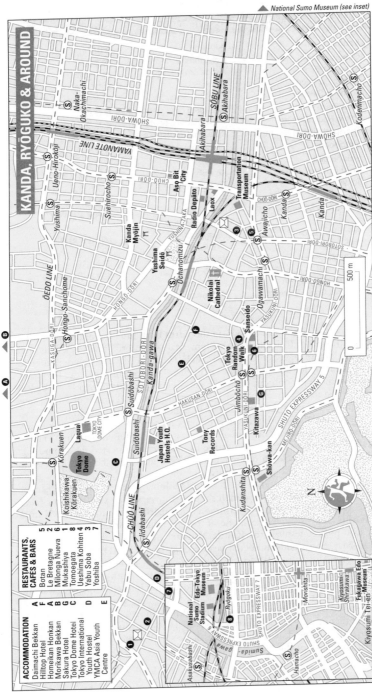

▲ National Sumo Museum (see inset)

Kanda	*Kanda*	神田
Ochanomizu	*Ochanomizu*	御茶の水
Kanda Myōjin	*Kanda Myōjin*	神田明神
Nikolai Cathedral	*Nikorai-dō*	ニコライ堂
Yushima Seidō	*Yushima Seidō*	湯島聖堂
Akihabara	*Akihabara*	秋葉原
Tokyo Radio Depāto	*Tokyo Radio Depāto*	東京ラジオデパート
Transportation Museum	*Kōtsū Hakubutsukan*	交通博物館
Jimbōchō	*Jimbōchō*	神保町
Suidōbashi	*Suidōbashi*	水道橋
Koishikawa-Kōrakuen	*Koishikawa-Kōrakuen*	小石川後楽園
Tokyo Dome	*Tōkyō Dōmu*	東京ドーム
Ryōgoku	*Ryōgoku*	両国
Edo–Tokyo Museum	*Edo–Tōkyō Hakubutsukan*	江戸東京博物館
Fukagawa Edo Museum	*Fukagawa-Edo Hakubutsukan*	深川江戸博物館
Kiyosumi Tei-en	*Kiyosumi Tei-en*	清澄庭園
Museum of Contemporary Art	*Tōkyō-to Gendai Bijutsukan*	東京都現代美術館
National Sumo Stadium	*Kokugikan*	国技館

Back at the river, some woods on the north bank hide the distinctive shrine of **Yushima Seidō** (daily 9.30am–4pm, May–Oct until 5pm; free), dedicated to the Chinese sage Confucius. The Seidō (Sacred Hall) was founded in 1632 as an academy for the study of the ancient classics at a time when the Tokugawa were promoting Confucianism as the state's ethical foundation. In 1691 the hall was moved to its present location, where it became an elite school for the sons of samurai and high-ranking officials, though most of these buildings were lost in the fires of 1923. Today, the quiet compound contains an eighteenth-century wooden gate and, at the top of broad steps, the Taisen-den, or "Hall of Accomplishments", where the shrine to Confucius is located. This imposing, black-lacquered building was rebuilt in 1935 to the original design; look up to see four panther-like guardians poised on the roof tiles.

Follow the road round to the north of Yushima Seidō to find a large, copper *torii* and a traditional wooden shop, Amanoya, selling sweet, ginger-laced sake (*amazaké*). Beyond, a vermilion gate marks the entrance to **Kanda Myōjin** (9am–4.30pm; free), one of the city's oldest shrines and host to one of its top three festivals, the **Kanda Matsuri** (see p.36), which takes place in mid-May every odd-numbered year. Founded in 730 AD, the shrine originally stood in front of Edo Castle, where it was dedicated to the gods of farming and fishing (Daikoku and Ebisu). Later, the tenth-century rebel Taira no Masakado – who was beheaded after declaring himself emperor – was also enshrined here; according to legend, his head "flew" to Edo, where he was honoured as something of a local hero. When Shogun Tokugawa Ieyasu was strengthening the castle's fortifications in 1616, he took the opportunity to move the shrine, but mollified Masakado's supporters by declaring him a guardian deity of the city.

Of the many Western architects invited by the Meiji government to Japan to help it modernize, the one considered to have had the greatest impact is Josiah Conder. When he arrived in 1877, a freshly graduated 25-year-old, his position was to teach architecture at what would become the Faculty of Engineering at Tokyo University. By the time he died in Tokyo in 1920 he had designed over fifty major buildings including the original Imperial Museum at Ueno, and the Nikolai Cathedral (see p.60) in Ochanomizu. His crowning glory is generally considered to be the Rokumeikan reception hall in Hibiya, a synthesis of Japanese and Western architectural styles. This was torn down in 1940, but a model of it can be seen in the Edo–Tokyo Museum (see p.60). His students Tatsuno Kingo and Katayama Tōkuma went on to design Tokyo Station and the Akasaka Detached Palace respectively.

In the West, Conder is perhaps best known for his study of Japanese gardens and his book *Landscape Gardens in Japan*, published in 1893. Kyū Iwasaki-tei in Ueno (see p.87) and Kyū Furukawa Gardens near Komagome (see p.95) are two houses he designed with gardens which are open to the public.

Akihabara and around

Some 500m southeast of Kanda Myōjin, following Yushima-zaka as it drops steeply downhill, a blaze of adverts and a cacophony of competing audio systems announce **Akihabara**. This is Tokyo's foremost discount shopping area for electrical and electronic goods of all kinds, from computers and DVDs to mobile phones and "washlets" – electronically controlled toilet-cum-bidets with an optional medical analysis function. Today's high-tech stores are direct descendants of a postwar black market in radios and radio parts that took place beneath the train tracks around Akihabara Station. You can recapture some of the atmosphere in the narrow passages under the tracks just west of the station, or among the tiny stalls of **Radio Depāto** – four floors stuffed with plugs, wires, boards and tools for making or repairing radios; follow the Sōbu line tracks west from Akihabara Station to find the store just off Chūō-dōri.

Cutting-edge technology of an earlier age is celebrated on the opposite bank of the Kanda-gawa in the **Transportation Museum** (Tues–Sun 9.30am–4.30pm; ¥310; ☎03/3251-8481, ⓦwww.kouhaku.or.jp). The highlight is the train section, where you'll find Japan's first steam locomotive, built in Britain in 1871, and a wooden passenger carriage used by Emperor Meiji in 1877, complete with carpets and silk padding. Best of all are the simulators with their levers, buttons and screens, where you can drive a suburban JR train or put a Shinkansen through its paces.

Suidōbashi and Jimbōchō

Two stops west of Akihabara, the Sōbu line rumbles into **Suidōbashi**, where the stadium and thrill rides of **Tokyo Dome City** (ⓦwww.tokyo -dome.co.jp) punctuate the skyline. The centrepiece is the plump, white-roofed **Tokyo Dome**, popularly known as the "Big Egg", Tokyo's major baseball venue and home ground of the Yomiuri Giants. The Dome's **Baseball**

Hall of Fame and Museum (Tues–Sun 10am–5pm, March–Sept until 6pm; ¥400; Ⓦwww.baseball-museum.or.jp) is for diehard fans only, who'll appreciate the footage of early games and all sorts of baseball memorabilia, including one of Babe Ruth's jackets.

On the west side of the site is the recently upgraded **LaQua** amusement park (daily 10am–10pm; Ⓦwww.laqua.jp). The highlight is Thunder Dolphin (¥1000), a high-tech rollercoaster guaranteed to get you screaming. If you haven't got the stomach for it the world's first spokeless ferris wheel (¥800) provides a gentler ride and plenty of time to take a photo of the passing view. The hokey 13 Doors (¥800), a Japanese house of horrors, also provides some goulish laughs. A one-day passport (¥4000; or ¥2800 after 5pm) gets you access to all the park's rides. Alternatively, skip the rides and soak away your stress at the excellent **Spa LaQua** (see opposite).

Immediately to the west of Tokyo Dome is **Koishikawa-Kōrakuen** (daily 9am–5pm; ¥300), a fine example of an early seventeenth-century stroll-garden. Winding paths take you past waterfalls, ponds and stone lanterns down to the shores of a small lake draped with gnarled pines and over daintily humped bridges, where each view replicates a famous beauty spot. Zhu Shun Shui, a refugee scholar from Ming China, advised on the design, so Chinese as well as Japanese landscapes feature, the most obvious being Small Lu-shan, represented by rounded hills of bamboo grass. The garden attracts few visitors, though intrusive announcements from Tokyo Dome, looming over the trees, mean it's not always totally peaceful. The main entrance gate lies in the garden's southwest corner, midway between Suidōbashi and Iidabashi stations; there's another entrance close by Tokyo Dome.

From Suidōbashi hop on the Toei Mita subway one stop, or walk 1km south down Hakusan-dōri to **Jimbōchō**, a lively student centre which is also home to dozens of secondhand **bookshops** around the intersection of Yasukuni-dōri and Hakusan-dōri. The best ones are along the south side of Yasukuni-dōri in the blocks either side of Jimbōchō subway station, where racks of dog-eared novels and textbooks sit outside shops stacked high with dusty tomes. Most of these are in Japanese, but some dealers specialize in English-language books – both new and old – while a bit of rooting around might turn up a volume of old photographs or cartoons in one of the more upmarket antiquarian dealers. Note that many shops close on either Sunday or Monday.

Ryōgoku and around

From Akihabara, hop on a Sōbu-line train two stops west across the Sumida-gawa to **Ryōgoku**, a sort of sumo town with shops selling outsize clothes and restaurants serving flavourful tureens of *chanko-nabe*, the wrestlers' traditional body-building stew. Three times each year major sumo tournaments fill the **National Sumo Stadium**, outside Ryōgoku Station's west exit, with a two-week pageant of thigh-slapping, foot-stamping and arcane ritual (see p.192 for more on sumo and buying tickets). The one-room historical **museum** (Mon–Fri 10am–4.30pm; closed during tournaments; free) beside the stadium is for diehard fans only; better to simply wander the streets immediately south of the train tracks. Until recently, this area housed many of the major "stables" where wrestlers lived and trained, but rising land prices have forced most of them out. Nevertheless, there's still a good chance of bumping into some

Until just a few decades ago, when people began installing bathrooms at home, life in Tokyo's residential neighbourhoods focused round the **sentō**, the public bath. Though you no longer find them every few blocks, a surprising number of bathhouses survive, of which we've given a sampler below. Take along your own soap, shampoo and a towel – or buy them at the door. See p.40 for tips on bathing etiquette.

The *sentō* have been recently joined by a couple of enormous **onsen** (hot spring) complexes: Spa LaQua in Suidōbashi and Oedo Onsen Monogatari in Odaiba. Both are much more expensive than a traditional *sentō* but offer extensive bathing facilities, a range of places to eat and relaxation areas with very comfortable reclining chairs.

Asakusa Kannon Onsen 2-7-26 Asakusa, Taitō-ku ☏03/3844-4141 (daily 6.30am–6pm; ¥700); Asakusa Station. This big, old ivy-covered bathhouse isn't the cheapest *sentō* around, but it's right next to Sensō-ji and uses real onsen water. The clientele ranges from *yakuza* to grannies – very Asakusa.

Azabu-Jūban Onsen 1-5-22 Azabu-Jūban, Minato-ku ☏03/3404-2610 (daily except Tues); Azabu-Jūban Station. Of the two options here, the casual ground-floor baths (3–11pm; ¥400) offer better value, while upstairs (11am–9pm; ¥1260, or ¥940 after 6pm) is a much classier affair. Either way, the brown, mineral-rich onsen water is scalding hot.

Jakotsu-yu 1-11-11 Asakusa, Taitō-ku ☏03/3841-8641 (daily except Tues 1pm–midnight; ¥400); Tawaramachi Station. Spruce bathhouse down a back alley just south of Rox department store – one bath is designed to give you a mild but stimulating electric shock. Each section has a small rock garden and a handy coin laundry in the changing room.

Ōedo Onsen Monogatari 2-57 Omi, Koto-ku ☏03/5500-1126, ⓦwww .ooedoonsen.jp (daily 11am–9pm; ¥2872, or ¥1987 after 6pm); Telecom Centre Station. More of a theme park than a bathhouse, this newly developed onsen on the southwestern edge of Odaiba goes in for nostalgic kitsch in a big way. Admission includes a colourful *yukata* and towels. There's an outdoor bath and various street performers keep the atmosphere jolly.

Rokuryū Mineral Spa 3-4-20 Ikenohata, Bunkyō-ku ☏03/3821-3826 (Tues–Sun 3.30–11pm; ¥400); Nezu Station. Another real onsen bath boasting a lovely traditional-style frontage. The interior is more ordinary, but clean and spacious.

Spa LaQua 1-1-1 Kasuga, Bunkyō-ku ☏03/3817-4173, ⓦwww.laqua.jp (daily 11am–9pm; ¥2300); Suidōbashi Station. By far the most sophisticated of Tokyo's bathing complexes, this new place spread over five floors (the entrance is on the 6th floor) uses real onsen water pumped from 1700m underground. Admission includes towels and loose pyjamas to wear around the complex. Access to the Healing Baden set of special therapeutic saunas costs ¥300 extra. It's also a great place to pass the time if you miss the last train home and don't want to fork out for a capsule or hotel.

Tokyo onsens and spas		
Asakusa Kannon Onsen	*Asakusa Kannon Onsen*	浅草観音温泉
Azabu-Jūban Onsen	*Azabu-Jūban Onsen*	麻布十番温泉
Jakotsu-yu	*Jakotsu-yu*	蛇骨湯
Ōedo Onsen Monogatari	*Ōedo Onsen Monogatari*	大江戸温泉物語
Rokuryū Mineral Spa	*Rokuryū Kōsen*	六龍鉱泉
Spa LaQua	*Supa Rakuwa*	スパラクワ

junior wrestlers in their *yukata* and wooden *geta* with slicked-back hair, popping out to a store or for a quick snack of *chanko-nabe*. If you're feeling peckish yourself, one of the best places to sample this traditional sumo hotpot packed with tofu and vegetables is *Tomoegata* restaurant (see p.159).

Edo–Tokyo Museum

You'll need plenty of stamina for the next stop, the **Edo–Tokyo Museum** (Tues–Sun 9.30am–5.30pm, Thurs & Fri until 8pm; ¥600; ☎3626-9974, ⓦwww.edo-tokyo-museum.or.jp), housed in a colossal building behind the Sumo Stadium; the ticket lasts a whole day, so you can come and go. The museum tells the history of Tokyo from the days of the Tokugawa shogunate to postwar reconstruction, using life-size replicas, models and holograms, as well as more conventional screen paintings, ancient maps and documents, with plenty of information in English. The museum starts on the sixth floor, where a bridge (a replica of the original Nihombashi; see p.58) takes you over the roofs of famous Edo landmarks – a Kabuki theatre, *daimyō* residence and Western-style office – on the main exhibition floor below. The displays then run roughly chronologically; they're particularly strong on life in Edo's Shitamachi, with its pleasure quarters, festivals and vibrant popular culture, and on the giddy days after 1868, when Japan opened up to the outside world.

Fukagawa Edo Museum and around

From the Edo-Tokyo Museum head to the nearby Ryōgoku metro station on the Ōedo line. Go two stops south to Kiyosumi-Shirakawa, then take exit A3 to emerge in front of the beautifully landscaped Edo-era garden, **Kiyosumi Tei-en** (daily 9am–5pm; ¥150). Surrounding a large pond, the gardens reflect the changing seasons and are particularly worth visiting in spring for their cherry blossoms and azaleas.

From the gardens head east along the charming shopping street where you'll find many traditional shops and a spruce public toilet (it's been voted one of the ten best in Japan); you won't miss it. Further along is the captivating **Fukagawa Edo Museum** (daily 9.30am–5pm, closed second and fourth Mon of the month; ¥300), which re-creates a Shitamachi neighbourhood. The museum's one-room exhibition hall could be a film set for nineteenth-century Edo and contains seven complete buildings: the homes of various artisans and labourers, a watchtower and storehouses. As you walk through the rooms furnished with the clutter of daily life, you're accompanied by the cries of street vendors and birdsong, while the lighting shifts from dawn through to a soft dusk. It's worth investing in their English-language guidebook (¥500) before going in.

Museum of Contemporary Art

Continue east from the Fukagawa Edo Museum until you reach the major road Mitsuni-dōri. A block south of here a severe glass-and-grey-steel building houses Tokyo's premier modern art venue, the **Museum of Contemporary Art** (Tues–Sun 10am–6pm, Fri until 9pm; ¥500, plus an additional charge for special exhibitions; ☎03/5245-4111, ⓦwww.mot-art-museum.jp). Inside, the vast white spaces provide the perfect setting for a fine collection of works by Japanese and Western artists (notably Roy Lichtenstein) from the post-1945 avant-garde through the 1950s abstract revolution to pop art, minimalism and beyond. Only 150 pieces are displayed at a time but you can see the rest of the collection (some 3500 items) in the audiovisual library. There are also bookstores, cafés, a well-stocked art library and an information centre. Note that the museum closes twice a year for two weeks while the permanent exhibits are changed, so it's a good idea to phone before setting off. The museum can also be reached from Kiba Station on the Tozai line from where it's a fifteen-minute walk north.

Akasaka and Roppongi

ightlife is what **Akasaka** and **Roppongi**, southwest of the Imperial Palace, are all about. After a hard day's work, the bureaucrats and politicians from nearby Kasumigaseki and Nagatachō head for glitzy Akasaka, home to many of Tokyo's luxury hotels and expense-account restaurants, while younger Japanese and *gaijin* party down in Roppongi, an area which has recently shifted up the Tokyo pecking order with the opening of the **Roppongi Hills** mega-development in 2003.

Roppongi Hills aside, there are a handful of sights to keep you occupied if you find yourself here during the day. Chief amongst these are Akasaka's premier shrine, **Hie-jinja**, with its attractive avenue of red *torii*; **Zōjō-ji**, near Roppongi, once the temple of the Tokugawa clan; and **Tokyo Tower**, arguably Tokyo's most easily recognizable sight, but no longer the highest viewing spot in the city.

Akasaka

Southwest of the Imperial Palace, beside the government areas of Kasumigaseki and Nagatachō, is **Akasaka**. This was once an agricultural area (*akane*, plants that produce a red dye were farmed here, hence the area's name, which means

Akasaka and Roppongi

Akasaka	*Akasaka*	赤坂
Akasaka Detached Palace	*Geihinkan*	迎賓館
Ark Hills	*Āku Hiruzu*	アークヒルズ
Hie-jinja	*Hie-jinja*	日枝神社
Suntory Museum of Art	*Santorii Bijutsukan*	サントリー美術館
Toyokawa Inari	*Toyokawa Inari-jinja*	豊川稲荷神社
Roppongi	*Roppongi*	六本木
Nogi-jinja	*Nogi-jinja*	乃木神社
Roppongi Hills	*Roppongi Hiruzu*	六本木ヒルズ
Tokyo Tower	*Tōkyō Tawā*	東京タワー
Zōjō-ji	*Zōjō-ji*	増上寺

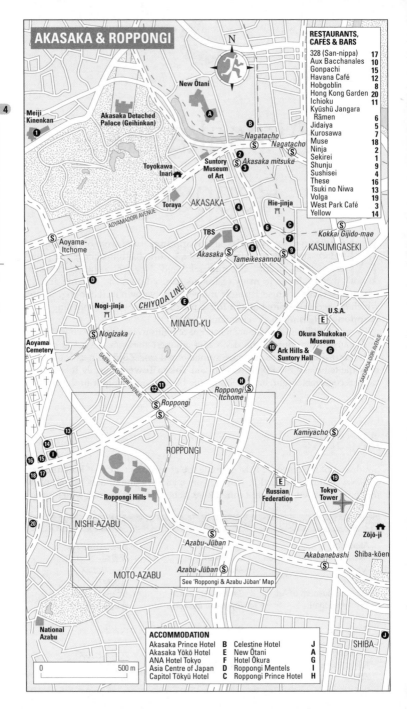

AKASAKA & ROPPONGI

N

RESTAURANTS,
CAFÉS & BARS

328 (San-nippa)	17
Aux Bacchanales	10
Gonpachi	15
Havana Café	12
Hobgoblin	8
Hong Kong Garden	20
Ichioku	11
Kyūshū Jangara Rāmen	6
Jidaiya	5
Kurosawa	7
Muse	18
Ninja	2
Sekirei	1
Shunju	9
Sushisei	4
These	16
Tsuki no Niwa	13
Volga	19
West Park Café	3
Yellow	14

Meiji
Kinenkan

New Ōtani

Akasaka Detached
Palace (Geihinkan)

Nagatacho

Nagatacho

Toyokawa
Inari

Suntory
Museum
of Art

Akasaka mitsuke

Toraya

AKASAKA

Hie-jinja

AOYAMADORI AVENUE

TBS

Kokkai Gijido-mae

KASUMIGASEKI

Aoyama-
Itchome

Akasaka

Tameikesannou

CHIYODA LINE

MINATO-KU

Nogi-jinja

U.S.A.

Aoyama
Cemetery

Nogizaka

Okura Shukokan
Museum

GAIEN-HIGASHI-DORI AVENUE

Ark Hills &
Suntory Hall

SAKURADA-DORI AVENUE

Roppongi
Itchome

Roppongi

ROPPONGI

Kamiyacho

Roppongi Hills

Russian
Federation

Tokyo
Tower

NISHI-AZABU

Azabu-Jūban

Zōjō-ji

MOTO-AZABU

Azabu-Jūban

Akabanebashi

Shiba-kōen

See 'Roppongi & Azabu Jūban' Map

National
Azabu

SHIBA

0   500 m

ACCOMMODATION

Akasaka Prince Hotel	B	Celestine Hotel	J
Akasaka Yōkō Hotel	E	New Ōtani	A
ANA Hotel Tokyo	F	Hotel Ōkura	G
Asia Centre of Japan	D	Roppongi Mentels	I
Capitol Tōkyū Hotel	C	Roppongi Prince Hotel	H

"red slope"), but subsequently developed as an entertainment district in the late nineteenth century, when *ryōtei* restaurants, complete with performing geisha, started opening to cater for the modern breed of politicians and bureaucrats. The area still has its fair share of exclusive establishments, shielded from the hoi polloi by high walls and even higher prices. Their presence, along with the headquarters of the TBS TV station and some of Tokyo's top hotels, lends Akasaka a certain cachet, though prices at many restaurants and bars are no worse than elsewhere in Tokyo.

Hie-jinja

At the southern end of Akasaka's main thoroughfare, Sotobori-dōri, stands a huge stone *torii* gate, beyond which is a picturesque avenue of red *torii* leading up the hill to the **Hie-jinja**, a Shinto shrine dedicated to the god Ōyamakui-no-kami, who is believed to protect against evil. Although the ferro-concrete buildings date from 1967, Hie-jinja's history stretches back to 830 AD, when it was first established on the outskirts of what would become Edo. The shrine's location shifted a couple more times before Shogun Tokugawa Ietsuna placed it here in the seventeenth century as a source of protection for his castle (now the site of the Imperial Palace). In February 1936, the Hie-jinja became the command centre for an attempted coup by a renegade group of 1400 soldiers, intent on restoring power to the emperor, who was being increasingly marginalized by the military-controlled government. Government buildings were seized and two former premiers and the inspector general of military training were killed before the insurrection crumbled after just four days. The soldiers surrendered and nineteen of their leaders were executed.

Hie-jinja hosts the **Sannō Matsuri** (June 10–16), one of Tokyo's most important festivals. The highlight is a parade on June 15 involving four hundred participants dressed in Heian-period costume and carrying fifty sacred *mikoshi* (portable shrines) – there's a festival every year, but the *mikoshi* parade only takes place every other year (in even-numbered years). The front entrance to the shrine is actually through the large stone *torii* on the east side of the hill, beside the *Capitol Tōkyū Hotel*. Fifty-one steps lead up to a spacious enclosed courtyard, in which roosters roam freely and salarymen bunk off work to idle on benches. To the left of the main shrine, look for the carving of a female monkey cradling its baby, a symbol that has come to signify protection for pregnant women.

The New Ōtani Hotel and around

Heading north from the shrine along Sotobori-dōri and across Benkei-bashi, the bridge that spans what was once the outer moat of the shogun's castle, you'll soon reach the **New Ōtani** hotel. Within its grounds is a beautiful traditional Japanese **garden**, originally designed for the *daimyō* Katō Kiyomasa, lord of Kumamoto in Kyūshū, over four hundred years ago. You can stroll freely through the garden or admire it while sipping tea in the *New Ōtani's* lounge. The hotel also has its own small **art gallery** (Tues–Sun 10am–6pm; ¥500, free to guests), with works by Japanese and European artists, including Chagall and Modigliani, and a tea-ceremony room, where tea is served in the traditional way (Thurs–Sat 11am–4pm; ¥1050).

Returning across the Benkei-bashi to the Akasaka Mitsuke intersection brings you to the Suntory Building, which houses the elegant **Suntory Museum of Art** on its eleventh floor (Tues–Sun 10am–5pm, Fri until 7pm;

¥500 or more depending on the exhibition; ℡03/3470-1073, ⓦwww
.suntory.co.jp/sma). As well as changing exhibitions of ceramics, lacquerware,
paintings and textiles, the museum has a traditional tea-ceremony room, where
tea and sweets are served for around ¥300.

Walking southwest from the museum along Aoyama-dōri, you'll soon
encounter the colourful **Toyokawa Inari** (also known as Myōgon-ji), an
example of a combined temple and shrine which was much more common
across Japan before the Meiji government forcibly separated Shinto and
Buddhist places of worship. The temple's compact precincts are decked with
red lanterns and banners and the main hall is guarded by statues of pointy-
eared foxes wearing red bibs – the messengers of the Shinto god Inari, found
at all Inari shrines.

Toyokawa Inari borders the extensive grounds of the grand, European-style
Akasaka Detached Palace (Geihinkan), which serves as the official State
Guest House. When it was completed in 1909, this vast building, modelled on
Buckingham Palace on the outside and Versailles on the inside, only had one
bathroom in the basement and the empress's apartments were in a separate
wing from her husband's; this was fine by the emperor since he was in the habit
of taking his nightly pick from the ladies-in-waiting. Some members of the
imperial family, including the crown prince, still live within the palace grounds,
which unfortunately puts it off limits to visitors.

Ark Hills and around

Returning to Sotobori-dōri and heading southeast past Hei-jinja brings you
to Roppongi-dōri. Turn south along this road to reach the **Ark Hills** complex, a precursor of the Mori Corporation's Roppongi Hills, housing the *ANA
Hotel* and the classical-music venue Suntory Hall (see p.180). Behind Ark Hills
and next to the *Hotel Ōkura* is the **Ōkura Shūkokan** art museum (Tues–Sun
10am–4.30pm; ¥500, free to hotel guests), established in 1917 by the self-styled
Baron Ōkura Tsuruhiko and housing an intriguing display of Oriental ceramics, paintings, prints and sculptures from a collection of over 1700 traditional
works of art. The museum is on the hill above Kamiyachō subway
station.

Roppongi

Around a kilometre south of Akasaka is **Roppongi**, meaning "six trees",
though there's hardly a twig in sight today. The area was once reputed to be
home to six *daimyō*, all of whom coincidentally had the Chinese character for
"tree" in their names. From the Meiji era onwards, Roppongi was a military
stamping ground, first for the imperial troops and then, during the American
Occupation, for the US forces. When the US army moved out in 1958, TV
Asahi moved in, the *gaijin* community started hanging out here and today's
entertainment district was born.

For the last decade Roppongi has been slipping downmarket, becoming pep-
pered with discount shops, pachinko parlours and karaoke clubs, while bounc-
ers hand out leaflets for strip joints and sleazy hostess clubs. In stark contrast
are the sleek precincts of nearby **Roppongi Hills**, a ¥280-billion complex of
offices, shops, residences and entertainment venues. Together with a proposed

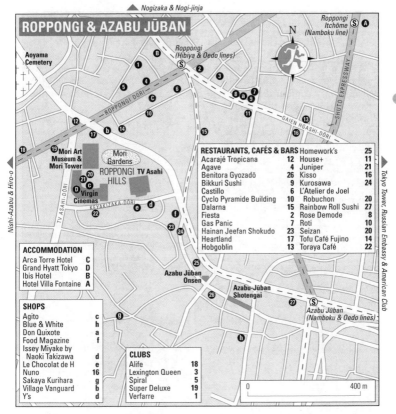

ROPPONGI & AZABU JŪBAN

Nogizaka & Nogi-jinja

Roppongi Itchōme **S** **A** (Namboku line)

Aoyama Cemetery

Roppongi (Hibiya & Oedo lines) **S**

N

ROPPONGI DŌRI

GAIEN HIGASHI-DŌRI

SHUTO EXPRESSWAY

Nishi-Azabu & Hiro-o ◄

Mori Art Museum & Mori Tower

Mori Gardens

ROPPONGI HILLS

TV Asahi

Virgin Cinemas

KEYAKIZAKA-DŌRI

TV ASAHI-DŌRI

Azabu Jūban Onsen

Azabu-Jūban Shotengai

Azabu Jūban (Namboku & Oedo lines) **S**

Tokyo Tower, Russian Embassy & American Club ►

RESTAURANTS, CAFÉS & BARS		Homework's	25
Acarajé Tropicana	12	House+	11
Agave	4	Juniper	21
Benitora Gyozadō	26	Kisso	16
Bikkuri Sushi	9	Kurosawa	24
Castillo	6	L'Atelier de Joel	
Cyclo Pyramide Building	10	Robuchon	20
Dalarna	15	Rainbow Roll Sushi	27
Fiesta	2	Rose Demode	8
Gas Panic	7	Roti	10
Hainan Jeefan Shokudo	23	Seizan	20
Heartland	17	Tofu Café Fujino	14
Hobgoblin	13	Toraya Café	22

ACCOMMODATION

Arca Torre Hotel	C
Grand Hyatt Tokyo	D
Ibis Hotel	B
Hotel Villa Fontaine	A

SHOPS

Agito	c
Blue & White	h
Don Quixote	a
Food Magazine	f
Issey Miyake by Naoki Takizawa	d
Le Chocolat de H	e
Nuno	16
Sakaya Kurihara	g
Village Vanguard	b
Y's	d

CLUBS

Alife	18
Lexington Queen	3
Spiral	5
Super Deluxe	19
Verfarre	1

0 _____ 400 m

4

AKASAKA AND ROPPONGI | Roppongi

new development for the old Defence Agency site on Gaien-Higashi-dōri and the construction of a major art museum closer to Nishi Azabu, Roppongi's future is looking much brighter. If you're up for a night of partying, it remains one of the best places in Tokyo to head for: see p.168 for bar reviews and p.177 for club reviews.

Roppongi Hills

Since its opening in April 2003, **Roppongi Hills** (Ⓦwww .roppongihills.com) has been a phenomenal success, clocking up one million visitors in its first three days alone. A large part of the development's popularity is down to its design, an apparently muddled mix of conflicting architectural styles which gives the complex a natural feel, as if it had evolved over a long period of time.

In fact, it took seventeen years for local property magnate Mori Minoru to realize his dream of an "Urban New Deal" for Tokyo. Part of this deal includes the liberal use of open space and greenery, so unusual in this land-starved city. There's a Japanese garden and pond, an open-air arena for free performances, several roof gardens and even a rice paddy on the roof of the Keyakizaka Complex above the state-of-the-art Virgin Cinema multiplex. The overhead

△ Tokyo Tower

utility cables that plague the rest of Tokyo have been banished, and funky street sculptures have been liberally applied, including Louise Bourgeois' **Maman**, an iconic giant bronze, stainless steel and marble spider, squatting at the base of the 54-storey, Kohn Pederson Fox-designed Mori Tower. If you approach Roppongi Hills through the main Metro Hat entrance from Roppongi Station you'll see the spider at the top of the escalators.

Directly ahead of the spider is the "Museum Cone", a glass structure enclosing a swirling staircase which forms the entrance to Roppongi Hills' highlight, the **Mori Art Museum** (MAM; daily 10am–10pm, Tues until 5pm, Fri & Sat until midnight; ¥1500; ☎03/6406-6100, ⓦwww .mori.art.museum). In line with Mori Minoru's philosophy of combining culture with commercialism in what he fancifully calls an "artelligent city", the prime top floors of the Mori Tower have been given over to the museum. MAM doesn't have its own collection but puts on exhibitions of works gathered from around Japan and abroad, with a particular focus on the best contemporary art and design, and on Asian artists. The museum also includes the **Tokyo City View** observation deck, Tokyo's highest viewpoint (daily 9am–1am; included in entrance to MAM, otherwise ¥1500); for an extra ¥500 you can go up onto the 270-metre-high roof, though it's only open when the weather is good.

Nogi-jinja to the Tokyo Tower

Beside the Roppongi exit of Nogizaka subway station is **Nogi-jinja**, a small shrine honouring the Meiji-era **General Nogi Maresuke**, a hero in both the Sino-Japanese and Russo-Japanese wars. When the emperor Meiji died, Nogi and his wife followed the samurai tradition and committed suicide in his house within the shrine grounds. The house is still here and is open just two days annually (12 & 13 Sept 9.30am–4.30pm; free); on other days you'll have to squint through the windows to catch sight of the general's blood-soaked shirt. On the second Sunday of every month, there's a good antique flea market in the shrine grounds.

Heading back to Roppongi crossing and continuing along Gaien-Higashi-dōri for around 1km will eventually bring you to the **Tokyo Tower** (daily 9am–10pm; main observatory ¥820, top observatory ¥1420; ☎03/3433-5111, ⓦwww.tokyotower.co.jp). Built during an era when Japan was becoming famous for producing cheap copies of foreign goods, this 333-metre red-and-white copy of the Eiffel Tower, opened in 1958, manages to top its Parisian role model by several metres. The uppermost observation deck, at 250m, has been supplanted as the highest viewpoint in Tokyo by the roof deck of Roppongi Hills' Mori Tower (which, incidentally, provides the best view of the Tokyo

Murakami Takashi

All over Roppongi Hills you'll see the colourful cartoon-like designs of leading contemporary artist **Murakami Takashi**. The 42-year-old artist describes his work as part of the "poku" movement, combining pop cultural references with those that would only interest a nerd, known as an *otaku* in Japanese. Designs such as a smiling cosmos flower and a blobby morphing character known as DOB have been a big hit, and Louis Vuitton have brought Murakami in to add technicolour allure to their luxury brand. One of Murakami's sculptural works (*Miss Ko2*) sold for $500,000 at an auction in New York, while his free plastic "snack toys", free with packs of chewing gum, have become collectors' items.

Tower, especially when illuminated at night). More attractions have been added over the years, including an aquarium (¥1000), a waxworks (¥870) and a holographic "Mystery Zone" (¥400), as well as the usual souvenir shops – to the point where the place feels more like an amusement arcade than the Eiffel Tower. There are good views of Tokyo Bay from here, but unless it's an exceptionally clear day, it's better to save your cash for a drink at one of the rooftop bars at any of a host of other city skyscrapers.

Zōjō-ji

Tokyo Tower stands on the eastern flank of **Shiba-kōen**, a park whose main point of interest is **Zōjō-ji**, the family temple of the Tokugawa clan. Zōjō-ji dates from 1393 and was moved to this site in 1598 by Tokugawa Ieyasu (the first Tokugawa shogun) in order to protect southeast Edo spiritually and provide a waystation for pilgrims approaching the capital from the Tōkaidō road. This was once the city's largest holy site, with 48 sub-temples and over a hundred other buildings. Since the fall of the Tokugawa, however, Zōjō-ji has been razed to the ground by fire three times, and virtually all the current buildings date from the mid-1970s.

The main remnant of the past is the imposing **San-gadatsu-mon**, a 21-metre-high gateway dating from 1612 and the oldest wooden structure in Tokyo. The name translates as "Three Deliverances Gate" (Buddhism is supposed to save believers from the evils of anger, greed and stupidity) and the gate is one of Japan's Important Cultural Properties. As you pass through, keep an eye out for the tower with a large bell, said to have been made from melted metal hairpins donated by the ladies of the shogun's court. Look out too for the pair of Himalayan cedar trees, one planted by US President General Grant when he visited the temple in 1879 and the other by the then Vice-President George Bush in 1982. Ahead lies the **Taiden** (Great Main Hall), while to the right are ranks of *jizō* statues, capped with red bonnets and decorated with plastic flowers and colourful windmills that twirl in the breeze. Amid this army of mini-guardians lie the remains of six shogun, behind a wrought-iron gate decorated with dragons.

5

Asakusa

Last stop on the Ginza line heading north, **Asakusa** is best known as the site of Tokyo's most venerable Buddhist temple, **Sensō-ji**, whose towering worship hall is filled with a continual throng of petitioners and tourists. Stalls before the temple cater to the crowds, peddling trinkets and keepsakes as they have done for centuries; old-fashioned craft shops display exquisite hair combs, paper fans and calligraphy brushes; and all around is the inevitable array of restaurants, drinking places and fast-food stands. It's this infectious, carnival atmosphere that makes Asakusa so appealing: this is the area of Tokyo where you'll find the most vivid reminders of Edo's Shitamachi and the popular culture it spawned – one which seems to be constantly in the throes of some celebration or other. The biggest bash is the Sanja Matsuri (see p.37), but there are numerous smaller festivals – ask at the **information centre** (daily 10am–8pm; ☎03/3842-5566) in front of Sensō-ji's main gate if there's anything in the offing; they also organize Sunday afternoon walking tours of the area with English-speaking guides (1.30pm & 3pm; free).

Sensō-ji

Walking west from the river or the Ginza line subway station, you can't miss the solid red-lacquer gate with its monstrous paper lantern that marks the southern entrance to **Sensō-ji**. This magnificent temple, also known as Asakusa Kannon, was founded in the mid-seventh century to enshrine a tiny golden image of Kannon, the goddess of mercy, which had turned up in the nets of two local fishermen. Though most of the present buildings are postwar concrete reconstructions, there's a great sense of atmosphere as you draw near the main hall with its sweeping, tiled roofs.

Getting to Asakusa by river

One of the best ways of getting to Asakusa is by river. Sightseeing ferries (known as *Suijū basu*, or "water buses") follow the Sumida-gawa north from Hama Rikyū Teien via Hinode Pier (see p.000 for details), then dock under Azuma-bashi, opposite Philippe Starck's eye-catching Flamme d'Or Building. Heading back downriver there are departures roughly every forty minutes (daily 9.50am–6.15pm, Sat & Sun until 6.55pm; ¥620 to Hama Rikyū Teien, ¥660 to Hinode Pier), though note that 3.25pm is usually the last departure stopping at Hama Rikyū Teien.

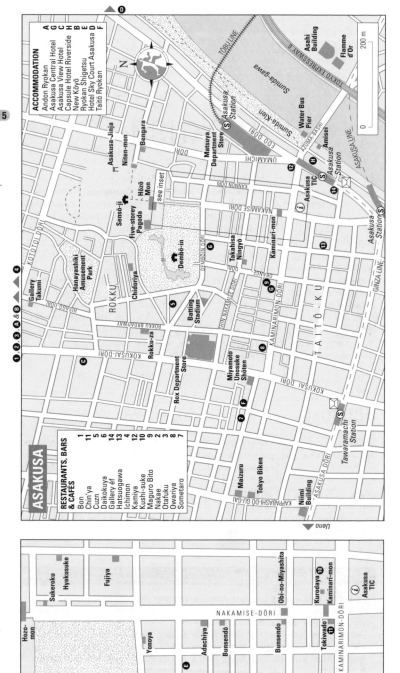

Asakusa

Asakusa	*Asakusa*	浅草
Asakusa-jinja	*Asakusa-jinja*	浅草神社
Gallery Takumi	*Gyararii Takumi*	ギャラリー匠
Kappabashi-dōgu-gai	*Kappabashi-dōgu-gai*	かっぱ橋道具街
Miyamoto Unosuke Shōten	*Miyamoto Unosuke Shōten*	宮本卯之助商店
Rox Dome Sugo Batting Stadium	*Sugō Battingu Sutajiamu*	スゴーバッティングスタジアム
Sensō-ji	*Sensō-ji*	浅草寺
Sumida-kōen	*Sumida-kōen*	隅田公園

The main approach starts under the great **Kaminari-mon**, or "Thunder Gate", named after its two vigorous guardian gods of Thunder and Wind (Raijin and Fūjin), and proceeds along Nakamise-dōri, a colourful parade of small shops packed with gaudy souvenirs, tiny traditional dolls, kimono accessories and sweet-scented piles of *sembei* rice crackers. A double-storied treasure gate, **Hōzō-mon**, stands astride the entrance to the main temple complex; the treasures, fourteenth-century Chinese sutras, are locked away on the upper floor. Its two protective gods – *Niō*, the traditional guardians of Buddhist temples – are even more imposing than those at Kaminari-mon; look out for their enormous rice-straw sandals slung on the gate's rear wall.

Beyond, there's a constant crowd clustered around a large, bronze incense bowl where people waft the pungent smoke – considered the breath of the gods – over themselves for its supposed curative powers. There's nothing much to see inside the temple itself, since the little Kannon – said to be just 7.5cm tall – is a *hibutsu*, a hidden image considered too holy to be put on view. The hall, however, is full of life, with the rattle of coins being tossed into a huge wooden coffer, the swirling plumes of incense smoke and the constant bustle of people coming to pray, buy charms and fortune papers or to attend a service. Three times a day (6am, 10am & 2pm) drums echo through the hall into the courtyard as priests chant sutras beneath the altar's gilded canopy.

Like many Buddhist temples, Sensō-ji accommodates Shinto shrines in its grounds, the most important being **Asakusa-jinja**, dedicated to the two fishermen brothers who netted the Kannon image, and their overlord. The shrine was founded in the mid-seventeenth century by Tokugawa Iemitsu and the original building still survives, though it's hard to tell under all the restored paintwork. More popularly known as Sanja-sama, "Shrine of the Three Guardians", this is the focus of the tumultuous **Sanja Matsuri**, Tokyo's biggest festival, which takes place every year on the third weekend in May. The climax comes on the second day, when over one hundred *mikoshi* (portable shrines) are manhandled through the streets of Asakusa by a seething crowd, among them the three *mikoshi* of Asakusa-jinja, each weighing around 1000kg and carried by at least seventy men.

Sensō-ji's eastern entrance is guarded by the attractively aged **Niten-mon**. Originally built in 1618, this gate is all that remains of a shrine honouring Tokugawa Ieyasu which was relocated to Ueno in 1651 after a series of fires. Niten-mon has since been rededicated and now houses two seventeenth-century Buddhist guardians of the south and east. The road heading east leads to a narrow strip of park, **Sumida-kōen**; the river here provides the stage for one of the city's great summer firework displays (*hanabi taikai*), held on the last Saturday of July.

Asakusa's traditional craft shops

Wander the arcades and backstreets of Asakusa and you'll come across all sorts of traditional **craft shops** which haven't changed much over the last hundred years. The following are just a selection of what's on offer.

Adachiya Nakamise-dōri, Taitō-ku ☎03/3844-1643 (daily 9am–6pm). This shop sells clothes for dogs – not exactly traditional, but in tune with the commercial (and sometimes kitsch) spirit of Asakusa.

Bengara 2-35-11 Asakusa, Taitō-ku (Mon–Wed, Fri & Sat 10am–6pm, Sun 11am–6pm). The best place to look for *noren*, the type of split curtain which can be seen hanging outside every traditional shop or restaurant.

Bunsendō Nakamise-dōri, Taitō-ku (daily 9am–6pm, closed one Mon each month). A specialist in high-quality paper fans.

Fujiya 2-2-15 Asakusa, Taitō-ku ☎03/3841-2283 (daily except Thurs 10am–6pm). Hand-printed cotton towels (*tenugui*) designed by octogenarian Kawakami Keiji. Some Fujiya towels are now collectors' items.

Hyakusuke 2-2-14 Asakusa, Taitō-ku (daily except Tues 11am–5pm). Geisha and Kabuki actors have been coming here for over a century to buy their cosmetics, including a skin cleanser made from powdered nightingale droppings.

Kurodaya 1-2-5 Asakusa, Taitō-ku ☎03/3844-7511 (Tues–Sun 11am–7pm). Kurodaya has been selling wood-block prints and items made of traditional *washi* paper since 1856.

Obi-no-Miyashita Nakamise-dōri, Taitō-ku ☎03/3844-0333 (daily 9am–6.30pm). Small shop selling handbags, cute teddy bears and other items made from beautiful pieces of kimono silk fabric, and *obi*, the decorated belts worn with kimono.

Sukeroku Nakamise-dōri, Taitō-ku (daily 10am–6pm). Pint-sized shop famous for its miniature, handmade plaster dolls in Edo-period costume.

Takahisa Ningyō Shin-Nakamise-dōri, Taitō-ku ☎03/3844-1257 (daily 10am–8pm). Rows of richly decorated battledores (*hagoita*), traditionally used by young girls playing shuttlecock at New Year.

Tokiwadō 1-3 Asakusa, Taitō-ku (daily 10am–6pm). Various types of *Kaminari okoshi* "thunder crackers" on sale beside Kaminari-mon gate.

Yonoya 1-37-10 Asakusa, Taitō-ku (daily except Wed 10am–6pm). Tokyo's finest hand-crafted boxwood combs and hair decorations.

Asakusa's traditional craft shops

Adachiya	*Adachiya*	安立屋
Bengara	*Bengara*	べんがら
Bunsendō	*Bunsendō*	文扇堂
Fujiya	*Fujiya*	ふじ屋
Hyakusuke	*Hyakusuke*	百助
Kurodaya	*Kurodaya*	くろだや
Obi-no-Miyashita	*Obi-no-Miyashita*	帯のみやした
Sukeroku	*Sukeroku*	助六
Takahisa Ningyō	*Takahisa Ningyō*	たかひさ人形
Tokiwadō	*Tokiwadō*	常盤堂
Yonoya	*Yonoya*	よのや

West of Sensō-ji

When Kabuki and *bunraku* were banished from central Edo in the 1840s they settled in the area known as **Rokku** ("Block 6"), between Sensō-ji and today's Kokusai-dōri. Over the next century almost every fad and fashion in popular entertainment started life here, from cinema to cabaret and striptease. Today a handful of the old venues survive, most famously **Rock-za**, with its nightly strip show, and there are loads of cinemas, pachinko parlours, gambling halls and drinking dives. It's not all lowbrow, though: several small theatres in the area, such as Asakusa Shingekijō, still stage *rakugo*, a centuries-old form of comic monologue where familiar jokes and stories are mixed with modern satire.

One block east of the Rox department store, look out for a giant baseball glove pinned to the front of a building – or listen for the crack of wood on leather. In a nation besotted with baseball but short on space, the answer is indoor batting cages, such as the ones here at this **Rox Dome Sugo Batting Stadium** (daily 10am–2am; from ¥300 for 16 balls; ☎03/3845-5515). The idea is to try and hit balls hurtling towards you at up to 130km per hour. It's tremendous fun, especially on weekdays when it's quieter, and a great way to work up a thirst.

From behind Rox the rather grandly named Rokku Broadway leads past betting shops and strip joints north into **Hisago-dōri**, a covered shopping street with a few interesting traditional stores. At the top end is **Gallery Takumi** crafts gallery (daily 10am–8pm; free; ☎03/3842-1990) – you can see different artisans at work here at weekends, while on weekdays there are video presentations about crafts production. Various items such as pottery, lacquerware and woodwork are on sale at their annex (daily except Tues 10am–6pm) a couple of doors further up the same street.

Drum Museum

The wide avenue of Kokusai-dōri forms the western boundary of Rokku. Near its southerly junction with Kaminarimon-dōri, just south from the Rox department store, the shop of **Miyamoto Unosuke Shōten** (daily except Tues 9am–6pm; ☎03/3842-5622, ⓦ www.miyamoto-unosuke.co.jp) is easily identifiable from the elaborate *mikoshi* in the window. The shop is an Aladdin's cave of traditional Japanese percussion instruments and festival paraphernalia: masks, *happi* coats (shortened kimono-style jackets), flutes, cymbals and, of course, all kinds of *mikoshi*, the largest with a price tag over ¥3 million. Since 1861, however, the family passion has been drums, resulting in an impressive collection from around the world which now fills the fourth-floor **Drum Museum** (Wed–Sun 10am–5pm; ¥300). There's every type of percussion material and, best of all, you're allowed to have a go on some. A red dot on the name card indicates those not to be touched; blue dots mean you can tap lightly, just with your hands; and the rest have the appropriate drumsticks ready and waiting.

Kappabashi

Continuing westwards from the Drum Museum brings you after a few blocks to another main road, Kappabashi-dōgu-gai. Locally known as **Kappabashi**, or "Kitchenware Town", this is the best-known of several wholesale markets in northeast Tokyo where you can kit out a whole restaurant. You don't have to be a bulk-buyer, however, and this is a great place to pick up unusual souvenirs, such as the plastic food displayed outside restaurants to tempt the customer.

This practice dates from the last century, originally using wax, but came into its own about thirty years ago when foreign foods were being introduced to a puzzled Japanese market. The best examples are absolutely realistic; try Maizuru (☎03/3843-1686) or Tokyo Biken (☎03/3842-5551) if you're looking for an unusual (but not cheap) souvenir. These are both open daily from 9am to 6pm, but note that many shops along here close on Sunday.

6

Ueno and around

Most people visit **Ueno** for its **park** (*kōen*), one of Tokyo's largest open spaces and home to a host of good museums, as well as a few relics from a vast temple complex that once occupied this hilltop. After a stroll through the park, your first stop should be the prestigious **Tokyo National Museum**, which alone could easily fill a day, though there's also a very worthy **Science Museum** and the more lively **Museum of Western Art**. Save an hour too for the endearing **Shitamachi Museum**, which harks back to Ueno's proletarian past.

Much of downtown Ueno has a rough-and-ready feel, especially round the station and the bustling **Ameyoko-chō market**, which extends south under the train tracks. Further west, there's a more sedate atmosphere in the **Kyū Iwasaki-tei Gardens**, set around one of Tokyo's few remaining Meiji-era mansions, and amongst the worshippers at **Yushima Tenjin** and the students at **Tokyo University**'s ivory towers.

North of the university campus are **Nezu** and **Yanaka**, inner Tokyo's most charmingly old-fashioned areas and a world away from the usual hustle and bustle of Tokyo. A highlight is the historic and tranquil shrine of **Nezu-jinja**, but the whole area is strewn with small temples, cemeteries and other attractions, such as the picturesque and historic **Yanaka Cemetery**, the beautiful **Asakura Sculpture Museum** and the old-style shopping street of **Yanaka Ginza**. There are also a couple of good traditional Japanese-style hotels around here (see p.144) for those who really want to soak up the Shitamachi atmosphere.

Some history

In 1624 the second shogun, Tokugawa Hidetada, chose Ueno hill for a magnificent temple to protect his castle's northeast quarter, traditionally the direction of evil forces. **Kan'ei-ji** became the city's prime Buddhist centre, with 36 sub-temples extending over nearly 300 acres. The complex incorporated the Tokugawas' mortuary temple and a major shrine dedicated to Ieyasu, first of the line, as well as the tombs of six subsequent shogun. When the shogunate collapsed early in 1868, this was the natural place for Tokugawa loyalists to make their last stand, in what became the Battle of Ueno. Though the shogun had already resigned and the castle surrendered peacefully, roughly two thousand rebel samurai occupied Kan'ei-ji until the emperor's army finally attacked. Whether it was fires caused by the shelling or deliberate arson on either side, nearly all the temple buildings were destroyed, although ironically Ieyasu's shrine was spared.

In 1873 the new Meiji government designated the now desolate hilltop one of Tokyo's first five **public parks**. Ten years later, a station was built nearby and

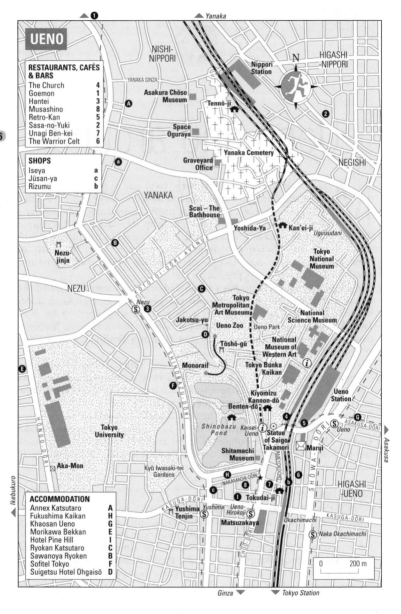

UENO

RESTAURANTS, CAFÉS & BARS

The Church	4
Goemon	1
Hantei	3
Musashino	8
Retro-Kan	5
Sasa-no-Yuki	2
Unagi Ben-kei	7
The Warrior Celt	6

SHOPS

Iseya	a
Jūsan-ya	c
Rizumu	b

ACCOMMODATION

Annex Katsutaro	A
Fukushima Kaikan	H
Khaosan Ueno	G
Morikawa Bekkan	E
Hotel Pine Hill	I
Ryokan Katsutaro	C
Sawanoya Ryoken	B
Sofitel Tokyo	F
Suigetsu Hotel Ohgaisō	D

for many years Ueno served as the terminus for northbound trains, bringing in migrants from the poor, northern provinces in search of jobs. For a brief period from 1869 to 1888 **Nezu** earned a certain notoriety for its licensed "pleasure quarters", though these were closed down soon after the Imperial University moved into the neighbourhood in the 1880s, as it was felt the students were being distracted from their studies.

Ueno was flooded with the destitute in 1945, when firebombs destroyed huge swathes of the city and thousands lived in the underground passages beneath the station or made makeshift homes in the park. For several years a **black market** flourished under the railway arches, reaching its peak as the economy boomed in the early 1950s. Though the market has largely been cleaned up and the *yakuza* are less obvious these days, this is still one of the cheapest places to shop in the city, and a world away from genteel Ginza.

Ueno

Although it's far from being the city's most attractive park, **Ueno Park** is where all Tokyo seems to flock during the spring cherry-blossom season. Outside this brief period, however, the park only gets busy at weekends, and during the week it can be a pleasant place for a stroll, particularly around the Shinobazu Pond – though you'll have to avert your eyes from the many homeless people camped out in tents amid the trees.

Ueno, Nezu and Yanaka

Ueno	*Ueno*	上野
Ameyoko-chō	*Ameyoko-chō*	アメ横丁
Bunka Kaikan	*Bunka Kaikan*	東京文化会館
Kyū Iwasaki-tei Gardens	*Kyū Iwasaki-tei Tei-en*	旧岩崎邸庭園
National Museum of Western Art	*Kokuritsu Seiyō Bijutsukan*	国立西洋美術館
National Science Museum	*Kokuritsu Kagaku Hakubutsukan*	国立科学博物館
Shinobazu Pond	*Shinobazu-no-ike*	不忍池
Shitamachi Museum	*Shitamachi Fūzoku Shiryōkan*	下町風俗資料館
Tokudai-ji	*Tokudai-ji*	徳大寺
Tokyo Metropolitan Art Museum	*Tōkyō-to Bijutsukan*	東京都美術館
Tokyo National Museum	*Tōkyō Kokuritsu Hakubutsukan*	東京国立博物館
Tokyo University	*Tōkyō Daigaku*	東京大学
Tōshō-gū	*Tōshō-gū*	東照宮
Ueno Park	*Ueno-kōen*	上野公園
Ueno Zoo	*Ueno Dōbutsuen*	上野動物園
Yushima Tenjin	*Yushima Tenjin*	湯島天神
Nezu	*Nezu*	根津
Nezu-jinja	*Nezu-jinja*	根津神社
Yoshida-ya	*Yoshida-ya*	吉田屋商店
Yanaka	*Yanaka*	谷中
Asakura Chōso Museum	*Asakura Chōso Hakubutsukan*	朝倉彫塑博物館
Space Oguraya	*Supēsu Oguraya*	すぺーす小倉屋
Tennō-ji	*Tennō-ji*	天王寺
Yanaka Cemetery	*Yanaka Reien*	谷中霊園

From Ueno Station there are two routes into the park: "Park Exit" takes you to the main, west gate where you'll also find an **information desk** (daily 9am–5pm); while the "Shinobazu Exit" brings you out closer to the southern entrance, above Keisei-Ueno Station, where trains depart for Narita Airport. On the southerly option, at the top of the steps leading up to the park from the street, stands a bronze statue of **Saigō Takamori** (see box below), out walking his dog.

As you follow the main path northwards, the red-lacquered **Kiyomizu Kannon-dō** comes into view on the left. Built out over the hillside, this temple is a smaller, less impressive version of Kyoto's famous Kiyomizu-dera temple, but has the rare distinction of being one of Kan'ei-ji's few existing remains, dating from 1631. The temple is dedicated to **Senju Kannon** (the thousand-armed Kannon), whose image is displayed only in February, although the second-rank **Kosodate Kannon** receives more visitors as the Bodhisattva in charge of conception. Hopeful women leave dolls at the altar during the year, following which the dolls are all burnt at a rather sad memorial service on September 25.

The temple faces westwards over a broad avenue lined with ancient cherry trees towards **Shinobazu Pond**. Once an inlet of Tokyo Bay, the pond is now a wildlife protection area and, unlikely as it may seem in the midst of a city, hosts a permanent colony of wild black cormorants as well as temporary populations of migrating waterfowl. A causeway leads out across its reeds and lotus beds to a small, leafy island occupied by an octagonal-roofed temple, **Benten-dō**, dedicated to the goddess of good fortune, water and music (among other things). Inside the dimly lit worship hall you can just make out Benten's eight arms, each clutching a holy weapon, while the ceiling sports a snarling dragon.

Head back into the park on the tree-lined avenue which marks the approach to Tokugawa Ieyasu's shrine, **Tōshō-gū**. Ieyasu died in 1616 and is buried in Nikkō, but this was his main shrine in Tokyo, founded in 1627 and rebuilt on a grander scale in 1651. For once it's possible to penetrate beyond the screened entrance and enclosing walls to take a closer look inside (daily 9am–4.30pm or 5pm, July & Aug until 6pm; ¥200). A path leads from the ticket gate clockwise round the polychrome halls and into the worship hall, whose faded decorative work contrasts sharply with the burnished black and gold of Ieyasu's shrine room behind. Before leaving, take a look at the ornate, Chinese-style front gate, where two golden dragons carved in 1651 by Hidari Jingorō – he of Nikkō's sleeping cat (see p.220) – attract much attention; so realistic is the carving that, according to local tradition, the pair sneak off at midnight to drink in Shinobazu Pond.

The last samurai

Saigō Takamori's life story was the inspiration for the Tom Cruise movie *The Last Samurai*. Born in 1827, the "Great Saigō", as he later became known, was leader of the Restoration army, which helped bring Emperor Meiji to power. Later, though, he grew increasingly alarmed at the loss of traditional values and eventually left the government to set up a military academy in his home town of Kagoshima in the southern island of Kyūshū. In January 1877 he led an army of 40,000 against the government in what came to be known as the Satsuma Rebellion. The imperial forces prevailed and on September 24, with the enemy closing in, a severely wounded Saigō asked one of his comrades to kill him. General Saigō's popularity was such, however, that he was rehabilitated in 1891 and his statue in Ueno Park was unveiled a few years later. A military uniform, however, was deemed inappropriate – hence the *yukata* and dog.

The seventeenth-century, five-storey pagoda rising above the trees to the north of Tōshō-gū is actually marooned inside **Ueno Zoo** (Tues–Sun 9.30am–5pm; ¥600; ℡03/3828-5171). Considering this zoo is over a century old and in the middle of a crowded city, it's less depressing than might be feared. In recent years they've been upgrading the pens – though they're still small and predominantly concrete – and there's plenty of vegetation around, including some magnificent, corkscrewing lianas. The main attractions are a new reptile house and the pandas, who snooze away on their concrete platform, blithely unaware they're supposed to be performing for the hordes of excited school children. As ever, weekends are the worst time, and it's a good idea to bring a picnic since food inside the zoo is expensive.

Tokyo National Museum

Dominating the northern reaches of Ueno Park is the **Tokyo National Museum** (Tues–Sun 9.30am–5pm, April–Sept Fri until 8pm; ¥420; ℡03/3822-1111, ⓦwww.tnm.go.jp), containing the world's largest collection of Japanese art, plus an extensive collection of Oriental antiquities. Displays are rotated every few months from a collection of 89,000 pieces, and the special exhibitions are usually also worth seeing if you can stand the crowds. Though the new galleries are a vast improvement, the museum style tends to old-fashioned reverential dryness. Nevertheless, among such a vast collection there's something to excite everyone's imagination.

It's best to start with the **Hon-kan**, the central building, where you'll find English-language booklets at the lobby information desk and a good museum shop in the basement. The Hon-kan presents the sweep of Japanese art, from Jōmon-period pottery (pre-fourth century BC) to early twentieth-century painting, via theatrical costume for Kabuki, Nō and *bunraku*, colourful Buddhist mandalas, *ukiyo-e* prints, exquisite lacquerware and even seventeenth-century Christian art from southern Japan.

In the building's northwest corner look out for a passage leading to the new **Heisei-kan**, where you'll find the splendid Japanese Archeology Gallery containing important recent finds. Though it covers some of the same ground as the Hon-kan, modern presentation and lighting really bring the objects to life – the best are refreshingly simple and burst with energy. Highlights are the chunky, flame-shaped Jōmon pots and a collection of super-heated Sue stoneware, a technique introduced from Korea in the fifth century. Look out, too, for the bug-eyed, curvaceous clay figures (*dogū*) of the Jōmon period and the funerary *haniwa* from the fourth to sixth centuries AD – these terracotta representations of houses, animals, musicians and stocky little warriors were placed on burial mounds to protect the deceased lord in the afterlife.

In the southwest corner of the compound, behind the copper-domed Hyōkei-kan of 1908, lurks the **Hōryū-ji Hōmotsu-kan**. This sleek new gallery contains a selection of priceless treasures donated over the centuries to Nara's Hōryū-ji temple. The most eye-catching display comprises 48 gilt-bronze Buddhist statues in various poses, each an island of light in the inky darkness, while there's also an eighth-century Chinese zither and an ink-stand said to have been used by Prince Shōtoku when annotating the lotus sutra.

The museum's final gallery is the **Tōyō-kan**, on the opposite side of the compound, housing a delightful hotchpotch of Oriental antiquities, with Javanese textiles and nineteenth-century Indian prints rubbing shoulders with Egyptian mummies and a wonderful collection of Southeast Asian bronze

Buddhas. The Chinese and, particularly, Korean collections are also interesting for their obvious parallels with the Japanese art seen earlier. If you've got the energy, it's well worth taking a quick walk through, though there's frustratingly little English labelling.

National Science Museum and National Museum of Western Art

In the park's northeast corner, a minute's walk from the National Museum, the **National Science Museum** (Tues–Sun 9am–4.30pm; ¥420; ☎03/3822-0111, ⓦwww.kahaku.go.jp/english/index.htm) is easily identified by a life-size statue of a romping blue whale outside. Compared with Tokyo's other science museum (see p.49), this one has fewer interactive exhibits but a great deal more information, some of it in English, covering natural history as well as science and technology. Best is the "Science Discovery Plaza", in the new building at the back, where pendulums, magnets, mirrors and hand-powered generators provide entertainment for the mainly school-age audience.

South of here is the **National Museum of Western Art** (Tues–Sun 9.30am–5pm, Fri until 8pm; ¥420; ☎03/3828-5131, ⓦwww.nmwa.go.jp), instantly recognizable from the Rodin statues populating the forecourt of the gallery designed by Le Corbusier and erected in 1959 to house the mostly French Impressionist paintings left to the nation by Kawasaki shipping magnate Matsukata Kōjirō. Since then, works by Rubens, Tintoretto, Max Ernst and Jackson Pollock have broadened the scope of this impressive collection.

Tokyo Metropolitan Art Museum and Shitamachi Museum

A short stroll west across the park towards the zoo is the **Tokyo Metropolitan Art Museum** (daily 9am–5pm, closed first and third Mon of the month; admission price varies; ☎03/3823-6921, ⓦwww.tobikan.jp), in a partly underground brick building. There are sometimes interesting temporary exhibitions here, but otherwise you can safely give it a miss.

At the southern end of the park, the **Shitamachi Museum** (Tues–Sun 9.30am–4.30pm; ¥300; ☎03/3823-7451) is set in a distinctive, partly traditional-style building beside Shinobazu Pond. The museum opened in 1980 to preserve something of the Shitamachi while it was still within living memory. A reconstructed merchant's shop-house and a 1920s tenement row, complete with sweet shop and coppersmith's workroom, fill the ground floor. The upper floor is devoted to rotating exhibitions focusing on articles of daily life – old photos, toys, advertisements and artisans' tools. All the museum's exhibits have been donated by local residents; you can take your shoes off to explore the shop interiors and it's also possible to handle most items. There's plenty of information in English, plus a well-produced museum booklet (¥400).

Ameyoko-chō

Ueno town centre lies to the south of the park, a lively mix of discount outlets, street markets, drinking clubs, a sprinkling of upmarket stores and craft shops, "soaplands" (a euphemism for brothels), love hotels and restaurants. While it's not strong on sophistication or culture, there's a greater sense of raw vitality here than elsewhere in Tokyo.

The biggest draw for both bargain-hunters and sightseers is the bustling **market** area south of Ueno Station, **Ameyoko-chō**, which extends nearly half a kilometre along the west side of the elevated JR train lines down to Okachimachi Station, spilling down side alleys and under the tracks. The name is an abbreviation of "Ameya Yokochō", or "Candy Sellers' Alley", dating from the immediate postwar days when sweets were a luxury and hundreds of stalls here peddled mostly sweet potatoes coated in sugar syrup. Since rationing was in force, black-marketeers joined the candy sellers, dealing in rice and other foodstuffs, household goods, personal possessions – whatever was available. Later, American imports also found their way from army stores onto the streets here, especially during the early 1950s Korean War. By then the market had been legalized, and over the years the worst crime has been cleaned up, but Ameyoko-chō still retains a flavour of those early days: gruff men with sand-paper voices shout out their wares; stalls selling bulk tea and coffee, cheap shoes, ready-peeled fruit, jewellery and fish are all jumbled up, cheek by jowl; and under the arches a clutch of *yakitori* bars still tempt the market crowds. In the thick of all this it's not surprising to stumble across a temple, **Tokudai-ji**, dedicated to a goddess offering prosperity and abundant harvests. Look out for the temple's colourful banners, up on the second floor two blocks before the southern limit of Ameyoko-chō.

Kyū Iwasaki-tei Gardens

The west side of central Ueno is dominated by seedy love hotels and dubious bars. A short walk past Yushima Station, however, you'll discover a remarkable remnant of a much more genteel past. The **Kyū Iwasaki-tei Gardens** (daily 9am–5pm; ¥400; ℡03/3823-8340, ⓦwww.tokyo-park.or.jp) date from 1896 and surround an elegant **house**, designed by British architect Josiah Conder (see box p.63), which combines a *café au lait*-painted, Western-style two-storey mansion with a traditional single-storey Japanese residence. The wooden Jacobean and Moorish-style arabesque interiors of the Western-style mansion are in fantastic condition – in stark contrast to the severely faded screen paintings of the Japanese section. The lack of furniture in both houses makes them a little lifeless, but it's nonetheless an impressive artefact in a city where such buildings are increasingly rare. You can take tea in the Japanese section (¥500) or sit outside and admire the tranquil gardens, which also combine Eastern and Western influences.

Yushima Tenjin and Tokyo University

Returning to Yushima Station from the gardens it's a short walk west to **Yushima Tenjin** (also known as Yushima-jinja), a shrine dedicated to Tenjin, the god of scholarship. The best time to visit is in late February when the plum trees are in blossom and candidates for university entrance exams leave mountains of *ema* (wooden votive tablets) inscribed with their require-ments.

The shrine stands a few minutes' walk south of the nation's top-ranking **Tokyo University**, whose graduates fill the corridors of power. Founded in 1869, Tōdai – as it's commonly known – occupies the former estate of the wealthy Maeda lords, though there's little sign of their mansion beyond a scummy pond and the one-storey, red-lacquer gate, **Aka-mon**, which forms the front (west) entrance into the university's sleepy and decidedly unkempt campus.

Nezu

The old Tokyo district of **Nezu**, meaning "Water's Edge", is a short walk north of Tōdai. Its main sight, the venerable, cedar-shaded shrine **Nezu-jinja**, lies five minutes' walk north of Nezu Station on the Chiyoda subway line, tucked to the west off Shinobazu-dōri. Nezu-jinja dates from the early eighteenth century when it was built in honour of the sixth Tokugawa shogun, Ienobu. The ornate and colourfully decorated shrine is notable for its corridor of vermilion *torii* and a hillside bedecked with some three thousand azalea bushes which bloom in a profusion of pinks and reds during late April and early May, attracting throngs of camera-toting visitors. At other times the shrine is serenely peaceful. While you're in the neighbourhood you may also want to visit the traditional *kushiage* restaurant *Hantei* (see p.163).

Returning to Nezu Station, head east along the major road Kototoi-dōri for around five minutes to reach **Yoshida-ya** (Tues–Sun 9.30am–4.30pm; free), an early twentieth-century sake store which was moved here in 1987 under the auspices of the Shitamachi Museum (see p.86). After a glimpse inside at the giant glass bottles, china barrels and other accoutrements of the trade, turn right at the crossroads and then, at the next corner on the left, look out for a bizarre little contemporary art gallery called **SCAI – The Bathhouse** (Tues–Sat noon–7pm; free; ☎03/3821-1144, ⓦwww.scaithebathouse.com), which occupies a 200-year-old public bath. Immediately uphill from here is the southern edge of Yanaka Cemetery (see below).

Yanaka

After the Long Sleeves Fire of 1657 (see History, p.272), many temples relocated to the higher ground of **Yanaka**, where they remain today, alongside old wooden buildings that seem to have miraculously escaped the ensuing centuries' various calamities. It's a charming area to explore on foot, and you could spend many hours rambling through its narrow, quiet streets, discovering small temples, shrines and traditional craft shops.

The area is dominated by **Yanaka Cemetery**, one of Tokyo's oldest and largest graveyards. If you're not walking here from Nezu, the cemetery is most easily reached from the west side of Nippori Station on the Yamanote line. A five-minute walk south of the Nippori entrance to the cemetery, you'll find one the area's most attractive temples, **Tennō-ji**, within the grounds of which is a large copper Buddha dating from 1690. Head southwest down the main cemetery avenue from here to reach the **graveyard offices** (daily 8.30am–5pm), where you can pick up a Japanese map of the plots locating various notables such as author Natsume Sōseki (see Contexts, p.279); the last Tokugawa shogun, Yoshinobu; and, in a separate fenced-off area, Archbishop Nikolai Kasatkin, founder of the Russian Orthodox Nikolai Cathedral (see p.60).

Return to the Nippori entrance to the cemetery, turn west and walk a few hundred metres to reach another of Yanaka's many gems, the **Asakura Chōso Museum** (Tues–Thurs, Sat & Sun 9.30am–4.30pm; ¥400; ☎03/3821-4549), the well-preserved home and studio of sculptor **Asakura Fumio** (1883–1964), often referred to as the Rodin of Japan. Completed in 1935, the house successfully combines a modernist concrete building, used by the artist as his studio, with a wood-and-bamboo Japanese-style home. A lovely Japanese garden occupies the centre, while on the roof of the studio is an equally delightful Western-style garden with great views across the rooftops. Many of Asakura's works are on display, including some incredibly lifelike sculptures of his beloved cats.

On leaving the museum, turn left and continue along an attractive residential street of two-storey wooden houses to reach **Space Oguraya** (Tues–Sun 10am–6pm, closed Tues July & Aug; free; ☎03/3828-0562), a pawnbroker's shop dating from 1847 which has now been reborn as a contemporary art gallery. The house includes a three-storey wooden *dozō* (storage house) and it's worth popping inside to see this lovingly preserved and increasingly rare type of architecture.

Retrace your steps towards Nippori, but instead of turning right at the junction towards the station head left and go down some stone steps to find the pedestrianized shopping street known as **Yanaka Ginza**. The antithesis of trendy Tokyo malls, this appealing shopping promenade is worth exploring to find small family businesses selling *sembei* (rice crackers), tofu and other food specialities. Sendagi Station on the Chiyoda subway line is close by.

Ikebukuro and northern Tokyo

M arsh and farmland until a hundred years ago, **Ikebukuro** is a product of the train age. Its first station was completed in 1903, and six lines now connect the area with central Tokyo and the low-cost dormitory suburbs to the north and east. Cheap accommodation and good transport have attracted an increasing number of resident expatriates, typically Chinese and Taiwanese, but also including a broad sweep of other nationalities, which lends Ikebukuro a faintly cosmopolitan air. It's not as trendy or hip as Shinjuku or Shibuya, and for the short-term visitor there are no compelling reasons to visit Ikebukuro. However, to some this very lack of star status and cool pretension is Ikebukuro's appeal.

Two vast department stores – Tobū and Seibu – square off against each other from opposite sides of Ikebukuro's confusing station. The area west of the train tracks, **Nishi–Ikebukuro**, is the more interesting to explore, particularly the wedge of streets spreading out towards the attractive **Rikkyō University** campus, if only for its plethora of bars and restaurants. Across the tracks,

Ikebukuro and around

Ikebukuro	*Ikebukuro*	池袋
Ancient Orient Museum	*Kodai Orienteki Hakabutsukan*	古代オリエント博物館
Japan Traditional Crafts Centre	*Zenkoku Dentōteki Kōgeihin Sentā*	全国伝統的工芸品センター
Metropolitan Art Space	*Tōkyō Geijutsu Gekijō*	東京芸術劇場
Rikkyō University	*Rikkyō Daigaku*	立教大学
Komagome	*Komagome*	駒込
Kyū Furukawa Gardens	*Kyū Furukawa Teien*	旧古河庭園
Rikugi-en	*Rikugi-en*	六義園
Sugamo	*Sugamo*	巣鴨
Kōgan-ji	*Kōgan-ji*	高岩寺
Kōshinzuka Station	*Kōshinzuka-eki*	庚申塚駅
Toden Arakawa Line	*Toden Arakawa sen*	都電荒川線

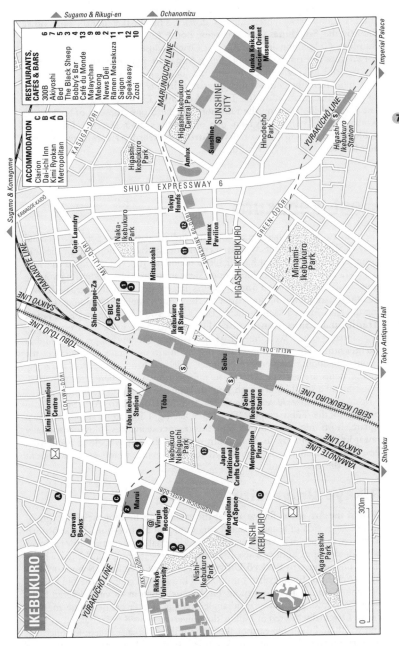

IKEBUKURO

▲ Sugamo & Rikugi-en   ▲ Ochanomizu

Imperial Palace ▶

RESTAURANTS, CAFÉS & BARS

300B	6
Akiyoshi	7
Bed	5
The Black Sheep	3
Bobby's Bar	4
Café du Monde	13
Malaychan	9
Mekong	8
News Deli	2
Rāmen Meisakuza	1
Saigon	11
Speakeasy	12
Zozoi	10

ACCOMMODATION

Clarion	C
Dai-ichi Inn	B
Kimi Ryokan	A
Metropolitan	D

▲ Sugamo & Komagome

MARUNOUCHI LINE

Bunka Kaikan & Ancient Orient Museum

SUNSHINE CITY

Sunshine 60

Higashi-Ikebukuro Central Park

Higashi-Ikebukuro Park

KASUGA-DŌRI

Hinodechō Park

YURAKUCHŌ LINE

Higashi-Ikebukuro Station

Amlux

SHUTO EXPRESSWAY 6

KAWAGOE-KAIDŌ

YAMANOTE LINE

SAIKYO LINE

TŌBU TŌJŌ LINE

Coin Laundry

MEIJI-DŌRI

Naka-Ikebukuro Park

Tōkyū Hands

Humax Pavilion

SUNSHINE 60-DŌRI

Mitsukoshi

HIGASHI-IKEBUKURO

GREEN-ŌDŌRI

Minami-Ikebukuro Park

Shin-Bungei-Za

BIC Camera

Ikebukuro JR Station

MEIJI-DŌRI

Tokyo Antiques Hall ▶

Kimi Information Centre

TOKIWA-DŌRI

Tōbu Ikebukuro Station

Tōbu

S

Seibu

S

Seibu Ikebukuro Station

SEIBU IKEBUKURO LINE

Shinjuku ▶

SAIKYO LINE

YAMANOTE LINE

Caravan Books

Marui

Virgin Records

Ikebukuro Nishiguchi Park

Japan Traditional Crafts Centre

Metropolitan Plaza

NISHIGUCHI KAISEI-DŌRI

YURAKUCHŌ LINE

RIKKYO-DŌRI

Rikkyō University

Metropolitan Art Space

Nishi-Ikebukuro Park

NISHI-IKEBUKURO

Agariyashiki Park

N

0   300m

Higashi-Ikebukuro is the main shopping centre and has good discount stores, with cameras and electronic goods at prices rivalling Akihabara. Apart from a pretty tacky entertainment district, Higashi-Ikebukuro's only other draw is the **Sunshine City** complex, home to the monstrous, sixty-storey Sunshine 60 building and the Ancient Orient Museum.

Two stops east on the Yamanote line is **Sugamo**, a popular gathering spot for Tokyo's old folk, who flock to visit the local temple, **Kōgan-ji**, where they seek relief from the gods for their physical ailments. From here it's a short walk to Kōshinzuka Station on the **Toden Arakawa Line** (see box, p.95), Tokyo's last tram service. Back on the Yamanote line head one stop east of Sugamo to Komagome to visit **Rikugi-en**, one of the city's most attractive Edo-period gardens, and the equally lovely **Kyū Furukawa Gardens**, combining Western and Japanese styles of horticulture.

West Ikebukuro

Ikebukuro Station handles around one million passengers per day – second only to Shinjuku – and its warren of connecting passages, shopping arcades and countless exits is notoriously difficult to negotiate. It's even worse on the west side, when the helpfully colour-coded signs mutate to blue, indicating you are now in Tōbu territory. **Tōbu** is Japan's largest department store, with over 80,000 square metres of floor space in three interconnected buildings, including the glass-fronted Metropolitan Plaza, where you'll find the excellent **Japan Traditional Crafts Centre** (daily 11am–7pm, every other Tues until 5pm; occasionally closed Wed; free; ℡03/5954-6066, Ⓦwww.kougei.or.jp/english/center.html). This has an extensive display of arts and crafts from all over the country, including lacquerware, ceramics, dolls and handmade paper, and many of the items are for sale. There's an information desk where the staff speak English and a small library with English-language books on traditional arts.

Both the nearby *Hotel Metropolitan* and **Metropolitan Art Space** also belong to the Tōbu empire. The latter, facing Tōbu store across an open square, hosts regular concerts and theatre performances, plus occasionally rewarding exhibitions. Its main claim to fame, though, is its long **escalator**, best experienced on the way down for a dizzying, ninety-second descent beneath the glass atrium.

Rikkyō University

Behind the Art Space, follow any of the small roads heading west through an area of lanes rich in restaurants and bars until you hit tree-lined Rikkyō-dōri. Turn left, in front of a white clapboard wedding hall, and continue for just over a hundred metres until you see a square, red-brick gateway on the left. This is the main entrance to **Rikkyō University**, founded as St Paul's School in 1874 by an American Episcopalian missionary. Through the gateway, the old university courtyard has an incongruous Ivy League touch in its vine-covered halls, white windows and grassy quadrangle, making it a favourite venue for film crews. Originally located in Tsukiji, the university moved to Ikebukuro in 1918 and weathered the 1923 earthquake with minimal damage except for one toppled gate tower; the lopsided look was left, so it's said, as a memorial to those who died, but a deciding factor was perhaps the sheer lack of bricks. Other

△ Expressway roads

original buildings include the congregation hall, now a nicotine-stained refectory opposite the main entrance, All Saint's Chapel and a couple of wooden missionary houses.

East Ikebukuro

Over on the east side of Ikebukuro Station, **Seibu** rules. This is the company's flagship store and was the largest in the country until Tōbu outgrew it a few years back. Though the group has been retrenching in recent years, Seibu has a history of innovation and spotting new trends. Apart from the main store, there are also branches of Parco, Loft and Wave, Seibu offshoots specializing in fashion, household goods and music respectively.

Heading east from Ikebukuro Station, you can't miss the monstrous sixty storeys of **Sunshine 60**, which at 240m was Japan's tallest building until it was pipped by Yokohama's Landmark Tower. Just in front is Toyota's **Amlux** car showroom (Tues–Sun 11am–8pm), one for diehard petrol-heads only. An underground passage leads from the basement here into the Sunshine 60 tower, just one of four buildings comprising the **Sunshine City** complex of shops, offices, exhibition space, a hotel and various cultural centres – though compared to the city's newer developments, it all looks rather dowdy. The tower's sixtieth-floor observatory (10am–8.30pm; ¥620) may be a shade higher than Shinjuku's rivals, but you have to pay, and unless it's a really clear day there's not a lot to see anyway.

Sunshine City's most easterly building, Bunka Kaikan, houses the **Ancient Orient Museum** (daily 10am–5pm; ¥500) on its seventh floor, displaying archeological finds from the Middle East (Syria in particular) and elsewhere. While there are the inevitable bits of old pot, the collection focuses on more accessible items such as statues, jewellery, icons and other works of art, including some superb Gandhara Buddhist art from Pakistan and a smiling, wide-eyed goddess made in Syria around 2000 BC.

Sugamo and Komagome

Two stops east of Ikebukuro on the Yamanote line is **Sugamo**. On the north side of the JR Station a shopping street, Jizō-dōri, branches left off the main road, marked by an arch with orange characters. The street is nicknamed *obāchan no Harajuku* or "old ladies' Harajuku", in ironic reference to Tokyo's epicentre of young fashion. Jizō-dōri is, of course, anything but fashionable; shops here sell floral aprons, sensible shoes, long johns and shopping trolleys, interspersed with speciality food stores, household products and pharmacies selling traditional and Western medicines.

This all arose because of a temple, **Kōgan-ji**, 100m up on the right, dedicated to "thorn-removing" Togenuki Jizō, who provides relief from both physical pain and the metaphorical suffering of the soul. In case a prayer doesn't work, people also queue up in front of a small Kannon statue, known as the Migawari Kannon, tucked into a corner of the temple forecourt. Each person in turn pours water over the statue and wipes whatever part of its anatomy corresponds to their own ailment, thus transferring it to the Kannon – until

Tokyo's last tramline

Early twentieth-century Tokyo boasted a number of tramlines, of which only the twelve-kilometre **Toden Arakawa Line** remains, running north from Waseda to Minowa-bashi. The most interesting section lies along a short stretch from **Kōshinzuka Station**, a fifteen-minute walk northwest of Sugamo Station, from where the line heads southwest towards Higashi-Ikebukuro, rocking and rolling along narrow streets and through Tokyo backyards. Most of the original tramlines were private enterprises – the Arakawa Line was built purely to take people to the spring blossoms in Asukayama Park – and have gradually been replaced with subways. Now the last of the *chin chin densha* ("ding ding trains"), as they're known from the sound of their bells, the Arakawa Line will probably survive for its nostalgia value if nothing else. All tickets cost ¥160, however far you go; you pay as you enter. Station signs and announcements are in English.

recently people used brushes but now it's hand towels only as the poor goddess was being scrubbed away. Despite the sad undertones, there's a good atmosphere, enlivened by a number of quack doctors who set up stalls outside.

Jizō-dōri continues north as far as Kōshinzuka Station, less than ten minutes' walk from the temple, where you can pick up a **tram** on the **Toden Arakawa Line** (see box above).

Rikugi-en

One stop east along the Yamanote line from Sugamo is **Komagome**. This is where you'll find **Rikugi-en** (daily 9am–5pm; ¥300), Tokyo's best surviving example of a classical Edo-period stroll-garden. It's also large enough to be relatively undisturbed by surrounding buildings and traffic noise. The entrance lies five minutes' walk south of the station on Hongō-dōri, taking a right turn one block before the next major junction.

In 1695 the fifth shogun granted one of his high-ranking feudal lords, **Yanagisawa Yoshiyasu**, a tract of farmland to the north of Edo. Yanagisawa was both a perfectionist and a literary scholar: he took seven years to design his celebrated garden – with its 88 allusions to famous scenes, real or imaginary, from ancient Japanese poetry – and then named it Rikugi-en, "garden of the six principles of poetry", in reference to the rules for composing *waka* (poems of 31 syllables). After Yanagisawa's death, Rikugi-en fell into disrepair until Iwasaki Yatarō, founder of Mitsubishi, bought the land in 1877 and restored it as part of his luxury villa. The family donated the garden to the Tokyo city authorities in 1938, since when it has been a public park.

Not surprisingly, few of the 88 landscapes have survived – the guide map issued at the entrance identifies a mere eighteen. Nevertheless, Rikugi-en still retains its rhythm and beauty, kicking off with an ancient, spreading cherry tree, then slowly unfolding along paths that meander past secluded arbours and around the indented shoreline of an islet-speckled lake. In contrast, there are also areas of more natural woodland and a hillock from which to admire the whole scene.

Kyū Furukawa Gardens

While you're in the Komagome area it would be a great shame to miss out on another beautifully maintained garden. Designed by Ogawa Jihei, a famed gardener from Kyoto, the **Kyū Furukawa Gardens** (daily 9am–5pm; ¥150) combine delightful Japanese-style grounds with an Italian-style terrace of rose beds and artfully shaped azalea bushes. The gardens fall down the hill from the mansion designed in 1914 by British architect Josiah Conder (see box on p.63), who was also responsible for the similar Kyū Iwasaki-tei house and gardens in Ueno (see p.87). It's possible to take tea and cake in the mansion and to go on a tour of the empty and frankly boring rooms – it's much more enjoyable to sample *matcha* and traditional Japanese sweets (¥500) in the tea house in the Japanese part of the garden. The best times to visit are in late April, when the azaleas bloom, and in mid-May, when the roses are out in full force. To reach the entrance to the gardens, walk back from Rikugi-en to Komagome Station and keep following Hongō-dōri uphill for about five minutes.

8

Shinjuku

F our stops south from Ikebukuro on the Yamanote line, and some 4km
due west of the Imperial Palace, **Shinjuku** is the modern heart of Tokyo.
The district has a long history of pandering to the more basic of human
desires, and a day and an evening spent in the area will show you Tokyo
at its best and worst – from the love hotels and hostess bars of Kabukichō to
the no-frills bars of Shomben Yokochō (Piss Alley) and the shop-till-you-drop
department stores and high-tech towers.

Shinjuku is split in two by a thick band of train tracks. The western half,
Nishi-Shinjuku, with its soaring skyscrapers, is a showcase for contemporary
architecture; the raunchier eastern side, **Higashi-Shinjuku**, is a nonstop red-
light and shopping district – though it's also home to one of Tokyo's most
attractive parks, **Shinjuku Gyoen. Shinjuku Station** itself is a messy
combination of three terminals (the main JR station, plus the Keiō and
Odakyū stations beside their respective department stores on the west side) and
connecting subway lines. There's also the separate **Seibu Shinjuku Station**,
northeast of the JR station. At least two million commuters are fed into these
stations every day and spun out of sixty exits, and the rivers of people constantly flowing along the station's many underground passages only add to the
confusion. It's easy to get hopelessly lost – if this happens, head immediately
for street level and get your bearings from the skyscrapers to the west.

Some history

The district takes its name from the "new lodgings" (*shin juku*) which were set
up west of the city centre in the late 1600s for travellers en route to Edo. These
were shut down in 1718 after a fracas in a brothel involving an influential
samurai and it took sixty years for Shinjuku to recover, by which time it had
become one of Edo's six **licensed quarters**, catering mainly to the lower
classes. By the late 1800s, the area had been nicknamed "Tokyo's anus", due to
the transportation of human waste through its streets to the countryside – and
had the most prostitutes of any area in the city.

A turning point came in 1885 when the opening of the railway encouraged
people to move out of the city into the increasingly fashionable western suburbs
– and the hordes of daily commuters passing through also made Shinjuku the
ideal location for the department stores which sprang up here during the early
twentieth century. The earthquake of 1923 left the area relatively unscathed, but
most of Shinjuku had to rebuild after the air raids of 1945 and there were plans
to relocate Tokyo's Kabuki theatre to the east side of the station. Such relatively
sophisticated entertainment was not really Shinjuku's style, however, so although
the area adopted the name **Kabukichō**, the black market stayed put, the red-light
trade resumed and the Kabuki theatre was rebuilt in Ginza.

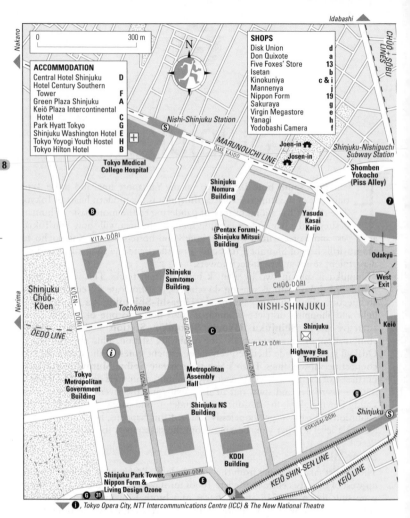

Idabashi

CHŪŌ + SŌBU LINES

Nakano

0   300 m

N

ACCOMMODATION
Central Hotel Shinjuku   D
Hotel Century Southern
  Tower   F
Green Plaza Shinjuku   A
Keiō Plaza Intercontinental
  Hotel   C
Park Hyatt Tokyo   G
Shinjuku Washington Hotel   E
Tokyo Yoyogi Youth Hostel   H
Tokyo Hilton Hotel   B

SHOPS
Disk Union   d
Don Quixote   a
Five Foxes' Store   13
Isetan   b
Kinokuniya   c & i
Mannenya   j
Nippon Form   19
Sakuraya   g
Virgin Megastore   e
Yanagi   h
Yodobashi Camera   f

Nishi-Shinjuku Station

MARUNOUCHI LINE

ŌME KAIDŌ

Joen-in

Josen-in

Shinjuku-Nishiguchi Subway Station

Shomben Yokocho (Piss Alley)

Tokyo Medical College Hospital

Shinjuku Nomura Building

Yasuda Kasai Kaijo

KITA-DŌRI

(Pentax Forum)-Shinjuku Mitsui Building

Odakyū

West Exit

Shinjuku Sumitomo Building

CHŪŌ-DŌRI

Shinjuku Chūō-Kōen

KŌEN-DŌRI

Tochōmae

GIJIDŌ-DŌRI

NISHI-SHINJUKU

Shinjuku

Keiō

ŌEDO LINE

HIGASHI-DŌRI

PLAZA DŌRI

Highway Bus Terminal

Tokyo Metropolitan Government Building

TOCHŌ-DŌRI

Metropolitan Assembly Hall

Shinjuku

Shinjuku NS Building

KOKUSAI-DŌRI

KDDI Building

Shinjuku Park Tower, Nippon Form & Living Design Ozone

MINAMI-DŌRI

KEIŌ SHIN-SEN LINE

KEIŌ LINE

Nerima

Tokyo Opera City, NTT Intercommunications Centre (ICC) & The New National Theatre

In the immediate postwar decades Shinjuku's seediness attracted a bohemian population of writers, students and radical intellectuals, who hung out in its jazz bars and coffee shops. In October 1968 passions bubbled over into riots and paving stones were ripped up and hurled at the police in an anti-Vietnam demo. On the western side of the station another type of revolution was under way. The area's first **skyscraper**, the 47-storey *Keiō Plaza Hotel*, opened in 1971 and was swiftly followed by several more earthquake-defying towers, while Tange Kenzō's Tokyo Metropolitan Government Building set the modernist seal on the area two decades later. It has since been joined by his Shinjuku Park Tower on the south side of Shinjuku Chūō-kōen and, further west, the arty performance halls of Tokyo Opera City and the New National Theatre, the latest attempt to bring respectability to the area.

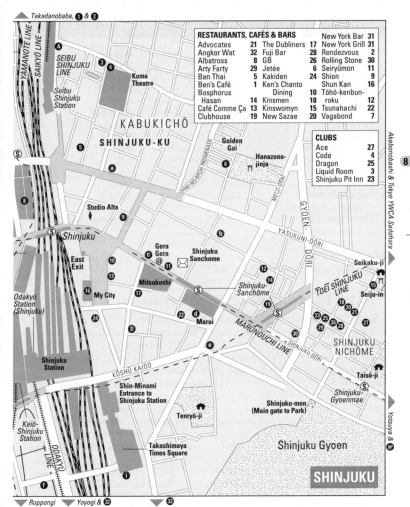

RESTAURANTS, CAFÉS & BARS

Advocates	21	New York Bar	31
Angkor Wat	32	New York Grill	31
Albatross	8	Rendezvous	2
Arty Farty	29	Rolling Stone	30
Ban Thai	5	Seiryūmon	11
Ben's Café	1	Shion	9
Bosphorus		Shun Kan	16
Hasan	14	Tōhō-kenbun-	
Café Comme Ça	13	roku	12
Clubhouse	19	Tsunahachi	22
The Dubliners	17	Vagabond	7
Fuji Bar	28		
GB	26		
Jetée	6		
Kakiden	24		
Ken's Chanto			
Dining	10		
Kinsmen	18		
Kinswomyn	15		
New Sazae	20		

CLUBS

Ace	27
Code	4
Dragon	25
Liquid Room	3
Shinjuku Pit Inn	23

Nishi-Shinjuku

West of the station, **Nishi-Shinjuku** is dominated by towers of glass, concrete and steel, including the vast Tokyo Metropolitan Government Building complex, from which the Tokyo prefecture is administered. Few are worth spending much time exploring, though most have free observation rooms on their upper floors, along with a wide selection of restaurants and bars with good views. Collectively, however, their impact is striking, mainly because their scale, coupled with the spaciousness of their surroundings, is so unusual for Tokyo – this is still predominantly a low-rise city. To reach Nishi-Shinjuku, either head for the west exit at Shinjuku Station and then go through the pedestrian tunnel beyond the two fountains in the sunken plaza

Shinjuku	*Shinjuku*	新宿
Golden Gai	*Gōruden Gai*	ゴールデン街
Hanazono-jinja	*Hanazono-jinja*	花園神社
Kabukichō	*Kabukichō*	歌舞伎町
Kinokuniya	*Kinokuniya*	紀伊国屋
New National Theatre	*Shin Kokuritsu Gekijō*	新国立劇場
Piss Alley	*Shomben Yokochō*	しょんべん横丁
Shinjuku Gyoen	*Shinjuku Gyoen*	新宿御苑
Shinjuku-Nichōme	*Shinjuku-Nichōme*	新宿二丁目
Shinjuku Park Tower	*Shinjuku Pāku Tawā*	新宿パークタワー
Sword Museum	*Tōken Hakubutsukan*	刀剣博物館
Taisō-ji	*Taisō-ji*	太宗持
Tokyo Metropolitan Government Building	*Tōkyō Tochō*	東京都庁
Tokyo Opera City	*Tōkyō Opera Shiti*	東京オペラシティ

in front of the Odakyū department store, or hop out of the subway at Tochōmae Station, on the Ōedo line.

Tokyo Metropolitan Government Building

On the left-hand side of Chūō-dōri as you emerge at the end of the tunnel is the monumental **Tokyo Metropolitan Government Building** (TMGB), a 400,000-square-metre complex designed by top Tokyo architect Tange Kenzō. Thirteen thousand city bureaucrats go to work each day at the TMGB, and the entire complex – which includes twin 48-storey towers, an adjacent tower block, the Metropolitan Assembly Hall (where the city's councillors meet) and a sweeping, statue-lined and colonnaded plaza – feels like Gotham City. Tange was actually aiming to evoke Paris's Notre Dame, and there's certainly something of that cathedral's design in the shape of the twin towers. But the building's real triumph is that it is unmistakably Japanese; the dense criss-cross pattern of its glass and granite facade is reminiscent of both traditional architecture and the circuitry of an enormous computer chip.

On the ground floor of the No.1 Tower you'll find the excellent Tokyo Tourist Information Centre (see Basics, p.19). Both the towers have identical free **observation rooms** on their 45th floors (Mon–Fri 9.30am–10pm, Sat & Sun 9.30am–7pm) and it's worth timing your visit for dusk, so you can see the multicoloured lights of Shinjuku spark and fizzle into action as the setting sun turns the sky a deep photochemical orange. The TMGB also has inexpensive cafés on the 32nd floor and the ground floor of the Metropolitan Assembly Hall. Free **tours** are available in English (Mon–Fri 10am–3pm) from the Tokyo Information Centre.

Shinjuku Park Tower

Just behind the TMGB is Shinjuku Chūō-kōen, a dusty park on the south side of which is **Shinjuku Park Tower**, another building across which Tange's modernist signature is confidently written. The style credentials of this complex of three linked towers, all topped with glass pyramids, are vouched for by the presence of the luxurious *Park Hyatt Hotel* (which occupies the building's loftiest floors), the Conran Shop and the **Living Design Centre Ozone** (daily except Wed 10.30am–6.30pm; entrance fee varies with exhibition; ☎03/5322-6500, ⓦwww.ozone.co.jp), a spacious museum specializing in interior design, with interesting, regularly changing exhibitions by both Japanese and Western designers. A regular free shuttle bus runs from opposite the Odakyū department store to the south side of the tower.

Tokyo Opera City and around

A ten-minute walk west of the Shinjuku Park Tower, and connected to Hatsudai Station on the Keiō line, is **Tokyo Opera City**, with 54 floors of offices, shops and restaurants. The best reason for visiting this 234-metre-high tower, which also has a state-of-the-art concert hall (see p.181), is to see what's showing at the **NTT Intercommunication Centre** (ICC; Tues–Sun 10am–6pm, Fri until 9pm; ¥800; ☎0120-144199, ⓦwww.ntticc.or.jp), on the fourth floor. This is the most innovative interactive exhibition space in Tokyo and there's almost always something interesting to see: past displays of "high-tech art" have included a soundproof room where you listen to your own heartbeat and light-sensitive robots you can control with your brain waves.

Directly behind Tokyo Opera City is the **New National Theatre**, an ambitious complex of three performing arts auditoria (see p.187). Returning to Hatsudai Station, duck south into the backstreets to find the small but intriguing **Sword Museum** (Tues–Sun 10am–4.30pm; ¥525; ☎03/3379-1386). This place is a must-see for fans of swashbuckling samurai dramas and Tarantino's *Kill Bill* films, and even if you're deteminedly anti-violence you'll still admire the incredible decorative detail on the blades, handles and sheaths of the lethal weapons displayed here.

Shomben Yokochō

Returning to the east side of Shinjuku Station, in the blocks between Keiō department store and the *Keiō Plaza Hotel* you'll find the long-distance bus station, the area's main post office and branches of top camera and electronics retailers, Yodobashi and Sakura (see p.202). Squashed up against the train tracks running north from the Odakyū department store are the narrow alleyways of the **Shomben Yokochō**, also known as Omoide Yokochō. The name of this cramped, four-block neighbourhood of ramshackle minibars and restaurants translates as "Piss Alley", but don't be put off exploring this atmospheric quarter – you're less likely to be ripped off for a drink here than in the similar Golden Gai district of Kabukichō. A pedestrian tunnel at the southern end of the alleys, just to the right of the cheap clothes outlets, provides a short cut to the east side of Shinjuku Station and Studio Alta.

Higashi-Shinjuku

Some days it seems as if all of Tokyo is waiting at Shinjuku's favourite meeting spot, beneath the huge TV screen on the **Studio Alta** building on the east (*higashi*) side of the JR station. It's worth bearing this in mind if you arrange to meet anyone there – a generally less crowded option is at the plaza opposite Studio Alta, from where you can soak up the supercharged atmosphere, especially at night, when the district is ablaze with neon. To the southeast of

Modern architecture in Tokyo

From the swirling rooftop of the National Yoyogi Stadium to the seemingly bubble-wrapped Prada building on Omotesandō, Tokyo has an astonishing array of **modern architecture**. Japan's top postwar architect, **Tange Kenzō**, has done more than most to define Tokyo's eclectic style – his monumental Tokyo Metropolitan Government Building in Shinjuku has been described as the last great edifice of postmodernism, though some would argue that he has gone one step further with the otherworldly Fuji TV building in Odaiba. Other works by Tange in Tokyo include the 1964 Olympic Stadium in Yoyogi and the United Nations University on Aoyama-dōri.

Tange is one of three Japanese architects to have received architecture's most prestigious international award, the Pritzker Prize. Another is **Andō Tadao**, former boxer and self-taught architect. His Collezione building, at the far east end of Omotesandō in Harajuku, is a good example of his liking for rough concrete and bold structural forms. He has also been commissioned to design the complex of shops and apartments replacing the now demolished Donjnkai Aoyama Apartments in the middle of Omotesandō. **Maki Fumihiko** is Japan's third Pritzker Prize winner. His work includes the futuristic Tokyo Metropolitan Gymnasium in Sendagaya, the Spiral Building near Omotesandō, with its deliberately fragmented facade, and the ambitious Hillside Terrace in ritzy Daikan'yama, a complex of homes, offices and shops developed over a 23-year period. Among other prominent Japanese architects, **Isozaki Arata**'s Ochanomizu Square Building, just north of the Imperial Palace, is a good example of how old and new architecture can be successfully combined. A similar synthesis is found in **Rokkaku Kijō**'s Tokyo Budōkan, the martial arts mecca, which visibly takes its inspiration from traditional Japanese art – in this case, paintings of overlapping mountains fading into the mists.

Many top foreign architects have used Tokyo as a canvas on which to work out their most extravagant designs. In Asakusa, look for **Philippe Starck**'s Super Dry Hall, with its enigmatic "golden turd" on the roof; and **Sir Norman Foster**'s Century Tower at Ochanomizu, which incorporates the vernacular design of the *torii*, ten of which appear to be piled on top of each other on the building's facade. Light floods into the soaring glass hall of **Rafael Viñoly**'s Tokyo International Forum in Yūrakuchō, while **Sir Richard Rogers's** Kabukichō Building, swathed in a framework of stainless-steel rods, is hidden on a Shinjuku side street. Most recently, in 2003, **Jacques Herzog** and **Pierre de Meuron** of Switzerland (the team responsible for London's Tate Modern) unveiled their stunning Prada building, a jewel-like edifice of rhomboid crystals, cuddled on one side by a velvety, moss-covered wall.

If you want to take a quick tour of Tokyo's modern architectural highlights, walk from Sendagaya Station on the Chūō line along Gaien-nishi-dōri to Aoyama-dōri, turn right and continue to the crossing with Omotesandō. From here you can either continue down to Shibuya, past Spiral Hall and the UN building or turn left to reach the Prada building and La Collezione. Either way, you'll have passed many of the best examples of modern Tokyo architecture. Although it misses out on some of the past decade's additions to the city's skyline, Tajima Noriyuki's illustrated, pocket-sized *Tokyo: A Guide to Recent Architecture* is still the best around.

here is **Shinjuku–dōri**, along which you'll find some of the classier department stores and shops, such as Mitsukoshi and **Isetan**, which has excellent food halls in its basement, a good range of restaurants on its top floor and an art gallery that frequently holds notable exhibitions (check local English-language newspapers and magazines for details). In addition, beneath the pounding feet of pedestrians on Yasukuni-dōri lies an extensive subterranean shopping complex, **Shinjuku Subnade**, while a tunnel with exits to all the major shops runs the length of Shinjuku-dōri from the main JR station to the Shinjuku-Sanchōme subway station.

Kabukichō to Takashimaya Times Square

Directly to the north of Studio Alta, across the wide boulevard of Yasukuni-dōri, lies the red-light district **Kabukichō**, at the heart of which is the Koma Theatre, where modern musicals and samurai dramas are performed. The tatty plaza in front of the theatre is lined with cinemas, many showing the latest Hollywood blockbusters, and the streets radiating around it contain a wide range of bars and restaurants. Stray a block or so further north and you're deep in the raunchier side of Kabukichō, with soaplands, hostess bars and girly shows lining the narrow streets. You stand a good chance of spotting members of the *yakuza* crime syndicates at work (the tight-perm hairdos and 1970s-style clobber are giveaway signs) around here, but the overall atmosphere is not unlike London's Soho, where the porn industry and illicit goings-on nestle unthreateningly beside less salacious entertainment.

Local shopkeepers come to pray for business success at Kabukichō's attractive **Hanazono-jinja**. This shrine predates the founding of Edo by the Tokugawa, but the current granite and vermilion buildings are modern recreations. It's worth paying a visit at night, when spotlights give the shrine a special ambience. From here, you're well poised to take a stroll through the **Golden Gai**, the low-rent drinking quarter where intellectuals and artists have rubbed shoulders with Kabukichō's demi-monde since the war. In this compact grid of streets there are around two hundred bars, no larger than broom cupboards and presided over by no-nonsense *mama-sans* and *masters*. You probably won't want to stop for a drink here unless you speak good Japanese: at most bars only regulars are welcome, while the others will fleece you rotten. There are, however, a couple of exceptions, listed on p.174. The cinderblock buildings are constantly under threat from both property developers and their own shoddy construction – they were never built to last this long, so catch them while they last and witness an increasingly rare side of Shinjuku's raffish past.

Shinjuku Gyoen and around

By contrast to the Golden Gai, the city's squeaky-clean future is on display at **Takashimaya Times Square**, a sleek shopping and entertainment complex which is shifting Shinjuku's focus away from Kabukichō. The complex is connected to the southern (Shin-Minami) entrance to Shinjuku Station by a broad wooden promenade and includes branches of the Takashimaya department store, interior design and handicrafts superstore Tōkyū Hands, and the vast seven-floor Kinokuniya bookstore. Inside the mall you'll also find **Shinjuku Joypolis** (daily 10am–11.15pm; ¥300), a high-tech amusement park of virtual-reality rides produced by Sega, and the **Tokyo IMAX Theatre** (¥1300), which screens 3-D films on its six-storey-high cinema screen.

Five minutes' walk east of Takashimaya Times Square, close by the Shinjuku-Gyoen-mae subway station, is the main entrance to **Shinjuku Gyoen** (Tues–Sun 9am–4.30pm, last entry 4pm; ¥200), the largest and arguably most beautiful gardens in Tokyo. The grounds, which once held the mansion of Lord Naitō, the *daimyō* of Tsuruga on the coast of the Sea of Japan, became the property of the Imperial Household in 1868, and the 150-acre park was opened to the public after World War II.

Apart from their spaciousness, the gardens' most notable feature is their variety of design. The southern half is traditionally Japanese, with winding paths, stone lanterns, artificial hills, islands in ponds linked by zigzag bridges and *Rakuutei*, a pleasant **teahouse** (10am–4pm; ¥700). At the northern end of the park are formal, French-style gardens, with neat rows of tall birch trees and hedge-lined flowerbeds. Clipped, broad lawns dominate the middle of the park, modelled on English landscape design. On the eastern flank next to the large greenhouse (Tues–Sun 11am–3.30pm), packed with subtropical vegetation and particularly cosy on a chilly winter's day, an imperial wooden **villa** from 1869 has been reconstructed (open second and fourth Sat of the month from 10am to 3pm). In spring, the whole park bursts with pink and white cherry blossoms, while in early November kaleidoscopic chrysanthemum displays and golden autumn leaves are the main attractions. There are several **cafés** within the gardens where you can grab a reasonable lunch for around ¥900, but it's much nicer to bring a picnic and relax in the tranquil surroundings. An alternative entrance to the gardens is through the western gate, a five-minute walk under and alongside the train tracks from Sendagaya Station.

Walking back towards Shinjuku Station will take you past the gay district of **Shinjuku Nichōme**. During the day the area is inconspicuous, but come nightfall the numerous bars (see p.183) spring into action, catering to every imaginable sexual orientation. Close by is **Taisō-ji**, a temple founded in 1668, which has the city's largest wooden statue of Yama, the King of Hell. The statue is in the temple building next to a large copper Buddha dressed in a red bib and cap. You have to press a button to illuminate the 5.5-metre Yama, whose fearsome expression is difficult to take seriously once you've spotted the offerings at his feet – a couple of tins of fruit are the norm.

9

Harajuku and Aoyama

South of Shinjuku lie the super-chic shopping and entertainment districts of **Harajuku** and **Aoyama**, a collective showcase for contemporary Tokyo fashion and style. Consumer culture reigns supreme in these streets, packed with smart cafés, designer boutiques and hip young spenders in search of the latest fashions and the most desirable labels. Harajuku caters to the younger, adventurous fashionista, while those with gilt-edged credit cards will feel more at home among the established fashion houses and antique shops of Aoyama. Even if shopping's not your bag, there are other good reasons for coming here, the best being the verdant grounds of the city's most venerable shrine, **Meiji-jingū**. Neighbouring **Yoyogi-kōen** was the focus of the 1964 Olympics, and several of the stadia surrounding it are a legacy of that event.

It's always rewarding strolling along **Omotesandō**, a tree-lined boulevard, often referred to as Tokyo's Champs Elysées, which links Harajuku and Aoyama. Just off Omotesandō are a clutch of worthwhile **galleries**: the Ōta Memorial Museum of Art, dedicated to *ukiyo-e* prints; the Nezu Museum of Art, with a wider focus on all types of Oriental art (and a charming traditional garden); and the anarchic and fun Design Festa Gallery. Finally, the peaceful grounds of **Aoyama Cemetery**, containing the graves of many Tokyo notables, are particularly worth strolling through during the cherry-blossom season, but are worth a visit at any time of year.

Meiji-jingū

Covering parts of both Aoyama and Harajuku is **Meiji-jingū**, Tokyo's premier Shinto shrine, a memorial to Emperor Meiji, who died in 1912, and his empress Shōken, who died in 1914. The shrine is split into two sections about a kilometre apart: the **Outer Garden**, between Sendagaya and Shinanomachi stations, contains the Meiji Memorial Picture Gallery and several sporting arenas, including the National Stadium and Jingū Baseball Stadium; while the more important **Inner Garden**, beside Harajuku Station, includes the emperor's shrine, the empress's iris gardens, the imperial couple's Treasure House and extensive wooded grounds.

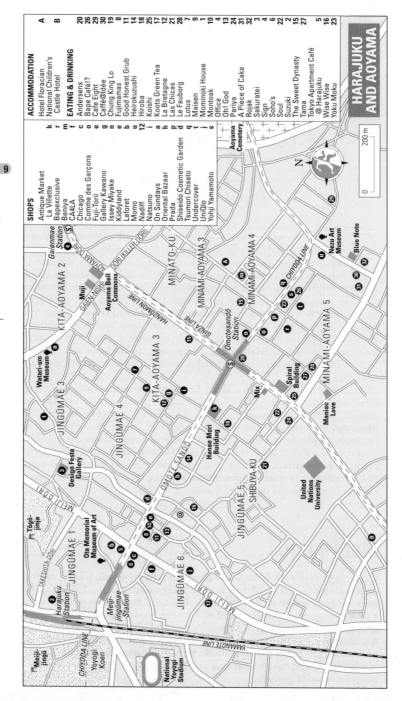

HARAJUKU AND AOYAMA

0   200 m

Aoyama	Aoyama	青山
Aoyama Cemetery	Aoyama Reien	青山霊園
National Children's Castle	Kodomo-no-shiro	こどもの城
Nezu Museum of Art	Nezu Bijutsukan	根津美術館
Spiral Hall	Supairaru Haru	スパイラルハル
Harajuku	Harajuku	原宿
Design Festa Gallery	Dezain Fesuta Gyararii	デザイン・フェスタ・ギャラリー
Meiji-jingū	Meiji-jingū	明治神宮
Meiji Memorial Picture Gallery	Meiji Kaigakan	明治絵画館
National Nō Theatre	Kokuritsu Nō Gekijō	国立能劇場
Omotesandō	Omotesandō	表参道
Ōta Memorial Museum of Art	Ōta Kinen Bijutsukan	太田記念美術館
Takeshita-dōri	Takeshita-dōri	竹下通り
Tōgō-jinja	Tōgō-jinja	東郷神社
Yoyogi-kōen	Yoyogi-kōen	代々木公園

Together with the neighbouring shrines to General Nogi and Admiral Tōgō (see p.110), Meiji-jingū was created as a symbol of imperial power and Japanese racial superiority. Rebuilt in 1958 after being destroyed during World War II, the shrine remains the focus of several annual **festivals** (see box on p.109). Apart from the festivals, Meiji-jingū is best visited midweek, when its calm serenity can be appreciated without the crowds.

The Outer Garden and around

The closest subway to the entrance to Meiji-jingū's Outer Garden is Aoyama Itchōme. The **Meiji Memorial Picture Gallery** (daily 9am–5pm; ¥500; ⓣ03/3401-5179, ⓦwww.meijijingu.or.jp/gaien/01.htm) lies at the northern end of a long gingko tree-lined approach road which runs beside the rugby and baseball stadiums northwest of the subway. The gallery has a stern, European-style exterior and a marble-clad entrance hall which soars up to a central dome. On either side are halls containing forty paintings which tell the life story of Emperor Meiji – more interesting for their depiction of Japan emerging from its feudal past than for their artistic merits.

Next to the gallery looms the 75,000-seater **National Stadium**, Japan's largest sporting arena, built for the 1964 Olympics. On the western side of the stadium – and best viewed from outside Sendagaya Station – is the Outer Garden's most striking feature: the **Tokyo Metropolitan Gymnasium**, designed by Maki Fumihiko (see box on p.102). At first glance the building looks like a giant alien spacecraft, though on closer examination it becomes obvious that the inspiration is a traditional samurai helmet. The corrugated stainless-steel-roofed building houses the main arena, while in the block to the right, crowned with a glass pyramid roof, are public swimming pools and a subterranean gym (entry ¥450).

Following the railway line and road west leads you to a sign pointing to the **National Nō Theatre**, set back from the street in a walled compound. Built in 1983, the theatre incorporates traditional Japanese architectural motifs, particularly in the design of its slightly sloping roofs. Nō, Japan's oldest and most stylized form of theatre, is something of an acquired taste, though if you want to give it a try this is one of the best places in which to see a production.

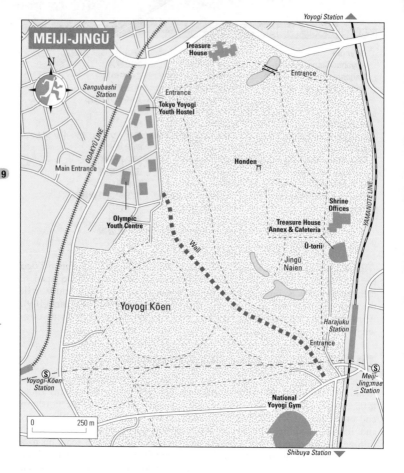

Return to the main road and follow the raised expressway as it crosses over the railway lines, then veer off left up the hill to Meiji-jingū's Inner Garden eastern entrance.

The Inner Garden

The most impressive way to approach the **Inner Garden** is through the southern gate next to Jingū-bashi, the bridge across from Harajuku's station, a toy-town-like building complete with mock-Tudor clock tower. From the gateway a wide gravel path runs through densely forested grounds to the twelve-metre-high **Ō-torii**, made from 1500-year-old cypress pine trees from Taiwan, the largest Myōjin-style gate in Japan. Just before the gate, on the right, is the **Bunkakan**, a new complex housing a restaurant, café, gift shop and the generally uninteresting annexe of the **Treasure House** (daily: April–Nov 8.30am–4pm; Jan–March & Dec 9.30am–3.30pm; ¥500 entry for both buildings); this is where you'll alight from your bus if you visit on an organized tour. To left of the Ō-torii is the entrance to the **Jingū Naien** (daily 8.30am–5pm;

¥500), a traditional garden – said to have been designed by the Emperor Meiji for his wife – which is at its most beautiful (and most crowded) in June, when over one hundred varieties of **irises**, the empress's favourite flowers, pepper the lush greenery with their purple and white blooms.

Returning to the garden's entrance, the gravel path turns right and passes through a second wooden *torii*, **Kita–mon** (north gate), leading to the impressive **honden** (central hall). With their Japanese cypress wood and green copper roofs, the buildings are a fine example of how Shinto architecture can blend seamlessly with nature. There are exits from the courtyard on its eastern and western flanks; follow either of the paths northwards through the woods to arrive at the pleasant grassy slopes and pond before the main **Treasure House** (same hours as annexe). Don't bother going in, though – the contents of the museum are no more thrilling than the lumpen grey concrete building that houses them.

Yoyogi-kōen

Apart from the wooded grounds of Meiji-jingū, **Harajuku** is also blessed with Tokyo's largest park, **Yoyogi-kōen**, a favourite spot for joggers and bonneted groups of kindergarten kids with their minders. Once an imperial army training ground, the park was dubbed "Washington Heights" after World War II, when it was used to house US military personnel. In 1964 the land was used for the Olympic athletes' village, after which it became Yoyogi-kōen. Two of the stadia, built for the Olympics, remain the area's most famous architectural features. The main building of Tange Kenzō's **Yoyogi National Stadium** is a dead ringer for Noah's ark, and its steel suspension roof was a structural engineering marvel at the time. Inside are a swimming pool and skating rink (Mon–Sat noon–8pm, Sun 10am–6pm; ¥900). The smaller stadium, used for basketball, is like the sharp end of a giant swirling seashell.

Omotesandō and around

Harajuku's most elegant boulevard, **Omotesandō**, leads from the entrance to Meiji-jingū to the cluster of contemporary designer boutiques on the other side of Aoyama-dōri. On either side are dense networks of streets, packed with funky little shops, restaurants and bars. One of the most famous roads is **Takeshita-dōri**, whose hungry mouth gobbles up teenage fashion victims as they swarm out of the north exit of Harajuku Station and spits them out the other end on Meiji-dōri minus their cash. Selling every kind of tat imaginable, the shops are hugely enjoyable to root around in and provide an intriguing window on Japanese teen fashion. On Sundays the crush of bodies on the street is akin to that on the Yamanote line at rush hour.

Serious bargain-hunters never miss out on the outdoor antiques market held on the first and fourth Sundays of each month in the precincts of **Tōgō-jinja**, just off Takeshita-dōri. The market sells everything from fine *tansu* (traditional Japanese chests) to old kimono and crockery. You'll need to know what you're looking for to avoid being ripped off, but it's also possible to snag bargains if you come at the end of the day when the stalls are packing up and the sellers are prepared to haggle. The **shrine** itself is dedicated to Admiral Tōgō Heihachirō, who led the victorious Japanese fleet against the Russians in the Russo–Japanese War of 1904–5, and has a pretty pond and garden fronting onto Meiji-dōri.

Walking back towards the crossing with Omotesandō, look out for Laforet, a trendy boutique complex, behind which is the excellent **Ōta Memorial Museum of Art** (Tues–Sun 10.30am–5pm; ¥500; ☎03/3403-0880, Ⓦwww.ukiyoe-ota-muse.jp). You'll have to leave your shoes in the lockers and put on slippers to wander the small galleries on two levels featuring *ukiyo-e* paintings and prints from the private collection of the late Ōta Seizō, the former chairman of the Tōhō Life Insurance Company. The art displayed comes from a collection of 12,000 pieces, including masterpieces by Utamaro, Hokusai and Hiroshige.

In complete contrast to all this is the **Design Festa Gallery** (daily 11am–8pm; free; ☎03/3479-1442, Ⓦwww.designfesta.com), a joyfully anarchic art space sprouting out of the funky backstreets of Harajuku like some bargain-basement Pompidou Centre. The gallery is an offshoot of Design Festa, Japan's biggest art and design event, held twice a year at Tokyo Big Sight (see p.127). It's hard to believe that beneath the day-glo paintings, graffiti, mad scaffolding and traffic cones, swarming over the building's front like some alien metal creeper, lies a block of ordinary apartments. Inside the art is no less eclectic, ranging from sculpture to video installations – even the toilet is plastered from floor to ceiling with artworks. Behind it is a good *okonomiyaki* café and bar. To find the gallery, take the street directly opposite the eastern Meiji-dōri end of Takeshita-dōri, then turn north at the second junction on your left.

Returning to Omotesandō and heading east, you'll pass Mori Building's latest project, the redevelopment of the **Dojunkai Aoyama Apartments** site, due to finish in 2006. Andō Tadao (see p.102), who has been charged with designing this new complex of shops and homes, plans to keep the complex low-rise, and also intends to reconstruct one of the original 1927 ivy-clad multi-family housing blocks that were a much-loved part of Omotesandō before being demolished in 2003.

Aoyama

Harajuku's funkiness gives way to Aoyama's sophistication as Omotesandō crosses Aoyama-dōri and becomes lined with top designer-label boutiques

111

△ Flea market, Harajuku

including **Prada**, which occupies an incredible glass-bubble building which is a tourist attraction in its own right.

At the T-junction, just beyond the Andō Tadao-designed Collezione building, turn right for the entrances to the **Nezu Museum of Art** (Tues–Sun 9.30am–4.30pm; ¥1000; ℡03/3400-2536, ⓦwww.nezu-muse.or.jp). The museum, founded by Nezu Kaichiro of Tobū railways and department store fame, houses a classy collection of Oriental arts. The best time to visit is the ten-day period at the end of April and beginning of May, when Ōgata Kōrin's exquisite screen paintings of irises are displayed. Otherwise, the museum's nicest feature is its garden, which slopes gently away around an ornamental pond and features several traditional teahouses.

Turning left at the end of Omotesandō, the road leads round into Tokyo's most important graveyard, officially entitled Aoyama Reien, but generally known as **Aoyama Bochi**. Everyone who was anyone, including Hachikō the faithful dog (see p.116), is buried here, and the graves, many decorated with elaborate calligraphy, are interesting in their own right. Look out for the section where foreigners are buried; their tombstones provide a history of early *gaijin* involvement in Japan. Despite it being a cemetery, many locals enjoy partying here during the *hanami* season under the candyfloss bunches of pink cherry blossoms.

If you don't want to explore the cemetery, an alternative route leads southwest from the Aoyama-dōri crossing with Omotesandō to pass (on your left) the **Spiral Building**, which includes a gallery, a couple of restaurants and a trendy card shop. The interior, with its sweeping, seemingly free-standing ramp walkway, is worth a look. The next major junction with Aoyama-dōri sees the start of **Kottō-dōri**, or antique street; you'll find several shops selling old (and generally overpriced) wares along here, as well as more designer boutiques as it heads towards Roppongi.

Keeping on Aoyama-dōri and moving closer to Shibuya you'll pass the funky **National Children's Castle** (Tues–Fri 12.30–5.30pm, Sat & Sun 10am–5pm; ¥500; ℡03/3797-5666, ⓦwww.kodomo-shiro.or.jp), marked by one of the bizarre, cartoon-like sculptures of Okumoto Taro. The very uncastle-like building houses a large kids' playground featuring a hotel and a swimming pool (¥300 extra).

Shibuya to Shinagawa

I
mmediately south of Harajuku is **Shibuya**, birthplace of a million-and-one
consumer crazes, where teens and twenty-somethings throng **Centre Gai**, the
shopping precinct that splits the district's rival department-store groups: **Tōkyū**
(who own the prime station site, the Mark City complex and the Bunkamura
arts hall) and **Seibu** (whose outlets include the fashionable, youth-oriented Loft
and Parco stores). Although there are a few interesting museums in the area – most
particularly the **Japan Folk Crafts Museum** – Shibuya is primarily an after-dark
destination, when the neon signs of scores of restaurants, bars and cinemas battle
it out with five-storey-tall TV screens for the attention of passers-by.

 Ebisu, just south of Shibuya, is the home of the old Yebisu brewery developed by owners Sapporo into **Ebisu Garden Place**, a forerunner of
Roppongi Hills and Shiodome as an integrated living, working, shopping and
entertainment area. Here you'll find the excellent **Tokyo Metropolitan
Photography Museum**. **Daikan'yama**, a pleasant stroll uphill to the west of
Ebisu, is one of Tokyo's classiest districts and a great place to chill out at a pave-
ment café or do a spot of window-shopping.

 A kilometre south of Ebisu, the mainly residential area of **Meguro** is home
to a couple of off-beat museums and the splendid wedding hall of **Meguro
Gajōen**, as well as the tranquil **National Park for Nature Study** and the
serene gardens of **Happōen**. Equally restrained and peaceful is the
Hatakeyama Collection of tea-ceremony implements, overlooking an
attractive traditional garden.

 East of Meguro is the transport and hotel hub of **Shinagawa**, the location of
one of the original checkpoints on the Tōkaidō, the major highway into Edo
during the reign of the shoguns. Nearby are the historic temple **Sengaku-ji**,
a key location in Tokyo's bloodiest true-life samurai saga, and the **Hara
Museum of Contemporary Art**, housing an interesting collection of modern art and a very pleasant café.

Shibuya

The plaza on the west side of Shibuya Station was the famous waiting spot of
Hachikō the dog (see box on p.116) and is the best place from which to take

Shibuya	*Shibuya*	渋谷
Bunkamura	*Bunkamura*	文化村
Dōgenzaka	*Dōgenzaka*	道玄坂
Hachikō	*Hachikō*	ハチ公
Japan Folk Crafts Museum	*Mingeikan*	民芸館
NHK Studio Park	*NHK Sutajio Pāku*	スタジオパーク
TEPCO Electric Energy Museum	*TEPCO Denryokukan*	電力館
Tobacco and Salt Museum	*Tabako-to-Shio-no-Hakubutsukan*	たばこと塩の博物館
Toguri Museum of Art	*Toguri Bijutsukan*	戸栗美術館
Tokyo Metropolitan Children's Hall	*Tōkyō-to Jidō Kaikan*	東京都児童会館
Ebisu	*Ebisu*	恵比寿
Tokyo Metropolitan Photography Museum	*Tōkyō-to Shashin Bijutsukan*	東京都写真美術館
Yebisu Garden Place	*Ebisu Gāden Pureisu*	恵比寿ガーデンプレイス
Daikan'yama	*Daikan'yama*	代官山
Meguro	*Meguro*	目黒
Happōen	*Happōen*	八芳園
Hatakeyama Collection	*Hatakeyama Kinenkan*	畠山記念館
Meguro Gajōen	*Meguro Gajōen*	目黒雅叙園
Meguro Parasitological Museum	*Meguro Kiseichū-kan*	目黒寄生虫館
National Park for Nature Study	*Kokuritsu Shizen Kyōikuen*	国立自然教育園
Tokyo Metropolitan Teien Art Museum	*Tōkyō-to Teien Bijutsukan*	東京都庭園美術館
Shinagawa	*Shinagawa*	品川
Hara Museum of Contemporary Art	*Hara Bijutsukan*	原美術館
Sengaku-ji	*Sengaku-ji*	泉岳寺
Sony Museum	*Sonii Myujiamu*	ソニーミュージアム

in the evening buzz. Head to the upper floors of the adjacent **Shibuya Mark City**, a restaurant and hotel complex, for a bird's-eye view of the area. Opposite, to the west, the 109 Building stands at the apex of Bunkamura-dōri and Dōgenzaka – the latter leads up to **Dōgenzaka**, one of Tokyo's most famous love-hotel disticts. This area is named after Owada Dōgen, a thirteenth-century highwayman who robbed travellers on their way through the then isolated valley.

Running parallel to the north of Bunkamura-dōri is the always-packed **Centre Gai**, where trend-obsessed Tokyo teens and twenty-somethings gather to create or spot the latest look – tiny dogs used as fashion accessories and brightly coloured shoes are the latest rage.

RESTAURANTS, CAFÉS & BARS

Belgo	21
Cantina	1
Christon Café	15
Coins Bar	2
Karaoke-kan	10
Lion	19
Moph	3
Nobu Tokyo	16
Miyoko	5
Pink Cow	4
Punraku	12
Secobar	22
Shizenkan II	20
Sonoma	13
Underground	6
Mr. Zoogunzoo	11
Xanadu	

CLUBS

Club Asia	14
Club Pure	7
Club Quattro	8
Harlem	18
La Fabrique	9
The Ruby Room	13
Simoon	23
Womb	17

SHOPS

HMV	o
Hysteric Glamour	a
Loft	k
Love Girls Market	q
Mandarake	j
Marui	i
Parco	f & g
Pink Dragon	b
Recofan	b
Seibu	h
Three Minute Happiness	n
Tōkyū	c
Tōkyū Hands	m & p
Tower Books	d
Tower Records	e

ACCOMMODATION

Arimax Hotel	A
Cerulean Tower Tōkyū Hotel	G
National Children's Castle Hotel	D
Shibuya Business Hotel	E
Shibuya Creston Hotel	F
Shibuya Excel Hotel Tōkyū	C
Shibuya Tōbu Hotel	B

Hachikō: a dog's life

The story of **Hachikō** the dog proves that fame in Japan comes to those who wait. Every morning, the Akita pup faithfully accompanied his master Ueda Eisaburō, a professor in the Department of Agriculture at the Imperial University, to Shibuya Station, and returned to the station in the evening to greet him. In May 1925, Professor Ueda died while at work, but Hachikō continued to turn up every day at the station. By 1934, Hachikō had waited patiently for nine years, and locals were so touched by the dog's devotion that a bronze statue was cast of him.

In 1935, Hachikō was finally united in death with his master and was buried with Ueda in Aoyama cemetery. The stuffed skin of a second dog was used to create a doppelgänger Hachikō, which can be seen at the National Science Museum. During World War II, the original Hachikō statue was melted down for weapons, but a replacement was reinstated beside the station in 1948. Today, this is the most famous rendezvous in all Tokyo, though the throngs of people around the small statue and the rats that rummage through the rubbish in the surrounding bushes mean that it's not a particularly convivial place to hang out.

Bunkamura and around

At the western end of Bunkamura-dōri is the main entrance to the **Bunkamura** (Ⓦ www.bunkamura.co.jp), an arts complex with an excellent gallery (showing temporary exhibitions of mainly Western art), a couple of cinemas, the 2000-seater Orchard Hall, home of the Tokyo Philharmonic Orchestra, and the Theatre Cocoon, which hosts some of the city's more avant-garde productions. The ticket counter is on the first floor (daily 10am–7.30pm; ℡ 03/3477-3244 for programme information).

Walk a few minutes uphill behind the Bunkamura to reach the **Toguri Museum of Art** (Tues–Sun 9.30am–5.30pm; ¥1030; ℡ 03/3465-0070, Ⓦ www .toguri-museum.or.jp), which displays Edo-era and Chinese Ming-dynasty (1368–1644) ceramics. Although it's not to everyone's taste (and entrance is pricey), this small but exquisitely displayed exhibition, comprising selections from a collection of some six thousand pieces, is worth the expense if you're interested in pottery. Carefully positioned mirrors enable you to inspect the fine detail of work on the underside of displayed plates and bowls, and there's a pretty garden beside the lobby which you can gaze out on while sipping tea or coffee.

Back down the hill, head to the road east of Centre Gai and climb the steps of **Spain-zaka**, with its emporia of ephemera. At the top of this narrow street are **Cinema Rise**, an imaginatively designed movie theatre which shows mainly foreign art-house films, and **Tōkyū Hands**, a giant handicrafts store, good for unusual souvenirs (see p.208).

North to NHK Studio Park

From Cinema Rise head east past the Parco fashion stores and walk up Kōen-dōri to find the quirky **Tobacco and Salt Museum** (Tues–Sun 10am–5.30pm; ¥100; ℡ 03/3476-2041). Take the lift to the fourth floor, which has temporary exhibitions, and work your way down past displays on the third, which focus on the harvesting of salt from the sea and other sources of sodium. The second floor has the tobacco exhibits, including two thousand packets from around the world, and dioramas showing how the leaves were prepared for smoking in the past. It's all in Japanese, and only on the ground floor are you actually allowed to light up a fag.

At the top of Kōen-dōri, 200m north of the Tobacco and Salt Museum and opposite the Shibuya Ward Office and Public Hall, is the NHK Broadcasting Centre, housing Japan's equivalent of the BBC. You can take an entertaining tour around part of the complex by visiting the **NHK Studio Park** (daily 10am–6pm, closed third Mon of the month; ¥200; ☎03/3485-8034, ⓦ www.nhk.or.jp/studiopark). Although it's all in Japanese, much of the exhibition is interactive: you get to try your hand as a newsreader and weather presenter and mess around on multimedia gadgets. Try out the 3-D screen TV, but read the English instructions first on how to contort your body to get the desired effect.

If you've got kids in tow, there are a couple of places worth searching out close by. On Fire Street, 100m east of NHK, the **TEPCO Electric Energy Museum** (daily except Wed 10am–6pm; free; ☎03/3477-1191, ⓦ www .denryokukan.com) has seven floors of exhibits relating to electricity. The English brochure says "Let's make friends with electricity" and TEPCO, Tokyo's power company, goes out of its way to convince you that this is possible, even to the extent of hosting free showings of Hollywood movies on Mondays. Look out for the laser that can etch your profile and name (in Japanese characters) onto a credit-card-sized piece of card.

Nip under the train tracks and across Meiji-dōri to reach **Tokyo Metropolitan Children's Hall** (daily 9am–5pm; free; ☎03/3409-6361, ⓦ www.jidokaikan.metro.tokyo.jp), an excellent government-sponsored facility for kids, including a rooftop playground, library, music room and craft-making activities.

Japan Folk Crafts Museum

Just two stops from Shibuya on the Keiō Inokashira line to Komaba-Tōdaimae Station, or a twenty-minute walk west of Dōgenzaka to Komaba-kōen, lies the very impressive **Japan Folk Crafts Museum** (or Mingeikan; Tues–Sun 10am–5pm; ¥1000; ☎03/3467-4527, ⓦ www.mingeikan.or.jp). Set in a handsome stone-and-stucco building, this is the best museum in the Shibuya area and a must-see for Japanese-craft fans, with an excellent collection of pottery, textiles and lacquerware. The gift shop is a fine source of souvenirs, and an annual competition and sale of new craft works is held between November 23 and December 3.

Opposite the museum stands a nineteenth-century **nagayamon** (long gate house), brought here from Tochigi-ken prefecture in northern Honshū by the museum's founder, Yanagi Soetsu, father of the famous designer Yanagi Sori.

Ebisu and Daikan'yama

Ebisu, less than 2km south of Shibuya, might not be quite so trendy as it once was, but it still has a buzz. There are many lively bars and stylish restaurants here with the main focus of the area being **Yebisu Garden Place**, a huge shopping, office and entertainment complex, connected to the station by a long moving walkway. The complex is built on the site of the nineteenth-century Sapporo brewery that was once the source of the area's fortunes, and includes the glitzy *Westin Hotel*, a 39-storey tower, cinema, performance hall and mock French chateau housing the top-notch *Taillevent Robuchon* restaurant. Slated by

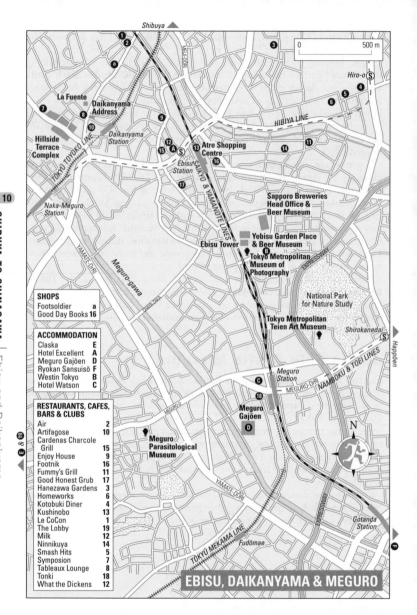

Shibuya

Hiro-o ⑤

La Fuente

Daikanyama
Address

Hillside
Terrace
Complex

Daikanyama
Station

HIBIYA LINE

TOKYO TOYOKO LINE

Atre Shopping
Centre

Ebisu
Station

Naka-Meguro
Station

Sapporo Breweries
Head Office &
Beer Museum

Yebisu Garden Place
& Beer Museum

Ebisu Tower

Tokyo Metropolitan
Museum of
Photography

YAMATE-DORI

Meguro-gawa

SAIKYO & YAMANOTE LINES

National Park
for Nature Study

Shirokanedai ⑤

Tokyo Metropolitan
Teien Art Museum

Happōen

NAMBOKU & TOEI LINES

SHOPS

| Footsoldier | a |
| Good Day Books | 16 |

ACCOMMODATION

Claska	E
Hotel Excellent	A
Meguro Gajōen	D
Ryokan Sansuisō	F
Westin Tokyo	B
Hotel Watson	C

Meguro
Station

MEGURO-DORI

Meguro
Gajōen

EXPRESSWAY

Gotanda
Station

MEGURO-D

**RESTAURANTS, CAFES,
BARS & CLUBS**

Air	2
Artifagose	10
Cardenas Charcole Grill	15
Enjoy House	9
Footnik	16
Fummy's Grill	11
Good Honest Grub	17
Hanezawa Gardens	3
Homeworks	6
Kotobuki Diner	4
Kushinobo	13
Le CoCon	1
The Lobby	19
Milk	12
Ninnikuya	14
Smash Hits	5
Symposion	7
Tableaux Lounge	8
Tonki	18
What the Dickens	12

Meguro
Parasitological
Museum

N

YAMATE-DORI

Fudōmae

TOKYU MEKAMA LINE

EBISU, DAIKANYAMA & MEGURO

professionals as an architectural disaster, Yebisu Garden Place is still worth visiting for a couple of interesting museums.

The best is the **Tokyo Metropolitan Photography Museum** (Tues–Sun 10am–6pm, Thurs & Fri until 8pm; admission charges vary; ☎03/3280-0031, ⓦwww.tokyo-photo-museum.or.jp), on the west side of the complex. This has excellent changing exhibitions of shots by major Japanese and Western

Beer in Japan

When **beer** was first brewed in Japan in Sapporo during the late nineteenth-century colonization period of Hokkaidō, the locals had to be bribed to drink it. These days, they need no such encouragement, knocking back a whopping seven million litres a year. Beer in Japan generally means lager, produced by the big-four brewers Asahi, Kirin, Sapporo and Suntory, who also turn out a range of ale-type beers (often called black beer), as well as half-and-half concoctions, which are a mixture of the two. The current bestseller is Asahi Superdry, a dry-tasting lager.

Standard-size cans of beer cost around ¥200 from a shop or vending machine, while bottles (*bin-biiru*) served in restaurants and bars usually start at ¥500. Draught beer (*nama-biiru*) is also sometimes available and, in beer halls, will be served in a *jokki*, which comes in three different sizes: *dai* (big), *chū* (medium) and *shō* (small).

In recent years, the big-four breweries have seen their monopoly on domestic sales eroded by cheap foreign imports and deregulation of the industry, which has encouraged local **microbreweries** to expand their operations. In Japanese, the new brews are called *ji-biiru* (regional beer), and although few have got their act together to produce really fine beers, their drinks are always worth sampling as an alternative to the bland brews of the big four. The microbreweries include T.Y. Harbour Brewery and Sunset Beach Brewing Company (see p.174).

photographers, along with study rooms and an experimental photography and imaging room. The museum's policy of concentrating on one photographer at a time in its frequently changing exhibitions allows you to see the artist's work develop and gain an understanding of the motivations behind it.

On the western side of the complex, behind the Mitsukoshi department store, the history of beer in Japan – and of the brewery that used to be here – is detailed at the lively **Yebisu Beer Museum** (Tues–Sun 10am–6pm; free; ☏03/5423-7255, ⓦwww.sapporobeer.jp/brewery/ebisu). Look out for the touchscreen video displays and a computer simulation, where one of the people taking part in the tour is chosen to be the leader of a virtual-reality tour around different aspects of the brewing process. There's also an opportunity to sample some of Sapporo's beers, at ¥200 for a small glass. If you have time, head for the restaurants on the 38th and 39th floors of the **Yebisu Tower**, next to the photography museum; you don't need to eat or drink here to enjoy the spectacular free views of the city.

Daikan'yama

A ten-minute stroll west along Komazawa-dōri from Ebisu Station, or one stop from Shibuya on the Tōkyū Tōyoko line, is **Daikan'yama**, home to some of the city's classiest homes, shops and watering holes – the village-like area's laid-back atmosphere is a refreshing break from the frenzy of nearby Shibuya. Daikan'yama's contemporary style has been defined by the smart **Hillside Terrace** complex, designed by Maki Fumihiko (see p.102). Strung along leafy Kyū-yamate-dōri, the various stages of Hillside Terrace were developed over nearly a quarter-century; the **Hillside Gallery** (Tues–Sun 10am–5pm; free), opposite the Danish Embassy, has interesting modern art exhibitions. Closer to the station are the smart **Daikan'yama Address** and **La Fuente** complexes, where you'll find more groovy boutiques and ritzy restaurants and cafés.

Meguro

The 500-metre walk between Ebisu Garden Place and Meguro Station takes you past a curious building with a giant red ball on its roof; it's a driving school. Once at Meguro Station follow the road southwest downhill, towards the towering complex of **Meguro Gajōen** (℡03/5434-3920, Ⓦwww.megurogajoen.co.jp), which replaced the original wedding hall, built at the turn of the century and known as Ryūgū-jō (Fairytale Dragon Palace). Something of the old wedding hall's fantastic nature remains in the many restored painted wooden carvings (huge *ukiyo-e*-style panoramas of kimonoed ladies and samurai warriors) and lacquer and mother-of-pearl inlaid scenes of flowers and birds, culled from the old building, which now decorate the enormous interior – big enough to host some twenty-odd weddings simultaneously. Visit at a weekend and the place buzzes with bridal parties. The complex has a hotel and several pricey restaurants, including a thatched farmhouse surrounded by a lush garden.

Return to Meguro-dōri and walk a few blocks further west across the Meguro-gawa and up the hill just beyond Yamate-dōri to reach the quirky **Meguro Parasitological Museum** (Tues–Sun 10am–5pm; free; ℡03/3716-1264). Any ideas you had of Japan being a healthy place to live will quickly be dispelled by these two floors of exhibits on parasites, which emphasize the dangers of creepy-crawlies in uncooked food. Exhibits include record-breaking tapeworms (one is 8.8m long), pickled in jars, along with some gruesome photographs of past victims, including one poor fellow whose swollen testicles scrape the ground.

Tokyo Metropolitan Teien Art Museum and the National Park for Nature Study

Heading east from Meguro Station along Meguro-dōri, past the raised Shuto Expressway, brings you to the elegant **Tokyo Metropolitan Teien Art Museum** (10am–6pm; closed second and fourth Wed of the month; entrance fee depends on the exhibition; ℡03/3443-0201, Ⓦwww.teien-art-museum.ne.jp). This Art Deco building was the former home of Prince Asaka Yasuhiko, Emperor Hirohito's uncle, who lived in Paris for three years during the 1920s, where he developed a taste for the European style. It's worth popping into for the gorgeous interior decoration and landscaped grounds with Japanese gardens, pond and tea-ceremony house (entry to gardens only is ¥200).

Next to the museum's grounds is the **National Park for Nature Study** (Tues–Sun 9am–4pm, May–Aug until 5pm; ¥200; ℡03/3441-7176, Ⓦwww.ins.kahaku.go.jp). This spacious park is an attempt to preserve the original natural features of the countryside before Edo was settled and developed into Tokyo. It partially succeeds – among the eight thousand trees in the park there are some that have been growing for five hundred years; frogs can be heard croaking amid the grass beside the marshy ponds; and the whole place is a bird-spotter's paradise. The best thing about the park is that entry at any one time is limited to three hundred people, making it one of the few public areas in Tokyo where you can really escape the crowds.

An alternative access point for the National Park for Nature Study is Shirokanedai Station, on the Namboku and Toei Mita subway lines.

Happōen and the Hatakeyama Collection

Shirokanedai Station is also the handiest jumping-off point for the lovely **Happōen** (daily 10am–5pm; free). The garden's name means "beautiful from any angle" and, despite the addition of a modern wedding hall on one side, this is still true. A renowned adviser to the shogunate, Hikozaemon Okubo, lived here during the early seventeenth century, although most of the garden's design dates from the early twentieth century when a business tycoon bought up the land, built a classical Japanese villa (still standing by the garden's entrance) and gave the gardens their present name. Take a turn through its twisting pathways and you'll pass two 100-year-old bonsai trees, a stone lantern said to have been carved eight hundred years ago by the Heike warrior Taira-no Munekiyo, and a central pond. Nestling amid the trees is the delightful **teahouse** (daily 11am–5pm; ¥800), where ladies in kimono will serve you *matcha* and *okashi*. At weekends the whole scene is enlivened by many smartly dressed wedding parties, lining up for group photos against the verdant backdrop.

Around 600m south of Happōen, in the midst of a quiet residential area, is another pretty Japanese garden overlooked by the formal *kaiseki-ryōri* restaurant *Hannya-en* (☎03/3441-1256) and the **Hatakeyama Collection** (Tues–Sun: April–Sept 10am–5pm; Oct–March 10am-4.30pm; ¥500; ☎03/3447-5787, Ⓦwww.ebara.co.jp/hatakeyama). Devoted to the art of the tea ceremony, this compact but appealing museum houses the collection of business magnate Hatakeyama Issei, who made his fortune manufacturing waste incinerators and pumps. Hatakeyama had exquisite taste and his collection contains many lovely pieces, including implements used in the tea ceremony and works of art. Hatakeyama also designed the building, which reflects the structure of a traditional teahouse, albeit on a much larger scale. Tea (¥400) is served in the exhibition hall until thirty minutes before closing.

Shinagawa

East of Meguro is the transport and hotel hub of **Shinagawa**, the location of one of the original checkpoints on the Tōkaidō, the major highway into Edo during the reign of the shoguns. Heading east from the Hatakeyama Collection, cross the busy main road, Sakurada-dōri, and keep going till you reach the compound containing the three *Prince* hotels. The hotels are built on the combined grounds of three imperial palaces, sold off after World War II; it's worth ducking into the *Takanawa Prince Hotel* and walking through the gardens, parts of which are unchanged since they were the property of the emperor's family, to see the **Kannon-dō**, a Kamakura-period temple rebuilt here in the 1954, and the neighbouring **Ean Tea House**, sadly not open to public viewing unless you can afford the ¥200,000 charged to rent it out for a meal or tea ceremony.

Down the hill is **Shinagawa Station**; the opening of a new Shinkansen station here in 2003 is revitalizing the area, mainly east of the tracks, where a clutch of modern towers reach for the sky, though none is particularly interesting to visit.

Around 800m south of Shinagawa Station, tucked into a quiet residential area, is a 1938 Bauhaus-style house which now contains the eclectic **Hara Museum of Contemporary Art** (Tues–Sun 11am–5pm, Wed until 8pm;

The 47 rōnin

Celebrated in Kabuki and *bunraku* plays, as well as on film, *Chūshingura* is a true story of honour, revenge and loyalty. In 1701, a young *daimyō*, Asano Takumi, became embroiled in a fatal argument in the shogun's court with his teacher and fellow lord Kira Yoshinaka. Asano had lost face in his performance of court rituals and, blaming his mentor for his lax tuition, drew his sword within the castle walls and attacked Kira. Although Kira survived, the shogun, on hearing of this breach of etiquette, ordered Asano to commit *seppuku*, the traditional form of suicide, which he did.

Their lord having been disgraced, Asano's loyal retainers, the **rōnin** – or master-less samurai – vowed revenge. On December 14, 1702, the 47 *rōnin*, lead by **Ōishi Kuranosuke**, stormed Kira's villa (the remains of which are in Ryōgoku), cut off his head and paraded it through Edo in triumph before placing it on Asano's grave in Sengaku-ji. Although their actions were in line with the samurai creed, the shogun had no option but to order the *rōnin*'s deaths. All 47 committed *seppuku* on February 14, 1703, including Ōishi's 15-year-old son. They were buried with Asano in Sengaku-ji, and today their graves are still wreathed in the smoke from the bundles of incense placed by their gravestones.

¥1000; ☏03/3445-0651, ⊕www.haramuseum.or.jp).The museum's small permanent collection includes some funky installations, such as *Rondo*, by Morimura Yasumasa, whose self-portrait occupies the downstairs toilet. The building itself, designed by Watanabe Jin, the architect responsible for Ueno's Tokyo National Museum and the Wakō department store in Ginza, is worth a look, as are the tranquil sculpture gardens overlooked by the museum's pleasant café.

While you're in this area you may care to drop by the **Sony Museum** (Mon–Fri 10am–5pm; free; ☏03/5448-4455, ⊕www.sony.co.jp/eco), at the Sony headquarters a five-minute walk northwest of the Hara Museum. It's fascinating to see how far devices such as the radios and recording equipment displayed here have developed in such a short period of time. For those interested in recycling there's also an interesting Environmental Exhibition Room, which details the company's environmental outlook and practices. From the museum it's a short walk west along Yatsuyama-dōri to Gotanda Station on the Yamanote line.

Sengaku-ji

Around a kilometre north of Shinagawa is the famous temple of **Sengaku-ji**, home to the graves of **Asano Takumi** and his **47 rōnin** (see box above); the closest station is Sengaku-ji on the Toei Asakusa line. Most of the temple was destroyed during the war and has since been rebuilt, but a striking gate dating from 1836 and decorated with a metalwork dragon remains. The statue and grave of **Ōishi Kuranosuke**, the avenging leader of the 47 *rōnin*, are in the temple grounds. A **museum** (daily 9am–4pm; ¥200; ☏03/3441-5560, ⊕www.sengakuji.or.jp) to the left of the main building contains the personal belongings of the *rōnin* and their master Asano, as well as a receipt for the severed head of Kira.

Bayside Tokyo

So thoroughly urban is Tokyo that it comes as something of a shock to many visitors (and some residents) that the city is actually beside the sea. Yet many of the *ukiyo-e* masterpieces of Hokusai and Hiroshige depict waterside scenes around **Tokyo Bay**, and several of the city's prime attractions are to be found here. The teeming fish market of **Tsukiji** provides a rowdy early-morning antidote to the serenity of the nearby traditional gardens, **Hama Rikyū Teien**. East of the market is **Tsukudashima**, a pocket of traditional wooden homes and shops dating from the Edo period, while, to the south, across the Rainbow Bridge, lie the modern waterfront city and pleasure parks of **Odaiba**, built on vast islands of reclaimed land.

Around 9km east from Tsukiji across Tokyo Bay, some of the city's older recreational facilities still pull in the crowds. The open spaces of **Kasai Rinkai-kōen** are a good place to catch the sea breeze, but the park's greatest attraction is its aquarium, and particularly the doughnut-shaped tuna tank, where silver shoals race round you at dizzying speeds. From the park, the Cinderella spires of **Tokyo Disney Resort** are clearly visible to the west. Though not everyone's cup of tea, this little bit of America can make a hugely entertaining day out, even if you're not travelling with kids.

Bayside Tokyo

Hama Rikyū Teien	*Hama Rikyū Teien*	浜離宮庭園
Kasai Rinkai-kōen	*Kasai Rinkai-kōen*	葛西臨海公園
Museum of Maritime Science	*Fune no Kagakukan*	船の科学館
Odaiba	*Odaiba*	お台場
Palette Town	*Pareto Toun*	パレットタウン
Rainbow Bridge	*Reinbō Buriji*	レインボーブリッジ
Sumiyoshi-jinja	*Sumiyoshi-jinja*	住吉神社
Tokyo Bay	*Tōkyō-wan*	東京湾
Tokyo Big Sight	*Tōkyō Bigu Saito*	東京ビッグサイト
Tokyo Central Wholesale Market	*Tōkyō Chūō Oroshiuri Ichiba*	中央卸売市場
Tokyo Disneyland	*Tōkyō Dizuniirando*	東京ディズニーランド
Tsukiji Hongan-ji	*Tsukiji Hongan-ji*	築地本願寺
Tsukudashima	*Tsukudashima*	佃島

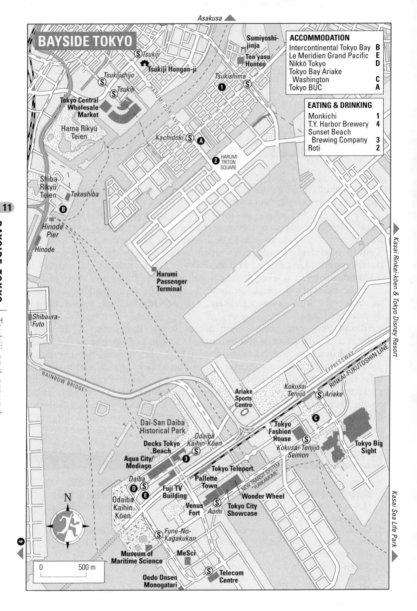

BAYSIDE TOKYO

ACCOMMODATION
Intercontinental Tokyo Bay   B
Le Meridien Grand Pacific   E
Nikkō Tokyo   D
Tokyo Bay Ariake
  Washington   C
Tokyo BUC   A

EATING & DRINKING
Monkichi   1
T.Y. Harbor Brewery   4
Sunset Beach
  Brewing Company   3
Roti   2

Asakusa

Sumiyoshi-jinja
Ten'yasu Honten
Tsukiji
Tsukiji Hongan-ji
Tsukijishijo
Tsukiji
Tsukishima
Tokyo Central Wholesale Market
Hama Rikyū Teien
Kachidoki
HARUMI TRITON SQUARE
Shiba Rikyū Teien
Takeshiba
Hinode Pier
Hinode
Harumi Passenger Terminal
Shibaura-Futo
RAINBOW BRIDGE
EXPRESSWAY
RINKAI-FUKUTOSHIN LINE
Ariake Sports Centre
Kokusai-Tenjijō
Ariake
Dai-San Daiba Historical Park
Odaiba Kaihin-Kōen
Decks Tokyo Beach
Aqua City/ Mediage
Daiba
Fuji TV Building
Odaiba Kaihin Kōen
Venus Fort
Aomi
Fune-No-Kagakukan
Museum of Maritime Science
MeSci
Oedo Onsen Monogatari
Telecom Centre
Tokyo Fashion House
Kokusai-Tenjijō Seimon
Tokyo Big Sight
Tokyo Teleport
Pallette Town
NEW TRANSIT SYSTEM "YURIKAMOME"
Wonder Wheel
Tokyo City Showcase

N

0   500 m

Kasai Rinkai-kōen & Tokyo Disney Resort

Kasai Sea Life Park

11

BAYSIDE TOKYO | Tsukiji and around

Tsukiji and around

A dawn visit to the vast **Tokyo Central Wholesale Market**, on the edge of Tokyo Bay, some 2km southeast of the Imperial Palace, is one of the highlights of any trip to Tokyo and a must for raw-fish fans, who can breakfast on the

124

freshest slices of sashimi and sushi. Covering 56 acres of reclaimed land south of Ginza, the market is popularly known as **Tsukiji** (Reclaimed Land), and has been here since 1923. The area it stands on was cleared in the wake of the disastrous Furisode (Long Sleeves) Fire of 1657. Tokugawa Ieyasu had the debris shovelled into the marshes at the edge of Ginza, thus providing his lords with space for their mansions and gardens. In the early years of the Meiji era, after the *daimyō* had been kicked out of Tokyo, the city authorities built a special residential area for Western expats here. The market relocated to this area from Nihombashi after the 1923 earthquake. There's talk of another move around 2015, and various locations across the bay are being debated.

Emerging from Tsukiji subway on the Hibiya line, you'll first notice the **Tsukiji Hongan-ji**, one of the largest and most Indian-looking of Tokyo's Buddhist temples. Pop inside to see the intricately carved golden altar and cavernous interior with room for a thousand worshippers. From the temple, the most direct route to the **market** is to continue along Shin-Ōhashi-dōri, crossing Harumi-dōri (the route from Ginza) and past the row of grocers and noodle bars. The sprawling bulk of the market is in the next block. At around 7am, Tokyo's restaurateurs and food retailers pick their way through the day's catch, which is put on sale at 1600 different wholesalers' stalls under the crescent-shaped hangar's roof.

Sloshing through the water-cleansed pathways, dodging the mini-forklift trucks that shift the produce around, and being surrounded by piled crates of seafood – some of it still alive – is what a visit to Tsukiji is all about. If you get peckish, head for the outer market area (Jōgai Ichiba), which is crammed with sushi stalls and noodle bars servicing the sixty thousand people who pass through here each day. Good choices include *Daiwa Zushi* and *Sushi-bun*, both open from 5.30am, and actually within the market, while *Tatsuzushi* and the more expensive *Sushisei* are in the block of shops between the market and Tsukiji Hongan-ji. Expect to pay around ¥2000 for a set course.

The closest **subway station** to the market is Tsukiji-Shijō (on the Ōedo line), but if you want to witness the frantic auctions that start at 5am you'll have to catch a taxi or walk to the market. If you can't make it that early, it's still worth coming here; the action in the outer markets continues through to midday.

Hama Rikyū Teien

The contrast between bustling Tsukiji and the traditional garden of **Hama Rikyū Teien** (Tues–Sun 9am–4.30pm; ¥300), less than a ten-minute walk east, couldn't be more acute. This beautifully designed park once belonged to the

Tsukiji facts and figures

Every day, bar Sundays and public holidays, 2300 tonnes of fish are delivered to Tsukiji from far-flung corners of the earth. Over four hundred different types of seafood come under the hammer, including eels from Taiwan, salmon from Santiago and tuna from Tasmania. But, as the market's official title indicates, fish is not the only item on sale at Tsukiji, which also deals in meat, fruit and vegetables.

The auctions, held at the back of the market, aren't officially open to the public, but no one will stop you slipping in quietly to watch the buyers and sellers gesticulating wildly over polystyrene crates of squid, sea urchins, crab and the like. The highlight is the sale of rock-solid frozen tuna, looking like steel torpedoes, all labelled with yellow stickers indicating their weight and country of origin. Depending on their quality, each tuna sells for between ¥600,000 and ¥1 million.

shogunate, who hunted ducks here. These days the ducks, protected inside the garden's nature reserve, are no longer used for target practice and only have to watch out for the large number of cats that wander the idly twisting pathways. There are three ponds, the largest spanned by a trellis-covered bridge that leads to a floating teahouse, *Nakajima-no-Chaya* (¥500 for tea). Next to the entrance is a sprawling, 300-year-old pine tree and a manicured lawn dotted with sculpted, stunted trees. One of the best times of year to come here is in early spring, when lilac wisteria hangs in fluffy bunches from trellises around the central pond. From the Tokyo Bay side of the garden, you'll get a view across to the Rainbow Bridge, and can see the floodgate which regulates how much sea water flows in and out of this pond with the tides. By far the nicest way of approaching the gardens is to take a ferry from Asakusa, down the Sumida-gawa (see p.27 for details).

Tsukudashima and around

Another rewarding diversion from Tsukiji, across the Sumida-gawa, is **Tsukudashima** (meaning "island of rice fields"), a tiny enclave of Edo-period houses and shops clustered around a backwater spanned by a dinky red bridge. Sheltering in the shadow of the modern River City 21 tower blocks, the area has a history stretching back to 1613, when a group of Ōsaka fishermen were settled on the island by the shogun. In addition to providing food for the castle, the fishermen were expected to report on any suspicious comings and goings in the bay. For their spiritual protection, they built themselves the delightful **Sumiyoshi-jinja**, dedicated to the god of the sea. The water well beside the shrine's *torii* has a roof with eaves decorated with exquisite carvings of scenes from the fishermen's lives. Every three years, on the first weekend in August, the shrine hosts the Sumiyoshi Matsuri **festival**, during which a special *mikoshi* (portable shrine) is dowsed in water as it is paraded through the streets; this is symbolic of the real dunking it would once have had in the river.

To reach Tsukudashima on foot, head for the Tsukuda-Ōhashi bridge, a ten-minute walk from Tsukiji subway station, past St Luke's Hospital. The area is easily spotted on the left side of the island as you leave the bridge and shouldn't take more than thirty minutes to explore. The closest **subway station** is Tsukishima, on the Yūrakuchō and Ōedo lines.

While you're out here, and for a complete contrast, you may also like to take a swing through another of Tokyo's new mini-city developments, **Triton Square** at Harumi (the closest subway station is Kachidoki, one stop south of Tsukishima on the Ōedo line), which boasts a pleasant riverside location and some relaxing places to sit outside and enjoy food or drink (including a branch of the popular Western-style restaurant *Roti*, see p.160). From here keep walking southwest and you'll eventually hit the end of the man-made island and a

Tsukadashima cuisine

Tsukudashima is famous for a couple of types of food. **Tsukudani** are delicious morsels of seaweed and fish preserved in a mixture of soy sauce, salt or sugar – eighteen different types of this speciality are served up at *Tensuya Honten* (see Shopping, p.207). Heading southwest from Tsukushima station you'll also find a shopping street packed with **okonomiyaki** and **monja** restaurants. If you want to chow down on these very Tokyo styles of batter pancake, then head for *Monkichi* (3-8-10 Tsukushima ☎03/3531-2380).

patch of open land beside Harumi Passenger Terminal, where long-distance ferries from all parts of Japan dock.

Odaiba

Returning to Tsukiji and heading west towards the raised Shuto Expressway will bring you to Shimbashi Station and the start of the Yurikamome monorail line out to **Odaiba**, an island of reclaimed land in Tokyo Bay. Odaiba means "cannon emplacements", referring to the defences set up in the bay by the shogun in 1853 to protect the city from Commodore Perry's threatening Black Ships (see p.272). The remains of the two cannon emplacements are now dwarfed by the huge landfill site – Rinkai Fukutoshin, of which Odaiba is a part – on which the Metropolitan Government set about constructing a 21st-century city in 1988. The economic slump and spiralling development costs slowed the project down and, when the Rainbow Bridge linking Odaiba to the city opened in 1993, the area was still a series of empty lots.

A decade on, Odaiba is yet to reach its full potential, but is still worth visiting; futuristic buildings linked by the zippy monorail, a man-made beach, parks and architectural wonders have turned the island into such a local hit that at weekends the monorail and shopping plazas are swamped with day-trippers. For overseas visitors its principal highlights are a couple of excellent museums and a raucous new onsen complex. At night, the illuminated Rainbow Bridge, giant technicolour ferris wheel and twinkling towers of the Tokyo skyline make Odaiba a romantic spot – you'll see plenty of canoodling couples staring wistfully at the glittering panorama.

The easiest way of reaching Odaiba is on the **Yurikamome monorail**, which arcs up to the Rainbow Bridge on a splendid circular line and stops at all the area's major sites, terminating at Ariake Station. Buying a one-day ticket for the monorail (¥800) is a good idea if you intend to see all the island – walking across Odaiba is a long slog. In addition, **trains** on the Rinkai line, linked with the JR Saikyo line, run to the central Tokyo-Teleport Station on Odaiba. **Buses** from Shinagawa Station, southwest of the bay, cross the Rainbow Bridge and run as far as the Maritime Museum, stopping at Odaiba Kaihin-kōen on the way. Alternatively, you can take a **ferry** from Hinode Sanbashi to either Ariake or the Maritime Museum via Harumi and Odaiba Kaihin-kōen – the journey costs just ¥520 and doubles as a quick, cut-price cruise of Tokyo Bay.

The following description of sights starts at the far south side of Odaiba and ends with a walk back across the Rainbow Bridge – easily the highlight of any trip out to this ultra-modern area.

Tokyo Big Sight and Palette Town

One stop from the monorail terminus at Ariake is the enormous and striking Tokyo International Exhibition Centre, better known as the **Tokyo Big Sight** (☎03/5530-1111, ⓦwww.bigsight.jp). Its entrance is composed of four huge inverted pyramids, and in front stands a 15.5-metre sculpture of a red-handled saw, sticking out of the ground as if left behind by some absent-minded giant. This is one of Japan's largest venues for business fairs and exhibitions; check their website for details of events, which include huge antique fairs and the twice-yearly Design Festa (see p.110).

Aomi Station is the stop for the vast **Palette Town** shopping and entertainment complex (ⓦ www.palette-town.com), which offers something for almost everyone. On the east side is potentially the most interesting piece of the package, the **Toyota City Showcase** (daily 11am–9pm; free), displaying Toyota's current range of cars. Enthusiasts will enjoy just strolling around this huge showroom, and you can also take part in the fuel-injected fun by signing up for various activities such as designing your own car using CAD technology, taking a ride in an electric vehicle (¥200) or a virtual-reality drive (¥500), or even selecting one of Toyota's current models and taking it for a test drive (¥300). Given the crowds, it's best to make advance bookings for some of these activities (ⓣ0070-800-849-000, ⓦ www.megaweb.gr.jp). Just behind the showroom are some more high-tech diversions, the best of which is the **Wonder Wheel** (daily 10am–10pm; ¥900), a candy-coloured ferris wheel, 115m in diameter, which takes sixteen minutes to make a full circuit.

The upper floor on the west side of Palette Town is dominated by **Venus Fort**, described as a "theme park for ladies" but basically a shopping mall designed as a mock Italian city, complete with piazza, fountains and Roman-style statues – even the ceiling is painted and lit to resemble a perfect Mediterranean sky from dawn to dusk. Most of the theme-style restaurants and shops here are totally bland (the exception is the Lab Labo area, where young designers offer their interior design and accessory creations), but the complex is worth swinging through if only to gawk at the sheer lunacy of it all. Downstairs is Sun Walk, a more restrained shopping mall, at the back of which you'll find the **History Garage** (daily 11am–10pm; free), displaying a good range of classic cars and including a gallery with around three thousand miniature cars and an extensive range of car-related books.

MeSci and the Museum of Maritime Science

West of Palette Town is a fat finger of reclaimed land partly covered by Tokyo's container port and overlooked by the **Telecom Centre**, a wannabe clone of Paris's Grande Arche at La Défense. The centre has a viewing platform on its 21st floor (¥600), but this can safely be skipped in favour of Tokyo's best science museum, the National Museum of Emerging Science and Innovation, or **MeSci** (daily except Tues 10am–5pm; ¥500; ⓣ03/3570-9151, ⓦ www.miraikan.jst.go.jp), which is chock-full of fascinating high-tech displays. Here you can learn about the latest in robot technology, superconductivity (including maglev trains), the environment, space and much more, as well as checking out the weather around the world by looking up at a giant sphere covered with one million light-emitting diodes and showing the globe as it appears from space that day. All displays have English explanations and there are also plenty of English-speaking volunteer guides on hand. Directly south of MeSci is the new spa complex, **Ōedo Onsen Monogatari** (see p.65 for details).

From MeSci it's a short walk to the excellent **Museum of Maritime Science** (Mon–Fri 10am–5pm, Sat & Sun 10am–6pm; ⓣ03/5550-1111, ⓦ www.funenokagakukan.or.jp), housed in a concrete reproduction of a 60,000-tonne cruise ship. The exhibits include many detailed model boats and the engines of a giant ship. Docked outside are a couple of real boats: the *Sōya*, which undertook scientific missions to the South Pole, and the *Yōtei Marine*, a ferry refitted as an exhibition space. Admission to the two ships only is ¥600; for the museum and the *Yōtei Marine* ¥700; for everything ¥1000. Within the

△ Wonder wheel

museum grounds you'll also find a couple of lighthouses, submarines, a flying boat and two open-air swimming pools (open July 18–Aug 31; ¥2800 including admission to the museum).

Head around the waterfront from the museum, past the curiously shaped triangular tower (an air vent for the road tunnel that goes under Tokyo Bay) to reach a park, **Odaiba Kaihin-kōen**. Across the bay, the lines of red cranes at the container port look like giraffes at feeding time.

The beach to Rainbow Bridge

As you turn the corner of the island and the Rainbow Bridge comes into view, Odaiba's man-made **beach** begins. As Japanese beaches go, it's not bad, but it's best avoided on sunny weekends, when you'll see more raw flesh than sand. Fronting the beach are the **Aqua City** and **Decks Tokyo Beach** shopping malls. Apart from trendy shops and restaurants, the former includes the Mediage multiplex cinema, while the latter has its own brewery and **Joypolis** (daily 10am–11.30pm; ¥500 admission only), a multi-storey arcade filled with Sega's interactive entertainment technology.

Next to the mall, a surreal aura hangs over Tange Kenzō's **Fuji TV Building**, a futuristic block with a huge metal sphere suspended in its middle – it looks like it's been made from a giant Meccano set. You can pay to head up to the 25th-floor **viewing platform** (Tues–Sun 10am–8pm; ¥500) or do the sensible thing and put the cash towards a cocktail in the Sky Lounge at the top of the neighbouring *Meridien Grand Pacific Hotel*, where the view is thrown in for free.

From the Sunset Beach row of restaurants beside the Decks Mall, you can walk across onto one of the shogun's gun emplacement islands, now a public park, or continue for an exhilarating walk along the **Rainbow Bridge**. This 918-metre-long, single-span suspension bridge has two levels, the lower for the waterfront road and the monorail, and the upper for the Metropolitan Expressway. On both sides is a pedestrian promenade linking the **observation rooms** (daily: April–Oct 10am–9pm; Jan–March, Nov & Dec 10am–6pm; ¥300) in the anchorages at either end of the bridge. The walk along the bridge takes about forty minutes and provides magnificent views across the bay, even as far as Mount Fuji if the sky is clear. One minute's walk from the exit from the shore-side observation room is the station for the monorail back to Shimbashi.

West across Tokyo Bay

West of Odaiba, older blocks of reclaimed land sporting dormitory towns, golf links and other recreational facilities jut out into Tokyo Bay. The prime attractions are **Kasai Rinkai-kōen**, a seaside park boasting one of Tokyo's biggest aquariums and a birdwatching centre, and the enormously popular **Tokyo Disneyland**. Though you probably won't have time to visit both in one day, these places are at adjacent stops on the JR Keiyō line from Tokyo Station. Coming from Odaiba, you can pick up the Keiyō line at Shin-Kiba Station.

Kasai Rinkai-kōen

Lying between its JR station and the sea, the flat expanse of **Kasai Rinkai-kōen** (open 24hr; free) isn't the most attractive of landscapes, but there's more to it than first appears. For many Tokyo families this is a favourite weekend spot – for picnicking, cycling or summer swimming from its small, crescent-shaped beach – while bird enthusiasts ogle waterbirds and waders in the well-designed bird sanctuary. The park's biggest draw, however, is its large aquarium, the **Tokyo Sea Life Park** (Tues–Sun 9.30am–5pm, last entry 4pm; ¥800), set under a glass-and-steel dome overlooking the sea. The first thing you meet coming down the escalators is two vast tanks of tuna and sharks, the aquarium's highlight; go down again and you stand in the middle of this fishy world, surrounded by 2200 tonnes of water. Smaller tanks showcase sea life from around the world, from flashy tropical butterfly fish and paper-thin seahorses to the lumpy mudskippers of Tokyo Bay. Not everyone is here to admire the beauty of the fish – as you walk round, listen out for murmurs of *oishii* (the Japanese equivalent of "delicious!"). The short videos on show in the 3-D theatre are in Japanese only, but worth catching for the visuals.

If you're heading back into central Tokyo from here, one of the nicest ways is to hop on a **ferry** for the 55-minute ride (¥800) via Ariake to Hinode Sanbashi near Hamamatsuchō. Boats leave hourly from the park's western pier, with the last departure at 5pm. See p.27 for further details.

Tokyo Disney Resort

The big daddy of Tokyo's theme parks, **Tokyo Disney Resort** (@www .tokyodisneyresort.co.jp) comprises two separate but adjacent attractions: **Tokyo Disneyland**, a pretty close copy of the Californian original, and the new **DisneySea Park**, a water- and world travel-themed area. The parks are plonked in commuter land a fifteen-minute train ride east of the city centre, and both follow the well-honed Disney formula of theme lands, parades and zany extravaganzas. Few people seem to have a good word for the DisneySea Park, but whatever your preconceptions, it's pretty hard not to have a good time overall.

You'll probably want to devote a whole day to each park to get your money's worth; a one-day "**passport**" for either costs ¥5500; a two-day passport to both parks is ¥9800; there are also a couple of discount passports available for Disneyland only if you enter later in the day. The resort is generally open from 8/9am to 10pm, but hours may vary and the park is occasionally closed for special events, so it's best to check beforehand by phone. The best option is to visit the **Tokyo Disney Resort Ticket Centre** (daily 10am–7pm; ☎03/3595-1777) in Yūrakuchō, where you can pick up an English leaflet and buy your

Tokyo for kids

Tokyo is a fantastic city for entertaining kids, so you needn't worry about bringing the young ones along. There's Disneyland, of course (see above), and the thrill rides at LaQua (see p.64), as well as the wonderful Ghibli Museum, Mitaka (see p.238), a short train ride from Shinjuku. If your children are 6 or under, the National Children's Castle (see p.112) and the Tokyo Metropolitan Children's Hall (see p.117) will keep them occupied for many an hour.

There's a whole swag of educational **museums**, the best ones being Ueno's National Science Museum (see p.86) and Odaiba's MeSci (see p.128), plus Ueno's zoo (see p.84) and the fabulous aquarium at Kasai Seaside Park (see above). See p.209 for a list of **shops** featuring the latest hit toys and Japanese crazes. For more information, the English-language website @www.tokyowithkids.com is an excellent resource.

tickets at the same time; the office is in the Hibiya Mitsui Building near Hibiya subway station.

The gates to Disneyland sit right in front of Maihama Station (on the JR Keiyō line). Inside, you'll find World Bazaar, with its shops and general services (pushchair rentals, bank, lockers and information), followed by the central plaza in front of Cinderella's castle, from where the six theme lands radiate. Tomorrowland's Star Tours and Space Mountain offer the most heart-stopping rides. Next door, DisneySea Park offers an additional 23 water-based attractions spread across seven zones and a grand European-style *Hotel MiraCosta*. A monorail encircles the two sites, stopping near Maihama Station at a shopping complex which is also home to the Art Deco *Disney Ambassador Hotel*, where real addicts can collect complimentary Mickey toiletries before breakfasting with the mouse himself. Expect long queues: Disneyland attracts over thirty thousand visitors per day on average, and many more over weekends and holidays.

Listings

Listings

12

Accommodation

Tokyo offers a wide range of **places to stay**, from first-class hotels to budget dorm bunks. The main difficulty is finding somewhere at an affordable price, particularly if you're on a limited budget or travelling alone. At all price levels, however, security and cleanliness are top-notch, and you'll nearly always find someone who speaks some English.

Whatever your budget, it's wise to **reserve** your first few nights' accommodation before arrival. This is especially true of the cheaper places, which tend to fill up quickly, particularly over national holidays and in late February, when thousands of students head to Tokyo for the university entrance exams. If you do arrive without a reservation, head for Narita Airport's tourist information desk, which handles hotel bookings (see "Arrival", p.22), or the Welcome Inn Reservation Centre (Mon–Fri 9.15–11.30am & 1–4.45pm; ℡03/3211-4201, Ⓦwww.jnto.go.jp), at the Tokyo Tourist Information Centre (see p.19).

What kind of place you stay in will depend on your budget. Basically the choice is between a standard, Western-style **hotel** a traditional family-run **ryokan** (see box overleaf), which is slightly cheaper, a **capsule hotel** (see p.145) and a **youth hostel** (see p.146). For tips on finding **long-term accommodation**, see p.146.

When choosing your **area**, bear in mind that central Tokyo, comprising Ginza, Nihombashi, Hibiya, Akasaka and Roppongi, is largely the domain of expensive, world-class establishments and upmarket business hotels. For cheaper rooms, there's a greater choice in Shinagawa, Shibuya and Shinjuku to the south and east, and especially in Ueno and Ikebukuro in the north. Also in the north, Asakusa is set slightly apart from Tokyo's main thrust, but offers a few well-priced rooms in an appealing area. In the last few years, several top-class establishments have sprung up in Tokyo's new suburban satellites, notably the Odaiba development in Tokyo Bay.

While most places listed below are within easy access of either a **subway** or **train station**, remember that trains stop running around midnight; if you're a night owl, aim to stay near one of the entertainment districts to avoid taxi fares. Our listings below show the nearest station for each hotel.

Accommodation taxes

There are various additional **taxes** to look out for when paying for accommodation in Tokyo (as throughout the rest of the country). Top-end hotels levy a service charge of ten to fifteen percent, while if your room costs over ¥15,000 per night (including service charges), an extra three percent will be added. In addition, if your room costs over ¥10,000 per night, there's a Tokyo Metropolitan Government tax to be paid of an additional ¥100 per night (or ¥200 per night if your room costs over ¥15,000).

All accommodation in this book has been graded according to the following **price codes**, which refer to the **cheapest double or twin room available** including taxes; note that rates may increase during peak holiday periods, in particular around Christmas and New Year, the Golden Week (April 29–May 5) and Obon (the week around August 15). In the case of hostels providing **dormitory accommodation**, we've given the price per person. Most hotels have **single rates**, which can be anything from half to three-quarters the double rate. Accommodation at some business hotels consists mainly of single rooms; at these places, we've also given the single rate, as well as a price code.

- ① under ¥6000
- ② ¥6000–8000
- ③ ¥8000–10,000
- ④ ¥10,000–12,000
- ⑤ ¥12,000–15,000
- ⑥ ¥15,000–20,000
- ⑦ ¥20,000–30,000
- ⑧ ¥30,000–40,000
- ⑨ over ¥40,000

Hotels and ryokan

Whether in the de luxe or business categories, **hotels** generally provide Western-style rooms with en-suite bathrooms, TV, phone and air-conditioning. In terms of room design many hotels are pretty characterless, and don't expect much space either; thanks to the city's notoriously high real-estate prices, everything is packed in with the greatest efficiency. A handful of new design-conscious hotels aside, you'll find far better value and more atmosphere at a traditional, family-run **ryokan**.

Staying in a ryokan

One of the highlights of a visit to Tokyo is staying in a **ryokan**, a family-run inn where you'll be expected to follow local custom from the moment you arrive.

Just inside the front door there's usually a row of **slippers** ready for you to change into. The bedrooms have rice-straw matting (tatami) on the floor and little else beyond a low table and dresser, plus a few cushions. The **bedding** is stored behind sliding doors during the day and laid out in the evening. In top-class establishments this is done for you, but elsewhere be prepared to tackle your own. There'll be a mattress (which goes straight on the tatami) with a sheet, a soft quilt to sleep under and a pillow stuffed with rice husks.

All ryokan provide a *yukata*, a loose cotton robe tied with a belt, and a short jacket in cold weather. The *yukata* can be worn in bed, when going to the bathroom and for wandering about the ryokan – many Japanese take an outdoor evening stroll in their *yukata* and wooden shoes (*geta*), kept in the entrance hall. It's important always to wrap the left side over the right; the opposite is used to dress bodies at a funeral. The traditional Japanese bath (*furo*) is a luxurious experience with its own set of rules (see p.40). There are usually separate **bathrooms** for men and women. If there's only one, either there'll be designated times for males and females, or guests take it in turn – it's perfectly acceptable for couples and families to bathe together, though there's not usually a lot of space.

Evening **meals** tend to be early, at 6pm or 7pm. Smarter ryokan generally serve meals in your room, while communal dining is the norm in cheaper places. **At night**, some ryokan lock their doors pretty early, so check before going out – they may let you have a key.

Akasaka and around

Akasaka Prince Hotel
赤坂プリンスホテル
1-2 Kioichō, Chiyoda-ku ⊤ 03/3234-1111,
Ⓦ www.princehotels.co.jp/english. Akasaka-
Mitsuke Station. See map p.68. Forty-storey
Tange Kenzō-designed tower with stunning
views, though the cool grey and white
interior is a bit chilly. The rooms will suit
fans of retro 1970s decoration. ❽

Akasaka Yōkō Hotel
赤坂陽光ホテル
6-14-12 Akasaka, Minato-ku ⊤ 03/3586-4050,
Ⓦ www.yokohotel.co.jp. Akasaka Station. See
map p.68. Pleasant mid-range hotel in a red-
brick building with a smart marble lobby
and simple rooms. The singles rates
(¥9500) are reasonable for the area. ❺

ANA Hotel Tokyo
東京全日空ホテル
1-12-33 Akasaka, Minato-ku ⊤ 03/3505-1111,
Ⓦ www.anahotels.com/tokyo. Tameiki-Sannō
Station. See map p.68. Conveniently located
midway between Akasaka and Roppongi,
this stylish hotel has attentive staff, a swimming pool, spacious public areas and good
views, especially towards Tokyo Tower. ❽

Asia Centre of Japan
ホテルアジア会館
8-10-32 Akasaka, Minato-ku ⊤ 03/3402-6111,
Ⓦ www.asiacenter.or.jp. Aoyama Itchōme or
Nogizaka stations. See map p.68. Recently
upgraded and a bargain for this area, so it
fills up quickly. The small, neat rooms are
Western style, and cheaper if you forego
en-suite bathrooms. Also has an
inexpensive café and good-value single
rates from ¥7800. ❺

Capitol Tōkyū Hotel
キャピトル東急ホテル
12-10-3 Nagatachō, Chiyoda-ku
⊤ 03/3581-4511, Ⓦ www.capitoltokyo
.com/english/index.html. Kokkaigijido-Mae
Station. See map p.68. Adjacent to
Hie-jinja, the flagship hotel of the Tōkyū
chain blends Japanese and Western styles
successfully, though some might find the
overall ambience a little dark. There's a
small traditional garden, an outdoor pool
in the summer and several restaurants
and bars. ❽

New Ōtani
ニューオータニ
4-1 Kioichō, Chiyoda-ku ⊤ 03/3265-1111,
Ⓦ www.newotanihotels.com. Akasaka-Mitsuke
Station. See map p.68. Mammoth hotel which
is a tourist attraction in its own right for its
traditional gardens. It also sports a staggering 36 restaurants and bars, a tea-ceremony room, art gallery, swimming pools,
tennis courts, and much more. Some
rooms have been gaudily refurbished, but
all are comfortable and most have great
views. ❼

Hotel Ōkura
ホテルオークラ
2-10-4 Toranomon, Minato-ku ⊤ 03/3582-0111,
Ⓦ www.hotelokura.co.jp/tokyo. Kamiyachō
Station. See map p.68. One of Tokyo's most
prestigious hotels, with a classic 1950s-
style lobby with low chairs and garden view,
although the guest-room decor lags behind
that of Tokyo's top contemporary design-
conscious hotels. ❼

Asakusa and around

Andon Ryokan
行燈旅館
2-34-10 Nihonzutsumi, Taitō-ku
⊤ 03/3873-8611, Ⓦ www.andon.co.jp. Minowa
Station. See map p.76. Tokyo's first designer
ryokan, this enticing place is set in a
traditional area five minutes' walk from
Minowa Station in an ultra-modern
building which glows invitingly like a
lantern. The tatami rooms are small and
all share common bathrooms, but come
equipped with DVD players. There's also a
jacuzzi spa you can book for private dips,
free Internet access and super-friendly
English-speaking staff. ❷

Asakusa Central Hotel
浅草セントラルホテル
Asakusa Sentoraru Hoteru
1-5-3 Asakusa, Taitō-ku ⊤ 03/3847-2222,
Ⓦ www.pelican.co.jp. Asakusa Station. See map
p.76. Modest business hotel which rises
above the competition thanks to its convenient location on Asakusa's main street,
its English-speaking staff and its small
but well-appointed rooms, all with TV and
telephone. ❹

Asakusa View Hotel
浅草ビューホテル
3-17-1 Nishi-Asakusa, Taitō-ku ⊤ 03/3847-1111,
Ⓦ www.viewhotels.co.jp/asakusa. Tawaramachi
Station. See map p.76.. Asakusa's grandest
hotel, all sparkling marble and chandeliers.
The rooms are less memorable than the
public areas, but there are great views from

the higher floors. The top-floor bar does a reasonable buffet lunch, and there's also a shopping arcade and swimming pool (a pricey ¥3000). **7**

New Kōyō
ニュー紅陽
2-26-13 Nihonzutsumi, Taitō-ku
ⓣ03/3873-0343, ⓦ www.newkoyo.com.
Minami-Senju Station. See map p.76.. This former day-labourers' flop house is well off the beaten track but popular among budget travellers and job-hunters for its ultra-cheap singles for just ¥2500 (there are no doubles). It's worth paying a little extra for a four-mat room (¥2700), though even these are pretty cell-like. There are reasonably clean communal baths, toilets and kitchen, plus coin laundry, Internet access and bike rental.

Ryokan Shigetsu
旅館指月
1-31-11 Asakusa, Taitō-ku ⓣ03/3843-2345,
ⓦ www.shigetsu.com. Asakusa Station. See map p.76.. Just off bustling Nakamise-dōri, this elegant ryokan is definitely the place to stay in Asakusa. Inside is a world of kimono-clad receptionists and tinkling *shamisen* music, but it's surprisingly affordable, with a choice of small Western- or Japanese-style rooms, all en suite. There's also a Japanese bath on the top floor with views over temple roofs. **6**

Hotel Sky Court Asakusa
ホテルスカイコート浅草
6-35-8 Asakusa, Taitō-ku ⓣ03/3875-4411,
ⓦ www1.ocn.ne.jp/~hsky21/Skycourt_Asakusa .htm. Asakusa Station. See map p.76.. Standard business hotel ten minutes' walk north of Asakusa Station; Hostelling International members pay a discounted rate of ¥5000 per night for a single en-suite room. There's also free email access and no curfew. **4**

Taitō Ryokan
対十旅館
2-1-4 Nishi-Asakusa ⓣ03/3843-2822, ⓦwww .libertyhouse.gr.jp. Tawaramachi Station. See map p.76.. This atmospheric, if somewhat dilapidated, wooden ryokan is turning into a quasi-*gaijin* house thanks to its central location, cheap prices (¥3000 per person) and enthusiastic English-speaking owner, who is a font of local knowledge. There are only seven tatami rooms (none en suite and all non-smoking), so you'll need to book ahead. **1**

Ginza, Shiodome and around

Four Seasons Hotel Tokyo at Marunouchi
フォーシーズンズホテル東京丸の内
Pacific Century Place Marunouchi, 1-11-1 Marunouchi, Chiyoda-ku ⓣ03/5222-7222,
ⓦ www.fourseasons.com. Tokyo Station. See map p.54. Chic interior design and a very handy location beside Tokyo Station are two pluses. But it's the little things – like asking when you'd like your room cleaned, giving you a choice of newspaper or having free bicycles on hand – that makes this intimate, 57-room hotel a top choice. **9**

Ginza Tōbu Hotel
銀座東武ホテル
6-14-10 Ginza ⓣ03/3546-0111, ⓦ www.tobuhotel .co.jp/ginza. Higashi-Ginza Station. See map p.54. Top-of-the-range business hotel which pre-serves a personal touch. Rooms are a decent size, well-furnished and reasonably priced, and there's a business centre, bar and restaurants. **8**

Ginza Yoshimizu
銀座吉水
3-11-3 Ginza, Chūō-ku ⓣ03/3248-4431,
ⓦ www.yoshimizu.com. Higashi-Ginza Station. See map p.54. Look for the bamboo sprouting in front of this new and very appealing – but quite traditional – ryokan, handily located a block from the Kabuki-za. Rooms are all Japanese-style, with tatami mats, a futon and a few antique furnishings; the cheapest rooms share bathrooms. Breakfast included. **7**

Imperial Hotel
帝国ホテル
1-1-1 Uchisaiwai-chō, Chiyoda-ku
ⓣ03/3504-1111, ⓦ www.imperialhotel.co.jp. Hibiya Station. See map p.54. Facing the Imperial Palace, this prestigious hotel offers spacious rooms, with good views from the newer and slightly pricier tower. Services include a business centre, amenity lounge for late/early arrivals, baby-sitting, swimming pool (¥1000), thirteen top-class restaurants, four bars, a tea-ceremony room (¥1500) and a shopping arcade. **9**

Palace Hotel
パレスホテル
1-1-1 Marunouchi, Chiyoda-ku ⓣ03/3211-5211,
ⓦ www.palacehotel.co.jp. Ōtemachi Station. See map p.54. One notch down from the *Imperial* (see above), this top-class hotel also over-looks the palace gardens, though it's a little less convenient. Rooms are fair-sized and

comfortably furnished, with minibar, TV and all the standard amenities. There are seven restaurants and three bars, plus a shopping arcade, business centre and well-stocked bookshop. ❽

Park Hotel Tokyo
パークホテル東京
Shiodome Media Tower, 1-7-1 Higashi Shinbashi, Minato-ku ☎03/6252-1111, ⓦwww .parkhoteltokyo.com. Shiodome Station. See map p.54. Classy new place with a soaring atrium and wow views on all sides. The standard rooms are a little on the small size but fairly priced for what you get. The lobby is on the 25th floor; take the lifts to the right as you enter the building. ❼

Royal Park Hotel
ロイヤルパークホテル
2-1-1 Kakigarachō, Chūō-ku ☎03/3667-1111, ⓦwww.royalparkhotels.co.jp/nihonbashi. Suitengūmae Station. See map p.54. Swish business hotel conveniently located next to Tokyo City Air Terminal (TCAT) and above the Hanzōmon subway line. The rooms are quite stylish, and facilities include restaurants and bars, a business centre, pool and gym. ❽

Royal Park Shiodome Tower
ロイヤルパーク汐留タワー
1-6-3 Higashi Shinbashi, Minato-ku ☎03/6253-1111, ⓦwww.royalparkhotels.co.jp/shiodome. Shiodome Station. See map p.54. New top-class hotel at the heart of the Shiodome complex with some nice contemporary design touches and free in-room Internet access. They also run the Mandara Spa, offering a range of (pricey) spa treatments – one way to soothe away the stresses of Tokyo. ❼

Tokyo BUC
東京ビュック
2-8-12 Kachidoki, Chūō-ku ☎03/5547-5660, ⓦwww.tokyo-buc.com. Kachidoki Station. See map p.124. One of the best-value business hotels in Tokyo, with spacious rooms and singles for ¥5460. The catch is that it's a members' hotel – the general public is only allowed to stay Friday to Monday and on public holidays. ❸

Yaesu Fujiya Hotel
八重洲富士屋ホテル
2-9-1 Yaesu, Chūō-ku ☎03/3273-2111, ⓦwww.yaesufujiya.com. Tokyo Station. See map p.54. Opposite the east entrance to Tokyo Station, this old-fashioned hotel offers professional service and

convenience rather than great value for money. ❻

Yaesu Terminal Hotel
八重洲ターミナルホテル
1-5-14 Yaesu, Chūō-ku ☎03/3281-3771, ⓕ3281-3089. Nihombashi Station. See map p.54. Welcoming business hotel offering good rates for such a central location, though the cheaper rooms are cramped. It's also situated in an appealing area, tucked among lively backstreets just northeast of Tokyo Station. ❻

Ikebukuro

Hotel Clarion
ホテルクレリオン
2-3-1 Ikebukuro, Toshima-ku ☎03/5396-0111, ⓦwww.clariontokyo.com. Ikebukuro Station. See map p.91. International-class hotel in a good location on the west side of Ikebukuro Station – well priced and with more character than its local rivals. ❼

Dai-ichi Inn Ikebukuro
第一イン池袋
1-42-8 Higashi-Ikebukuro ☎03/3986-1221, ⓦwww.daiich-hotels.co.jp. Ikebukuro Station. See map p.91. This mid-range business hotel offers mainly single and twin rooms. Prices are reasonable, with a discount if you book online. ❻

Kimi Ryokan
貴美旅館
2-36-8 Ikebukuro, Toshima-ku ☎03/3971-3766, ⓦwww.kimi-ryokan.jp. Ikebukuro Station. See map p.91. With doubles from ¥6500 and singles at ¥4500, this is a great-value institution on Tokyo's budget scene and a good place to meet fellow travellers – but you'll need to book well ahead. It's tricky to find, in the backstreets of west Ikebukuro, and there's a 1am curfew. ❷

Hotel Metropolitan
ホテルメトロポリタン
1-6-1 Nishi-Ikebukuro, Toshima-ku ☎03/3980-1111, ⓦwww.itbc.co.jp/hotel. Ikebukuro Station. See map p.91. Also known as the *Crowne Plaza Metropolitan Tokyo*, Ikebukuro's plushest hotel has all the facilities you'd expect, including limousine bus connections to Narita Airport. The rooms are comfortable and well priced, and it's located on the more interesting west side of Ikebukuro. ❼

Kanda, Hongo and around

Hilltop Hotel
山の上ホテル
1-1 Kanda-Surugadai, Chiyoda-ku
ⓣ03/3293-2311, ⓦ www.yamanoue-hotel.co.jp.
Ochanomizu Station. See map p.61. Perched on
a small rise above Meiji University, this small
1930s hotel was formerly the commissioned officers' quarters under the
Occupation, and then became the haunt of
famous writers, notably Mishima. Its rooms
are far from Tokyo's grandest, but there are
Art Deco touches and a friendly welcome –
and oxygen and negative ions are pumped
around the premises. ❼

Homeikan Honkan and Daimachi Bekkan
鳳名館本館
大町別館
5-10-5 Hongo, Bunkyō-ku ⓣ03/3811-1187,
ⓦ www1.odn.ne.jp/homeikan. Ochanomizu
Station. See map p.61. The Meiji-era
Homeikan Honkan is the only inn in the city
that's a listed cultural property, but it's the
sister establishment across the road,
Daimachi Bekkan, that's the real looker, with
its ancient carpentry and ryokan design.
There are no en-suite bathrooms, but all
rooms have tatami mats and some have
window-cased balconies overlooking an
exquisite Japanese garden. ❹

Morikawa Bekkan
森川別館
6-23-5 Hongo, Bunkyō-ku ⓣ03/3811-8171,
ⓦ www1.odn.ne.jp/homeikan. Tōdai-Mae
Station. See maps pp.61 & 62. Part of the
same group as the *Homeikan Honkan*, this
elegant traditional hotel was built to
resemble the best of Kyoto's ryokan. It's
close by Tokyo University and some other
interesting buildings, including the church-
like Buddhist temple of Kyūdo Kaikan and a
Meiji-era wooden apartment block. ❹

Sakura Hotel
サクラホテル
2-21-4 Kanda-Jimbōchō ⓣ03/3261-3939,
ⓦ www.sakura-hotel.co.jp. Jimbōchō Station.
See map p.61. Cherry-pink building a
couple of blocks south of Yasukuni-dōri.
The rooms are boxy and all share
common bathrooms, but they're spotless
and good value for such a central location. Choose between singles (around
¥761), bunk-bed twins (¥8400) and dormitory bunks (¥3800 per person). Also
has a cheap café. ❸

Tokyo Dome Hotel
東京ドームホテル
1-3-61 Koraku, Bunkyō-ku ⓣ03/5805-2222,
ⓦ www.tokyodome-hotels.co.jp. Suidōbashi
Station. See map p.61. Good value both for its
central location and high-quality, larger-
than-average rooms – hence it's often full,
particularly if there's a big game or event on
at the neighbouring stadium. There's an
outdoor pool (¥161) from mid-July to the
end of August. ❼

YMCA Asia Youth Centre
YMCAアジアユースセンター
2-5-5 Sarugakuchō, Chiyoda-ku ⓣ03/3233-
0611, eayc@ymcajapan.org/ayc/jp. Suidōbashi
Station. See map p.61. Tucked away in the
backstreets, and open to both men and
women. The rooms, mostly single, are a bit
worn and gloomy, but all come with bathroom and TV. Weekend rates start at
around ¥5000 for a single, rising to ¥6300
on weekdays; there's a small discount for
YMCA members. ❸

Meguro

Claska
クラスカ
1-3-18 Chuo-chō, Meguro-ku ⓣ03/3719-8121,
ⓦ www.claska.com. Meguro Station. See map
p.118. This old hotel, in a rather far-flung
corner of Meguro-ku (you'll need to take a
bus or taxi from Meguro Station), has been
given a top-notch contemporary makeover
and is now one of the best of Tokyo's small
but growing band of designer hotels, with a
chic café-bar-bookstore in the lobby, an
exhibition space and even a dog-grooming
parlour. There are just eight individually and
appealingly decorated rooms (including two
singles for ¥11,650). ❼

Meguro Gajoen
目黒雅叙園
1-8-1 Meguro, Meguro-ku ⓣ03/5434-3837,
ⓦ www.megurogajoen.co.jp. Meguro Station.
See map p.118. No expense is spared in the
rooms (all suites) at this luxurious hotel,
attached to the amazing wedding hall of the
same name (see p.118). There's a choice of
either Western or Japanese room – the
latter are better, with their own sauna,
hinoki wood baths and tiny gravel gardens
outside the windows. ❽

Hotel Watson
ホテルワトソン
2-26-5 Kami-Ōsaki, Shinagawa-ku

ⓣ03/3490-5566. Meguro Station. See map
p.118. Sleek business hotel with friendly
English-speaking management and
decent-sized rooms with TV and
minibar. ⑥

Nezu and Yanaka

Annex Katsutaro
アネックス勝太郎
3-8-4 Yanaka, Taitō-ku ⓣ03/3828-2500,
ⓦwww.katsutaro.com. Sendagi Station. See
map p.82. Modern sister establishment to
the traditional *Ryokan Katsutaro* (see
below), this good-value place is in the
heart of a very convivial neighbourhood
and close to the subway and JR lines.
There's free Internet access and a coin
laundry on site. ④

Ryokan Katsutaro
旅館勝太郎
4-16-8 Ikenohata, Taitō-ku ⓣ03/3821-9808,
ⓦwww.katsutaro.com. Nezu Station. See map
p.82. A good alternative if *Sawanoya* (see
below) is full, handily located within walking
distance of Ueno Park. It's a homely place
with just seven slightly faded tatami rooms,
some with bath, and laundry facilities. ③

Sawanoya Ryokan
澤の屋旅館
2-3-11 Yanaka, Taitō-ku ⓣ03/3822-2251,
ⓦwww.sawanoya.com. Nezu Station. See map
p.82. Welcoming ryokan with good-value,
traditional tatami rooms, all with washbasin,
TV, telephone and air-conditioning, though
only two are en suite. The owner, Sawa-
san, is something of a local character, and
his son performs lion dances for guests.
The surrounding streets are worth
exploring and Ueno Park is within walking
distance. ③

Suigetsu Hotel Ohgaisō
水月ホテル鴎外荘
3-3-21 Ikenohata, Taitō-ku ⓣ03/3822-4611,
ⓦwww.ohgai.co.jp. Nezu Station. See map p.82.
One of very few mid-range hotels with a
Japanese atmosphere. Its three wings,
containing a mix of Western and tatami
rooms, are built around the Meiji-period
house and traditional garden of novelist
Mori Ōgai. ④

Odaiba and Tokyo Bay

Hotel Inter-Continental Tokyo Bay
ホテルインターコンチネンタル東京ベイ

1-16-2 Kaigan, Minato-ku ⓣ03/5404-2222,
ⓦwww.ichotelsgroup.com. Hinode Station. See
map p.124. Luxury hotel with views across
the bay to the Rainbow Bridge and inland
to Tokyo Tower, and rooms decorated in
earthy tones. It's ten minutes' walk from
Hamamatsuchō Station or two minutes'
from Hinode Station on the Yurikamome
monorail. ⑧

Le Meridien Grand Pacific
ホテル・グランパシフィック・メリディアン
2-6-1 Daiba, Minato-ku ⓣ03/5500-6711,
ⓦwww.lemeridien.com/japan/tokyo. Daiba
Station. See map p.124. The traditional
European style of this luxury hotel's interior
sits somewhat uncomfortably with the
futuristic architecture of Odaiba, but the
rooms are fair value and there are lots of
facilities, including a gallery with changing
exhibitions. ⑧

Hotel Nikkō Tokyo
ホテル日光東京
1-9-1 Daiba, Minato-ku ⓣ03/5500-5500,
ⓦwww.hnt.co.jp/english/index.htm. Daiba
Station. See map p.124. Modern works of art
adorn the walls, and there are great views
of the Rainbow Bridge and the city across
Tokyo Bay. Rooms are spacious and have
small balconies. ⑧

Tokyo Bay Ariake Washington Hotel
東京ベイ有明ワシントンホテル
3-1 Ariake, Minato-ku ⓣ03/5564-0111,
ⓦwww.ariake-wh.com. Kokusai-tenjijō Seimon
Station. See map p.124. Best value for the
Odaiba area, this upmarket chain hotel has
decent-sized rooms and is also home to
Georgetown, a good buffet restaurant and
ji-biru bar. ⑥

Roppongi and around

Arca Torre Hotel
ホテルアルカトーレ六本木
6-1-23 Roppongi ⓣ03/3404-5111, ⓦwww
.arktower.co.jp. Roppongi Station. See map p.71.
There are plenty of single rooms at this
new, centrally located business hotel; the
more expensive ones face out onto
Roppongi-dōri (which is odd, since this is
the noisy side of the hotel); the standard
double rooms are small. Handily located for
the area's nightlife. ⑥

Celestine Hotel
セレステンホテル
3-23-1 Shiba, Minato-ku ⓣ03/5441-4111,
ⓦwww.celestinehotel.com. Shiba-kōen Station.

See map p.68. In a business area south of Shiba-kōen, this classy new hotel has a pleasant lounge and secluded Moorish-style garden. The rooms are a good size and nicely decorated. They also have one fully accessible room for disabled travellers. ⑧

Grand Hyatt Tokyo
グランドハイアット東京
6-10-3 Roppongi, Minato-ku ☎ 03/4333-1234, Ⓦ www.grandhyatttokyo.com. **Roppongi Station. See map p.71.** The most glamorous of Tokyo's clutch of recently opened swanky hotels. The rooms' standout design uses wood and natural fabrics and the latest in technology, including flat-screen TVs. The Beckhams stayed here – the modern equivalent of an imperial endorsement. ⑨

Hotel Ibis
ホテルアイビス
7-14-4 Roppongi, Minato-ku ☎ 03/3403-4411, Ⓦ www.ibis-hotel.com. **Roppongi Station. See map p.71.** A stone's throw from Roppongi crossing; the lobby is on the fifth floor, where there's also Internet access. The cheapest doubles are small but bright and have TV and fridge – one of the best deals in the area – and there are friendly English-speaking staff. ⑤–⑦

Mentels Roppongi
ホテルメンテルス六本木
1-11-4 Nishi-Azabu, Minato-ku ☎ 03/3403-7161. **Roppongi Station. See map p.68.** Standard business hotel with old-fashioned, reasonably sized Western rooms, as well as a few Japanese-style ones. The location, right on Roppongi-dōri and close to Nishi-Azabu crossing, is ideal for those who want to party. The cheapest singles are under ¥8700. ⑤

Roppongi Prince Hotel
六本木プリンスホテル
3-2-7 Roppongi, Minato-ku ☎ 03/3587-1111, Ⓦ www.princehotels.co.jp/english/. **Roppongi Station. See map p.68.** Popular with celebrities, the main feature in this hotel – designed by top architect Kurokawa Kisho and set in a quiet area of Roppongi – is its atrium and amoeba-shaped swimming pool, overlooked by the guest rooms. ⑦

Hotel Villa Fontaine Roppongi
ホテルヴィラフォンテーヌ六本木
1-6-2 Roppongi, Minato-ku ☎ 03/3560-1110, Ⓦ www.villa-fontaine.co.jp. **Roppongi-Itchōme Station. See map p.71.** Very stylish business hotel tucked into a corner of the Izumi Garden development directly above the

subway station. The larger-than-average rooms are pleasantly decorated and have free LAN Internet connections; rates include a buffet breakfast. ⑥

Shibuya, Aoyama and Ebisu

Arimax Hotel
アリマックスホテル
11-15 Kamiyama-chō, Shibuya-ku ☎ 03/5454-1122, Ⓦ www.arimaxhotelshibuya .co.jp. **Shibuya Station. See map p.115.** There's a classic European feel to this elegant boutique hotel a short walk from the action in Shibuya. English is spoken and it's all very professional. The suites come with their own cosy sauna. ⑦

Cerulean Tower Tōkyū Hotel
セルリアンタワー東急ホテル
26-1 Sakuragaoka-chō, Shibuya-ku ☎ 03/3476-3000, Ⓦ www.ceruleantower -hotel.com. **Shibuya Station. See map p.115.** Stylish new addition to the Tōkyū chain's clutch of hotels in this area. Some rooms have bathrooms with a glittering view of the city, and there's a pool and gym (free to guests on the executive floor, otherwise ¥2000), several restaurants, a jazz club plus a nō theatre in the basement. ⑦

Hotel Excellent
ホテルエクセレント
1-9-5 Ebisu-nishi, Shibuya-ku ☎ 03/5458-0087, Ⓕ 5458-8787. **Ebisu Station. See map p.118.** Standard business hotel – nothing flash, but reasonably priced for such a handy location. ⑤

Hotel Floracian
ホテルフロラシオン
4-17-58 Minami-Aoyama, Minato-ku ☎ 03/3403-1541, Ⓦ www.floracian-aoyama.com. **Omotesandō Station. See map p.106.** In a quiet residential area, with high-standard Western-style rooms and a convenient location, handy for the designer end of Omotesandō. ⑤

National Children's Castle Hotel
こどもの城ホテル
5-53-1 Jingūmae, Shibuya-ku ☎ 03/3797-5677. **Shibuya Station. See maps pp.106 & 115.** On the sixth and seventh floors of this complex devoted to kids' entertainment (but you don't have to have children to stay here), offering large and comfy rooms and inexpensive singles (though without windows). ⑤

Shibuya Business Hotel
渋谷ビジネスホテル

1-12-5 Shibuya ⓣ03/3409-9300,
ⓕ3409-9378. Shibuya Station. See map p.115.
Apart from a capsule hotel, the cheapest
deal you'll find in this pricey but happening
part of town – meaning it often gets
booked up. Set in a quiet location
behind the post office. ⑤

Shibuya Creston Hotel
渋谷クレストンホテル
10-8 Kamiyamachō, Shibuya-ku ⓣ03/3481-
5800, ⓦwww.crestonhotel.co.jp. Shibuya
Station. See map p.115. Upmarket business
hotel with larger-than-normal rooms and a
discreet, club-like atmosphere. Near NHK
at the quiet end of Shibuya. ⑦

Shibuya Excel Hotel Tōkyū
渋谷エクセルホテル東急
1-12-2 Dōgenzaka, Shibuya-ku ⓣ03/5457-0109,
ⓦwww.tokyuhotels.co.jp. Shibuya Station. See
map p.115. High-tech fixtures and contemporary furnishings complement this new
skyscraper hotel atop the Shibuya Mark
City complex. Better value than the nearby
Shibuya Tōkyū Inn and women get a floor
to themselves. ⑦

Shibuya Tōbu Hotel
渋谷東武ホテル
3-1 Udagawachō, Shibuya-ku ⓣ03/3476-0111,
ⓦwww.tobuhotel.co.jp/shibuya. Shibuya Station.
See map p.115. Pleasant chain hotel, well
located near Shibuya's department stores,
with friendly service and a good range of
restaurants. ⑥

Westin Tokyo
ウェスティン東京
1-1-4 Mita, Meguro-ku ⓣ03/5423-7000,
ⓦwww.westin.co.jp. Ebisu Station. See map
p.118. In the Yebisu Garden Palace development, this opulent hotel is decorated in Art
Nouveau style; the spacious rooms have
high ceilings and plush furnishings. Guests
have access to the Yebisu Gardens gym
and pool for a fee. ⑨

Shinagawa and around

Keihin Hotel
京浜ホテル
4-10-20 Takanawa, Minato-ku ⓣ03/3449-5711,
ⓦwww.keihin-hotel.co.jp. Shinagawa Station. See
colour map at back of book. Small, old-fashioned
hotel directly opposite the station. There are
some Japanese-style rooms (starting at
¥12,000) which are good value if shared. ⑤

Le Meridien Pacific Tokyo
ホテルパシフィック東京

3-13-3 Takanawa, Minato-ku ⓣ03/3445-6711,
ⓦwww.lemeridien.com/japan/tokyo. Shinagawa
Station. See colour map at back of book. A
minute's walk from the west entrance of
Shinagawa Station, this luxury hotel has
good-size rooms, Japanese gardens, an
outdoor pool and several restaurants. ⑦

New Takanawa Prince Hotel
新高輪プリンスホテル
3-13-1 Takanawa, Minato-ku ⓣ03/3442-1111,
ⓦwww.princehotels.co.jp/english/index1.html.
Shinagawa Station. See colour map at back of
book. The best of the three *Prince* hotels in
Shinagawa. The sedate lobby overlooks the
elegant gardens created for Prince Takeda,
and there's a swimming pool in summer. ⑧

Ryokan Sansuisō
旅館山水荘
2-9-5 Higashi-Gotanda, Shinagawa-ku
ⓣ03/3441-7475, ⓕ3449-1944. Gotanda Station.
See colour map at back of book. Homely and
spotless ryokan. Only a few of the tatami
rooms have en-suite bath, and no meals are
available. It's a five-minute walk from the
station, near the Gotanda Bowling Centre.
Good-value singles start at ¥4900. ③

The Strings Hotel
ザ・ストリングスホテル
Shinagawa East One Tower, 2-16-1 Konan,
Minato-ku ⓣ03/4562-1111, ⓦwww
.stringshotel.com. Shinagawa Station. See colour
map at back of book. Super-smart hotel
hidden away on the 26th floor and upwards
of one of Shinagawa's new brace of towers.
The airy atrium lobby with its water, wood
and stone combination evokes Japan, but
in a thoroughly modern way. If you're not
staying, afternoon tea (¥2500) at either of
its restaurants is a good way to soak up
the atmosphere. ⑧

Takanawa Tōbu Hotel
高輪東武ホテル
4-7-6 Takanawa, Minato-ku ⓣ03/3447-0111,
ⓦwww.tobuhotel.co.jp/takanawa. Shinagawa
Station. See colour map at back of book.
Small, sleek business hotel; rates include
Western-style buffet breakfast in the
ground-floor café. It's five minutes' walk
up the hill from the station. ⑦

Tōyoko Inn Shinagawa-eki Takanawaguchi
東京国際ユースホステル
4-23-2 Takanawa ⓣ03/3280-1045, ⓦwww.toyoko-
inn.co.jp. Shinagawa Station. See colour map at
back of book. Handy branch of this bargain
business hotel chain that doesn't stint on
room features (including trouser press and

LAN sockets for free Internet access). Rates include a continental breakfast and there are free Internet terminals in the lobby. ❸

Shinjuku

Central Hotel Shinjuku
セントラルホテル新宿
3-34-7 Shinjuku, Shinjuku-ku ☎03/3354-6611, Ⓕ3355-4245. Shinjuku Station. See map p.98. The elegant lobby sets the tone at this classy, boutique-style hotel in an ultra-convenient location. Also has non-smoking rooms. ❻

Hotel Century Southern Tower
ホテルセンチュリーサザンタワー
2-2-1 Yoyogi, Shinjuku-ku ☎03/5354-0111, Ⓕ5354-0100, ⓦwww.southerntower.co.jp. Shinjuku Station. See map p.98. Part of the new Odakyū Southern Tower complex, this smart, stylish hotel has better-value room rates than many of its older rivals in Nishi-Shinjuku. The views overlooking the station lend the place a *Blade Runner*-ish feel. ❼

Keiō Plaza Intercontinental Hotel
京王プラザイナター–コンチネンタルホテル
2-2-1 Nishi-Shinjuku, Shinjuku-ku ☎03/3344-0111, ⓦwww.keioplaza.co.jp. Shinjuku Station. See map p.98. Though it's long since been knocked off its perch as the tallest, most glamorous hotel in Shinjuku, the *Keiō* nevertheless retains some of its original cachet. Rooms on the western side have great views across the Tokyo Metropolitan Government Building. There's an outdoor pool in summer but it's often in the shade. ❻

Park Hyatt Tokyo
パークホテル東京
3-7-1-2 Nishi-Shinjuku, Shinjuku-ku ☎03/5322-1234, ⓦwww.parkhyatttokyo.com. Tochō-mae Station. See map p.98. Famous for its key role in the recent hit movie *Lost In Translation*, this is easily the best of Nishi-Shinjuku's luxury hotels; the huge rooms and decor are the epitome of sophistication, and the restaurants and spa, pool and fitness centre, occupying the pinnacles of Tange Kenzō's tower, have breathtaking views on all sides. ❾

Shinjuku Washington Hotel
新宿ワシントンホテル
3-2-9 Nishi-Shinjuku, Shinjuku-ku ☎03/3343-3111, ⓦwww.shinjuku-wh.com. Tochō-mae Station. See map p.98. Business hotel in the building with the porthole

windows. The lobby is on the third floor, where there are automated check-in machines (as well as humans) dishing out electronic key cards for the compact, good-value rooms. You may also find yourself in the nearby Annex building. ❻

Tokyo Hilton Hotel
東京ヒルトンホテル
6-6-2 Nishi-Shinjuku, Shinjuku-ku ☎03/3344-5111, ⓦwww.hilton.com. Tochō-mae Station. See map p.98. In the slinky, wave-like building behind the more traditional skyscrapers of Nishi-Shinjuku. Rooms have nice Japanese design touches, such as *shōji* (paper screens) on the windows. Renowned for its buffet breakfast and lunch and afternoon tea spreads. ❽

Ueno

Fukushima Kaikan
ふくしま会館
2-12-14 Ueno, Taitō-ku ☎03/3834-6221. Yushima Station. See map p.82. Friendly, functional hotel, and the staff speak some English. There's a choice of Western- or Japanese-style rooms – the latter are quite roomy and many have great views across Shinobazu pond. ❺

Khaosan Ueno
ホテルパインヒル
4-2-3 Higashi-Ueno, Taitō-ku ☎03/3842-8286, ⓦwww.khaosan-tokyo.com. Ueno Station. See map p.82. New, spotlessly clean hostel (dorm beds only; ¥2000per night) within spitting distance of Ueno Station. The rooms are stuffed with bunk beds and very cramped, but it's the cheapest place to bed down in Tokyo, and there's free Internet access and the use of a kitchen, too. They also run a long-stay hostel in Asakusa (2-1-5 Kaminarimon, Taitō-ku ☎03/3842-8286), in a great position overlooking the Sumida-gawa.

Hotel Pine Hill
ホテルパインヒル
2-3-4 Ueno, Taitō-ku ☎03/3836-5111, Ⓕ3837-0080. Ueno-Hirokōji Station. See map p.82. The best value among the clutch of ordinary, mid-range business hotels in central Ueno. Rooms are small but adequate. ❻

Sofitel Tokyo
ソフィテル東京
2-1-48 Ikenohata, Taitō-ku ☎03/5685-7111, ⓦwww.sofiteltokyo.com. Yushima Station. See

map p.82. Unmissable landmark tower – it's the one that looks like a kid's Lego project – though it's a darn sight more attractive on the inside. The recently renovated rooms are all tastefully done out in sepia tones and there are some lovely views of the park. ❼

Ueno First City Hotel
上野ファーストシティホテル

1-14-8 Ueno, Taitō-ku ☎03/3831-8215. Yushima Station. See map p.82. Spruce, reasonably priced and friendly little business hotel on the western edge of Ueno offering a choice of Japanese- and Western-style rooms, all en suite. Take exit 6 of Yushima Station, turn right and right again at the traffic lights. ❺

Capsule hotels

Further down the price scale are Tokyo's **capsule hotels**, rows of coffin-like tubes with just enough room to sit up in, containing a mattress, with a TV and radio built into the plastic surrounds. The "door" consists of a plastic curtain – which won't keep out the loudest snores – and you're completely sealed away from the outside world and daylight, making alarm clocks a necessity for waking up early. Capsule hotels are generally clustered around major train stations and cater mainly to salarymen – often in various states of inebriation – who've missed the last train. Staying in a capsule provides a quintessentially Japanese experience, but they won't suit everyone – claustrophobics and anyone over two metres tall should give them a miss – and note also that the majority are for men only. It's possible to reserve ahead should you wish to stay longer than a single night.

Capsule Inn Akasaka
かぷせるイン赤坂
6-14-1 Akasaka, Minato-ku ☎03/3588-1811. Akasaka Station. See map p.68. Clean, men-only capsule hotel with a large lounge and communal bathrooms. There are 280 capsules, so you shouldn't have a problem if you turn up late at night without a booking. Check in from 5pm; check out by 10am. ¥3500 per person.

Capsule Hotel Riverside
カプセルホテルリバーサイド
2-20-4 Kaminarimon ☎03/3844-1155, ℱ3841-6566. Asakusa Station. See map p.76. One of the cheapest capsule deals in Tokyo. It's mainly for men (there are just fifteen capsules for women on a separate floor). Basic English spoken. ¥2900 per person.

Love hotels

Love hotels – where you can rent rooms by the hour - are another wonderful hybrid which can be a source of cheap accommodation for the adventurous. Generally located in entertainment districts, such as Shibuya, Shinjuku, Ueno and Ikebukuro, they are immediately recognizable from their ornate exteriors, incorporating cupids, crenellations or, most incongruously, the Statue of Liberty, and a sign quoting prices for "rest" or "stay". They're not as sleazy as they might sound and the main market is young people or married couples taking a break from crowded apartments. There's now a trend to call them fashion hotels, in acknowledgement of the fact that it's usually the more discerning, trend-conscious woman who makes the room choice.

All kinds of tastes can be indulged at love hotels, with rotating beds in mirror-lined rooms being almost passé in comparison to some of the fantasy creations on offer. Some rooms even come equipped with video cameras so you can take home a souvenir of your stay. You usually choose your room from a back-lit display indicating those still available – the best contain moving beds, lurid murals and even swimming pools – and then negotiate with a cashier lurking behind a tiny window – eye-to-eye contact is avoided to preserve modesty. Though daytime rates are high (from about ¥4000 for 2hr), the price of an overnight stay can cost the same as a basic business hotel (roughly ¥5000–7000). The main drawback is that you can't check in until around 10pm.

Capsule Land Shibuya
カプセルランド渋谷
1-19-14 Dōgenzaka, Shibuya-ku
ⓣ**03/3464-1777,** ⓦ**www.capsule-land.com.**
Shibuya Station. See map p.114. Easy-to-find
men-only capsule hotel at the top of the
Dōgenzaka. Also has "semi-double" rooms
for singles (including women) and couples,
but they're very cramped. ❷

Fontaine Akasaka
フォンテーヌ赤坂
4-3-5 Akasaka, Minato-ku ⓣ**03/3583-6554.**
Akasaka-Mitsuke Station. See map p.68. One of
the more expensive capsule hotels, but a
touch more respectable than most, and
takes both men and women. ¥4800 for
men, ¥4500 for women.

Green Plaza Shinjuku
グリーンプラザ新宿
1-29-2 Kabukichō, Shinjuku-ku ⓣ**03/3207-4923.**
Shinjuku Station. See map p.98. The lobby is
on the fourth floor of this large men-only
capsule hotel (has room for 660 guests),
with friendly staff and a good fitness and
sauna area. The roof-top spa baths cost
extra. ¥4000 per person.

Youth hostels

Apart from the capsule hotels, the cheapest option for budget travellers is to
stay in one of Tokyo's two city-centre **youth hostels**. They're both clean and
efficient and have excellent facilities, though they impose an evening curfew
and, usually, a maximum stay of three nights. Japan Youth Hostels also has a
contract with Sky Court hotels to provide higher-standard hotel-style accommodation at favourable rates.

Tokyo International Youth Hostel
東京国際ユースホステル
18F Central Plaza Building, 1-1 Kaguragashi,
Shinjuku-ku ⓣ**03/3235-1107,** ⓦ**www**
.tokyo-yh.jp/eng/e_top.html. Iidabashi Station.
See map p.61. On a clear winter's day you
can see Mount Fuji from this smart hostel
above Iidabashi Station. Each bunk (¥3500
per night) has its own curtains and locker,
and there are IDD phones, a members'
kitchen and laundry facilities. Reception is
open 3pm to 9.30pm and there's a
10.30pm curfew. Exit B2b from the subway
brings you straight up into the lift lobby;

alternatively, from the JR station's west exit,
turn right into the Ramla Centre and keep
straight ahead to find the lift.

Tokyo Yoyogi Youth Hostel
東京代々木ユースホステル
3-1 Kamizonochō, Shibuya-ku ⓣ**03/3467-9163,**
ⓦ**www.tokyo-yh.jp/eng. Sangūbashi Station.**
See maps pp.98 & 108. Comfortable, single
rooms only (¥4000) at this modern hostel
which is part of the Olympic Youth Centre,
and in a complex of buildings at the top of
the hill. Guests must be out between 9am
and 4pm, and there's a vague 10pm
curfew. Book well in advance.

Long-term accommodation

The recent recession has caused rents in Tokyo to drop slightly and it's said that
landlords are becoming more flexible on the question of "key money" (usually
one or two months' non-refundable rent when you move in). However, you'll
still face a lot of competition when looking for **long-term accommodation**, not to mention endemic prejudice towards renting to non-Japanese. Be
prepared for a long haul to get your own place.

Most newcomers start off in what's known as a **gaijin house** – a privately
owned house or apartment consisting of shared or private rooms with
communal kitchen and bathroom. They're usually rented by the month,
though if there's space, weekly or even nightly rates may be available. Tokyo has
a wide range of such places, from total fleapits to the almost luxurious, though
the best places are nearly always full. Decent places include *Taitō Ryokan*
(ⓣ03/3843-2822, ⓦwww.libertyhouse.gr.jp; see map p.76) in Asakusa; and

Sakura House (@www.sakura-house.com; see map p.98), with properties near Shinjuku and in other areas. For other options scan the English-language press, particularly *Metropolis*, or contact the Kimi Information Centre (8F Oscar Building, 2-42-3 Ikebukuro ⊤03/3986-1604, @www.kimiwillbe.com; see map p.91.), which runs a useful letting agency. Monthly rates start from ¥30,000–40,000 per person for a shared room and ¥50,000–60,000 for a single. A deposit may also be required.

To find your own **apartment** it helps enormously to have a Japanese friend or colleague to act as an intermediary, or you could try an agent such as Kimi (see above). When you've found a place, apart from the first month's rent you should be prepared to pay a deposit of one to two months' rent in addition to key money and a month's rent in commission to the agent. Rentals in Tokyo start at ¥50,000–60,000 per month for a one-room box.

⓲

Eating and drinking

T okyo is one of the world's greatest cities for **eating** and **drinking**, but deciding what to eat and where to go can be a bewildering experience. Besides the problem of working out what's on the menu (or even on your plate), you're also swamped with choice – there are around 300,000 places to eat, from simple street food vendors to classy restaurants. Choose any country, from Belarus to Vietnam, and you're likely to find their cuisine somewhere in the city. And, of course, there are endless renditions and permutations of Japanese favourites such as sushi, ramen, tempura and *yakitori*.

With so many options, there's no need to panic about **prices**. Tokyo has a plethora of reliable noodle bars, *shokudō* and chain restaurants where the Japanese go when they need to fill up without fear of the cost; many are clustered around and inside train stations. There's also an abundance of fast-food options (see box opposite) and a wide variety of chain cafés (see box on p.164) offering light meals.

Drinking establishments run the gamut from shoebox-sized bars for regular patrons only (all of whom will have a bottle with their name on it kept at the bar for safekeeping) to the sophisticated cocktail lounges at top hotels. Many traditional-style pubs (*izakaya*) and live music venues often serve decent grub too. Beer remains the most popular drink, but you shouldn't leave Tokyo without sampling some of the many different sake (rice wine) which are available.

Meals

The traditional Japanese **breakfast** is a gut-busting combination of miso soup, fish, pickles and rice, though many Japanese now prefer a quick *kō hii* and *tō suto* (coffee and toast), served at most cafés on the "morning service" menu. Many ryokan and top hotels offer a choice between Western- and Japanese-style breakfast.

Hardly any of the locals linger over **lunch**, usually taken around noon – but that's no reason why you should follow suit. You could grab a sandwich, but it's better to go for a hearty meal at a restaurant, all of which offer set menus (called *teishoku*), usually around ¥1000 for a couple of courses, plus a drink, and rarely topping ¥3000 per person. This is also the best time to sample the food at top restaurants if you're on a budget, with some great deals available.

At any time of day you'll catch people snacking in stand-up noodle bars – often found around train stations – and beside the revolving conveyor belts of cheap sushi shops. **Dinner**, the main meal of the day, can be eaten as early as 6pm (with many places taking last orders around 9pm), although Tokyo is better served than most places in Japan when it comes to late-night dining.

13

EATING AND DRINKING | Meals

Fast-food city

Too much to do in Tokyo and too little time to do it? No need to hang about eating – do as Tokyoites do and grab some fast food or food to go. **Convenience stores** such as Seven-Eleven, AM/PM and Lawson sell a wide range of snacks and meals round the clock, which can be heated up in the shop's microwave or reconstituted with hot water. For more upmarket goodies, make your way to the basement food halls of the major department stores, where you'll also find good **bentō** (set boxes of food). For Japanese **fast food**, head for *Yoshinoya*, which serves reasonably tasty *gyūdon* (stewed strips of beef or pork on rice), and *Tenya*, which offers a similar low-cost deal for tempura and rice dishes. You'll find branches of both all over the city, as well as numerous *McDonald's* and *KFC*s; a good local chain is *Mos Burger*, serving up rice burgers, carrot juice and green *konnyaku* jelly (a root vegetable).

The latest fast-food hits include **soup** and decent Western-style **sandwiches** – something Tokyo's been lacking for a while. *Soup Stock Tokyo* (Ⓦ www.soup-stock -tokyo.com) serves steaming mugs of hearty broths; you'll find them all over Tokyo, including Ueno Station (see map p.82), Roppongi Hills (B2F Hollywood Plaza, map p.71), the Maru Building in Marunouchi (map p.54), and the Coredo Building in Nihombashi (map p.54), among other locations. Upmarket sandwiches are available from *Benugo* (Ⓦ www.benugo.co.jp), in Yebisu Garden Place (map p.118), Akasaka (map p.68) and Shiodome (map p.54). For a Hawaiian twist on the sandwich and burger genre, try the very tasty offerings at *Kua 'Aian* (Ⓦ www .four-seeds.co.jp), currently one of the most popular places in the city: you'll find them on the corner of Aoyama-dōri and Koto-dōri in Aoyama (map p.106) and in the Marunouchi Building, Marunouchi (map p.54), among other places.

With traditional Japanese cuisine you'll usually get all your courses at the same time, but at more formal places rice and soup are always served at the end of the meal.

For more information on Tokyo's restaurants, check out the free weekly magazine *Metropolis* or some of the websites listed in the box in Basics on p.21. The *Zagat Survey of Tokyo Restaurants* (¥1500) is the most up-to-date guidebook; you can also read their listings at Ⓦ www.zagat.com. **Reservations** are advisable for many places, especially on Friday, Saturday and Sunday nights; we've given phone numbers in the listings below – also useful if you get lost and need to ring for directions.

Restaurants

With so much competition in the food stakes, it's perhaps not surprising that many Tokyo restaurants are concentrating on decor to give them a wow-factor edge. On the one hand you have contemporary design stunners like *Daidaiya* and *Shunju*; on the other, themed dining fantasies such as *Seiryūmon*, *Ninja* and *Christon Café*.

If you're not bothered about design, Tokyo has several unpretentious **restaurant chains** worth checking out. For **Indian** food, *Moti*, with outlets in Roppongi and Akasaka, is a long-time local favourite. For good **Italian** dishes, head for *Capricciosa*, with branches all over the city – its sign is in elongated *katakana* on a green, red and white background. Branches of the casual, American-style *News Deli* (Ⓦ www.sunrisejapan.com /restaurants) can also been found all over the city, including Aoyama,

In most restaurants, before you start eating you'll be handed an *oshibori*, a damp, folded hand towel, usually steamed hot, but sometimes cold in summer. Use the towel to clean your hands and then fold it for the waiter to remove later. When the food arrives, you can wish your companions *bon appétit* by saying *itadakimas*.

Chopsticks (*hashi*) come with their own set of rules. Don't stick them upright in your rice – an allusion to death (relatives traditionally pass pieces of bone from the cremation pot to the funeral urn with long chopsticks). If you're taking food from a shared plate, turn the chopsticks around and use the other end to pick up. Never cross your chopsticks when you put them on the table and don't use them to point at things. When eating soupy noodles you can enjoy a good slurp, and it's fine to drink directly from the bowl.

When you want the **bill**, say *o-kanjō kudasai* (bill please); the usual form is to pay at the till on the way out. Tipping is not expected, but it's polite to say *gochisō-sama deshita* (that was delicious) to the waiter or chef.

Daikan'yama, Ikebukuro and Shinjuku.

Among the **Japanese chains** to look out for are *Sushisei* (see opposite), a classy sushi restaurant, and *Kushinobō* (see p.155), the folk craft-decorated *kushikatsu* (deep-fried morsels on skewers) restaurant. The *Gonpachi*, *La Bohème*, *Monsoon* and *Zest* chains are all run by the same company (Wwww.global-dining.com) and can be relied on for value and late-night dining in chic settings. There are branches of all four in Ginza, Harajuku, Shibuya, Nishi-Azabu and Daikan'yama.

If you can't decide what to go for, make your way to the restaurant floors of the major **department stores** and **shopping malls**, such as Ebisu's Yebisu Garden Place (map p.118), Shiodome (map p.54), My City in Shinjuku (map p.98) and Roppongi Hills (map p.71), where there are enough options to keep you busy eating for weeks. At these places you'll find a wide choice of cuisines and dining atmospheres under one roof, often with plastic food displays in the windows and daily specials. Also, don't overlook the good-value **family restaurants**, such as *Royal Host* (in Shinjuku, Shinagawa and Takodanobaba, among other locations) and *Jonathan's* (Shinjuku, Harajuku, Asakusa), which serve both Western and Japanese dishes and have easy-to-choose-from picture menus; most are open 24 hours, too.

Restaurant prices

The **restaurants** in the listings below have been graded as **inexpensive** (under ¥1000 for a meal without alcohol); **moderate** (¥1000–4000); **expensive** (¥4000–6000); and **very expensive** (over ¥6000). The cheapest time to eat out is lunchtime, when even the priciest places offer good-value set meals, and you'd be hard-pressed to spend over ¥2000. **Tipping** is not expected, but **consumption tax** (five percent) can push up the total cost (although it's sometimes included in the prices). Some restaurants and bars serving food, especially those in hotels, add on a **service charge** (typically ten percent). Make sure you have cash to hand; payment by **credit card** is becoming more common, but is generally restricted to upmarket restaurants and hotels.

Akasaka

Aux Bacchanales
Ō bakunaru

2F Ark Mori Building, 1-12-32 Akasaka, Minato-ku ☎03/3582-2225; Roppongi-Itchōme Station; see map p.68. Daily 10am–midnight. Tucked away in the Ark Hills complex, opposite Suntory Hall, this is one of Tokyo's most authentic Parisian-style brasseries – their *steak frite* is the real thing – and it's a pleasant spot to hang out sipping coffee or red wine. Moderate.

Kyūshū Jangara Rāmen
九州じゃんがらーメン

2-12-8 Nagatachō, Chiyoda-ku ☎03/3595-2130; Tameike-Sannō Station; see map p.68. Mon–Fri 11am–3pm & 5pm–12.30am. On Sotobori-dōri, near the entrance to the Hie-jinja, this funky noodle bar serves up large bowls of Kyūshū-style ramen (Chinese noodles) in three types of soup: fish, mild and light, and greasy garlic, from ¥550, with beer at ¥450. Also has branches in Akihabara (3-11-6 Soto-Kanda, Chiyoda-ku ☎03/3512-4059), Ginza (7-11-10 Ginza, Chūō-ku ☎03/3289-2307) and Harajuku (1-13-21 Jingūmae, Shibuya-ku ☎03/3404-5572), on Omotesandō near Harajuku Station. Inexpensive.

Jidaiya
時代屋

3-14-3 Akasaka, Minato-ku ☎03/3588-0489; Akasaka Station; see map p.68. Mon–Fri 11.30am–2.30pm & 5pm–4am, Sat & Sun 5–11pm. Charming farmhouse-style *izakaya* in the heart of Akasaka, all dark wood, tatami and traditional ornaments. There's an English menu to help you select between the wide range of dishes, including a wild boar stew for ¥4000 and *kaiseki*-style course for ¥8000. Lunch is a much better deal at under ¥1000. There's also a branch in Roppongi (B1 Uni Roppongi Building, 7-15-17 Roppongi, Minato-ku ☎03/3403-3563) Expensive.

Kurosawa
黒澤

2-7-9 Nagatachō, Chiyoda-ku ☎03/3580-9638; Tamekei-Sannō Station; see map p.68. Mon–Fri 11.30am–3pm, 5–10pm, Sat noon–9pm. Slightly pricey but very tasty *soba* noodles and pork *sukiyaki* dishes are served at this atmospheric restaurant with a design inspired by the sets from Akira Kurosawa's movies *Yojimbo* and *Red Beard*. They also have a cute restaurant specializing in *udon* noodles near Roppongi Hills (6-11-16 Roppongi, Minato-ku ☎03/3403-9638; see map p.71). Moderate.

Ninja
忍者

1F Akasaka Tokyū Building, 2-14-31 Nagatachō, Chiyoda-ku ☎03/5157-3936; Akasaka-Mitsuke Station; see map p.68. Daily 5.30pm–4am. Dark, twisting corridors; waiters who jump out of secret doorways; a magician who does amazing tricks at your table – all this and more makes up the fun dining experience at this upmarket *ninja*-themed *izakaya*. The modern Japanese cuisine comes in small but tasty portions. Moderate to expensive.

Shunju
春秋

27th Floor, San'nō Park Tower, 2-11-1 Nagatachō, Chiyoda-ku ☎03/3592-5288; Tamekei-Sannō Station; see map p.68. Mon–Sat 11.30am–2.30pm, 5–11pm. You've perhaps read their cookbook, now try the real thing. This is the modern Japanese dining experience *par excellence*, matching stylish contemporary interior design with food made from the freshest seasonal ingredients. Set menus kick off at ¥6000 (plus twenty percent in service and taxes). There's also the more casual *Kitchen Shunju* (☎03/5369-0377; see map p.98) in Shinjuku's My City department store. Expensive to very expensive.

Sushisei
寿司清

3-11-4 Akasaka, Minato-ku ☎03/3582-9503; Akasaka Station; see map p.68. Mon–Sat 11.30am–2pm, 5–10pm. One of the city's best sushi restaurant chains, which means you may have to wait to be served at peak times. Per-piece charges start at ¥100, much less than at similar à la carte *sushi-ya*. There are also branches in Tsukiji, close to the market (4-13-9 Tsukiji, Chūō-ku ☎03/3541-7720), and in Roppongi Hills (see *Seizan*, p.160). Moderate.

West Park Café
Uesuto Pāku Kafue

2F Akasaka Tōkyū Plaza, 2-14-3 Nagatachō, Chiyoda-ku ☎03/3580-9090; Akasaka Mitsuke Station; see map p.68. Mon–Fri 11.30am–11pm, Sat & Sun 11.30am–3pm. Relaxed American-style deli-café, with an outdoor terrace and an airy interior. Good for light meals and weekend brunches. There are other branches a five-minute walk west of Yoyogi-kōen at 23-11 Moto-Yoyogichō, and on the fifth floor of the Maru Building, Marunouchi (map p.54). Moderate.

Despite being the home of macrobiotic cooking, **vegetarianism** isn't a widely practised or fully understood concept in Japan. You might ask for a vegetarian (*saishoku*) dish in a restaurant and still be served something with meat or fish in it. If you're a committed vegetarian, things to watch out for include *dashi* stock, which contains bonito (dried tuna), and most breads and cakes, which can contain lard. Omlettes too can often contain chicken stock. To get a truly vegetarian meal you will have to be prepared to spell out exactly what you do and do not eat when you order. The Tokyo Veg website (🅦 www.tokyoveg.com) has some useful general information in English, plus a few restaurant recommendations on its info board section. Also check out the reviews in this chapter for *Bon* (see opposite), *Café Eight* (see below), Hiroba (see below), *Mominoki House* (see below), *Nataraj* (p.157), *Shizenkan II* (p.161), and *Shunju* (p.151).

Aoyama and Harajuku

Café Eight
Kafe Ēto
4-27-15 Minami-Aoyama, Minato-ku ☎03/5464-3207; Omotesandō Station; see map p.106. Daily 11am–11pm, closed third Wed of month. On the third floor of the same building as the stylish furniture and homeware shop Time and Style, this cute café serves a healthy, veggie-based menu – no animal products are used, so it's perfect for vegetarians and vegans. Inexpensive.

Chung King Lo
Chungu Kingu Ro
3-14-17 Minami-Aoyama, Minato-ku ☎03/5771-0338; Omotesandō Station; see map p.106. Daily 11.30am–11pm. Modern Chinese café and bar, part of the Idée design group, tucked away in the backstreets at the designer end of Omotesandō. Given that it's oh so stylish, it's actually not bad value, and the food is fine. Good for a quiet drink too. Moderate.

Fujimamas
Fujimamamsu
6-3-2 Jingūmae, Shibuya-ku ☎03/5485-2262; Meiji-jingūmae Station; see map p.106. Mon–Fri noon–3pm & 6–11pm, Sat & Sun noon–4pm & 6–11pm. There's a bit more style than sub-stance to the East–West fusion food at this popular place, but it's generally good value and the menu (desserts are headed "Oh, I just couldn't . . . but I will!") is a hoot. Moderate.

Heirokuzushi
平禄寿司
5-8-5 Jingūmae, Shibuya-ku ☎03/3498-3968; Meiji-jingūmae Station; see map p.106. Daily 11am–9pm. Perennially popular *kaitenzushi*

(conveyor-belt sushi) restaurant in a prime position on Omotesandō. Plates range from ¥120 to ¥240. Inexpensive.

Hiroba
広場
3-8-15 Kita-Aoyama, Minato-ku ☎03/3406-6409; Omotesandō Station; see map p.106. Daily 11am–10pm. Hearty lunch buffets for ¥1200. It's at the Crayon House natural food shop, just off Omotesandō around the corner from the Hanae Mori Building. Moderate.

Las Chicas
Rasu Chikasu
5-47-6 Jingūmae, Shibuya-ku ☎03/3407-6865; Omotesandō Station; see map p.106. Daily 11am–11pm. There are few nicer places to dine on a summer's night than in the enchanting courtyard here, and there's also a spacious indoor restaurant and a lively bar (with an Internet terminal). Food is Italian-fusion, supported by some fine Antipodean wines. Moderate.

Maisen
マイ泉
4-8-5 Jingūmae, Shibuya-ku ☎03/3470-0071; Omotesandō Station; see map p.106. Daily 11am–10pm. Set in an old bathhouse, this long-running *tonkatsu* restaurant serves up great-value set meals. Moderate.

Mominoki House
モミノキハウス
2-18-5 Jingūmae, Shibuya-ku ☎03/3405-9144; Meiji-jingūmae Station; see map p.106. Mon–Sat 11am–11pm. Lots of natural ingredients are used at this macrobiotic restaurant on the quiet side of Harajuku. Plants, paintings and jazz add to the atmosphere, and a good lunch can be had for around ¥1500. Moderate.

Nobu Tokyo
Nobu Tōkyō

6-10-17 Minami-Aoyama, Minato-ku ☎03/5467-0022; Omotesandō Station; see map p.115. Mon–Fri 11.30am–2.30pm & 6–11pm, Sat & Sun 6–11pm. Japanese–Peruvian fusion cuisine by superstar chef Nobu Matsuhisa – try the signature black cod with miso – served in what looks like a luxurious family diner, with big pink rose prints, expensive black leather seats and an open kitchen with chefs in baseball caps. The lunch set for ¥3000 is the best deal. Expensive.

Pariya
パリヤ

3-12-14 Kita Aoyama, Minato-ku ☎03/3486-1316; Omotesandō Station; see map p.106. Daily 11.30am–2.30pm & 6–11pm. Three Bapa Papa character dolls greet you at this fun eatery, just off Aoyama-dōri, where you can choose from a wide range of ingredients and cooking methods to make up your meal. The English menu explains how it all works, or you could come for lunch when a good-value spread is laid out. Moderate.

Rojak
Rojaku

6-3-14 Minami-Aoyama, Minato-ku ☎03/3409-6764; Omotesandō Station; see map p.106. Daily noon–4pm, 6pm–midnight. Tucked away down a cul-de-sac near the *Blue Note Tokyo* jazz club, this place does appealing and reasonably priced Asian/organic food and has a very cosy library-style bar with sofas. There's also a new branch in Roppongi Hills (Hillside complex ☎03/5770-5831). Moderate to expensive.

Sakuratei
さくら亭

3-20-1 Jingūmae, Shibuya-ku ☎03/3479-0039; Meiji-jingūmae Station; see map p.106. Daily 11.30am–11pm. Funky cook your own *okonomiyaki* and *yakisoba* joint behind the weird and wonderful Design Festa gallery (see p.110). From 11.30am to 3pm you've got ninety minutes to eat as much as you like for ¥980, and it's just as good value at night. Inexpensive.

Tama
たま

5-9-8 Minami-Aoyama, Minato-ku ☎03/3406-8088; Omotesandō Station; see map p.106. Daily 11.30am–2.30pm & 6–11pm. Decent choice of traditional Japanese dishes with subtle twists served in a minimalist, smooth concrete setting. The extensive sake selection changes monthly and the menu is in English. Moderate.

Underground Mr Zoogunzoo
Undagurando Misuta Zugunzu

B1 Aoyama City Building, 2-9-11 Shibuya, Shibuya-ku ☎03/3400-1496; Omotesandō Station; see map p.115. Tues–Sun 6–11pm. The earthy tones and baked mud walls of this narrow basement space conjure up the Australian outback, while the menu also reflects the tastes of down-under, with Pacific-rim fusion cuisine and an extensive selection of Antipodean wines. Expensive.

Asakusa and around

Bon
ぼん

1-2-11 Ryusen, Taitō-ku ☎03/3872-0375; Iriya Station; see colour map at back of book. Daily except Tues noon–3pm & 5–7pm. A rare chance to sample *fucha shojin-ryōri*, an exquisite, totally vegetarian style of Zen Buddhist cooking. The setting, a charming old Japanese house, and the calm service, make it an experience not to be missed. Moderate to expensive.

Chin'ya
ちんや

1-3-4 Asakusa, Taitō-ku ☎03/3841-0010; Asakusa Station; see map p.76. Daily except Wed 11.45am–9pm. Founded in 1880, this famous, traditional *shabu-shabu* and *sukiyaki* restaurant offers basic menus from ¥3000. It occupies seven floors, with cheaper, more casual dining in the basement. Moderate to expensive.

Daikokuya
大黒屋

1-38-10 Asakusa, Taitō-ku ☎03/3844-1111; Asakusa Station; see map p.76. Daily except Thurs 11.30am–8.30pm. There's always a queue at lunchtime at this Meiji-era tempura restaurant set in an attractive old building opposite Dembō-in garden. The speciality is *tendon*, a satisfying bowl of shrimp, fish and prawn fritters on a bed of rice (from ¥1400). The tatami room upstairs tends to be less hectic. Try the annex around the corner (1-31-10 Asakusa ☎03/3844-2222; closed Tues) if the main restaurant is busy or closed. Moderate.

Hatsuogawa
初小川

2-8-4 Kaminarimon, Taitō-ku ☎03/3844-2723;

Asakusa Station; see map p.76. Mon–Sat noon–2pm & 5–8pm, Sun 5–7.30pm. Look for the profusion of potted plants outside this tiny, rustic *unagi* (eel) restaurant – it's very foreigner-friendly and a lovely place to experience this most luscious of Japanese dishes. Moderate.

Maguro Bito

まぐろ人

1-5 Asakusa, Taitō-ku ☎03/3844-8736; Asakusa Station; see map p.76. Daily 11am–10pm. Fuji-TV viewers voted this the top *kaiten-zushi* shop in Japan, and it's easy to see why: the quality of fish and other ingredients is excellent, the turnover fast and the decor on the ritzy side. Expect a queue, but it moves fast. Electronically price-coded plates range from ¥130 to ¥400. There's also a stand-up/take-away branch opposite Kaminari-mon. Inexpensive.

Nakae

中江

1-9-2 Nihonzutsumi, Taitō-ku ☎03/3872-5398; Minowa Station. Tues–Sun 11.30am–2pm & 5–10pm; see colour map at back of book. This venerable restaurant specializes in dishes made with horse meat, including *sukiyaki* – an unusual delight, although it won't be to everyone's taste. The interior, decorated with beautiful ink paintings of horses, looks pretty much like it did a century ago when the whole area was a thriving red-light district.

Otafuku

大多福

1-6-2 Senzoku, Taitō-ku ☎03/3871-2521; Iriya Station; see colour map at back of book. Mon–Sat 5–11pm, Sun 5–10pm; closed Mon April–Sept.

Customers have been coming to this charming restaurant for over eighty years to sample its delicious selection of *oden* dishes, including rarities such as shark, both flesh and bone. Wash it all down with a beaker of pine-scented *tarozake* (sake). Some Japanese would help here, but the staff are very friendly and you can sit at the counter and point at what you want in the bubbling brass vats. Moderate to expensive.

Owariya

おわり屋

1-7-1 Asakusa, Taitō-ku ☎03/3845-4500; Tawaramachi Station; see map p.76. Daily except Fri 11.30am–8.30pm. This restaurant, with classy calligraphy on the walls, has been dishing up delicious soba in all its variations for over a century. Inexpensive to moderate.

Sometaro

染太郎

2-2-2 Nishi-Asakusa, Taitō-ku ☎03/3844-9502; Tawaramachi Station; see map p.76. Daily noon–10pm. Homely restaurant specializing in *okonomiyaki*, cheap and filling savoury pancakes cooked on a hotplate. One good-sized bowl costs from ¥400, depending on your ingredients, or try your hand at *yaki-isoba* (fried noodles) from ¥580. There's a book of English instructions and plenty of people to offer advice. To find it look for a bamboo-fenced garden and lantern halfway up the street. Inexpensive.

Ebisu, Hiro-o and Meguro

Cardenas Charcole Grill
Kādeinasu Chyākōru Guriru

see map p.76

Dining on the water

Yakatabune lunch and dinner cruises on the Sumida-gawa and in Tokyo Bay are a charming Tokyo dining institution that few short-term visitors get around to experiencing. These low-slung traditional boats lit up with paper lanterns can accommodate anything from 16 to 100 people. The boats of **Amisei** (☎03/3844-1869) set off from the southwest side of Azumabashi bridge, Asakusa. Their ninety-minute lunch cruises cost ¥6300, while a two-hour evening cruise costs ¥8000, including all the tempura you can eat. More lavish menus can be ordered for higher prices and, naturally, the charges skyrocket for cruises on the night when Asakusa holds its annual fireworks extravaganza in July. **Funasei Yakatabune** cruises (☎03/5479-2731, ⓦwww.funasei.com) run out of Kita-Shinagawa and offer a choice of Japanese- and Western-style menus for around ¥10,000 per person. More affordable are the **Tsukishima** cruises (☎03/3533-6699), where the meal features the local culinary speciality, *monjayaki*, a thin batter pancake similar to *okonomiyaki*; cruises kick off at around ¥5000 per person, including all you can eat and drink.

13

EATING AND DRINKING | Restaurants

1-12-14 Ebisu Nishi, Shibuya-ku ⊕03/5428-0779; Ebisu Station; see map p.118. Mon–Fri 11.30am–2pm & 5.30pm–2am, Sat & Sun 5.30pm–2am. This dramatic, multi-level basement space showcases some of Tokyo's best contemporary fusion cuisine – the fishcakes in *uni* sauce look like spiky sea urchins and taste fantastic. Moderate to expensive.

Ebisu Tower
Ebisu Tawā
Yebisu Garden City; Ebisu Station; see map p.118. Daily 11.30am–3pm & 5–11pm. Two floors of restaurants with great views across the city. Try *Yebisu* (⊕03/5420-1161), on the 39th floor, a classy *yakitori-ya* with sets for around ¥1000; or *Chibo* (⊕03/5424-1011), a fun Ōsaka-style *okonomiyaki* restaurant on the 38th. Moderate.

Fummy's Grill
Fumiizu Guriru
2-1-5 Ebisu, Shibuya-ku ⊕03/3473-9629; Ebisu Station; see map.118. Daily 1.30pm–2am. Nouvelle cuisine, minus the skimpy portions, served in a casual setting with a small open terrace overlooking a quiet street. They also offer a weekend brunch for ¥1300. Moderate.

Good Honest Grub
Gudo Honesuto Gurabu
1-11-11 Ebisu Minami, Shibuya-ku ⊕03/3710-0400; Ebisu Station; see map p.118. Daily 11.30am–2am. This relaxed, brightly decorated place serves up just what the name says: chunky sandwiches, big salads and sizeable plates of pasta. The fruit shakes and slurpies are good, and they also have organic wine. There's another, roomier branch in Harajuku (2F Harajuku Belle Pia, 6-6-2 Jingūmae, Shibuya-ku ⊕03/3406-6606). Inexpensive to moderate.

Homework's
Hōmuwākusu
5-1-20 Hiro-o, Shibuya-ku ⊕03/3440-4560; Hiro-o Station; see map p.118. Mon–Sat 11am–9pm, Sun 11am–6pm. This popular pit stop at the end of Hiro-o's main shopping street does good, chunky, home-made burgers – and the French fries are well up to scratch, too. There's another branch near Roppongi Hills (1-5-8 Azabu-Jūban, Minato-ku ⊕03/3405-9884; map p.9). Moderate.

Hong Kong Garden
Hongu Kongu Gāden
4-5-2 Nishi-Azabu, Minato-ku ⊕03/3486-3711; Hiro-o Station; see map.68. Mon–Fri 11.30am–3pm & 5.30–10.30pm, Sat & Sun 11.30am–4.30pm & 5.30–10.30pm. Chinese restaurants in Tokyo don't come much bigger than this lively place. The steaming dishes include lunch and dinner eat-all-you-like dim sum and other options for ¥3000–4000. Moderate to expensive.

Kushinobō
串の坊
6F Atre, 1-5-5 Ebisu, Shibuya-ku ⊕03/5475-8415; Ebisu Station; see map p.118. Daily 11.30am–9pm. This *kushiage* restaurant has a cosy, folk-craft ambience and does great-value lunch sets from under ¥1000, as well as lots of interesting deep-fried nibbles on skewers. There are other branches around the city, including at Roppongi (2F 7&7 Building, 7-14-18 Roppongi), which specializes in *fugu*; Shibuya (5F J&R Building, 33-12 Udagawachō); and Shinjuku (1-10-5 Kabukichō). Moderate.

Ninnikuya
ニンニク屋
1-26-12 Ebisu, Shibuya-ku ⊕03/3446-5887; Ebisu Station; see map p.118. Tues–Sun 6.30pm–10.30pm. Tokyo's original garlic restaurant, and still one of the best. Virtually everything on the menu is cooked with the pungent bulb, and the buzzing atmosphere in the long dining room with large shared wooden tables can't be beaten. Moderate to expensive.

Tonki
とんき
1-1-2 Shimo-Meguro, Meguro-ku, ⊕03/3491-9928; Meguro Station; see map p.118. Daily except Tues 4–10.45pm. Tokyo's most famous *tonkatsu* restaurant, where a seemingly telepathic team make order of chaos. You'll need to queue up outside the main branch, west of the station, which is only open from 4pm; for lunch, go to *Tonki Annex* on the east side of the station, across the plaza on the second floor of the corner building. Moderate.

Ginza, Shiodome and Yūrakuchō

There are plenty of restaurants to choose from in the new Coredo, Marunouchi Building and Shiodome complexes (all on Ginza map p.54). The more adventurous will want to muck in with the locals at the numerous *yakitori* bars nestling under the railway tracks between Yūrakuchō and Shimbashi stations.

Afternoon Tea Baker and Diner
Afutanūn Chi Bēka ando Daina
2-3-6 Ginza, Chūō-ku ☎03/5159-1635; Ginza-Itchōme Station; see map p.54. Mon–Fri 11.30am–2.30pm & 5.30–10.30pm, Sat & Sun 11.30am–2.30pm & 5.30–9pm. Stylish department store restaurant set up with the help of British celeb chef, Jamie Oliver – his simple but inventive grub kicks off at ¥3500 for three courses at lunch or ¥5000 for four courses at dinner. Moderate to expensive.

Aroina Tabeta
あろいなたべた
3-7-11 Marunouchi, Chiyoda-ku ☎03/5219-6099; Yūrakuchō Station; see map p.54. Daily 24 hours. Note the big ¥500 sign – that's the price you'll pay for all food, including set lunches, at this basic Thai eatery under the tracks. The cooking is heavy on the chilli (a surprise in Tokyo) but tasty, and great value for what you get. Inexpensive.

Atariya
当リヤ
3-5-17 Ginza, Chūō-ku ☎03/3564-0045; Ginza Station; see map p.54. Mon–Sat 4.30–11pm. One of the more reasonable places to eat in Ginza, this small, workaday restaurant, marked by a big red lantern, has an English menu and is a good introduction to *yakitori* bars. Moderate.

Daidaiya
橙家
2F Ginza Nine Building, 8-5 Ginza-nishi ☎03/5537-3566; Shimbashi Station; see map p.54. Daily 5pm–1am. In a city of stunning restaurant interiors, this one really knocks your socks off. The food is "nouvelle japonaise", with items such as foie gras on lotus root cakes, as well as a good sushi and tempura selection. Be sure to book. There are other spectacular branches in Shinjuku (☎03/5362-7173) and Akasaka's Belle Vie complex (☎03/3588-5087). Expensive.

Edo-gin
江戸銀
4-5-5 Tsukiji, Chūō-ku ☎03/3543-4401; Tsukiji Station; see map p.54. Daily 11am–9.30pm. Over one hundred chefs slice fish for hordes of customers who pack out *Edo-gin* and its three satellite shops. The portions are reckoned to be among the largest in the city, and certainly make the traditional one-bite technique of eating sushi difficult. The ¥1000 *teishoku* is the best bet for lunch. Moderate to expensive.

En
えん
42nd Floor, Shiodome City Centre, 1-5-2 Higashi Shimbashi, Minato-ku ☎03/5537-2096; Shiodome Station; see map p.54. Daily 11.30am–2pm, 5–11pm. This upmarket Japanese *izakaya* has rustic stylings, a menu with a wide range of vegetable and fish dishes and killer views across to Hama Rikyū Teien and the bay. Moderate.

Farm Grill
Famu Guriru
2F Ginza Nine, 3-8-6 Ginza, Chūō-ku ☎03/5568-6156; Shimbashi Station; see map p.54. Daily 11.30am–11pm. Pay as you enter for this popular California-style buffet located under the expressway. It's ¥1000 at lunch or ¥2500 for dinner, and there's a 2hr time limit. Drinks are not included, but in the evening you can opt for a ¥3800 *nomihodai* (drink as much as you like) which includes wine, whisky, coffee and a choice of fifty cocktails. Moderate.

G-Zone
Ji Zon
1-2-3 Ginza, Chūō-ku; Ginza-Itchōme Station; see map p.54. Daily 11am–4am. The Global Dining group has gathered together all its concept restaurants at this complex beneath the Shuto Expressway – from the ye olde Japanese-style *Gonpachi* (☎03/5524-3641) at one end to the faux-European *La Bohème* (☎03/5524-3616) at the other, with the Mexican *Zest Cantina* (☎03/5524-3621) and Southeast Asian *Monsoon Café* (☎03/5524-3631) in the middle. Moderate to expensive.

Little Okinawa
Ritoru Okinawa
8-7-10 Ginza, Chūō-ku ☎03/3572-2930; Shimbashi Station; see map p.54. Mon–Fri 5pm–3am, Sat & Sun 4pm–midnight. The welcome at this cosy Okinawan restaurant is as warm as it would be in the southern islands. Try Ryūkyū dishes such as *chanpuru* and the strong tipple *awamori*. There's an English menu, but the Japanese one has photos. Moderate.

Mango Tree Tokyo
Mango Torii Tōkyō
35F Marunouchi Building, 2-4-1 Marunouchi,

Chiyoda-ku ☎ 03/5224-5489; Tokyo Station; see map p.54. Daily 11am–4pm, 5–11pm. Stylish Thai restaurant with branches in Bangkok and London. Its delicious lunchtime buffet (¥2685) is one of the best ways to enjoy the view from the top of the Marunouchi Building.

Matsumotorō
松本楼
1-2 Hibiya-kōen, Chiyoda-ku ☎ 03/3503-1415; Hibiya Station; see map p.54. Daily 11am–5pm. The food is pretty standard, but on a sunny day it's a pleasure to sit in the garden terrace of this venerable restaurant which is as old as Tokyo's first Western-style park, in which it is located.

Nair's
Nairu
4-10-7 Ginza, Chūō-ku ☎ 03/3541-8246; Higashi-Ginza Station; see map p.54. Daily except Tues 11.30am–9.30pm, Sun until 8.30pm. This Tokyo institution has been going since 1949, and although it's perhaps not the best Indian around, the Kerala home cooking is tasty and reasonably cheap for Ginza, even if the decor is on the tacky, Bollywood side. Moderate.

Nataraj
Nataraju
7-9F Ginza Kosaka Building, 6-9-4 Ginza ☎ 03/5537-1515; Ginza Station; see map p.54. Daily 11.30am–11pm. Vegetarians will want to check out this reasonably classy Indian chain restaurant, which does a fine range of veg curries and naan breads. It's in the same building as *Tsukiji Tama-zushi* (see below). Moderate.

Nylon
Nairon
B2 Caretta Shiodome, 1-8-2 Higashi-Shinbashi, Minato-ku ☎ 03/5537-5646; Shiodome Station; see map p.54. Daily 11.30am–11pm. Mediterranean restaurant with a breezy hint of the Aegean in its design. The lunch buffet (¥1500; Mon–Fri 11.30am–1.50pm, Sat & Sun 11am–2.20pm) offers a selection of pizza, pasta, rice and salad dishes that is one of the better deals in the Shiodome area, and at night you can enjoy a bucket of mussels from ¥1200. Moderate.

Robata Honten
爐端本店
1-3-8 Yūrakuchō, Chiyoda-ku ☎ 03/3591-1905; Hibiya Station; see map p.54. Daily 5–11pm. The delicious food at this rustic *izakaya* (look for the basket of veggies outside) is

laid out in big plates for you to see – order what you fancy and the genial, kimono-clad owner will whisk it off to be prepared. Moderate.

Taimeiken
たいめいけん
1-12-10 Nihombashi, Chūō-ku ☎ 03/3271-2464; Nihombashi Station; see map p.54. Mon–Sat 11am–9pm. Tokyoites swoon at the nostalgia of one of Tokyo's original Western-style restaurants, whose *omu-raisu* (rice-stuffed omelette) featured in the movie *Tampopo* (see p.189). Old waiters in bow ties and waitresses in pinstripe overalls bustle about the cheap and cheerful cafeteria downstairs serving large portions of curry rice, *tonkatsu* and noodles. There's a more expensive restaurant above. Inexpensive to moderate.

Takara
Takara
B1F Tokyo International Forum, 3-5-1 Marunouchi, Chiyoda-ku ☎ 03/5223-9888; Yūrakuchō Station; see map p.54. Mon–Fri 11.30am–2.30pm, 4–11pm, Sat & Sun 11.30am–10pm. A striking red communal table defines this modern *izakaya*, specializing in sake and serving excellent modern Japanese cuisine – try their substantial lunch sets. John Gautner, Tokyo's *gaijin* sake guru, holds monthly seminars on *nihonshu* here.

Tenmaru
天マル
6-9-2 Ginza, Chūō-ku ☎ 03/3289-1010; Ginza Station; see map p.54. Mon–Sat 11.30am–3pm & 5–9pm, Sun 11am–9pm. Consistently good tempura restaurant in a basement just off Chūō-dōri. Expect to spend at least ¥2000 per head. English menu available. Moderate.

Torigin Honten
鳥ぎん本店
B1, 5-5-7 Ginza, Chūō-ku ☎ 03/3571-3333; Ginza Station; see map p.54. Daily 11.30am–10pm. Bright, popular restaurant serving *yakitori* and *kamameshi* (kettle-cooked rice with a choice of toppings), tucked down an alley two blocks east of Ginza's Sony Building among a clutch of cheeky copycat rivals. Good for a snack or a full meal, particularly if you opt for *kamameshi* or a weekday lunch set, both from around ¥800. The English menu makes it a lot easier. Inexpensive to moderate.

Tsukiji Tama-zushi Ginza Rabi-ten
築地玉寿司

5F, 6-9-5 Ginza, Chūō-ku ☏03/3574-9635; Ginza Station; see map p.54. Daily 5.30pm–2am. Despite the plush surroundings, prices are very reasonable at this retro-glam restaurant on three floors with a glitzy sushi bar on the sixth floor and a more soothing, Japanese-style "sushi corner" on the fourth. Plates cost ¥100–500 for the basic *nigiri-zushi*. Moderate.

Ikebukuro

Akiyoshi
秋吉

3-30-4 Nishi-Ikebukuro, Toshima-ku ☏03/3982-0601; Ikebukuro Station; see map p.91. Daily 5pm–midnight. Unusually large *yakitori* bar with a good atmosphere and a helpful picture menu. You might have to queue at peak times for the tables, but there's generally space at the counter. Inexpensive.

Malaychan
マレーチャン

3-22-6 Nishi-Ikebukuro, Toshima-ku ☏03/5391-7638; Ikebukuro Station; see map p.91. Mon–Sat 11am–2.30pm & 5–11pm, Sun 11am–11pm. Unpretentious Malay restaurant dishing up decent food, from grilled fish on banana leaf and *mee goreng* to winter steam boats. The beer pitchers are good value, or throw in a Singapore Sling and you can still eat well for around ¥2000. Weekday lunch menus from ¥800. Inexpensive to moderate.

Mekong
メコン

B1, 3-26-5 Nishi-Ikebukuro, Toshima-ku ☏03/3988-5688; Ikebukuro Station; see map p.91. Daily except Tues lunchtime 11.30am–2.30pm & 5–11pm. The decor may not be much to rave about, but the tastes and aromas will take you straight back to Thailand. The lunchtime buffet is a steal at ¥1050; at other times you can eat well for around ¥2000 per head from their picture menu. Moderate.

Rāmen Meisakuza
ラーメン名作座

1-14 Higashi-Ikebukuro, Toshima-ku; Ikebukuro Station; see map p.91. Daily 11am–4am. Fans of the Chinese-style soupy noodle dish should head straight to this narrow alley on the east side of the station towards Sunshine City. Seven outlets serve up variations on the theme,

with *Hinano* (☏03/3986-2327) doing a low-cholesterol version, and *Maguroya* (☏03/5956-3455) offering Tsukiji-style ramen made with a tuna-fish-head soup and liberal seafood and fish toppings. Inexpensive.

Saigon
サイゴン

3F, 1-7-10 Higashi-Ikebukuro, Toshima-ku ☏03/3989-0255; Ikebukuro Station; see map p.91. Mon–Fri noon–2.30pm & 5–10.30pm, Sat & Sun 11.30am–10.30pm. Friendly, unpretentious place serving authentic Vietnamese food, even down to the 333 beer. *Banh xeo* (sizzling pancake with a spicy sauce) or *bunh bo* (beef noodle soup) are recommended, with a side dish of *nem* (spring rolls) if you're really hungry. Weekday lunchtime sets are excellent value at ¥750. Inexpensive to moderate.

Kanda, Kagurazaka and Ryōgoku

Botan
ぼたん

1-15 Kanda-Sudachō, Chiyoda-ku ☏03/3251-0577; Awajichō Station; see map p.61. Mon–Sat 11.30am–9pm (last order 8pm). Chicken *sukiyaki* is the order of the day at this atmospheric old restaurant tucked into the backstreets of Kanda. There's no choice and it's certainly not cheap at just over ¥7000 a head, but this is the genuine article, where the chicken, vegetables and tofu simmer gently over individual braziers in small rooms. Very expensive.

La Bretagne
ラブルターニュ

4-2 Kagurazaka, Shinjuku-ku ☏03/3478-7855; Iidabashi Station; see map p.61. Tues–Sat 11.30am–10.30pm, Sun 11.30am–9pm. Attractive French-run restaurant, down a little dead-end street with tables outside, offering authentic crepes and buckwheat *galettes*. Also serves salads, lunchtime sets (around ¥1500) and daily specials. There's another branch just off Omotesandō (4-9-8 Jingūmae, Shibuya-ku ☏03/3478-7855; map p.106). Moderate.

Mukashiya
昔屋

5-12 Kagurazaka, Shinjuku-ku ☏03/3267-9595; Iidabashi Station; see map p.61. Mon–Fri 5–11pm, Sat 5–10.30pm. Big, old-style *iza-kaya* with a rustic flavour. The speciality food is *yakitori* – try their own *Mukashi-yaki*, made of soya bean skins, or choose from the English menu. Moderate.

Tomoegata

巴潟

2-17-6 Ryōgoku, Sumida-ku ⊤ 03/3632-5600; Ryōgoku Station; see map p.61. Tues–Sun 11.30am–10pm. In the heart of sumo territory, this is a good place to sample the wrestlers' protein-packed meat, seafood and vegetable stew, *chanko-nabe*. For ¥2800 you can have the full-blown meal cooked at your table, though most people will find the smaller, ready-made version (¥840; lunch only) more than enough. It's two blocks south of the station, and easy to spot from its parade of colourful flags; there's a new annexe on the north side of the street. Inexpensive to moderate.

Yabu Soba

やぶそば

2-10 Kanda-Awajichō, Chiyoda-ku ⊤ 03/3251-0287; Awajichō Station; see map p.61. Daily 11.30am–8pm. Connoisseurs travel a long way to slurp the noodles here and to listen to the cheerful waiting staff's distinctive singsong cries. You might have to wait at busy times, but it doesn't take long, and there's an attractive garden to admire. Prices start at around ¥600. Inexpensive to moderate.

Yoshiba

吉葉

2-14-5 Sumida Yokoami, Sumida-ku, ⊤ 03/3623-4480; Ryōgoku Station; see map p.61. Daily 11.30am–1.30pm, 5–10pm. Set in an old sumo *dojo* (practice hall) – book ahead for the prime tables around the practice ring. This is the best place to come for *chanko-nabe* (from ¥2000), including 17 different ingredients, or there's a set menu for ¥6000 per person. On Monday, Wednesday and Friday there's live singing of traditional songs. Expensive.

Roppongi, Nishi-Azabu and Azabu-Jūban

Benitora Gyōzadō

紅虎餃子堂

2-5-1 Azabu-Jūban, Minato-ku ⊤ 03/5474-0364; Azabu-Jūban Station; see map p.71. Daily 11.30am–11pm. Known for its pan-fried *gyoza* (dumplings) and luscious pork black bean sauce, this is one of Tokyo's better Chinese restaurants. The atmosphere is fun and welcoming and there's an English menu.

Bikkuri Sushi

びっくり寿司

3-14-9 Roppongi, Minato-ku ⊤ 03/3403-1489; Roppongi Station; see map p.71. Daily 11am–5am. Conveyor-belt sushi on the corner of Gaien Higashi-dōri, opposite the Roi Building. The long opening hours make this a popular spot with clubbers hanging out for the first trains of the day. Dishes start at ¥130. Inexpensive.

Cyclo Piramide Building

Shikuro Piramido Biru

6-6-9 Roppongi, Minato-ku ⊤ 03/3478-4964; Roppongi Station; see map p.71. Daily 11.30am–3pm & 5–10.30pm. Stylish Vietnamese restaurant serving some tasty offerings although they lack an authentic tang. Expensive.

Dalarna

ダーラナ

5-9-19 Roppongi, Minato-ku ⊤ 03/3478-4690; Roppongi Station; see map p.71. Mon–Sat noon–3pm & 6–9.30pm. This intimate Swedish restaurant offers yummy meatballs with lingonberry jam, gravlax and other Scandinavian dishes. There are good lunch deals and the set dinner is ¥3500. Moderate.

Gonpachi

権八

1-13-11 Nishi-Azabu, Minato-ku ⊤ 03/5771-0170; Roppongi Station; see map p.68. Daily 11.30am–5pm. The monumental *kura* (storehouse) at Nishi-Azabu crossing looks as if it's somehow survived since the Edo period, but it's actually one of the newest on the block and is only supposed to be a temporary structure. Inside, take your pick between soba and grilled items on the ground and second floors, while on the third it's sushi. President Bush Jnr ate here, but don't let that put you off – it has a wonderful Samurai drama atmosphere. There's also a branch in *G-Zone* in Ginza (see p.156). Moderate.

Hainan Jeefan Shokudo

海南鶏飯食堂

6-11-16 Roppongi, Minato-ku ⊤ 03/5474 3200; Roppongi Station; see map p.71. Daily 11.30am–2pm & 6–10pm. The menu at this smart new eatery at the quiet end of Roppongi Hills is made up of Singaporean hawker favourites. The portions aren't huge but it's all tasty and well done and the service is very friendly. Moderate.

Havana Café

Habana Kafe

4-12-2 Roppongi, Minato-ku ☎03/3423-3500; Roppongi Station; see map p.68. **Daily noon–5am.** There's more of a Tex-Mex than a Cuban lilt to the menu at this brightly decorated café away from the main Roppongi drag. The portions are large, the prices reasonable and there's a happy hour from 5pm to 7pm. Moderate.

Ichioku

一億

4-4-5 Roppongi, Minato-ku ☎03/3405-9891; Roppongi Station; see map p.68. **Daily 5pm–3am, Sun until 11pm.** At the Nogizaka end of Roppongi – look for the green, yellow and red front of this funkily decorated *mukokuseki* (no nationality) *izakaya*. Many swear by the cheese *gyoza* and tofu steaks, but there's plenty more to choose from on the picture menu. Dishes are made from organically grown vegetables. Moderate.

Juniper

Junipā

4F Grand Hyatt Tokyo, 6-10-3 Roppongi, Minato-ku ☎03/4333-8888; Roppongi Station; see map p.71. **Daily 11.30am–11pm.** The *Grand Hyatt* has an excellent range of restaurants, and although it's invidious to choose one, *Juniper* is the most original, offering cuisine with a Scandinavian twist in a chic, casual atmosphere. They also have outdoor seating in the Roppongi Hills atrium. Expensive.

Kisso

吉左右

B1 Axis Building, 5-17-1 Roppongi, Minato-ku ☎03/3582-4191; Roppongi Station; see map p.71. **Mon–Sat 11.30am–2pm & 5.30–10pm.** Wonderful place to sample *kaiseki-ryōri* (see box opposite), the menus for which change to reflect the seasons. Lunch sets are a bargain at ¥1200 to ¥2500; evening set meals, including at least nine different dishes, start at ¥8000. The decor features modern furnishings with traditional touches, including giant ikebana displays and waitresses in kimono. Very expensive.

L'Atelier de Joel Robuchon

Raterieru de Joeru Robushon

2F Roppongi Hills Hillside, 6-10-1 Roppongi, Minato-ku ☎03/5772-7500; Roppongi Station; see map p.71. **Daily 11.30am–2.30pm, 6–10pm.** Of all the many, many restaurants in Roppongi Hills, this is the one that has created the biggest buzz – and the longest queues, since they have a no-bookings

policy. Be patient or lucky and you'll eventually get a seat at the long counter facing onto the open kitchen and be able to see what all the fuss is about, as black-garbed chefs create mini-culinary masterpieces before your very eyes. The six-course menu is ¥6000, but it's possible to treat yourself to a couple of the *dégustation*-size dishes for less. Expensive to very expensive.

Rainbow Roll Sushi

Rēnbo Roru Sushi

2F Monteplaza, 1-10-3 Azabu-Jūban ☎03/5572-7689; Azabu-Jūban Station; see map p.71. **Daily 11.30am–2pm & 6–11pm.** Sushi gets a contemporary makeover at this sleekly designed restaurant where fish is often the last thing you'll find in your California-style roll. They do great cocktails too. Moderate.

Roti

Rote

1F Piramide Building, 6-6-9 Roppongi, Minato-ku ☎03/5785-3671; Roppongi Station; see map p.71. **Mon–Fri 11.30am–3pm & 6–11pm, Sat noon–5pm & 6–11pm, Sun 10am–3pm & 6–10pm.** You'd better be hungry before dining at this "modern American brasserie" because the portions are huge. You could easily share their speciality – rotisserie chicken, which is well worth the ¥2000 asking price – or any of their other grilled meat dishes. They also serve fine microbrew beers and a tempting range of desserts. There's another branch at the Harumi Triton complex (1-8-16 Harumi, Chūō-ku ☎03/5144-8275; map p.124). Moderate.

Seizan

清山

Roppongi Hills West Walk 5F, 6-10-1 Roppongi, Minato-ku ☎03/5772-2077; Roppongi Station; see map p.71. **Daily 11am–11pm.** Part of the venerable Sushisei chain (see Akasaka), this is the best sushi place in Roppongi Hills, with a great lunch set for ¥1300 as well as dinner sets from ¥1800. Ask to sit at the counter if you want to order directly from the chefs.

Volga

Boruga

3-5-14 Shiba Koen, Minato-ku ☎03/3433-1766; Kamiyachō Station; see map p.68. **Daily 11am–2.30pm & 5–11pm.** Outside is a camp, onion-domed facade, inside it's like entering a set from *Dr Zhivago*, all heavy velvet and

Kaiseki-ryōri: Japanese haute cuisine

Japan's finest style of cooking, **kaiseki-ryōri**, comprises a series of small, carefully balanced and expertly presented dishes. Though never cheap, it's a dining experience which shouldn't be missed while in Tokyo. *Kaiseki-ryōri* began as an accompaniment to the tea ceremony and still retains the meticulous design of that elegant ritual. At the best *kaiseki-ryōri* restaurants the atmosphere of the room in which the meal is served is just as important as the food, which will invariably reflect the best of the season's produce; you'll sit on tatami, a scroll decorated with calligraphy will hang in the *tokonoma* (alcove) and a waitress in kimono will serve each course on beautiful china and lacquerware. For such a sublime experience you should expect to pay ¥10,000 or more for dinner, although a lunchtime *kaiseki* bentō is a more affordable option. Good *kaiseki-ryōri* restaurants to try include **Kisso** in Roppongi (see opposite), **Kakiden** (see overleaf) and the *Park Hyatt*'s **Kazue** (see overleaf) in Shinjuku.

gilt. There are over twenty different types of vodka, and a menu which embraces standard Russian dishes such as *borsch* and *piroshki*. There's often live music, too. Expensive.

Shibuya

Christon Café
Karisuton Kafe
B1F, 2-10-7 Dogenzaka, Shibuya-ku ☏03/5728-2225; Shibuya Station; see map p.115. Mon 5–11pm, Tues–Sun 5pm–5am. This basement restaurant could be the set for a Hammer horror movie shot in a Gothic cathedral, though the nicely presented Asian fusion food won't scare you. There's another branch in Shinjuku (☏03/5287-2426). Moderate.

Le CoCon
Re Kokon
US Building, 2-8 Uguisudani-chō, Shibuya-ku ☏03/5459-5366; Shibuya Station; see map p.118. Daily 11.30am–3pm & 6pm–midnight. One of the most unusual Tokyo design restaurants. For wannabe Hobbits, the mud-pod dining booths in the basement are the place for a cosy dinner, while those who don't want to be cocooned will appreciate the friendly atmosphere and tetrahedron wood design of the ground-floor bar. The French-style food is very tasty. Expensive.

Miyoko
妙高
1-17-2 Shibuya, Shibuya-ku ☏03/3499-3450; Shibuya Station; see map p.115. Mon–Fri 11.30am–2pm and 5–9pm, Sat 11.30am–2pm. You really can't go wrong with the hearty metal bowls of *Yamanashi-ken* flat *udon*

noodles in a rich *nabe* stew – just the ticket on a chilly day. Or try the cold noodle dishes in summer. Look for the water wheel outside. Moderate.

Punraku
プンラク
8F Q-Front Building, 21-6 Udagawa-chō, Shibuya-ku ☏03/5459-2601; Shibuya Station; see map p.115. Daily noon–2.30pm, 5pm–1am. Convivial and airy modern Japanese restaurant on the top floor of the glass-fronted building diagonally across from the station. There's an English menu and the prices aren't outrageous. It's also a supprisingly quiet place for lunch given how busy it is outside. Moderate.

Shizenkan II
自然観パート2
Royal Building, 3-9-2 Shibuya, Shibuya-ku ☏03/3486-2661; Shibuya Station; see map p.115. Mon–Sat 11.30am–8pm. Health-food restaurant and shop, on the Ebisu side of Shibuya Station, serving a decent set lunch for ¥1000, with lots of brown rice and small vegetable dishes. Moderate.

Sonoma
Sonoma
2-25-17 Dōgenzaka, Shibuya-ku ☏03/3462-7766; Shibuya Station; see map p.115. Mon–Thurs & Sun 11.30am–midnight, Fri & Sat 11.30am–4am. Very much a *gaijin* hangout but none the worse for that, with decent and good-value fusion food. If you eat here you can get into the funky *Ruby Room* club (see p.178) upstairs for free. It's a little hidden away: look for the first alley off to the right of Dōgenzaka as you wall up the hill from the station. Moderate.

Shinjuku and around

Angkor Wat
アンコールワット
1-38-13 Yoyogi, Shibuya-ku ☏ 03/3370-3019;
Yoyogi Station; see map p.98. Mon–Fri
11am–2pm & 5–11pm, Sat & Sun 5–11pm.
Tokyo's best Cambodian restaurant. Tell the
waiters your price limit and let them bring
you a selection of dishes (¥3000 per head
is more than enough). The sweetly spicy
salads, soups and vegetable rolls are all
excellent. It's a five-minute walk west of
Yoyogi Station; look for the pottery elephant
outside the entrance on a side street.
Moderate.

Ban Thai
Ban Tai
1-23-14 Kabukichō, Shinjuku-ku
☏ 03/3207-0068; Shinjuku Station; see map
p.98. Mon–Fri 11.30am–3pm & 5–11.45pm, Sat
& Sun 11.30am–11.45pm. Shinjuku's most
famous Thai restaurant, serving authentic
dishes at moderate prices. It's on the third
floor of a building surrounded by the
screaming neon strip joints of Kabukichō.
Moderate.

Bosphorus Hasan
Bosuforusu Hasan
3-6-11 Shinjuku, Shinjuku-ku ☏ 03/3354-7947;
Shinjuku-Sanchōme Station; see map p.98.
Daily 6–11pm. On the second floor, this
long-running restaurant serves very good
Turkish food in a casual atmosphere that's
evocative of the country, right down to the
occasional belly-dancing performances.
Moderate.

Kakiden
柿でん
8F Yasuyo Building, 3-37-11 Shinjuku, Shinjuku-
ku ☏ 03/3352-5121; Shinjuku Station; see map
p.98. Daily 11am–9pm. One of the best
places in Tokyo to sample *kaiseki-ryōri*,
Japanese haute cuisine. There's a lunch for
¥4000, but you won't regret investing in the
eighteen-course dinner for ¥8000. There
are live performances on the thirteen-
stringed *koto* from 6pm to 8pm. Very
expensive.

Ken's Chanto Dining
Kenzu Chanto Dainingu
B1, FF Building, 3-26-8 Shinjuku, Shinjuku-ku
☏ 03/5363-0336; Shinjuku Station; see map
p.98. Daily 11.30am–2.30pm & 5pm–midnight.
Korean-influenced modern Japanese
restaurant, with an elegant contemporary

design and dishes like *kimchee*-stuffed
cabbage rolls and tuna *sashimi* with organic
vegetables. Expensive.

New York Grill
Nyu Yōku Guriru
Park Hyatt Tower, 3-7-1-2 Nishi-Shinjuku
☏ 03/5323-3458; Tochōmae Station; see map
p.98. Daily 11.30am–2.30pm & 5.30–10.30pm.
Stylish 52nd-floor restaurant where the
great views, huge portions and bustling
atmosphere make for a memorable eating
experience. The ¥5000 lunch is worth
forking out for. Bookings essential. The
hotel's *kaiseki-ryōri* restaurant *Kazue*
(☏ 03/5323-3460) is also excellent.
Expensive to very expensive.

Seiryūmon
青龍門
3/4F Shinjuku Remina Building, 3-17-4 Shinjuku,
Shinjuku-ku ☏ 03/3355-0717; Shinjuku-
Sanchōme Station; see map p.98. Mon–Fri
6pm–5am, Sat 5pm–5am, Sun 5pm–midnight.
One of Tokyo's first theme restaurants, and
still going strong. This branch of the
Chinese–Taiwanese chain replicates a
Shanghai opium den circa 1840. You dine
inside cages and there's a mock secret
entrance to the restaurant. Moderate to
expensive.

Shion
しおん
1-25 Kabukichō, Shinjuku-ku; Shinjuku Station;
see map p.98. Daily 11.30am–11pm. Round the
corner from *Kirin City* on the west side of
Shinjuku, this is one of the area's cheapest
conveyor-belt sushi operations. There's
often a queue, but it moves quickly. Plates
cost ¥100 or ¥200 each, and you can order
beer and sake. Inexpensive.

Shun Kan
しゅんかん
7F/8F My City, 3-38-1 Shinjuku, Shinjuku-ku;
Shinjuku Station; see map p.98. Daily
11.30am–10pm. The My City department
store has given its restaurant floors a super-
snazzy makeover, worth seeing in itself. The
more populist seventh floor has walls decorated with an ingenious range of items –
from old video recorders to flattened card-
board boxes; the eighth floor is all zen cool-
ness. Among the wide range of restaurants
it's worth checking out *Kowloon Ten Shin*
(☏ 03/5360-8191) for an all-you-can-eat
Chinese and dim sum buffet (lunch/dinner
¥1800/2800), *Kitchen Shunju*, the
Okinawan *Nabbie and Kamado*

(☎03/5379-1070) and the Korean *Saikaho*. Moderate.

Tsunahachi
つな八

3-31-8 Shinjuku. Shinjuku-ku ☎03/3352-1012; Shinjuku Station; see map p.98. Daily 11.15am–10pm. The main branch of the famous tempura restaurant almost always has a queue outside, though you're likely to get seated quickly if you settle for the upstairs rooms away from the frying action. Everything is freshly made, and even with the ¥1300 set (including soup, rice and pickles) you'll be full. Moderate.

Takadanobaba

Cambodia
カンボジャ

2F Yoshino Building, 3-10-14 Takada, Toshima-ku ☎03/3209-9320; Takadanobaba Station; see colour map at back of book. Mon–Sat 11.30am–2pm & 5–11pm. Popular Cambodian café, serving a spicy variation on *okonomiyaki* pancakes and Khmer-style curries – the picture menu makes ordering easy. From the station, head east along Waseda-dōri for two blocks, then turn north; the restaurant is on the second floor just after the comic bookstore. Moderate.

Rendezvous
ランデヴー

B1 Yanagiya Building, 2-18-6 Takadanobaba, Shinjuku-ku ☎03/5285-0128; Daily 1pm–midnight. Takadanobaba Station; see colour map at back of book. Small, friendly café serving the most authentic Burmese food among the cluster of places catering to the area's expat Burmese community. Try the *lape-toh* (fermented tea-leaf salad) or *mohinga* (noodles in a spicy, thick broth). Moderate.

Ueno, Nezu and around

Goemon
五右衛門

1-1-26 Hon-Komagome, Bunkyō-ku ☎03/3811-2015; Hon-Komagome Station; see colour map at back of book. Mon–Fri noon–2pm & 5–10pm, Sat noon–8pm. Cooking with tofu is raised to a fine art here in a delightful setting straight out of a woodblock print. Dine in one of the wooden pavilions fronting the rock garden and gurgling fountain, if possible. The set menu for lunch starts at ¥2700, while dinner costs from ¥5500. Expensive to very expensive.

Hantei
はん亭

2-12-15 Nezu, Bunkyō-ku ☎03/3828-1440; Nezu Station; see map p.82. Tues–Sat noon–2.30pm & 5–10pm, Sun noon–2.30pm & 4–9.30pm. Stylish dining in a beautiful, three-storey wooden house. There's only one dish, *kushiage* – deep-fried skewers of crunchy sea food, meat and vegetables with special dipping sauces – served in combination plates, six at a time: ¥2700 for the first plate; ¥1300 thereafter, until you say stop. Moderate to expensive.

Musashino
武蔵野

2-8-11 Ueno, Bunkyō-ku ☎03/3831-1672; Ueno-Hirokōji Station; see map p.82. Daily 11.30am–10pm. Ueno is famed for its *tonkatsu* (breaded pork cutlets), worth trying at this traditional restaurant behind bamboo screens and pot plants, which serves big, thick, melt-in-the-mouth slabs for reasonable prices. Choose between standard *rōsu* or fillet, at around ¥1500 including soup, rice and pickles. They also serve fried prawns (*ebi-fry*). Moderate.

Retro-kan
Retoro-kan

Ueno Station; see map p.82. Handy if you're waiting for a train, this recently renovated restaurant mall attached to Ueno Station is home to some stylish places. *Coca* on the first floor has an eclectic world cuisine menu, while the neighbouring *Tsuki-no-Shizuku* serves handmade tofu, among other Japanese dishes. There are also branches of *Hard Rock Café* and the British chain pub *Rose & Crown*. Moderate.

Sasa-no-yuki
笹乃雪

2-15-10 Negishi, Taitō-ku ☎03/3873-1145; Uguisudani Station; see map p.82. Tues–Sun 11am–9pm. Three centuries ago, the chef here was said to make tofu like "snow lying on bamboo leaves", and both the name and the quality have survived, though the old wooden house is now marooned among flyovers. Inside, it's nowhere near as fancy as *Goemon* (see opposite), but calm prevails over the tatami mats as you feast on delicately flavoured silk-strained tofu. There are three menus (from ¥1600 at lunch for three varieties of tofu), with the emphasis on flavour rather than quantity. Dinner set menus start at ¥3500. Moderate.

Unagi Ben-kei
鰻弁慶
4-5-10 Ueno, Bunkyō-ku ☎ 03/3831-2283;
Okachimachi Station; see map p.82. Daily
11.30am–9pm, closed third Mon of month. Eel
(*unagi*) is the order of the day at this
informal traditional restaurant on three floors
– try their *unagi donburi* lunchtime set for a
taster (¥1050; Mon–Sat). They also do well-
priced *sukiyaki* and *shabu shabu* meals
(from ¥1260 for lunch), as well as tempura,
sashimi and so forth. An English menu is
available. Moderate.

Cafés and teahouses

Tokyo's **café scene** was revolutionized in the early 1990s with the advent of
the cheap chain coffee shop (see box below). For all the convenience of these
operations, you shouldn't miss sampling at least one of Tokyo's old-style
Japanese cafés, or **kissaten**, where the emphasis is on service and creating an
interesting, relaxing space, using quirky decor and unusual music, for example.
You'll pay more at the *kissaten* than at the newer chain cafés, but many of
these places, such as Shibuya's *Lion*, have become institutions. If you want to
mingle with the city's beautiful people, cafés in Omotesandō and
Daikan'yama are the places to hang out. Just remember to take your time,
since you've rented the table rather than paid for a quick pick-me-up. Apart
from drinks, many of the cafés listed below also serve a fine selection of food
and are good places for snacks and light meals.

Teahouses are much thinner on the ground, and your only real chance of
attending a traditional Japanese tea ceremony will be at the *Imperial*, *New Ōtani*,
the *Ōkura* hotels (see p.137 and p.138). For pretty settings, try the
teahouses in Shinjuku Gyoen, Happōen, Kyū Iwasaki-tei Gardens and Kyū
Furukawa Gardens. It's worth noting that while cafés often keep late hours, teahouses are strictly a daytime affair. The listings below give the nearest subway
or train station.

Tokyo's chain cafés

Of the many **chain cafés** now liberally spread around the city, *Renoir* and *Almond*,
with its famous branch at Roppongi crossing, are the oldest survivors. However,
with their stuck-in-the-1970s decor, such places are now overshadowed by bright
upstarts such as *Café Veloce*, *Doutor*, *Mister Donuts* and *Tully's*. These serve
straightforward "blend" (medium-strength) coffee and tea from as little as ¥180,
plus a decent range of pastries, sandwiches and other snacks – particularly *Mister
Donuts*, which is also one of the few places to offer free coffee refills. All are ideal
for breakfast or a quick snack. The chain cafés *Giraffe* and *Pronto* also transform
into bars in the evening, serving reasonably priced alcoholic drinks and nibbles.

From just one outlet in 1996, *Starbucks* now seems to be everywhere; for sheer
location-power, check out the branch overlooking the crossing at Shibuya Station
(although unlike other branches, this one only serves the more expensive, large-
size coffees). For a less mercenary approach, nip across to another recent foreign
import, *Segafredo Zanetti*, in the Shibuya Mark City complex (there are others in
Hiro-o, Shinagawa and Shinjuku). This famous Italian-brand coffee shop has more
Euro-chic and serves decent *panini*, beer and pear schnapps. Not to be outdone,
the local biggie, *Doutor*, has very stylish branches in Shibuya, just north of Tower
Records, and at *Le Café Doutor Espresso*, at the main Ginza crossing opposite the
department store Wakō.

Cafés

Andersens
Anderusen

5-1-26 Aoyama, Minato-ku ☎03/3407-3333;
Omotesandō Station; see map p.106. Daily
7am–10pm. This Tokyo outpost of
Hiroshima's famed Swedish-style bakery
has an excellent range of pastries and
sandwiches and a reasonably priced
sit-down café – a good option for breakfast
and lunch.

Bape Café!?
Bepu Kafe!?

B1F, 5-3-18 Minami-Aoyama, Minato-ku
☎03/5778-9726; Omotesandō Station; see map
p.106. Daily 11am–8pm. Part of the
designer/DJ Nijo's booming A Bathing Ape
empire of trendy streetwear (see
"Shopping", p.205), this design-driven
café-bar is a fun and suprisingly good-
value place for a drink, with everything at
¥500. Their lunch sets for ¥1000 are also
great.

Ben's Café
Benzu Kafe

1-29-21 Takadanobaba, Shinjuku-ku
☎03/3202-2445, ⓦwww.benscafé.com;
Takadanobaba Station; see colour map at back of
book. Daily 11.30am–midnight. Any time is a
good time to visit this laid-back New York-
style café with its fine range of coffees,
drinks and snacks. Check the website for
details of art events, comedy and poetry
reading nights. Also has an Internet terminal.

Café Comme Ça
Kafe Komu Sa

3-26-6 Shinjuku, Shinjuku-ku ☎03/5367-5551;
Shinjuku Station; see map p.98. Daily noon–8pm.
Serving delicious cakes, this place is in the
trendy Five Foxes Store, with stark concrete
surfaces enlivened by paintings of Buddhist
deities and piles of coloured powder as
bright as the clothes downstairs.

Café du Monde
Kafe Chu Mondo

Spice 2 Building, 1-10-10 Nishi-Ikebukuro,
Toshima-ku; Ikebukuro Station; see map p.98.
Mon–Fri 8.30am–10.30pm, Sat & Sun
9am–10.30pm. Bright, modern New Orleans-
style coffee shop specializing in authentic
chicory coffee and *beignets* (doughnuts
fried in cotton-seed oil) with various dipping
sauces.

Caffé@Idée
Kafe@Idē

6-1-16 Minami-Aoyama, Minato-ku
☎03/3409-6744; Omotesandō Station; see map
p.106. Daily 11.30am–11.30pm. On the top
floor of a trendy interior design store, this is
a popular place for lunch, with Italian-
influenced food and good desserts. In the
evening it becomes a bistro, and there's
also a cigar bar.

Cantina
Kanchina

B1 Shibuya Homes Building, 2-1 Udagawa-chō,
Shibuya-ku ☎03/5489-2433; Shibuya Station;
see map p.115. Tues–Sun 11am–11pm. Kids
will love this café-diner which combines
drinks and Western-style food with movie
tie-in toys (some for sale). There's lots of
movie memorabilia, plus monitors screening
videos, while a Harrison Ford waxwork
props up the bar.

Gallery éf
Garuri Efu

2-19-18 Kaminarimon, Taitō-ku ☎03/3841-9079;
Asakusa Station; see map p.76. Daily except
Tues, café & gallery 11am–7pm, bar 6pm–midnight. This café-bar is one of Asakusa's
trendiest hangouts, with decent lunch sets
for around ¥900. It's worth popping into if
only to see the miraculous survival of the
kura (traditional storehouse) hidden at the
back, which now houses a very eclectic
gallery.

Lion
ライオン

2-19-13 Dōgenzaka, Shibuya-ku
☎03/3461-6858; Shibuya Station; see map
p.115. Daily 11am–10.30pm. Not a place for
animated conversations, this Addam's
Family-style institution amid the love hotels
of Dōgenzaka is where salarymen and pen-
sioners come to quietly appreciate classical
music with their coffee – hardly strong stuff,
since many of the clients seem to be
asleep. Seats are arranged to face a pair of
enormous speakers.

Lotus
ロータス

4-6-8 Jingūmae, Shibuya-ku ☎03/5772-6077;
Omotesandō Station; see map p.106. Daily
10am–4am. Long opening hours, an
appealing light meal menu and a quietly
trendy vibe make this café a prime choice
for the style mavens of Harajuku.

Milonga Nueva
ミロンガヌォーバ

1-3 Kanda-Jimbōchō, Chiyoda-ku
☎03/3295-1716; Jimbōchō Station; see map

p.61. Mon–Sat 10.30am–11pm, Sun 11.30am–7pm. Tucked away on the alley running parallel to Yasukuni-dōri, this rustic café serves up tango music along with its café au lait.

Montoak

Montoaku

6-1-9 Jingūmae, Shibuya-ku ☎ **03/5468-5928; Meiji-Jingūmae Station; see map p.106. Daily 10am–11pm.** Snooty but stylish watering hole that's the Omotesandō café-bar of the moment, with a glass facade facing onto Harajuku's famous shopping street. DJs create a suitable loungy vibe, and there's live music sometimes at weekends.

Moph

Mofu

1F Sibuya Parco Part-1, 15-1 Udagawa-chō, Shibuya-ku ☎ **03/5456-8244; Shibuya Station; see map p.115. Daily 11am–10pm.** Trendy self-service café on the ground floor of the Parco fashion store where you can get a good set of three types of tasty tapas-like nibbles plus a drink for ¥680.

Paul

Paru

1-11 Marunouchi, Chiyoda-ku ☎ **03/5208-8418; Tokyo Station; see map p.54. Daily 10am–9pm.** The main branch of the respected French bakery, on the ground floor of Pacific Century Place, the smart glass tower next to Tokyo Station. The baguettes, croissants and the like are *très authentique*.

A Piece of Cake

A Piisu obu Kēku

6-1-19 Minami-Aoyama, Minato-ku ☎ **03/5466-0686; Omotesandō Station; see map p.106. Daily except Tues 11am–7pm.** Looking out onto the small, funky sculpture garden in front of the Okumoto Taro Memorial Museum (he's the designer of the cartoon-like statue in front of Shibuya's Children's Castle), this very laid-back place has some interesting choices including traditional Indian *chai* and mulled wine.

Tofu Café Fujino

Tofu Kafe Fujino

1F Hollywood Beauty Plaza, 6-4-1 Roppongi, Minato-ku ☎ **03/5771-0102; Roppongi Station; see map p.71. Daily 8am–11pm.** Cute bunnies are the mascot at this fun modern café. Soy milk is used in all drinks and there's a variety of other tofu-based desserts. Their lunch box for ¥900 is good value, or you could go for a black sesame soy milk smoothie (¥600).

Tokyo Apartment Café @ Harajuku

Tōkyō Apātomento Kafe @ Harajuku

1F Green Fantasia, 1-11-11 Jingūmae, Shibuya-ku ☎ **03/3401-4101; Meiji-Jingūmae Station; see map p.106. Daily 11am–4am.** Coming here is like going to a party at your best friend's retro pad, and you can drink a coffee or cocktail in the closet, kitchen, study or dining room. Also does a good range of food, with nothing above ¥1000.

Ueshima Kohiten

上島麿

3-12-1 Kanda-Ogawamachi, Chiyoda-ku ☎ **03/3294-7223; Jimbōchō Station; see map p.61. Daily 7.30am–8pm.** One of the more conveniently located of the area's varied cafés, with comfy seats, an English menu, a good range of breakfast deals and reasonable cheap coffee (from ¥230 a cup) – it's been brewing its own brand since 1933.

Yoku Moku

ヨクモク

5-3-3 Minami-Aoyama, Minato-ku ☎ **03/5485-3330; Omotesandō Station; see map p.106. Daily 10am–7pm.** Hushed café in tune with the elegant sensibilities of this designer-shop end of Omotesandō. There are courtyard tables and a shop selling nicely packaged and expensive cakes, biscuits and chocolates.

Zozoi

ぞぞい

3-22-6 Nishi-Ikebukuro, Toshima-ku ☎ **03/5396-6676; Ikebukuro Station; see map p.91. Daily noon–10pm.** Sheepskin-covered stools and glass-sculpted tulips are part of the eclectic decor at this amiable café offering home-made cakes and biscuits, and a pleasant view onto the park.

Teahouses

Artifagose

Arutofagosu

20-23 Daikan'yama, Shibuya-ku ☎ **03/5489-1133; Daikan'yama Station; see map p.118. Daily 11am–8pm.** Occupying a prime al fresco spot in the heart of ritzy Daikan'yama, with a wide range of fine Darjeeling and other teas, plus bread and excellent cheese.

Cha Ginza

茶銀座

5-5-6 Ginza, Chiyoda-ku ☎ **03/3571-1211; Ginza Station; see map p.54. Tues–Sun 10am–6pm.** This tea shop offers a pleasing new take on the business of sipping *sencha*; ¥500 gets you two cups of the refreshing green stuff, plus sweet and sour nibbles and a taste of beer or wine first to allow you to savour the contrast. Iron walls add a contemporary touch and the rooftop area, open in clement weather, is the place to hang out with those Tokyo ladies who make shopping a career.

Koots Green Tea
Kūtosu Guriin Chi
6-27-4 Jingūmae, Shibuya-ku ☎03/5469-3300. Meiji-jingūmae Station; see map p.106. Daily 10am–10pm. In a quiet location just off Meiji-dōri, this green-tea café borrows an awful lot of the *Starbucks* concept, with *matcha* and *sencha* in multiple hot and cold combos, plus traditional snack foods – *onigiri*, salads and a few sweets.

Suzuki
寿々木
1-15-4 Jingūmae, Shibuya-ku ☎03/3404-8007; Harajuku Station; see map p.106. Mon–Sat 10.30am–8pm, Sun 10.30am–7pm. Tucked behind teeming Takeshita-dōri, but a million miles away in atmosphere, this shop specializes in *okashi* sweets, with tatami rooms, *fusuma* (rice paper and wood) screens and manicured gardens to gaze on. A frothy *matcha* (powdered green tea) and one pick from the sweets costs ¥900.

The Sweet Dynasty
Za Suwīto Dainasuchi
3-5-14 Kita-Aoyama, Minato-ku ☎03/5786-1555; Omotesandō Station; see map p.106. Daily

11am–10pm. This classy branch of a top Hong Kong café has been a huge hit with its Chinese teas and sweets, including a luscious mango pudding. They do dim sum, too.

Toraya Café
Toraya Kafe
Keyakizaka-dōri, 6-12-2 Roppongi, Minato-ku ☎03/5789-9811; Roppongi Station; see map p.71. Daily 10am–10pm. Tucked away amid the sleek designer shops of Roppongi Hills' Keyakizaka-dōri, this café specializes in Japanese teas and sweets – though as with anything trendy in these parts, there's often a long queue for a seat.

Wise Wise
Waizu Waizu
5-12-7 Jingūmae, Shibuya-ku ☎03/5467-7003; Omotesandō Station; see map p.106. Tues–Sun 11am–8pm. Tucked away at the rear of the Wise Wise designer interior store, this refined but unstuffy café specializes different green teas from across Japan, each served with a small plate of rice cracker snacks.

Yamamotoyama
山本山
2-5-2 Nihombashi, Chūō-ku ☎03/3281-0010; Nihombashi Station; see map p.54. Daily 10am–6pm. You can sip all grades of green tea at the back of this venerable and very traditional tea merchant's shop, served with either a sweet rice cake (from ¥600) or rice cracker (from ¥400).

The way of tea

Whenever you sit down in a restaurant or visit a Japanese home, you'll be offered a small cup of slightly bitter green tea, *ocha* (honourable tea), which is always drunk plain. Teas are graded according to their quality. *Bancha*, the cheapest, is for everyday drinking and, in its roasted form, is used to make the smoky *hōji-cha*, or mixed with popped brown rice for the nutty *genmaicha*. Medium-grade *sencha* is served in upmarket restaurants or to favoured guests, while top-ranking, slightly sweet *gyokuro* (dewdrop) is reserved for special occasions. *Matcha*, the powdered form of green tea, is very strong and can be quite bitter; it's usually served in tea ceremonies.

Tea was introduced to Japan from China in the ninth century and was popularized by Zen Buddhist monks, who appreciated its caffeine kick during their long meditation sessions. Gradually, tea-drinking developed into a formal ritual known as *cha-no-yu*, the **tea ceremony**, whose purpose is to heighten the senses within a contemplative atmosphere. In its simplest form the ceremony takes place in a tatami room, undecorated save for a hanging scroll or display of *ikebana* (traditional flower arrangement). Using beautifully crafted utensils of bamboo, iron and rustic pottery, your host will whisk *matcha* into a thick, frothy brew and present it to each guest in turn. Take the bowl in both hands, turn it clockwise a couple of inches and drink it down in three slow sips. It's then customary to admire the bowl while nibbling on a dainty sweetmeat (*wagashi*), which counteracts the tea's bitter taste.

Bars and izakaya

The authentic Japanese **bar** – smoky, cramped, exclusively male and always expensive – is the **nomiya**, often containing nothing more than a short counter bar, generally run by a *mama-san*, a unique breed who both charm and terrorize their customers, and who are less likely to rip you off if you speak some Japanese (but that's no guarantee). If you're game, try the *nomiya* under the tracks at Yūrakuchō, along Shinjuku's Shomben Yokochō (Piss Alley) and Golden Gai, and on Nonbei Yokochō, the alley running alongside the train tracks just north of Shibuya Station.

The major breweries have their own reliable chains of **izakaya** (Japanese pubs), which are generally quite large, serve a good range of drinks and bar snacks and often have a lively atmosphere. Ones to look out for include *Kirin City*, in Ginza, Harajuku and Shinjuku; the *Hub* in Ueno, Ikebukuro, Shibuya and Shinjuku; Sapporo's *Lions Beer Hall* in Ebisu, Ginza, Ikebukuro and Shinjuku; the identikit Oirish bar *The Dubliners* in Akasaka, Ikebukuro and Shinjuku; and the faux-Victorian British pub the *Rose & Crown* at Yūrakuchō, Shinbashi and Shinjuku.

Roppongi has easily Tokyo's greatest concentration of foreigner-friendly *gaijin* bars, though many are closed on Sunday. If there's live music you'll often pay for it through higher drinks prices or a **cover charge** – also see the reviews for *What the Dickens* (p.180) and *The Fiddler* (p.179). Some regular bars also have cover charges (and *izakaya* almost always do, though you'll usually get a small snack served with your first drink), but there's plenty of choice among those that don't, so always check the deal before buying your drink.

Opening hours are generally daily from 5pm to around midnight Sunday to Thursday, and until 4am or 5am on Friday and Saturday. *Nomiya* stay open as long as there are customers.

Akasaka and Roppongi

Acarajé Tropicana
Akaraje Toropikana
B2F Edge Building, 1-1-1 Nishi-Azabu, Minato-ku
☎03/3479-4690; Roppongi Station; see map
p.71. Closed Mon. Join the all-night Brazilian line-dancing sessions at this popular Latin American-style basement bar-restaurant just off Roppongi-dōri.

Agave
Agabe
B1F Clover Building, 7-15-10 Roppongi, Minato-ku ☎03/3497-0229; Roppongi Station; see map

Beer gardens

A Tokyo summer is invariably a hot and sticky experience, but there is compensation in the form of the **outdoor beer gardens** which sprout around the city from June through to the end of August. Look for the red lanterns and fairy lights on the roofs of buildings or in street-level gardens and plazas.

Two of the nicest – in real gardens – are *Hanezawa Gardens*, 3-12-15 Hiro-o, Shibuya-ku (daily 5–11pm; ☎03/3400-2013) and *Sekirei*, at the Meiji Kinenkan building, 2-2-23 Moto-Akasaka, Minato-ku (Mon–Sat 4.30–10.30pm, Sun 5.30–10.30pm; ☎03/3746-7723; see map p.69). Both are open from June to August; *Sekirei* has the added bonus of classical Japanese dance performances (*Nihon Buyō*) nightly at around 8pm.

Kudan Kaikan, 1-6-5 Kudan-minami, Chiyoda-ku also has a good beer garden on its roof from mid-May to the end of August (Mon–Fri 5pm–10pm, Sat & Sun 5–9pm; ☎03/3261-5521). Wednesday is usually ladies night, when women can drink as much as they like for ¥1000.

p.71. **Closed Sun.** One for tequila- and cigar-lovers, this atmospheric basement bar packs an authentic Latin American tang, with 400 varieties of the Mexican tipple on their shelves and a humidor bulging with stogies.

Castillo
Kasuchiro
6-1-8 Roppongi, Minato-ku ☎03/3475-1629; Roppongi Station; see map p.71. **Closed Sun.** If you never got over the disco craze of the 1970s and 1980s, this cosy bar, around the corner from Roppongi crossing, is the place for a boogie. They also run a *gaijin*-house guesthouse.

Fiesta
Fiesuta
5F Taimei Building, 3-11-6 Roppongi, Minato-ku ☎03/5410-3008; Roppongi Station; see map p.71. *Gaijin*-friendly karaoke bar (see box p.172) with 10,000 songs in languages other than Japanese and a dartboard to keep you amused. The ¥3000 cover charge includes three drinks

Gas Panic
Gasu Paniku
50 Togensha Building, 3-15-24 Roppongi, Minato-ku ☎03/3405-0633, ⓦwww.gaspanic.co.jp; Roppongi Station; see map p.71. Popular and grungy bar, and although it's just about the last word in sleaze (drunken *gaijin* males groping scantily clad Japanese girls), virtually everyone passes through here at least once. There's also a branch in Shibuya, at the station end of Centre Gai (☎03/3462-9042).

Heartland
Harutorando
1F Roppongi Hills West Walk, 6-10-1 Roppongi, Minato-ku ☎03/5772-7600; Roppongi Station; see map p.71. There's usually standing room only at this über-trendy but friendly bar in the northwest corner of Roppongi Hills. Sink one of their trademark green bottled beers and watch arty videos on the panoramic plasma screen behind the bar. Also opens for lunch.

Hobgoblin
Hobogoborin
Aoba Roppongi Building, 3-16-33 Roppongi, Minato-ku ☎03/3568-1280; Roppongi Station; see map p.71. British microbrewery Wychwood serves up its fine ales at this spacious bar that's fast become a Roppongi classic – which means you'll be part of a very boozy, noisy crowd of *gaijin*

at weekends and on nights when there are major football and other sports matches on their big-screen TVs. Its real strength is its hearty and very comforting English pub-style food, including pies and fish and chips. They also run *Legend Sports Bar* in the same building, a casual American-style bar festooned with photos of sporting heroes. There's a smaller *Hobgoblin* in Akasaka (B1 Tamondo Building, 2-13-19 Akasaka, Minato-ku ☎03/6229-2636; see map p.68) and a new branch in Shibuya.

House+
Hausu+
12F Roi Building, 5-5-1 Roppongi, Minato-ku ☎03/3402-2871; Roppongi Station; see map p.71. High above Roppongi's more dubious bars lies this curious mix of contemporary *izakaya*, secondhand clothes store and CD listening space – the brightly coloured Scandinavian-style furnishings give it the feel of an iza-ikea.

Rose Demode
Rosu Demode
3-13-9 Roppongi, Minato-ku ☎03/5474-1436; Roppongi Station; see map p.71. Quietly sophisticated bars with a laid-back vibe and room to breath are not Roppongi's usual stock in trade, which makes this convivial place quite a find. The ideal spot for a late-night tête-à-tête.

These
Tēzē
2-13-19 Nishi-Azabu, Minato-ku ☎03/5466-7331; Roppongi Station; see map p.68. **Closed Sun.** On the second floor, this lounge bar-cum-library, pronounced "Tay-Zay", is a cool hang-out for a quiet drink or a light late-night bite to eat. Ask them to show you their "secret room".

Tsuki no Niwa
月の庭
Nishi-Azabu, Minato-ku ☎03/5413-1741; Nogizaka Station; see map p.71. **Closed Sun.** The lovely, spotlit garden, viewed from the tatami room and the bar, is the highlight of this stylish, sedate *izakaya*. Their Japanese food is palatable, if a little pricey, and there's an English menu.

Aoyama and Harajuku

Office
Ofuisu
2-7-18 Kita-Aoyama, Minato-ku ☎03/5788-1052; Gaienmae Station; see map

If you're out drinking with Japanese, remember to pour your colleagues' drinks, but never your own; they'll take care of that. In fact, you'll usually find your glass being topped up after every couple of sips, making it difficult to judge how much you've imbibed.

You can make a toast by lifting your glass and saying "kampai".

In small bars, regular customers keep a bottle of their favourite tipple behind the counter with their name on it.

In *nomiya* and small bars you'll probably be served a small snack or a plate of nuts with your first drink, whether you've asked for it or not; this is often the flimsy excuse for the cover charge added onto the bill at the end.

p.71. This trendy fifth-floor bar is for those who, when they leave the office, don't really want to leave the office. Huddle round the photocopier, squat at childishly low tables and knock back the booze without the boss raising an eye. On the ground level of the same building, its sister bar *Sign* has a DJ to keep punters grooving along nicely.

Oh! God
Ō Gado
6-7-18 Jingūmae, Shibuya-ku ☎03/3406-3206; Meiji-Jingūmae Station; see map p.71.
Basement bar in the same complex as the *La Bohème* and *Zest* restaurants. The real attraction is the free movies screened nightly, although you won't see anything up to date. Drinks start at around ¥700 and there are two pool tables. It's a good post-club venue, since it's open till around 6am.

Soho's
Sohozu
4F V28 Building, 6-31-17 Jingūmae, Shibuya-ku ☎03/5468-0411; Meiji-Jingūmae Station; see map p.71. Upmarket, sophisticated bar and restaurant in a modernist curved building overlooking the Omotesandō–Meiji-dōri crossing, with killer views towards Shinjuku.

Soul
ソウル
3-12-3 Kita-Aoyama, Minato-ku ☎03/5466-1877; Omotesandō Station; see map p.71. Closed Sun. Popular *izakaya* just off Aoyama-dōri opposite Spiral Hall. The menu is in Japanese, but you can point to the large plates of spicy food on the counter.

Asakusa

Cuzn
Kuzun
1-41-8 Asakusa, Taitō-ku ☎03/3842-3223;

Asakusa Station; see map p.76. Tucked away on a quiet Asakusa street behind the Rox department store, this friendly, rustic bar has a comfy sofa area, free Internet access and sometimes shows soccer games on its big screen.

Ichimon
一文
3-12-6 Asakusa, Taitō-ku ☎03/3875-6800; Tawaramachi Station; see map p.76. Traditional *izakaya*, with a cosy, rustic atmosphere, specializing in various types of sake and dishes made with a range of unusual meats including ostrich, turtle, crocodile and whale. Payment is by wooden tokens which you purchase on entering.

Kamiya
神谷
1-1-1 Asakusa, Taitō-ku ☎03/3841-5400; Asakusa Station; see map p.76. Closed Tues. A feature of Asakusa since 1880, this was Tokyo's first Western-style bar. It's also known for its Denkibran ("electric brandy"), first brewed in 1883 when electricity was all the rage, which is made up of a small shot of gin, wine, Curaçao and brandy – it's a potent tipple, though they also make a weaker version. The ground floor is the liveliest and most informal; pay at the cash desk as you enter for your first round of food and drinks.

Daikan'yama, Ebisu, Hiro-o and Meguro

Enjoy House!
Enjoyu Hausu
2F Daikan'yama Techno Building, 2-9-9 Ebisu-Nishi, Shibuya-ku ☎03/5489-1591; Ebisu Station; see map p.118. The unique look here is zebra prints, low velour sofas, red lace curtains and tons of shiny disco balls. The

master wears shorts and Jackie Onassis-style sunglasses. Busy at weekends with a suitably young and attitude-free crowd.

Footnik

Futoniku

1F Asahi Building, 1-11-2 Ebisu, Shibuya-ku ☎03/5795-0144; **Ebisu Station; see map p.118.** Located a short walk east of Ebisu Station, this is Tokyo's only bar devoted to soccer. There's a game or two on the big screen every night, but for popular matches you'll have to pay an entry charge. Japanese movies with subtitles are also screened occasionally, and there's reasonable food.

Kotobuki Diner

Kotobuki Daina

5-3 Hiro-o, Shibuya-ku ☎03/3473-5463; **Hiro-o Station; see map p.118.** Lively, modern *izakaya* on two floors, with a ground-floor bar open to the street in the summer. It's popular with expats, and there's an English menu running the gamut from Mexican-style taco rice to crab pasta.

The Lobby

Za Robi

1-3-18 Chūō-chō, Meguro-ku ☎03/5773-8620; **Meguro Station; see map p.118.** Not a very original name for the lobby bar and café of the hip hotel *Claska*, but the smooth-as-Sinatra vibe – created by the same team behind the trendy *Office* and *Sign* bars in Aoyama (see above) is spot-on.

Smash Hits

Sumashu Hitsu

B1, M2 Hiro-o Building, 5-2-26 Hiro-o, Shibuya-ku ☎03/3444-0432; **Hiro-o Station; see map p.118. Closed third Mon of month.** This basement bar, designed as a mini-amphitheatre, is the place for karaoke exhibitionists keen to perform in front of a crowd – and with 12,000 English songs to choose from, plus many in other languages, you'll never be stuck for a tune. Entrance costs ¥3000, including two drinks.

Symposion

Shinposhiamu

17-16 Sarugaku-chō, Shibuya-ku ☎03/5458-6324; **Daikan'yama Station; see map p.118.** Pure *belle époque* restaurant and bar with French-influenced food and classy wines – you almost expect Toulouse-Lautrec and a troupe of girls to come high-kicking through the Art Nouveau doors.

Tableaux Lounge

Taburē Raunji

Sunroser Daikan'yama B1, 11-6 Sarugaku-chō,

Shibuya-ku ☎03/5489-2202; **Daikan'yama Station; see map p.118.** Ritzy lounge bar with padded leather chairs and bar and lots of chandeliers.

Yebisu Beer Station

Yebisu Biya Sutēshon

Yebisu Garden Place, Ebisu, Shibuya-ku; Ebisu Station; see map p.118. Sapporo's office and shopping development hosts several bars and *izakaya*, plus a spacious beer garden in summer.

Ginza and around

300 Bar

Sanbyaku Bā

B1F Fazenda Building, 5-9-11 Ginza, Chūō-ku ☎03/3572-6300; **Ginza Station; see map p.54.** The new, bargain-basement face of Ginza – a standing-only bar where all the drinks are ¥300.

Kagaya

かがや

B1F Hanasada Building, 2-5-12 Shinbashi, Minato-ku ☎03/3591-2347, ⓦ www1.ocn.ne.jp/~kagayayy; **Shinbashi Station; see map p.54.** English-speaking crazy guy Mark runs this simple basement bar as if he's hosting an 8-year-old's birthday party with alcohol. We're not going to give too much away since it would spoil the fun – which you will certainly have. Around ¥3000 will get you plenty of drink, food and side-splittingly silly games. Bookings recommended.

Lion

Raion

7-9-20 Ginza, Chūō-ku ☎03/3571-2590; **Ginza Station; see map p.54.** Opened in 1934, this baronial beer hall, flagship of the Sapporo chain, is a rather grand place with its dark tiles and mock wood-panelling. There are Germanic-style snacks on offer, and a restaurant upstairs.

Old Imperial Bar

Orudo Imupīriaru Bā

Imperial Hotel, 1-1-1 Uchisaiwaichō, Chiyoda-ku ☎03/3504-1111; **Hibiya Station; see map p.54.** This recreated bar is all that remains in Tokyo of Frank Lloyd Wright's Art Deco *Imperial Hotel* from the 1920s (you can find the front and lobby in the Meiji Mura park near Nagoya in central Honshū), and the low tables, booths and dim lights make it perfect for a quiet assignation. Ask the waiter to let you see the photo books of how the hotel once looked.

EATING AND DRINKING | Bars and izakaya

Karaoke bars

The Japanese were partial to a good singsong long before **karaoke**, literally "empty orchestra", was invented, possibly by an Ōsaka record store manager in the early 1970s. The machines, originally clunky eight-track tape players with a heavy-duty microphone, have come a long way since then and are now linked up to videos which screen the lyrics punters croon along to and feature a range of effects to flatter the singer into thinking their caterwauling is harmonious. Not for nothing have karaoke machines been dubbed the "electronic geisha".

In the mid-1980s, the whole industry, which earns ¥1 trillion a year, was boosted by the debut of the **karaoke box**, a booth kitted out with a karaoke system and rented out by groups or individuals wanting to brush up on their singing technique. These boxes have proved particularly popular with youngsters, women and families who shied away from the smoky small bars frequented by salarymen that were the original preserve of karaoke. Amazingly, research has shown that the introduction of karaoke has coincided with a significant drop in the number of drunks taken into protective custody by the police, with salarymen drinking less as they relax over a rousing rendition of *My Way*.

If you fancy joining in the sing-a-thon, there are multiple opportunities in Tokyo, the most *gaijin*-friendly being **Smash Hits** in Hiro-o (see p.171), **Fiesta** in Roppongi (see p.169) and **Karaoke-kan** in Shibuya (see p.173). Otherwise you could try one of many bars in the **Big Echo** chain – their signs are in English and they are generally found near stations; look for the one at Shinbashi (1-12-5 Shinbashi ℡03/3289-8800). They have plenty of songs in English and charge by the customer and by the hour.

Shin Hi No Moto
新日の基
1-chōme Yūrakuchō, Chiyoda-ku
℡03/3214-8012; Yūrakuchō or Hibiya stations; see map p.54. Lively, traditional *izakaya* under the tracks just south of Yūrakuchō Station. One of the few places to try the excellent Sapporo Red Star beer, or cheap, strong *shōchū* (grain liquor). The manager's English, so tell him what you'd like to eat and your budget. The fish comes fresh from Tsukiji.

Town Cryer
Taun Kuraiya
B1 Hibiya Central Building, 1-2-9 Nishi-Shinbashi, Minato-ku ℡03/3519-6690; Ōtemachi Station; see map p.54. Closed Sat & Sun. "Genuine British pub" (well, it's got beams and horse brasses) run by the team behind Ebisu's *What the Dickens!*, which means the hearty meals can be relied on to be filling.

Ikebukuro

300B
Sanbyaku B
3-29 Nishi-Ikebukuro; Ikebukuro Station; see map p.91. Big, bubbling *izakaya*, popular with a young crowd for its cheap prices and good food. There are two *300B*s on opposite sides of the road – this is the one (no.1) with the dried whale's penis hanging in the entrance.

The Black Sheep
Za Buraku Shiipu
B1, 1-7-12 Higashi-Ikebukuro, Toshima-ku ℡03/3987-2289; Ikebukuro Station; see map p.91. Tiny, lively, friendly bar down a dark alleyway – the perfect place for a low-brow, high-fun night out on the Ikebukuro tiles.

Bobby's Bar
Bobiizu Bā
3F Milano Building, 1-18-10 Nishi-Ikebukuro, Toshima-ku ℡03/3980-8875; Ikebukuro Station; see map p.91. There's a pleasant welcome at this *gaijin*-friendly bar run by the eponymous Bobby. Regular patrons give their home-made samosas the thumbs up.

Speakeasy
スピーキージー
B2, 1-21-1 Higashi-Ikebukuro, Toshima-ku ℡03/5985-8177; Ikebukuro Station; see map p.91. This spacious, low-lit take on a very cool New York drinking dive circa 1929 is liveliest on Friday and Saturday nights, when there's a DJ. They serve modern

Sake

Japan's most famous alcoholic beverage, **sake** is made from rice, water, a microbe known as *koji*, and yeast – according to legend the ancient deities brewed it from the first rice of the new year. Although sake has now been overtaken by beer as Japan's most popular tipple, over ten thousand different brands of the clean-tasting rice wine are still produced throughout the country by some two thousand breweries.

Sake primarily comes either in sweet (*amakuchi*) and dry (*karakuchi*) varieties. If you're after the best quality, connoisseurs recommend going for *ginjō-zukuri* (or *ginjō-zō*), the most expensive and rare of the *junmai-shu* pure rice sake. Some types of sake are cloudier and less refined than others, while a few are aged.

In restaurants and *izakaya* you'll be given the choice of drinking your sake warm (*atsukan*) in a small flask (*tokkuri*), or cold (*reishu*) – the latter is usually the preferred way. Sake is sometimes served in a small wooden box with a smidgen of salt on the rim of the box to counter the sweet taste. Glasses are traditionally filled right to the brim and are sometimes placed in a saucer to catch any overflow; they're generally small because, with an alcohol content of fifteen percent or more, sake is a strong drink – and it goes to your head even more quickly if drunk warm.

For more on sake check out the books and informative website (ⓦwww .sake-world) of long-time resident *gaijin* expert John Gautner, who often holds seminars on sake at the *Takara izakaya* in Yūrakuchō.

---

izakaya-style food for around ¥2000 a head, and their own beer.

Shibuya

Belgo
Berugo
B1F Ichigokan Building, 3-18-7 Shibuya, Shibuya-ku ☏03/3409-4442; Shibuya Station; see map p.115. Closed third Sun of month. European beer bar with lots of Belgian beers – the dark, slimline, multi-level basement space feels a bit like a medieval dungeon.

Coins Bar
Koinzu Bā
300 B1 Noa Shibuya Building, 36-2 Udagawa-chō, Shibuya-ku ☏03/3463-3039; Shibuya Station; see map p.115. The choice at this friendly basement bar is simple: ¥300 for any drink or plate of food, or ¥2500 for as much as you like of either over two and a half hours. Given how cheap it is, it's surprisingly stylish, making it a top choice if you're on a budget.

Karaoke-kan
カラオケ館
K&F Building, 30-8 Udagawachō, Shibuya-ku ☏03/3462-0785; Shibuya Station; see map p.115. On Centre Gai, this typical karaoke bar is the one in which Bill Murray sere-naded Scarlett Johansson in *Lost in*

Translation; ask for rooms 601 or 602, where they shot the movie.

Pink Cow
Pinku Kau
Villa Moderna, 1-3-18 Shibuya, Shibuya-ku ☏03/3406-5597, ⓦ www.thepinkcow.com; Shibuya Station; see map p.115. Now in a new and easier-to-find location, this funky haven for local artists and writers has a good range of imported wines and also runs a Friday and Saturday night home-cooked buffet for ¥2500. Call for details of other regular events, such as DJ nights.

Secobar
Sekobā
3-23-1 Shibuya, Shibuya-ku ☏03/5778-4571; Shibuya Station; see map p.115. Happening bar beneath the JR tracks which hosts some interesting club nights (for which there's usually a cover charge).

Xanadu
Zanadu
B1F Hontis Building, 2-23-12 Dōgenzaka, Shibuya-ku ☏03/5489-3750; Shibuya Station; see map p.115. Kublai Khan's pleasure dome it certainly ain't, but to most of the up-for-it *gaijin* and young Japanese crowd such things hardly matter. The place keeps going all night long at weekends, when the cover charge is at least ¥1000 (including a drink).

Shinjuku and around

Albatross
アルバトロス
1-2-11 Nishi-Shinjuku, Shinjuku-ku
Ⓣ**03/3342-5758; Shinjuku Station; see map**
p.98. Groovy little bar (with an art gallery
upstairs) set amidst the many small bars
and *yakitori* joints of the Shomben
Yokochō alley immediately north of the
station.

Clubhouse
Kurabuhausu
3F Marunaka Building, 3-7-3 Shinjuku, Shinjuku-
ku Ⓣ**03/3359-7785; Shinjuku-Sanchōme**
Station; see map p.98. This spacious sports
bar has a jolly atmosphere and a policy of
being cheaper than the Roppongi competition, with fine fish 'n' chips (¥800), plus a
good selection of vegetarian dishes.

The Dubliners
Za Daburnāzu
2F Shinjuku Lion Hall, 3-28-9 Shinjuku,
Shinjuku-ku Ⓣ**03/3352-6606; Shinjuku Station;**
see map p.98. Popular branch of Irish bar
chain, with Guinness and Kilkenny bitter on
tap and Irish stew on the menu. Good for a
quiet lunch or coffee as well as a rowdy
night's drinking.

Jetée
ジュテ
2F, 1-1-8, Kabukichō, Shinjuku-ku
Ⓣ**03/3208-9645; Shinjuku-Sanchōme Station;**
see map p.98. Closed Sun. Run by Kawai-san,
a Francophile *mama-san* whose passion for
films and jazz are combined in this tiny,
quintessential Golden Gai bar – but don't
bother turning up during May, when she
decamps to the Cannes Film Festival.
Cover charge ¥1000.

New York Bar
Nyu Yōku Bā
Park Hyatt Hotel, 3-7-1-2 Nishi-Shinjuku,
Shinjuku-ku Ⓣ**03/5323-3458; Tochōmae Station;**
see map p.98. Top-class live jazz music plus
the glittering night view of Shinjuku are the
attractions of this sophisticated bar
attached to the *Park Hyatt's New York Grill*.
Movie buffs can relive scenes from *Lost in
Translation* here.

Rolling Stone
Rōringu Sutōn
B1 Ebichu Building, 3-2-7 Shinjuku, Shinjuku-ku
Ⓣ**03/3354-7347; Shinjuku-Sanchōme Station;**
see map p.98. Conversation is out, ear-
splitting rock music is in at this long-running

rock 'n' roll bar – which becomes a sweaty
hell hole every weekend for those who can't
think of anything better to do than mosh
their way to the bar. The table charge is at
least ¥300; on Friday and Saturday expect
to pay ¥2000 entry including two drinks.

Tōhō-kenbun-roku
東方見聞録
3-6-7 Shinjuku, Shinjuku-ku Ⓣ**03/5367-3188;**
Shinjuku-Sanchōme Station; see map p.98.
Ultra-stylish chain *izakaya*, on the fourth
floor above a pachinko parlour, with cosy
wood and tatami booths around a radio-
actively green glass pond. The speciality is
yakitori, and the cold sake comes in a large
pottery cup overflowing into a saucer. ¥300
cover charge. There are two other branches
in Shinjuku, plus further ones in Ginza,
Shibuya and Aoyama.

Vagabond
バガボンド
1-4-20 Nishi-Shinjuku, Shinjuku-ku
Ⓣ**03/3348-9109; Shinjuku Station; see map**
p.98. Shinjuku institution where Matsuoka-
san plays the genial host, greeting guests
and sometimes playing along with the jazz
pianists who tinkle the ivories every night.
There's a ¥500 cover charge, but the drinks
are good value and the atmosphere is
priceless. Also has a downstairs bar,
without live music.

Tokyo Bay

Sunset Beach Brewing Company
Sanseto Biichi Buruin Kanpanii
1-6-1 Decks Tokyo Beach, Odaiba
Ⓣ**03/3599-6655; Odaiba Kaihin-kōen Station;**
see map p.124. The beer here is actually
made in the mall – either sample a couple
of glasses at the stand-up bar or venture
inside for a so-so all-you-can-eat buffet.
The real attraction, however, is the view of
the Rainbow Bridge across Tokyo Bay –
sipping a beer on the terrace here on a
summer evening is a delight.

T.Y. Harbor Brewery
T.Y. Hābā Burureri
Bond St, 2-1-3 Higashi-Shinagawa,
Shinagawa-ku Ⓣ**03/5479-4555; Tennoz Isle**
Station; see map p.124. Take the monorail
from Hamamatsuchō to reach this
microbrewery, in a converted Bayside
warehouse, which also has an outdoor
deck and a so-so Californian-cuisine
restaurant. The very respectable real ales

include amber ale, porter, wheat beer and California pale ale.

Ueno

The Church
Za Chachu
B1, 1-57 Ueno-kōen, Ueno, Taitō-ku ⓣ03/5807-1957; Ueno Station; see map p.82. Basement space hard by the station with a vaguely ecclesiastical theme and a reasonable range of British ales, mostly bottled, plus pub-style food. They often have Japanese and overseas bands and solo musicians performing.

The Warrior Celt
Za Uoriä Keruto
3F Ito Building, 6-9-22 Ueno ⓣ03/3841-5400; Ueno Station; see map p.82. Things can get pretty raucous at this good-time bar in the thick of Ueno. Prime ingredients are a fine range of beers, a nightly happy hour (5–7pm), live bands (Fri & Sat from 8.30pm) and, last but not least, Ladies Night on Thursdays (all drinks ¥500). Add fish 'n' chips – or a mean hummus – and you're away.

EATING AND DRINKING | Bars and izakaya

Clubs and live music

Tokyo is as important a venue on the international clubbing scene as London and New York, and you'll find all the latest sounds covered, from acid jazz to techno, trance and drum 'n' bass, with overseas DJs regularly jetting in to play gigs at the top clubs. The chameleon-like nature of the city's nightlife, fuelled by an insatiable appetite for new trends, means that Tokyo is one of the most exciting, but also most unpredictable, places in the world to party, and while some **clubs** weather the vagaries of fashion, it pays to consult the media before heading out. Check the local listings websites (see p.21) and look for the free monthly booklet of DJ schedules and discount coupons put out by the Club Information Agency (CIA, ⓦ www.ciajapan.com) which is available at clubs and shops such as Tower Records. Most major clubs also have their own website, where you'll find their schedules. Among the top local DJs at the moment are Ken Ishii, well known for his techno sets, the hard- house-loving Ko Kimura, and Krash, who spins hip-hop, which has become wildly popular through Japanese bands such as Dragon Ash.

If you prefer dancing, or just listening, to **live music**, then Tokyo is also well stocked with options – the city has an incredibly varied appetite for music from all corners of the globe, as a trip to any of the city's major CD emporiums will prove. It's not surprising, therefore, that top acts are keen to include the capital on their schedules, and on many nights of the week you can take your pick of anything from Beethoven to Beatles tribute bands or traditional Japanese ballads to contemporary jazz.

Clubs

All clubs levy a **cover charge**, typically ¥2500–3000, which usually includes tick-ets for your first couple of drinks. You can often save a small amount if you pick up a flyer for the club from one of the record shops or boutiques around town, or look for the discount coupons in the CIA booklet. With the exception of *Velfare* (see opposite), most clubs don't really get going until after 11pm, especially at weekends, and most stay open until around 4am. There's also a growing number of **recovery parties** (again, see *Velfare* and *Maniac Love*), kicking off at 6am. All the clubs listed below are open daily unless stated otherwise in the reviews.

Aoyama

Maniac Love
Maniaku Rabu
B1, 5-10-6 Minami-Aoyama, Minato-ku

ⓣ 03/3406-1066, ⓦ www.maniaclove.com; Omotesandō Station; see map p.106. Small but happening basement club just off Kotto-dōri, playing everything from ambient and acid jazz to hard house and garage.

Hardcore clubbers adore its sound system, lighting and early-morning (5/6am) raves.

Mix
Mikusu
3-6-19 Kita-Aoyama, Minato-ku
℡ 03/3797-0551, ⓦ www.at-mix.com;
Omotesandō Station; see map p.106. This long and narrow basement space on Aoyama-dōri hosts an arty crowd at weekends who don't seem to mind being squashed in like sardines to enjoy the infectious mix of soul and reggae.

Roppongi

Alife
Araifu
1-7-2 Nishi-Azabu, Minato-ku ℡ 03/5785-2531,
ⓦ www.e-alife.net; Roppongi Station; see map p.71. Closed Mon–Wed & Sun. Stylish new presence on the club scene. The ground-floor café-bar is a good place to chill out after you've worked up a sweat on the large dance floor below.

Muse
Muzu
1-13-3 Nishi-Azabu, Minato-ku ℡ 03/5467-1188;
Roppongi Station; see map p.68. A pick-up joint, but an imaginatively designed one, with lots of interesting little rooms to explore or canoodle in. There's also a groovy dance area at the back which gets packed at the weekends.

328
San-nippa
3-24-20 Nishi-Azabu, Minato-ku
℡ 03/3401-4968; Roppongi Station; see map p.68. Long-standing DJ bar in a basement next to the police box at Nishi-Azabu crossing. More laid-back than many other late-night Roppongi options, but can still get packed out at weekends.

Spiral
Supairaru
B1 TSK Building, 7-15-30 Roppongi, Minato-ku
℡ 03/5786-4412, ⓦ www.club-spiral.jp;
Roppongi Station; see map p.68. This basement venue specializes in psychedelic trance and has hip-hop every Thursday. Also hosts the gay hard-house and trance events Red and Goldfinger.

Super Deluxe
Supā Derakusu
B1, 3-1-25 Nishi-Azabu, Minato-ku
℡ 03/5412-0515, ⓦ www.super-deluxe.com;
Roppongi Station; see map p.71. Closed Sun.

This arty club bills itself as a place for "thinking, drinking people" and hosts a wide variety of arty events. The toilets– an art project in themselves – are something to behold, and the atmosphere is remarkably relaxed.

Velfarre
Berufāre
7-14-22 Roppongi, Minato-ku ℡ 03/3402-8000,
ⓦ http://velfarre.avex.co.jp; Roppongi Station;
see map p.71. Going strong for over a decade now, this glitzy and monolithic club – one of the largest in Asia – cost its investors ¥4 billion. It's often packed by 9pm, since it shuts at no later than 1am. Hosts recovery parties on Sunday from 6am.

Yellow (also known as Space Lab Yellow)
Ierō
1-10-11 Nishi-Azabu, Minato-ku
℡ 03/3479-0690, ⓦ www.space-lab-yellow.com;
Roppongi Station; see map p68. Look for the blank yellow neon sign and go down to the basement to discover one of Tokyo's most enduring clubs, offering a range of music on different nights, with mainly techno and house at weekends.

Shibuya

Air
Eru
B1 Hikawa Building, 2-11 Sarugaku-chō,
Shibuya-ku ℡ 03/5784-3386, ⓦ www.air-tokyo
.com; Shibuya Station; see map p.118. South of the station on the way to Ebisu, this eclectic club has a great sound system but is only open for special events; look out for flyers.

Club Asia
Kurabu Ashia
1-8 Maruyamachō, Shibuya-ku ℡ 03/5458-1996,
ⓦ www.clubasia.co.jp; Shibuya Station; see map
p.115. Long-running techno-trance club in the heart of the Dōgenzaka love-hotel district, with several dance floors and an attached al fresco Asian restaurant. Popular place for one-off events such as gigs by visiting DJs and special club nights.

Club Pure
Kurabu Pūru
32-7 Udagawa-chō, Shibuya-ku ℡ 03/3477-7077,
ⓦ www.clubpure.com; Shibuya Station; see map
p.115. This offshoot of Yokohama's most successful *gaijin*-friendly club has already gained a reputation as a fun place to dance to hip-hop and R&B.

Harlem
Hāremu

Dr Jeekan's Building, 2-4 Maruyama-chō, Shibuya-ku ☎03/3461-8806, ⓦ www.harlem.co.jp; Shibuya Station; see map p.115. Spacious two-floor club specializing in hip-hop, rap and R&B – come to check out Japanese wannabe Eminens dressed up in baggy trousers and baseball caps.

La Fabrique
Ra Faburiku

B1F Zero Gate, 16-9 Udagawa-chō, Shibuya-ku ☎03/5428-5100; Shibuya Station; see map p.115. Although you can come here for dinner (their speciality is *flammekueche*, wafer-thin pizza from Alsace), the main selling point is their French house nights (Fri & Sat; entrance ¥3000). It's smart, a bit snooty and oh so Parisian. A similar mix of restaurant and club is offered at the sister establishment, *Le Faubourg*, in Aoyama (5-8-1 Minami-Aoyama ☎03/5468-3636, see map p.106), which also has French house nights on Friday and Saturday.

The Ruby Room
Za Rubi Rūmu

2-25-17 Dōgenzaka, Shibuya-ku ☎03/3462-7766; Shibuya Station; see map p.115. Cosy, groovy club upstairs from the casual California diner *Sonoma* (see p.161). Eat in the diner and you'll get in without having to pay the cover charge.

Simoon
Shimūn

3-26-16 Shibuya, Shibuya-ku ☎03/5774-1669, ⓦ www.simoon.net; Shibuya Station; see map p.115. Occupying two compact basement spaces, hard-house and techno nights are *Simoon*'s main strengths. There's a good-sized dance floor and comfy couches for post-dancing lounging.

Womb
Uoūmu

2-16 Maruyama-chō, Shibuya-ku ☎03/5459-0039, ⓦ www.womb.co.jp; Shibuya Station; see map p.115. By central Tokyo standards this counts as a big club, with a spacious dance floor, enormous glitterball and a pleasant chill-out space. Top DJs work the decks, but be warned that at big events it can get dangerously crowded.

Shinjuku and Ikebukuro

Bed
Bedo

B1 Fukuri Building, 3-29-9 Nishi-Ikebukuro ☎03/3981-5300, ⓦ www.ikebukurobed.com; Ikebukuro Station; see map p.115. About as hip as nightlife gets in Ikebukuro. The mix of hip-hop, reggae, R&B, and occasional drum 'n' bass keeps things jumping until 5am. Also stages live shows.

Code
Kodo

4F Shinjuku Toho Kaikan, 1-19-9 Kabukichō, Shinjuku-ku ☎03/3209-0702, ⓦ www .clubcomplexcode.com; Shinjuku Station; see map p.115. Hidden inside a Kabukichō building is one of Japan's biggest clubs, with room for two thousand people and three dance floors, including an enormous main dance area surrounded by giant video screens.

Liquid Room
Rikido Rūmu

7F Shinjuku HUMAX Pavilion, 1-20-1 Kabukichō, Shinjuku-ku ☎03/3200-6831, ⓦ www .liquidroom.net; Shinjuku Station; see map p.115. There are all kinds of music genres on different nights at this trendy live house and club in the heart of Shinjuku. Check local media and flyers for details.

Tokyo Bay

Ageha
Ageha

Studio Coast, 2-2-10 Shin-kiba, Kōtō-ku ☎03/5534-2525, ⓦ www.ageha.com; Shin-Kiba Station; see map p.124. This giant warehouse space has been transformed into an ultra-cool mega-club with several dance areas, an outdoor pool, a sound system guaranteed to send your whole body shimmering and a roster of high-profile events. The major problem is its remote location way across Tokyo Bay. There's a free shuttle bus to and from the east side of Shibuya Station – check the website for details and make sure you turn up at least half an hour before you want to depart to get a ticket to board the bus.

Live music

Pop and rock are usually played in "live houses", most of which are little more than a pub with a small stage. There are also several larger venues where top local and international acts do their thing, most notably the cavernous Tokyo Dome in Suidōbashi, affectionately known as the "Big Egg", and the Nippon Budōkan, where the Beatles played. Tickets for concerts can be bought through ticket agencies – see "Directory" p.211.

Jazz and blues are incredibly popular in Tokyo, with scores of clubs across the city. The city is equally well served with **classical music** venues and there are usually one or two concerts of Western classical music every week, either by one of Tokyo's several resident symphony orchestras or by a visiting group, as well as occasional performances of **opera**. Tickets are available from the relevant box office or a ticket agency (see p.212), though they tend to be pricey (starting at around ¥3000) and are often scooped up as soon as they go on sale. However, a limited number of cheap seats (sometimes half-price) often go on sale on the day of the performance – be prepared to queue.

If you get the chance, catch a concert of **traditional Japanese music**, played on instruments such as the *sakuhachi* (flute), the *shamisen* (a kind of lute that is laid on the ground), and *taiko* (drum). Top groups to watch out for include Kodō, the theatrical drumming ensemble who occasionally play Tokyo venues, such as the Bunkamura in Shibuya.

Rock and pop

Cavern Club
Kabēn Kurabu
5-3-2 Roppongi, Minato-ku ☎03/3405-5207; Roppongi Station. A meticulous re-creation of the Beatles' Liverpool venue, with pretty decent Beatles cover bands providing the entertainment. Entrance charge ¥1500.

Club Citta
クラブチタ
4-1-26 Ogawachō, Kawasaki ☎044/246-8888; ⓦhttp://clubcitta.co.jp; Kawasaki Station. One of Tokyo's major live-music venues, in the suburb-city of Kawasaki, hosting a variety of local and international rock bands. Ticket prices vary depending on the act. It's a five-minute walk south of the station, which is around 20 minutes from central Tokyo.

Club Quattro
Kurabu Kuatoro
5F Quattro Building, 32-13 Udagawa-chō, Shibuya-ku ☎03/3477-8750, ⓦwww .net-flyer.com; Shibuya Station; see map p.115. Intimate rock-music venue which hosts both well-known local and international acts. Tends to showcase up-and-coming bands and artists.

Crocodile
Korokodairu
6-18-8 Jingūmae, Shibuya-ku ☎03/3499-5205, ⓦwww.music.co.jp/~croco; Meiji-Jingūmae Station; see map p.115. You'll find everything from samba to blues and reggae at this long-running basement space on Meiji-dōri between Harajuku and Shibuya. Cover charge ¥2000–3000. Gigs are also broadcast live on the Internet.

Cyber
Saibā
B1, 1-43-14 Higashi-Ikebukuro ☎03/3985-5844, ⓦwww.explosionworks.net/cyber; Ikebukuro Station. Dark, throbbing rock dive among the soaplands and love hotels north of Ikebukuro Station – the bands are variable, though you might strike lucky. Concerts start around 5.30pm. Entry ¥2000 and up, depending on the act.

The Fiddler
Za Fidorā
B1F, 2-1-2 Takadanobaba, Shinjuku-ku ☎03/3204-2698, ⓦwww.thefiddler.com; Takadanobaba Station. British pub (aka *The Mean Fiddler*) with rock and blues bands most evenings and occasional English comedy nights. Also serves fish 'n' chips and shepherd's pie, while pints of Guinness and Bass go for ¥900. It's at the intersection of Waseda-dōri and Meiji-dōri. No cover charge.

Milk

みるく

B1 Roob 6 Building, 1-13-3 Ebisu-Nishi, Shibuya-ku ☎03/5458-2826, Ⓦwww .milk-tokyo.com; Ebisu Station; see map p.118. Live house and club which packs in a lively crowd – if you get bored with the live thrash rock bands, check out the dildos and other sex toys in the kitchen cabinet. Entrance charge ¥3000–3500 Fri & Sat (including two drinks); around ¥2000 on other nights. Check the website for discount coupons to their events.

What the Dickens!

Wato Za Jikinzu

4F Roob 6 Building, 1-13-3 Ebisu-Nishi, Shibuya-ku ☎03/3780-2099, Ⓦwww .ookawara-kikaku.com/dickens; Ebisu Station; see map p.118. There's live music nightly at this olde English pub complete with beams and candle-lit nooks, with draught Guinness and Bass pale ale (¥950 a pint, ¥600 a half). The food – a range of hearty pies served with potatoes, veggies and bread – is also worth coming for.

Jazz and blues

Blue Note

Burū Nōto

6-3-16 Minami-Aoyama, Minato-ku ☎03/5485-0088, Ⓦwww.bluenote.co.jp; Omotesandō Station; see map p.106. Closed Sun. Tokyo's premier live-jazz venue, part of the international chain, attracts world-class performers at top ticket prices. Entry from ¥6000 (including one drink), depending on the acts.

Blues Alley Japan

Burūsu Arīi, Nihon

B1 Hotel Wing International Meguro, 1-3-14 Meguro, Meguro-ku ☎03/5496-4381, Ⓦwww.bluesalley.co.jp; Meguro Station; see map p.118. This offshoot of the Washington DC blues and jazz club occupies a small basement space near the station. Admission charges depend on the act.

JZ Brat

JZ Burato

2F Cerulean Tower Tōkyū Hotel, 26-1 Sakuragaoka-ch, Shibuya-ku ☎03/5728-0168, Ⓦwww.jzbrat.com; Shibuya Station; see map p.115. Swanky new jazz club in Shibuya's top hotel, with a spacious contemporary design and a respectable line-up of artists. Cover charge from ¥3000.

New York Bar

Nyū Yōku Bā

Park Hyatt Hotel, 3-7-1-2 Nishi-Shinjuku, Shinjuku-ku ☎03/5322-1234; Tochō-mae Station; see map p.98. Top-class live jazz plus a glittering night view of Shinjuku are the attractions of this sophisticated bar attached to the Park Hyatt's New York Grill. There's a ¥2000 cover charge, or it's free if you eat at the New York Grill.

Shinjuku Pit Inn

Shinjuku Pito In

B1 Accord Shinjuku Building, 2-12-4 Shinjuku, Shinjuku-ku ☎03/3354-2024, Ⓦwww.pit-inn.com; Shinjuku Station; see map p.98. Serious, long-standing jazz club which has been the launch platform for many top Japanese performers and which also attracts overseas acts.

Classical music and opera

Casals Hall

Kaserusu Hōru

1-6 Kanda-Surugadai, Chiyoda-ku ☎03/3294-1229; Ochanomizu Station; see map p.61. Set inside the Ochanomizu Square Building, designed by top architect Arata Isozaki, this is a major venue for piano recitals, chamber music and small ensembles.

NHK Hall

NHK Hōru

2-2-1 Jinnan, Shibuya-ku ☎03/3465-1751; Harajuku or Shibuya stations; see map p.106. One of Tokyo's older auditoria for classical concerts, but still well thought of and home to the highly rated NHK Symphony Orchestra. It's next to the NHK Broadcasting Centre, south of Yoyogi-kōen.

Orchard Hall

Ōchyādo Hōru

2-24-1 Dōgenzaka, Shibuya-ku ☎03/3477-9111, Ⓦwww.bunkamura.co.jp; Shibuya Station; see map p.115. In the Bunkamura Centre, up the slope from central Shibuya, this large concert hall hosts a wide range of classical music performances throughout the year.

Suntory Hall

Santorii Hōru

Ark Hills, 1-13-1 Akasaka, Minato-ku ☎03/3505-1001, Ⓦwww.suntory.co.jp/suntoryhall; Roppongi-Itchōme Station; see map p.68. Reputed to have the best acoustics in the city, this elegant concert hall has one of the world's largest pipe organs, sometimes used for free lunchtime recitals; check their website for details of this and other events.

Tokyo Bunka Kaikan
東京文化会館
5-45 Ueno, Taitō-ku ☎ 03/3828-2111,
ⓦ www.t-bunka.jp; Ueno Station; see map p.82.
Recently refurbished, the largest classical music hall in the city has a busy and varied schedule of performances. Classical music buffs should enquire about joining their music library, which holds over 100,000 recordings, books and scores.

Tokyo International Forum
Tōkyō Kokusai Fuōramu
3-5-1 Marunouchi, Chiyoda-ku ☎ 03/5221-9000,
ⓦ www.tif.or.jp; Yūrakuchō Station; see map

p.54. The Forum's four multi-purpose halls (including one of the world's largest auditoria, with over five thousand seats) host an eclectic mix of performing arts, from opera to Kabuki.

Tokyo Opera City
Tōkyō Opera Shitei
3-20-2 Nishi-Shinjuku, Shinjuku-ku
☎ 03/5353-9999, ⓦ www.operacity.jp
/en/concert.html; Hatsudai Station; see map
p.98. This stunningly designed concert hall, with a giant pipe organ, seats over 1600 and has excellent acoustics – though despite its name it hosts only music concerts, not full-blown opera. There's a more intimate recital hall too.

CLUBS AND LIVE MUSIC | Live music

Gay and lesbian Tokyo

C ompared to other big Japanese cities such as Ōsaka, Tokyo's **gay and lesbian** scene, centred on the district of **Shinjuku Nichōme** (see map p.98), is relatively open and friendly, and it's completely out of the closet as far as the rest of the country is concerned. Even so, don't expect the same level of openness as in London, San Francisco or Sydney; gay life in Tokyo is a low-key affair and it's very rare to find same-sex couples parading their love on the streets.

Despite there being an honourable tradition of male homosexuality in Japan, with some ancient Buddhist sects believing that love among men was preferable to love between the sexes, such attitudes don't make much of an impression these days – at least not publicly. There is still a huge amount of pressure put on men and women to marry, this being an almost essential step along the career ladder at many corporations, and such expectations keep many Japanese gays in the closet. This said, in recent times homosexuality has come to be seen as trendy, particularly in the major cities and among the cash-rich group of young working women known as OLs, or "office ladies", whose tastes drive a million marketing campaigns. Comic books and movies with homosexual characters have been a huge success with OLs, who swoon over the gay romances. There are gay and transvestite TV celebrities and even bars in Tokyo staffed by cross-dressing women, who flatter and fawn over their female customers in only a slightly more macho way than bona fide hostesses do over salarymen.

First held in 1995, the **Tokyo Gay and Lesbian Parade** (Ⓦ www.tlgp.org/eng) has been known to attract three thousand marchers and many more spectators, but has yet to establish itself as an annual event (there was no parade in 2003 and 2004).

In contrast, on the second to last weekend of August a hugely popular **matsuri** is held in Nichōme with drag shows and dancing in the street. The annual **Tokyo International Lesbian and Gay Video and Film Festival** (Ⓦ www.tokyo-lgff.org), based in Aoyama's Spiral Hall usually held in late July, is also a permanent fixture, and well worth attending if you're in town, showing films from around the world with English subtitles.

There are several monthly gay and lesbian **dance events** held at clubs around the city, including *Ageha, Code, Liquid Room* and *Spiral* (see "Clubs", pp.177–178, for details); the last regularly hosts the main **women–only** club night Goldfinger (Ⓦ www.goldfinger-party.com) on the last Friday of the

Whilst you're highly unlikely to encounter any problems as a gay traveller in Tokyo, you may find it difficult to break into any local gay scene without having some contacts. The Web is a good place to start looking; the best site is ⓦwww.utopia-asia.com/tipsjapn.htm, which covers gay life in Japan and lists bars and clubs in Tokyo.

International Gay Friends is a networking group for gays which organizes support groups for men and women. To contact them, write to if/Passport, CPO 180, Tokyo 100-91 or call ☏03/5693-4569.

GayNet Japan (ⓦwww.gnj.or.jp) has some discussion groups that you may find useful.

For details of the lesbian scene contact **OCCUR (Japan Association for the Lesbian and Gay Movement)**, 2nd Floor, Ishikawa-Building, 6-12-11 Honcho Nakano, Tokyo 164 ☏03/3383-5556, ℉3229-7880, a grass-roots gay activist organization and sponsor of the annual Tokyo International Lesbian and Gay Video and Film Festival.

month and the gay hard-house night Red (ⓦwww.joinac.com/red) on the second Saturday of the month. The *Tokyo Journal* has some details of gay venues in its Cityscope listings, and *Metropolis* (see p.34) is another good source of information about specific dance events.

Bars and clubs

The vast majority of gay and lesbian bars and clubs are located in **Shinjuku Nichōme**. They're generally open daily from the late afternoon to the early hours of the morning. We've noted in the reviews where a venue is exclusively gay or lesbian; otherwise, the following bars and clubs accept all-comers.

Ace
Esu
B2 Dai-ni Hayakawaya Building, 2-14-6 Shinjuku, Shinjuku-ku ☏03/3352-6297; Shinjuku-Sanchōme Station; see map p.98. House and garage rule at this predominantly gay basement club next to the cruising park in Nichōme.

Advocates
アドボカト
7th Tenka Building, 2-18-1 Shinjuku, Shinjuku-ku ☏03/3358-3988; Shinjuku-Sanchōme Station; see map p.98. *The* place to see and be seen around Nichōme, with the area's most casual vibe – although the bar itself is barely big enough for ten people, which is why scores of patrons hang out on the street corner outside. Not to be confused with *Advocates Bar*, round the corner, where there's often a hefty cover charge for the drag show, and where they sometimes hold women-only nights.

Arty Farty
Ātē Fātē
2F Dai 33 Kyutei Building, 2-11-7 Shinjuku, Shinjuku-ku ☏03/5362-9720; Shinjuku-Sanchōme Station; see map p.98. Artily designed bar with a younger clientele and a small dance floor. The music is generally handbag house and disco.

Dragon
ドラゴン
B1F Accord, 2-12-4 Shinjuku, Shinjuku-ku ☏03/3341-0606; Shinjuku-Sanchōme Station; see map p.98. It gets hot and sweaty on weekend nights down in this unpretentious club opposite *GB*. Porn movies play behind the industrial-design bar and the patrons whoop it up to dance anthems played through a dodgy PA. Admission ¥1000 men, ¥2000 women, including one drink.

Fuji Bar
Fuji Bā
2-12-16 Shinjuku, Shinjuku-ku ☏03/3354-2707;

Shinjuku-Sanchōme Station; see map p.98. This cosy karaoke bar (¥100 per song) in the basement of a building around the corner from *GB* has a wide selection of English songs, in case you're in the singing mood, and attracts a mixed crowd.

GB
Jiibii
B1 Business Hotel T Building, 2-12-3 Shinjuku, Shinjuku-ku ☎03/3352-8972; Shinjuku-Sanchōme Station; see map p.98. Only for the boys, this smoky basement bar is a long-standing pick-up joint for Japanese and foreigners. The
initials stand for Ginger Bar, after Hollywood dance icon Ginger Rogers. Women are only allowed in on Halloween.

Kinsmen
キンズメン
2F, 2-18-5 Shinjuku, Shinjuku-ku ☎03/3354-4949; Shinjuku-Sanchōme Station; see map p.98. Long-running and unpretentious bar – you're as likely to be carousing with a mixed group of office workers here as with a drag queen. Check out their famous ikebana flower displays.

Kinswomyn
Kinzu Uimin
3F Dai-ichi Tenka Building, 2-15-10 Shinjuku, Shinjku-ku ☎03/3354-8720; Shinjuku-Sanchōme Station; see map p.98. Tokyo's top women-only bar, which has a more relaxed ambience (and lower prices) than many of Nichōme's other lesbian haunts. Drinks are ¥700 and there's no cover charge.

Koishi
Koishi
5-9-15 Minami-Aoyama, Minato-ku ☎03/3409-1592; Omotesandō Station; see map p.106. Mon–Sat 6.30–11pm. On the corner of Kottō-dōri and Aoyama-dōri, this laid-back basement *izakaya* is run by gay owners and frequented by the fashion and show-biz crowd who hang out at this stylish end of Omotesandō.

New Sazae
ニューさざえ
2F Ishikawa Building, 2-18-5 Shinjuku, Shinjuku-ku ☎03/3354-1745; Shinjuku-Sanchōme Station; see map p.98. The antithesis of cool, this grungy, graffitied bar is nonetheless a welcoming place to everyone from bright-eyed *gaijin* to hard-bitten drag queens.

Theatre and cinema

hough language can be a problem when it comes to exploring Tokyo's **theatre**, colourful extravaganzas like **Takarazuka** or the more traditional **Kabuki** are enjoyable, and even the notoriously difficult **Nō** and **Butō** are worth trying once. Tokyo can also be a surprisingly good place for **English-language drama** – though it may not seem the obvious place to seek out a Shakespeare tragedy or an Ibsen revival, major international theatre groups often pass through on their foreign tours, although tickets tend to be expensive and hard to come by. **Information** about current and upcoming performances is available in the English-language press and from the Tokyo TIC (see p.19). As for film, there are plenty of multi-screen **cinemas** showing the latest Hollywood blockbusters – usually with Japanese subtitles – while a decent number of smaller cinemas show independent and art-house releases. See the "Directory", p.211, for details of **ticket agencies**.

Traditional theatre

Kabuki is by far the most accessible of Japan's traditional performing arts and its dramatic plots, full of larger-than-life heroes, are easy to follow even without understanding a word of the dialogue. Performances last three or four hours, but single-act tickets are available at the Kabuki-za (see below). Puppet theatre, **bunraku**, predates Kabuki but shares many of the same story lines. Don't expect the same lightning drama as in Kabuki – the puppets need three people to manipulate them – but the artistry of the puppeteers is astounding. Even most Japanese find **Nō**, the country's oldest form of theatre, unfathomable. Its highly stylized, painfully slow movements and archaic language don't make for a rip-roaring theatrical experience, though some find the rarefied style incredibly powerful. **Kyōgen**, short satirical plays with an earthy humour and simple plots, liven up the intervals. If you want to try Nō or Kyōgen, it's worth asking at the TIC about free performances by amateur groups.

Cerulean Tower Nō Theatre
セルリアンタワー能楽堂
26-1 Sakuragaoka-chō, Shibuya-ku
℡03/3477-6412, ⓦ www.ceruleantower.com
/english; Shibuya Station. Tokyo's newest Nō theatre, inside this luxury hotel, provides the elegant setting for both professional and amateur Nō and kyōgen performances.`

Kabuki-za
歌舞伎座
4-12-15 Ginza, Chūō-ku ℡03/5565-6000,
ⓦ www.shochiku.co.jp/play/kabukiza/theater;
Higashi-Ginza Station. Tokyo's main Kabuki theatre stages two programmes every day during the first three weeks of the month, usually at 11am and 4.30pm. Prices start at around ¥2500 for the full programme, or you

can buy one-act tickets (usually under ¥1000) at the theatre. Details, including a brief English synopsis, are available at the theatre or Tokyo TIC, and you can rent earphone guides (¥650, plus ¥1000 deposit; not available for one-act seats). A pair of binoculars is useful – inevitably the cheapest seats are way up at the back.

Kanze Nō-gakudō
観世能楽堂
1-16-4 Shōtō, Shibuya-ku Ⓣ03/3469-5241; Shibuya Station. The home theatre of Kanze, the best-known of Tokyo's several Nō troupes, and one of the city's most traditional Nō theatres.

Kokuritsu Gekijō
国立劇場
4-1 Hayabusachō, Chiyoda-ku Ⓣ03/3230-3000, Ⓦwww.jac.go.jp/english/index.html; Hanzōmon Station. Tokyo's National Theatre puts on a varied programme of traditional dance and music, including Kabuki, *bunraku*, court music and dance in its two auditoria. English-language programmes and earphones (¥650, plus

¥1000 deposit) are available, and tickets start at around ¥1500 for Kabuki and ¥4400 for *bunraku*.

Kokuritsu Nō-gakudō
国立能楽堂
4-18-1 Sendagaya, Shibuya-ku Ⓣ03/3423-1331, Ⓦwww.jac.go.jp/english/index.html; Sendagaya Station. The Kokuritsu Nō-gakudō (National Nō Theatre) hosts Nō performances several times a month, while printed English explanations of the plot help you make some sense of what's going on. The theatre is five minutes' walk southwest of Sendagaya Station.

Shimbashi Embujō
新橋演舞場
6-18-2 Ginza, Chūō-ku Ⓣ03/3541-2600, Ⓦwww.shochiku.co.jp/play/index.html; Higashi-Ginza Station. This large theatre on the eastern edge of Ginza stages a range of traditional dance, music and theatre, including the "Super-Kabuki" (Kabuki with all the bells and whistles of modern musical theatre) extravaganzas of impressario Ichikawa Ennosuke.

Contemporary and international theatre, dance and comedy

Apart from Japanese transfers of hit Broadway shows by the likes of Andrew Lloyd Webber, the most entertaining popular theatrical experience you can have in Tokyo is **Takarazuka** (see box opposite), the all-singing, all-dancing, all-female revue which appears occasionally at the Takarazuka Theatre. Keep an eye out as well for performances of **Butō** (or *Butoh*). This highly expressive dance form, inspired by visiting American performers in the early 1950s, is minimalist, introspective, and often violent or sexually explicit. There are a handful of groups in Tokyo and it's not to everyone's taste, but shouldn't be missed if you're interested in modern performance art. Both Takarazuka and Butō have entered the mainstream, but there's plenty happening on the fringes. Tiny Alice and the Japan Foundation Forum are prime places to catch Japanese-language **avant-garde theatre**, while every autumn (mid-Oct to mid-Dec) the **Tokyo International Festival of Performing Arts** (Ⓦwww1.biz.biglobe.ne.jp/~tif) showcases the best on the current scene.

Tokyo is also on the tour circuit of many **international theatre companies**, who often appear at the Tokyo Globe or Shinjuku's New National Theatre (see opposite), though seats sell out months in advance for the bigger names. Easier to come by are tickets for the amateur dramatic group **Tokyo International Players** (Ⓦwww.tokyoplayers.org), which has been going for over a century, feeding off the ever-changing cast of foreign acting talent that passes through the city. Check the English-language press for details of their shows – productions, mounted four or five times a year, are usually staged at the American Club in Kamiyachō (Ⓣ03/3224-3670). Also look out for productions by the new, semi-professional **Intrigue Theatre** (Ⓦwww.intriguetheatre.com).

The all-female world of Takarazuka

There's a long tradition of men performing female roles in Japanese theatre, acting out a male fantasy of how women are supposed to behave. It's not so strange, then, that actresses playing idealized men have struck such a chord with contemporary female audiences. Along with the glitter, this has been the successful formula of the 700-strong all-female **Takarazuka Review Company**, founded in 1914 in the town of the same name, 20km northwest of Ōsaka.

The company's founder, Kobayashi Ichizū, was mightily impressed by performances of Western operas he'd seen in Tokyo. He sensed that Japanese audiences were ripe for lively Western musical dramas, but he also wanted to preserve something of Japan's traditional theatre, too. So, as well as performing dance reviews and musicals, Takarazuka also act out classical Japanese plays and have developed shows from Western novels, including *Gone with the Wind* and *War and Peace*.

Thousands of young girls apply annually to join the troupe at the age of 16, and devote themselves to a punishing routine of classes that will enable them to embody the "modesty, fairness and grace" (the company's motto) expected of a Takarazuka member. They must also forsake boyfriends, but in return are guaranteed the slavish adoration of an almost exclusively female audience who go particularly crazy for the male impersonators or *otoko-yaku*.

For **comedy** in English, the **Tokyo Comedy Store** (Ⓦwww .tokyocomedy.com) hosts shows at *Bar Isn't It* in Roppongi on the first and third Thursday of the month, while the **Punchline Comedy Club** (Ⓦwww.punch-linecomedy.com/Tokyo) occasionally brings top foreign talent to *Pizza Express* (3F, 4-30-3 Jingūmae, Shibuya-ku ☎03/5775-3894). Finally, the **Tokyo Cynics** offer pud-style hit-and-miss stand-ups at *The Fiddler* in Takadanobaba (see p.179) on the second Tuesday of the month.

Dentsu Shiki Theatre Umi (SEA)
電通四季劇場海
1-8-2 Higashi-Shimbashi, Minato-ku
☎0120-489444, Ⓦwww.shiki.gr.jp; Shiodome Station. Part of the Shiodome development, this new state-of-the-art theatre has been hosting *Mamma Mia!* since its opening in December 2000 and is likely to for several years to come.

Japan Foundation Forum
国際交流フォーラム
1F Akasaka Twin Tower, 2-17-22 Akasaka, Minato-ku ☎03/5562-3892,
Ⓦwww.jpf.go.jp/e/others/forum.html; Tameikesannō Station. Established in 1994 to promote international cultural exchange, the forum stages a variety of events including performances by international – mainly Asian – theatre groups, and also hosts contemporary art installations from time to time.

New National Theatre
新国立劇場
1-20 Honmachi, Shinjuku-ku ☎03/5352-9999,
Ⓦwww.nntt.jac.go.jp; Hatsudai Station. Just

behind Tokyo Opera City, the New National Theatre comprises three stages specially designed for Western performing arts, including opera, ballet, dance and drama.

Setagaya Public Theatre
世田谷パブリックシアター
4-1-1 Tasihido, Setagaya-ku ☎03/5432-1526,
Ⓦwww.setagaya-ac.or.jp/sept; Sangenjaya Station. One of Tokyo's most watchable contemporary theatre companies stages productions such as their adaptation of Haruki Murakami's book, *The Elephant Vanishes*, a co-production with Theatre de Complicité, which has toured internationally to much acclaim.

Shiki Gekijō
しき劇場
1-10-48 Kaigan, Minato-ku ☎0120-489444,
Ⓦwww.shiki.gr.jp; Hamamatsuchō or Takeshiba stations. There are two modern theatres here – named Spring and Autumn – one hosting big Western musicals, the other home-grown productions.

Takarazuka Gekijō
宝ずか劇場
1-1-3 Yūrakuchō, Chūō-ku ☏ 03/5251-2001;
Hibiya Station. Mostly Hollywood musicals
punched out by a huge cast in fabulous
costumes to an audience of middle-aged
housewives and star-struck teenage girls.
The theatre, opposite the *Imperial Hotel*,
also stages regular Takarazuka performances (see box, p.187) as well as conventional dramas.
Terpsichore
テルプシコーレ
3-49-15 Nakano, Nakano-ku ☏ 03/3383-3719;
Nakano Station. The most active of Tokyo's
Butō venues, comprising a tiny theatre

beside the tracks just west of Nakano
Station.
Theatre Cocoon
シアターコくーン
2-24-1 Dōgenzaka, Shibuya-ku ☏ 03/3477-9111;
Shibuya Station. Part of Shibuya's
Bunkamura arts centre, this modern theatre
hosts some of Tokyo's more accessible
fringe productions.
Tiny Alice
タイニアリス
2-13-6 Shinjuku-ku ☏ 03/3354-7307; **Shinjuku-
Sanchōme Station.** Well-known for its cutting-
edge Japanese and Asian performance art,
and for its summer theatre festival.

Cinema

Tokyoites are avid movie-goers, though a trip to the **cinema** (*Eiga-kan*) is far
from cheap – around ¥1800, or ¥2500 for *shiteseki* (reserved seats). The best
time to catch a movie is on Cinema Day, generally the first day of the month,
when all **tickets** cost ¥1000. You can cut the cost somewhat by buying
discount tickets in advance from a ticket agency such as CN Playguide and
Pia. Note that the last show is generally around 7pm, and that if it's a popular
new release you'll need to be at the cinema well before the start time to get a
decent seat, or sometimes any seat at all.

Of the city's several **film festivals**, the biggest is the **Tokyo International
Film Festival** (Ⓦ www.tiff-jp.net), held each November at the Bunkamura
(see p.116) and other cinemas around Shibuya. Although it's increasingly
becoming a vehicle for promoting major releases from the US, this is still one
of the few opportunities you'll have for catching Japanese and world cinema
with English subtitles, not to mention seeing some films that would never get
a general release. Also worth catching is the annual **Tokyo Lesbian and Gay
Film Festival** (see "Gay and lesbian Tokyo", p.182).

Listings are published on Thursday in the *Daily Yomiuri* and every Friday in
Metropolis, which also has reviews as well as maps locating all the major
cinemas. Apart from those listed here, which tend to specialize in independent
movies, there are many more cinemas in Ginza, Ikebukuro, Shibuya and
Shinjuku, mostly showing the latest Hollywood blockbusters. And don't forget
the big-screen experiences at Tokyo's two IMAX theatres, in Shinjuku and
Ikebukuro.

Le Cinéma
ルシネマ
Tōkyū Bunkamura, 2-24-1 Dōgenzaka, Shibuya-
ku ☏ 03/3477-9264, Ⓦ www.b-lecinema.com;
Shibuya Station. Upmarket filmhouse within
the Bunkamura arts complex with two
screens. It's the main venue for the Tokyo
International Film Festival (see above).
Cinema Qualité
シネマクアリテ
Musashinokan Building, 3-27 Shinjuku, Shinjuku-

ku ☏ 03/3354-5670; Shinjuku Station. Three
screens at this complex on the east side of
Shinjuku Station behind the Mitsukoshi
department store. Often screens classic
revivals as well as independent European
hits.
Cinema Rise
ルシネマ
13-17 Udagawa-chō, Shibuya ☏ 03/3464-0052,
Ⓦ www.cinemarise.com; Shibuya Station.
Sleek, avant-garde-looking cinema with

two screens, which focuses on successful independent movies from around the world.

Ciné Saison
シネセゾン渋谷
Shibuya 6F The Prime Building, 2-29-5 Dōgenzaka, Shibuya-ku ☎03/3770-1721; Shibuya Station. Comfy cinema which showcases a wide range of films, including classic revivals from the 1960s and 1970s.

Hibiya Chanter
日比谷シャンテ
Hibiya Chanter Building, 1-2-2 Yūrakuchō, Chiyoda-ku ☎03/3591-1511, ⓦwww.toho.co.jp; Hibiya and Yūrakuchō stations. The three large cinemas at this complex screen many of the higher-profile, mainstream American and British releases.

Iwanami Hall
岩波ホール
2-1 Kanda-Jimbōchō, Chiyoda-ku ☎03/3262-5252, ⓦwww.iwanami-hall.com; Jimbōchō Station. Long -established venue which has a policy of screening non-commercial European films from places as diverse as Greece and Poland, as well as quirky Japanese movies.

National Film Centre
国立フイルムセンター
3-7-6 Kyōbashi, Chūō-ku ☎03/3272-8600, ⓦwww.momat.go.jp; Kyōbashi Station. A treasure-trove for film lovers, with a gallery showing film-related exhibitions and two small cinemas screening retrospectives from their 17,000 archived movies. Most

Tokyo in the movies

The Oscar-winning success of *Lost in Translation* has probably done more to promote Tokyo as a tourist destination than any other movie (or indeed government-sponsored ad campaign) of recent times. But Sofia Coppola's love poem to the city is far from the only movie to put Tokyo in the spotlight.

Godzilla, King of the Monsters (1956). Classic story of a giant mutant lizard, born after a US hydrogen bomb test in the Bikini Atoll, which ends up running amok in Tokyo. The film was such a hit that it went on to spawn a long line of sequels, the latest (the 28th in the series) was released at the end of 2004.

Lost in Translation (Sofia Coppola; 2003). Few films have so accurately captured contemporary Tokyo as this stylish comedy drama, with Bill Murray and Scarlett Johansson teetering on the brink of romance in and out of Shinjuku's *Park Hyatt Hotel*.

Tampopo (Itami Jūzō; 1985). Tampopo, the proprietress of a noodle bar, is taught how to prepare ramen that has both sincerity and guts in this comedy about Japan's gourmet boom. From the old woman squishing fruit in a supermarket to the gangster and his moll passing a raw egg sexily between their mouths, this is packed with memorable scenes guaranteed to get the tummy rumbling.

Tōkyō Monogatari (*Tokyo Story*; Ozu Yasujirō; 1954). The most popular of Ozu Yasujirō's films, although it may appear tedious to audiences brought up on Hollywood action movies. An elderly couple travel to Tokyo from their seaside home in western Japan to visit their children and grandchildren. The only person who has any time for them is Noriko, the widow of their son Shōji killed in the war. On their return, the mother falls ill and dies. That's about it for plot, but the simple approach of Ozu to the themes of loneliness and the breakdown of tradition, and the sincerity of the acting make the film a genuine classic.

Until the End of the World (Wim Wenders; 1993). Rambling Millennium angst road movie with an interesting premise, but gets bogged down during its Australian Outback section. The Japan scenes, contrasting frantic Tokyo and the soothing countryside, are among the best. Also stars the great actor Ryū Chishū, who played the father in Ozu's *Tokyo Story*.

You Only Live Twice (Lewis Gilbert; 1967). Sean Connery's fifth outing as 007 has Bondo-san grappling with arch-enemy Blofeld and sundry Oriental villains in Tokyo and the Japanese countryside. Fun escapism, packed with glamorous girls and cool gadgets, including a mini-helicopter in a suitcase (with rocket launchers, of course).

are Japanese classics, though they occasionally dust off their collection of foreign movies.

Shin-Bungei-za
新ぶんげいざ

3F Maruhan-Ikebukuro Building, 1-43-5 Higashi-Ikebukuro, Toshima-ku ℡ **03/3971-9422,** Ⓦ **www.shinbungeiza.com; Ikebukuro Station.** Repertory theatre; screenings include matinée double bills. The ¥1300 six-month membership includes one ticket, a monthly newsletter and regular discounts on admission.

Virgin Cinemas Roppongi
ヴァージンシネマズ六本木

Roppongi Hills, Roppongi, Minato-ku ℡ **03/5775-6090,** Ⓦ **www.tohocinemas.co.jp; Roppongi Station.** State-of-the-art multiplex cinema with bookable seats (no more rushing to grab the best spot), late-night screenings and popular Japanese movies with English subtitles. Tickets (¥3000) include a drink.

Waseda Shochiku
早稲田松竹

1-5-16 Takadanobaba, Shinjuku-ku ℡ **03/3200-8968. Takadanobaba Station.** Popular with students from the nearby university, this cinema is cheaper (¥1300) and less fancy others in town, but still shows a decent selection of mainstream and non-commercial releases.

Yebisu Garden Cinema
恵比寿ガーデンシネマ

Yebisu Garden Place, 4-20 Ebisu, Shibuya-ku ℡ **03/5420-6161; Ebisu Station.** There are two screens at this modern cinema in the Yebisu brewery development, showing an interesting range of classy Hollywood and British releases.

17

Sports and martial arts

The Japanese take their sport very seriously, and it's not uncommon for parts of Tokyo to come to a complete standstill during crucial moments of a major baseball (*yakyu*) game as fans gather around television screens in homes, offices, shops, bars – even on the street. **Baseball** is the city's biggest sporting obsession, and it's rare to find anyone who doesn't support one of Tokyo's two main teams, the Yomiuri Giants and the Yakult Swallows. Hot on baseball's heels is **soccer**, which since the launch of the professional J-League in 1993 has enjoyed phenomenal success, boosted by Japan's co-hosting of the 2002 World Cup.

Although its popularity is slipping (see box, p.193), **sumo wrestling** also has a high profile, with big tournaments (*bashō*) televised nationwide and wrestlers enjoying celebrity status. **Martial arts** such as aikido, judo and karate, all traditionally associated with Japan, are far less widely practised, though Tokyo, with its numerous *dōjō* (practice halls), is the best place in the country to watch or learn about these ancient fighting ways. Many *dōjō* allow visitors in to watch practice sessions.

Check the local media, such as *The Japan Times* and *Metropolis*, for details of events. To get tickets it's best to approach one of the major **advance ticket agencies**. Major games and events sell out fast, so a second approach is to go directly to the venue on the day and see if you can get a ticket from the box office or a tout outside; expect to pay well over the odds if it's a key game. For details of ticket agencies, see "Directory", p.212.

Baseball

If you're in Tokyo during the **baseball** season (April–Oct), think about taking in a professional match; even if you're not a fan, the buzzing atmosphere and audience enthusiasm can be infectious. As well as the professional leagues (of which there are two, Central and Pacific), there's the equally, if not more, popular All-Japan High School Baseball Championship, and you might be able to catch one of the local play-offs before the main tournament held each summer in Ōsaka; check with the tourist office for details.

Tickets, available from the stadia or at advance ticket booths, start at around ¥1500 and go on sale on the Friday two weeks prior to a game. For

more information on Japan's pro baseball leagues, check out Ⓦ www.inter
.co.jp/Baseball.

Tokyo Dome
東京ドーム
1-3 Koraku, Bunkyō-ku Ⓣ **03/3811-2111,**
Ⓦ **www.tokyo-dome.co.jp/dome; Suidōbashi**
Station. This huge covered arena, affectionately nicknamed the "Big Egg", is home to
the Yomiuri Giants
baseball team, one of the league's most
popular, and is a great place to take in a
night game (*naitā*).

Jingū Baseball Stadium
神宮技場
13 Kasumigaoka, Shinjuku-ku Ⓣ **03/3404-8999;**
Gaienmae Station. One of the stadia
grouped in Meiji-jingū's Outer Gardens,
this is the home ground of Tokyo's second
professional baseball team, the Yakult
Swallows.

Soccer

The **J-League**, Japan's first professional football league, launched amid a
multi-billion-yen promotional drive in 1993, has firmly captured the public's
imagination – not to mention wallet, with its glitzy range of associated
merchandise. Following on from the success of the World Cup 2002, hosted
jointly by Japan and Korea, the game is now a huge crowd-puller; games are
held between March and October, with a summer break in August.

The J-League's original ten teams have now multiplied into two leagues of
28 teams in total. Sixteen clubs play in the J1 league, twelve in the J2; all
participate in the JL Yamazaki Nabisco Cup and there are a host of other cups
and contests. The two main stadia – Ajinomoto and Saitama – home grounds
of two of the key J-League teams, are a little way out of Tokyo. For full details
of the J-League in English, including match reports, visit Ⓦ www
.j-league.or.jp/english/index.html.

Ajinomoto Stadium
味の素スタジアム
376-3 Nishimachi, Chofu Ⓣ **0424/40-0555,**
Ⓦ **www.ajinomotostadium.com; Tobitakyu**
Station. Head west of Tokyo on the Keiō line
to reach this new stadium, home to FC
Tokyo and Tokyo Verdy.

National Stadium
国立競技場
10 Kasumigaoka-chō, Shinjuku-ku
Ⓣ **03/3403-1151; Sendagaya Station.** Big
Japanese and international games are held

at this huge oval stadium built for the 1964
Olympics and seating 75,000 people.
Tickets cost from ¥2000.

Saitama Stadium
埼玉スタジアム
2002 500 Nakanoda, Saitama Ⓣ **048/812-2002,**
Ⓦ **www.stadium2002.com. Urawa Misono**
Station. The home of the Urawa Reds, this
is Japan's largest soccer-only stadium,
seating 64,000, and was the venue for the
2002 World Cup semi-final.

Sumo

Japan's national sport, **sumo**, developed out of the divination rites performed
at Shinto shrines, and its religious roots are still apparent in the various rituals
which form an integral part of a *bashō* (tournament). Two huge wrestlers,
weighing on average 170 kilos each and wearing nothing but a hefty loincloth,
face off in a small ring of hard-packed clay; the loser is the first to step outside
the rope or touch the ground with any part of the body except the feet. Bouts
are often over in seconds, but the pageantry and ritual make for a surprisingly
absorbing spectacle.

The trouble with sumo

In a neat reversal of Japan's appropriation of baseball and export of professional players to the US league, four of sumo's most revered stars of recent years were born abroad. Both the top-ranked yokuzuna Konishiki (a.k.a. the "dump truck") and Akebono, who retired in 1998 and 2001 respectively, were born in Hawaii; the 237-kilo Musashimaru, a yokuzuna since 1999, hails from American Samoa; while Asashoryu – a relative lightweight at 137kg, who became the 68th yokuzuna in Feburary 2003 – was born Dolgorsuren Dagvadorj in Ulan Bator, Mongolia.

The success of the foreign wrestlers is just one of the factors that is said to be turning Japanese off the 1500-year-old sport. At recent bouts there have been large chunks of unsold seats – unthinkable in the past – and even TV viewing figures are down as younger Japanese tune into soccer instead. The Japan Sumo Association finds itself in a bind. On the one hand they have tried to limit the number of foreign wrestlers to help preserve the sport's Japanese character. On the other, they are acutely aware that fewer young Japanese wish to submit to the punishing regime needed to become a top sumo wrestler. And so the keen young foreigners may just prove to be sumo's saviours.

Finding enough people to fight is only one of the Sumo Association's problems. The other is dealing with wrestlers like Asashoryu who flout the game's strict code of behaviour. The Mongolian yokuzuna has been known to show his emotions on winning or losing a bout – very much a no-no – and his out-of-the-ring antics keep Japan's scandal rags very happy. Given sumo's slipping profile, however, this may be just the sort of publicity the sport needs to keep it in the public's increasingly unappreciative eye.

Each year three major *bashō* take place in Ryōgoku's National Stadium (see p.64). At other times it's possible to watch practice sessions (*keiko*) at the stables (*heya*) where the wrestlers live and train. These sessions take place in the early morning (usually from around 5am or 6am to 10.30am) except during and immediately after a *bashō* or when the wrestlers are out of town; visitors are expected to watch in silence and women must wear trousers. A few stables accept visitors without an appointment, but it's safest to double-check first with the Tokyo TIC to make sure they're actually training that day. Recommended stables to try are: Dewanoumi Beya (2-3-15 Ryōgoku, Sumida-ku; ☎03/3631-0090) and Kasugano Beya (1-7-11 Ryōgoku, Sumida-ku; ☎03/3631-1871). You can pick up Japanese-only maps of the stables from the Ryōgoku Station ticket window.

For further information about tournaments, tickets and related events, consult the Nihon Sumō Kyōkai website (@www.sumo.or.jp) or pick up a copy of *Sumo World* magazine (@www.sumoworld.com).

Kokugikan
国技館
1-3-28 Yokoami, Kōtō-ku ☎03/3623-5111;
Ryōgoku Station. The National Sumo Stadium is the venue for Tokyo's three *bashō* during the middle fortnights of January, May and September. Tickets go on sale a month before each tournament; they're available from a ticket agency (see p.212) or line up early – before 8am – outside the stadium box office for one of the unreserved tickets which are sold on the day (¥2100); note that tickets are particularly hard to come by on the first and last days.

Aikido

Half sport, half religion, **aikido** (which translates as "the way of harmonious spirit") blends elements of judo, karate and kendo into a form of self-defence without body contact. It's one of the newer martial arts, having only been created in Japan earlier last century and, as a rule, is performed without weapons. For a painfully enlightening and humorous take on the rigours of aikido training, read Robert Twigger's *Angry White Pyjamas* (see Contexts, p.277).

The International Aikido Federation
合気道本部道場
17-18 Wakamatsuchō, Shinjuku-ku
☎03/3203-923, 🌐www.aikikai.or.jp;
Wakamatsu-Kawada Station. You'll also find

the Aikikai Hombu Dōjō at the same address and telephone number, where visitors are welcome to watch practice sessions.

Judo

Probably the martial art most closely associated with Japan, **judo** is a self-defence technique that developed out of the Edo-era style of fighting called *jujutsu*. Judo activities in Japan are controlled by the All-Japan Judo Federation.

All-Japan Judo Federation
全日本柔道連盟
Kodokan 1-16-30 Kasuga, Bunkyō-ku
☎03/3818-4199, 🌐www.judo.or.jp; Kasuga or Kōrakuen Stations. This *dōjō* has a spectators' gallery open to visitors free of charge (Mon–Fri 6–7.30pm, Sat 4–5.30pm). There's also a hostel here where you can stay if you have an introduction from an authorized judo body or an approved Japanese sponsor.

Nippon Budōkan Budo Gakuen
日本武道館
2-3 Kitanomaru-kōen, Chiyoda-ku
☎03/3216-5143. Kudanshita Station. Around fifty free martial arts exhibition matches are held at this large octagonal arena, an important centre for all martial arts, as well as judo. Within the Budōkan, there's also a school where you can catch practice sessions (Mon–Fri 5–8pm, Sat 2–6.30pm).

Karate

Karate has its roots in China and was only introduced into Japan in 1922. Since then the sport has developed into many different styles, all with governing bodies and federations based in Tokyo.

Japan Karate Association
日本空手協会
4F Sanshin Building, 29-33 Sakuragaoka-chō, Shibuya-ku ☎03/5459-6226; Shibuya Station. The home of the world's largest karate association. You can watch classes here (generally Mon–Sat 10.30–11.30am & 5–8pm), but it's best to call first.

Japan Karatedō Federation
全日本空手道連盟
6F, 2 Nippon Zaidan Building, 1-11-2 Toranomon, Minato-ku ☎03/3503-6640, 🌐www.karatedo.co.jp; Toranomon Station. This umbrella organization can advise on the main styles of karate and the best places to see practice sessions or take lessons. Call from Monday to Friday, between 9am and 5pm.

Kendo

Kendo ("the way of the sword") is Japanese fencing using a long bamboo weapon (the *shinai*) or the metal *katana* blade. This fighting skill is the oldest in Japan, dating from the Muromachi period (1392–1573). It was developed as a sport in the Edo period and is now watched over by the All-Japan Kendo Federation.

All-Japan Kendo Federation
All-Japan Kendo Federation
Nippon Budōkan, 2-3 Kitanomaru-kōen, Chiyoda-ku ☎03/3211-5804/5, ⓦwww.kendo.or.jp; **Kudanshita Station.** Practice sessions aren't generally open to the public here, but you might be lucky enough to catch the All-Japan Championships held in Tokyo each December, or the children's kendo competition in January, both held at the Budōkan.

(18) Shopping

Cruising the boutiques and fashion malls whilst toting a couple of designer-label carrier bags is such a part of Tokyo life that it's hard not to get caught up in the general enthusiasm. There are shops to suit every taste and budget, from swanky department stores and craft shops stuffed with all kinds of tempting curiosities to hushed antiques shops and rag-bag flea markets.

As the capital of world cool, the city is a prime hunting ground for the latest electronic gadgets, electrical equipment and cameras, as well as fashions that are so next year – if not next decade – elsewhere. CDs may be slightly less expensive than at home, and the selection of world music, jazz and techno in particular takes some beating. Foreign-language books and magazines are less well represented and can be very pricey. There are also some wonderful crafts shops and very quirky souvenir and novelty stores. Antique and bargain hunters shouldn't miss out on a visit to one of the city's flea markets, which if nothing else can turn up some unusual souvenirs and presents.

In general, **opening hours** are from 10am or 11am to 7pm or 8pm. Most shops close one day a week, not always on Sunday, and smaller places often shut on public holidays.

Though it's always worth asking, few shops take **credit cards** and fewer still accept cards issued abroad, so make sure you have plenty of cash. See p.29 for details of **consumption tax**.

Where to shop

Ginza remains the preserve of the city's conservative elegance, and is still regarded as Tokyo's traditional shopping centre, although it's been over-shadowed by the ritzy emporia of **Roppongi Hills** of late. **Shinjuku** has long put up a strong challenge, with an abundance of department stores and malls offering everything under one roof. Young and funky, **Shibuya** and **Harajuku** are probably the most enjoyable places to shop: even if you don't want to buy, the passing fashion parade doesn't get much better. The haute couture boutiques along **Omotesandō** and in nearby **Aoyama** provide a more rarefied shopping experience, while, of the northern districts, **Asakusa** figures highly for its crafts shops, particularly those on and around Nakamise-dōri. Ueno is home to the lively **Ameyoko-chō** market, while **Ikebukuro** is famous for its plethora of discount stores and the Sunshine City complex. Also worth a look are Yebisu Garden Place at **Ebisu** and Venus Fort, a shopping mall dedicated to women, out at **Odaiba**.

Tokyo also has a number of wholesale districts that can be fun to poke around. The most famous are **Tsukiji** fish market, **Kappabashi** ("Kitchenware Town"), the bookstores of **Jimbōchō** and **Akihabara**'s electrical emporia. North of Asakusabashi Station, **Edo-dōri** and its backstreets specialize in traditional Japanese dolls, while further north again the area called **Kuramae** is "Toy Town", where shops sell fireworks, fancy goods and decorations, as well as toys of every description. Immediately east of Ueno's mainline station along Shōwa-dōri, slick-haired guys in leathers stalk the rows of sleek machines in "**Motorbike Town**" (Baiku Taun).

For a somewhat more relaxed shopping experience, head out to one of the residential neighbourhoods such as Daikan'yama, Naka-Meguro and Shimo-Kitazawa, all a short train ride from Shibuya. **Daikan'yama** is smart and often expensive, but its village atmosphere is appealing, and it's a good place to check out up-and-coming Japanese designers. The next stop along the Tokyū-Tōyoko line from Shibuya (it's also on Hibiya metro line) is **Naka-Meguro**, where a host of funky fashion shops line the streets beside the Meguro-gawa. **Shimo-Kitazawa** has a studenty, bohemian air and any number of boutiques, some selling secondhand clothes, where you can scoop big-name labels at bargain prices – and keep an eye open too for fashion and art creations by local students. To get there, take the Keiō-Inokashira line four stops from Shibuya, or the Odakyū line six stops from Shinjuku.

Antique and flea markets

There's at least one **flea market** in Tokyo every weekend, though you'll need to arrive early for any bargains; see below for a round-up of the main venues and ask at the TIC (see p.19) for the current schedule. Alternatively, head for the permanent **antique halls**, also listed below, which gather various dealers under one roof, and where you'll come across fine, hand-painted scrolls, and intricate *netsuke* or samurai armour among a good deal of tat.

For a really wide selection of antiques there are several good fairs. One of the biggest is the **Heiwajima Zenkoku Komingu Kottō Matsuri**, which takes place over three days about five times a year (usually in Feb/March, May, June, Sept and Dec) at the Ryūtsū Centre (6-1-1 Heiwajima, Ōta-ku ☎03/3980-8228), one stop on the monorail from Hamamatsuchō to Haneda. Also recommended is **Yokohama Kottō World** (Pacifico Yokohama, 1-1-1 Minato Mirai, Nishi-ku ⓦ home.att.ne.jp/sigma/y-world/; entry ¥1000) held in Yokohama for three days, generally in April and November.

Duty-free shopping

Foreign visitors can buy **duty-free** items (that is, without consumption tax), but only in certain tourist shops and the larger department stores. Perishable goods, such as food, drinks, tobacco, cosmetics and film, are exempt from the scheme, and most stores only offer duty-free if your total spend in one shop on a single day exceeds ¥10,000. The shop will either give you a duty-free price immediately or, in department stores especially, you pay the full price first and then apply for a refund at their "tax-exemption" counter. The shop will attach a copy of the customs document (*warriin*) to your passport, to be removed by customs officers when you leave Japan. Note, however, that you can often find the same goods elsewhere at a better price, including tax, so shop around first.

Antique Market La Villette

アンティークマーケツトハナイモリビル

Hanae Mori Building, 3-6-1 Kita-Aoyama, Minato-ku; Omotesandō Station; see map p.106. Daily 11am–8pm (although some shops close on Thurs). Permanent stalls selling an expensive assortment of Japanese and Western antiques. Each stall has its own speciality – woodblock prints, ceramics, jewellery and so on.

Antiques Mall Ginza

アンティークマール銀座

1-13-1 Ginza, Chūō-ku ⓦ www.antiques-jp.com; Ginza-Itchōme Station; see map p.54. Daily except Wed 11am–7pm. Upmarket collection of classy antiques spread across three floors, though few bargains.

Hanazono-jinja

花園神社

5-17-3 Shinjuku, Shinjuku-ku; Shinjuku-Sanchōme Station; see map p.98. Sun dawn to dusk. You're more likely to find junk than real antiques at this market, but its setting in the grounds of a shrine on the west side of Shinjuku is attractive.

Nogi-jinja

乃木神社

8-11-27 Akasaka, Minato-ku. Nogizaka Station; see map p.68. Second Sun of each month from dawn to dusk. Around thirty vendors gather at this lively flea market offering the usual assortment of old kimono, bric-a-brac and the like.

Ōedo Antique Fair

大江戸骨董市

Tokyo International Forum, 3-5-1 Marunouchi, Chiyoda-ku; Yūrakuchō Station; see map p.54. Third Sunday of the month from dawn to late afternoon. One of the largest regular flea markets with many vendors offering real antiques and interesting curios. Don't expect any bargains, though.

Tōgō-jinja

東郷神社

1-5-3 Jingūmae, Shibuya-ku. Harajuku Station; see map p.106. Sun 4am–3pm. One of Tokyo's best flea markets, with around 150 vendors and a good range of inexpensive items that make great souvenirs. It's held on the first, fourth and fifth (if there is one) Sundays of the month, but is cancelled if it's wet.

Tokyo Antiques Hall

東京ふ億クラフトアンヂアンティークハルズ

3-9-5 Minami-Ikebukuro, Toshima-ku; Ikebukuro Station; see map p.91. Daily except Thurs 11am–7pm. Over thirty stalls, selling everything from boxes of dog-eared postcards to original ukiyo-e and magnificent painted screens.

Arts, crafts and souvenirs

While most department stores have a reasonable **crafts** section, it's a lot more fun rummaging around in Tokyo's specialist shops. The largest concentration is in **Asakusa** (see box on p.78), though a few still survive in the thick of Ginza and Nihombashi. If money is no object, head for the arcades in the big hotels, such as the *Imperial* (see p.138), *Ōkura* (see p.137) and *New Ōtani* (see p.137), where you can pick up luxury gifts, from Mikimoto pearls to Arita porcelain.

All the following outlets are good places to hunt for **souvenirs**, from cheap and cheerful paper products, whacky novelties and toys to satin-smooth lacquerware and sumptuous wedding kimono. Keep an eye out, too, for the ubiquitous "¥100 Shops" (everything at ¥100), which can yield amazing gizmos for next to nothing.

Beniya

Beniya

4-20-19 Minami-Aoyama, Minato-ku ⓣ 03/3403-8115; Omotesandō Station; see map p.106. Daily except Thurs 10am–7pm. One of Tokyo's best range of folk crafts (mingei) from around the country. They also stage craft exhibitions from time to time.

Blue & White

Buru & Uaito

2-9-2 Azabu-Jūban, Minato-ku ⓣ 03/3451-0537; Azabu-Jūban Station; see map p.71. Mon–Sat 10am–6pm. Quirky shop specializing in blue-and-white-coloured products made in Japan, including yukata, furoshiki (textile wrapping cloths), quilts, pottery and traditional decorations.

Fuji-Torii
Fuji-Torii

6-1-10 Jingūmae, Shibuya-ku ℡03/3400-2777;
Meiji-jingūmae Station; see map p.106. Daily
except Tues 11am–7pm, closed third Mon of
month. Omotesandō shop specializing
in *ukiyo-e*, plus other artworks and
antiques.

Iseya
Iseya

2-18-9 Yanaka, Taitō-ku ℡03/3823-1453;
Sendagi Station; see map p.82. Daily
10am–6pm. One of the colourful craft shops
that make Yanaka such a delightful part of
Tokyo to explore. This one specializes in
chiyogami – brightly coloured and patterned
paper products.

Itō-ya
Itō-ya

2-7-15 Ginza, Chūō-ku ℡03/3561-8311; Ginza
Station; see map p.54. Mon–Sat 10am–7pm,
Sun 10.30am–7pm. This wonderful stationery
store (Itō-ya 1), with nine floors and two
annexes (Itō-ya 2 & 3), is great for a whole
range of souvenirs such as traditional
washi paper, calligraphy brushes, inks and
so on. There are also branches in Shibuya
(2-24-1 Shibuya, Shibuya-ku), Shinjuku
(1-1-3 Nishi-Shinjuku, Shinjuku-ku) and
Ikebukuro (1-1-25 Nishi-Ikebukuro,
Toshima-ku).

Japan Traditional Craft Centre
全国伝統的工芸品センター

Metropolitan Plaza Building, 1-11-1 Nishi-
Ikebukuro, Toshima-ku ℡03/5954-6066,
ⓦwww.kougei.or.jp; Ikebukuro Station; see map
p.91. Daily 11am–7pm. This centre showcases the works of craft associations
across the nation, offering everything from
finely crafted chopsticks to elegant lacquerware and metalwork.

Jūsan-ya
Jūsan-ya

3-45-4 Yushima, Bunkyō-ku ℡03/3831-3238;
Yushima Station; see map p.82. Mon–Sat
10am–6pm. Take exit 2 from Yushima Station
and duck into the backstreets to find this
tiny shop where a craftsman sits making
beautiful boxwood combs – just as succes-
sive generations have done since 1736.

Natsuno
Natsuno

6-7-4 Ginza, Chūō-ku ℡03/3569-0952; Ginza
Station; see map p.54. Daily 10am–8pm.
This place boasts an incredible collection
of over a thousand types of chopsticks,
plus chopstick rests and rice bowls.
Prices range from ¥200 up up to
¥60,000 for a pair made from ivory. They
have another store just off Omotesandō
(4-2-17 Jingūmae, Shibuya-ku;
℡03/3403-6033; see map p.106).

Nihon Mingeikan
民芸館

4-3-33 Komaba, Meguro-ku ℡03/3467-4527;
Komaba-Tōdaimae Station; see map p.115.
Tues–Sun 10am–5pm. The gift shop of the
Japan Folk Crafts Museum may be a bit
out of the way, but they have original pottery and prints to die for and it's a fine
source of souvenirs. If you're in town, don't
miss their annual sale of new work (Nov
23–Dec 3).

Oriental Bazaar
Orientaru Bazā

5-9-13 Jingū-mae, Shibuya-ku
℡03/3400-3933; Meiji-jingūmae Station; see
map p.106. Daily except Thurs 10am–7pm. A
bit of a tourist trap, but its prime location
on Omotesandō makes this a very
popular, one-stop souvenir emporium,
selling everything from secondhand
kimono to origami paper.

Shōeidō
Shōeidō

8-2-8 Ginza, Chūō-ku ℡03/3572-6484;
Shimbashi Station; see map p.54. Mon–Fri
10am–7pm. High-class incense shop offering
the sweet-smelling aromas of a renowned
Kyoto incense maker.

Takumi
Takumi

8-4-2 Ginza, Chūō-ku; Mon–Sat 10am–7pm;
Shimbashi Station; see map p.54. Folk-craft
shop chock-a-block with bags, baskets,
pots, toys and fabrics.

S Watanabe
渡邊木版美術画補

8-6-19 Ginza, Chūō-ku ℡03/3571-4684;
Shimbashi Station; see map p.54. Mon–Sat
9.30am–8pm. Small shop specializing in
woodblock prints at a range of prices and
with both modern and traditional designs,
including original *ukiyo-e* as well as
reproductions of famous artists.

Books and magazines

Buying foreign-language books in Tokyo is likely to make a large impact on your wallet, but it can be enjoyable to browse the city's major **bookstores**. Most big hotels have bookstores stocking English-language books on Japan and a limited choice of fiction, as well as imported newspapers and magazines. Bookworms should also rummage around the **secondhand bookstores** of Jimbōchō, north of central Tokyo on the Hanzōmon, Mita and Shinjuku subway lines.

Caravan Books
Karaban Bukusu
2-21-5 Ikebukuro, Toshima-ku ℡03/5951-6404, ⓦwww.booksatcaravan.com; Ikebukuro Station; see map p.91. Mon–Thurs 11am–8pm, Fri & Sat 11am–9pm, Sun noon–6pm. Very good secondhand bookstore with a pleasant garden café tucked away in the backstreets on the west side of the station. Check their website for details of monthly wine and cheese evenings (usually held on Fridays).

Good Day Books
Gudo Dē Bukusu
1-11-2 Ebisu, Shibuya-ku ℡03/5421-0957, ⓦwww.gooddaybooks.com; Ebisu Station; see map p.118. Mon & Wed–Sat 11am–8pm, Sun 11am–6pm. On the third floor of the building next to the *Footnik* bar, this is nirvana for homesick bookworms, with Tokyo's best selection of secondhand books.

Kinokuniya
紀伊国屋
Takashimaya Times Square, Annex Building, 5-24-2 Sendagaya, Shinjuku-ku ℡03/5361-3301; Shinjuku Station; see map p.98. Daily 10am–8pm, closed one Wed each month. The sixth floor of Kinokuniya's seven-storey outlet offers Tokyo's best (but far from cheapest) selection of foreign-language books and magazines. Its original shop on Shinjuku-dōri – whose forecourt is still a favourite meeting spot – is also worth a browse.

Kitazawa
北沢
2-5 Jimbōchō, Chiyoda-ku ℡03/3263-0011; Jimbōchō Station; see map p.61. Mon–Sat 10am–6pm. The stately granite- and brick-fronted building houses one of the area's best selection of English-language titles among dozens of secondhand stores in Jimbōchō. It's on Yasukuni-dōri, just west of the junction with Hakusan-dōri.

Manga

All types of drawn cartoons, from comic strips to magazines, are known as **manga**, and together they constitute a multi-billion-yen business that accounts for around a third of all published material in Japan. The best seller is *Shukan Shōnen Jump*, a weekly which regularly shifts five million copies, but there are hundreds of other titles, not to mention the popular daily strips in newspapers.

Although manga are targeted at a cross-section of society – and sometimes cater to less wholesome tastes – comic books are frequently used to explain complicated current affairs topics and to teach high-school subjects.

Manga have become a recognized art form and top artists are respected the world over. The "god of manga", **Tezuka Osamu**, created *Astro Boy* and *Kimba, the White Lion* in the 1960s and went on to pen more challenging work such as the adventures of the mysterious renegade surgeon Black Jack and the epic war-time saga *Adorufu ni Tsugu* (*Tell Adolf*).

Manga are available just about everywhere, from train station kiosks to bookstores, and there's a useful website for the serious fan at ⓦwww.kodanclub.com. One good Tokyo shop to try is **Mandarake** (B2F Shibuya Beam Building, 31-2 Udagawa-chō, Shibuya-ku ℡03/3477-0777), near Shibuya Station, which sells a wide range of secondhand manga as well as character dolls and figures, posters, cards and even costumes if you fancy dressing up as your favourite manga character.

Maruzen

丸善

Maru Building, 2-4-1 Marunouchi 2, Chiyoda-ku ☎03/5220-7551; Tokyo Station; see map p.54. Mon–Sat 10am–8pm, Sun 10am–7pm. Stocks a wide range of imported and locally produced books, with a strong showing in art and design, and magazines in a variety of languages. You can buy traditional *washi* paper in the basement and there's a small crafts gallery on the fourth floor.

Nadiff

Najifu

4-9-8 Jingūmae, Shibuya-ku ☎03/3403-8814; Omotesandō Station; see map p.106. Daily 11am–8pm. Known for its good selection of art and photography books, as well as art supplies, avant-garde and world music selections, gallery and chill-out café.

On Sundays

On Sandeizu

Watari-um Museum of Contemporary Art, 3-7-6 Jingūmae, Shibuya-ku ☎03/3470-1424; Gaienmae Station; see map p.106. Tues–Sun 11am–8pm. This stylish bookstore inside one of the city's more avant-garde galleries offers Tokyo's best choice of art, photography and architecture books, plus a fabulous selection of postcards.

Tokyo Random Walk

Tōkyō Randomu Uaruku

1-3 Kanda-Jimbōchō, Chiyoda-ku ☎03/3291-7071; Jimbōchō Station; see map p.61. Mon–Sat 10.30am–8pm, Sun 11am–7pm. The bookstore of the long-running Japan-based English-language publisher Charles Tuttle, stocking a wide range of books by Tuttle and other publishers. Check the second floor for discounted books.

Tower Books

Tawā Bukusu

7F Tower Records, 1-22-14 Jinnan, Shibuya-ku ☎03/3496-3661; Shibuya Station; see map p.115. Daily 10am–10pm. The cheapest prices and best selection of imported books, magazines and papers, including an excellent travel guidebook section. Tower Records in Shinjuku and Ikebukuro (see p.209) stock a more limited range.

Cameras, computers and electronic goods

Shinjuku is Tokyo's prime area for **cameras** and photographic equipment, though **Ikebukuro** also has a solid reputation for new and secondhand deals at reasonable prices.

Akihabara boasts Tokyo's biggest concentration of stores selling **electronic goods**, mostly concentrated along a small stretch of Chūō-dōri and its side streets, all within walking distance of Akihabara Station (on the JR Yamanote and Hibiya subway lines). Anything you can plug in is available from a bewildering array of stores split into several outlets, with multiple floors selling overlapping product ranges. There are also plenty of discount stores in **Shinjuku, Ikebukuro** and **Shibuya**.

Before buying electrical goods, do compare prices – many shops are willing to bargain – and make sure there's the appropriate voltage switch (the Japanese power supply is 100v). For English-language instructions, after-sales service and guarantees, stick to export models, which you'll find mostly in the stores' duty-free sections.

Apple Ginza Store

Apuru Ginza Sutoru

3-5-12 Ginza, Chūō-ku ☎03/5189-8200, ⓦwww.apple.com/retail/jp/ginza; Ginza Station; see map p.54. Daily 10am–9pm. Apple's first dedicated store in Japan is an impressive shrine to its highly desirable products, with free Internet access on the fifth floor.

BIC Camera

Biku Kamera

1-11-1 Yūrakuchō, Chiyoda-ku ☎03/5221-1111; Yūrakuchō Station; see map p.54. Daily 10am–8pm. Housed in the old Sogō department store, the main branch of BIC offers hard-to-beat prices for cameras, audio and electronic goods – practically any gizmo you want can be found here, plus (strangely enough) discounted wine and liquor. Also branches in Ikebukuro (1-41-5 Higashi-Ikebukuro, Toshima-ku), Shinjuku (3-26 Shinjuku, Shinjuku-ku) and Shibuya (1-5 Dōgenzaka, Shibuya-ku).

Laox
Raokusu
1-2-9 Soto-Kanda, Chiyoda-ku ℡03/3253-7111; Akihabara Station; see map p.61. Mon–Sat 10am–8pm, Sun 10am–7.30pm. One of the most prominent names in Akihabara and probably the best place to start shopping: prices are reasonable, they have a well-established duty-free section with English-speaking staff, and nine stores where you can buy everything from pocket calculators to plasma-vision TVs.

Sakuraya
Sakuraya
1-1-1 Nishi-Shinjuku, Shinjuku-ku ℡03/5324-3636; Shinjuku Station; see map p.98. Daily 10am–8pm. Next to the Odakyū department store is the flagship store of this camera and electronics chain, which has several branches around Shinjuku, including one across the road from main rival Yodobashi Camera. There's a good selection of equipment and prices are keen.

Shimizu Camera
Shimizu Kamera
4-3-2 Ginza, Chūō-ku ℡03/3564-1008; Ginza Station; see map p.54. Mon–Sat 10am–7pm, Sun 10.30am–6pm. Reputable used-camera specialist in the backstreets of Ginza two blocks west of Mikimoto's pearl shop.

Sofmap
Sofumapu
3-8-3 Marunouchi, Chiyoda-ku ℡03/5219-1801, ⓦwww.sofmap.com; Yūrakuchō Station; see map p.54. Daily 11am–9pm. Electronic megastore with a good reputation for computers and related goods; it's on the ground floor of the building which also houses a giant Muji outlet.

Yamagiwa
Yamagiwa
4-1-1 Soto-Kanda, Chiyoda-ku ℡03/3255-3111; Akihabara Station; see map p.61. Mon–Fri 10.30am–8pm, Sat & Sun 10am–8pm. Highly rated store with a duty-free section on the sixth floor, selling a broad range of electronic products at bargain prices.

Yodobashi Camera
Yodobashi Kamera
1-11-1 Nishi-Shinjuku, Shinjuku-ku ℡03/3346-1010; Shinjuku Station; see map p.98. Daily 9.30am–9pm. Claiming to be the world's largest camera shop, this place offers decent reductions and stocks the broadest range. There's a smaller branch in Ueno.

Department stores

You can find almost anything you're looking for in Tokyo's massive **department stores**, from the impressive basement food halls right up through fashion, crafts and household items to the restaurant floors. These places are more likely to have English-speaking staff and a duty-free service (see box on p.197) than smaller stores, though prices do tend to be slightly above average. Their sales, particularly of kimono, can offer great bargains; look for adverts in the English-language press.

Isetan
伊勢丹デパート
3-14-1 Shinjuku, Shinjuku-ku ℡03/3352-1111, ⓦwww.isetan.co.jp; Shinjuku Station; see map p.98. Daily except Wed 10am–7.30pm. This stylish department store is one of the best in Shinjuku, with an emphasis on well-designed local goods and a reputation for promoting up-and-coming fashion designers; the newly renovated annex building housing men's clothing and accessories is particularly chic. Their free I-Club service will provide you with English-speaking shopping assistants.

Matsuya
松屋デパート
3-6-1 Ginza, Chūō-ku ℡03/3567-1211, ⓦwww.matsuya.com; Ginza Station; see map p.54. Daily 10am–8pm. More downmarket than many other big department stores, Matsuya has a decent choice of traditional crafts and household goods at competitive prices. There's another branch in Asakusa (1-4 Hanakawado, Taitō-ku).

Matsuzakaya

松坂屋デパト

3-29-5 Ueno, Taitō-ku ⓣ03/3832-1111,
ⓦ www.matsuzakaya.co.jp; Ueno-Hirokōji
Station; see map p.82. Mon–Sat 10am–7.30pm,
Sun 10am–7pm. Three-hundred-year-old
store with a not-surprisingly fusty air, similar
in style to Matsuya. There's another branch
in Ginza (6-10-1 Ginza, Chūō-ku
ⓣ03/3572-1111; Ginza Station; see
map p.54).

Mitsukoshi

三越デパト

1-4-1 Nihombashi-Muromachi ⓣ03/3241-3311,
ⓦ www.mitsukoshi.co.jp; Mitsukoshi-mae
Station; see map p.54. Daily 10am–7pm.
Tokyo's most prestigious and oldest department store is elegant, spacious and
renowned for its high-quality merchandise –
including a good range of traditional household items such as lacquerware and
pottery, as well as kimono, *obi* (the broad
decorative belts worn with kimono) and
other accessories. There are other
branches across Tokyo including in Ginza
(4-6-16 Ginza, Chūō-ku ⓣ03/3562-1111;
Ginza Station; see map p.54), Ikebukuro (1-
5-7 Higashi-Ikebukuro, Toshima-ku
ⓣ03/3987-1111; Ikebukuro Station; see
map p.91) and Shinjuku (3-29-1 Shinjuku,
Shinjuku-ku ⓣ03/3354-1111; Shinjuku
Station; see map p.98).

Seibu

西武デパト

1-28-1 Minami-Ikebukuro, Toshima-ku
ⓣ03/3981-0111, ⓦ www.seibu.co.jp; Ikebukuro
Station; see map p.91. Daily 10am–8pm.
Sprawling department store with a reputation for innovation, especially in its homeware store Loft and fashion offshoot Parco,
whose racks and shelves groan with state-
of-the-art ephemera; there are also a
cluster of Seibu, Loft and Parco stores in
Shibuya (see p.115).

Takashimaya

高島屋デパト

2-4-1 Nihombashi, Chūō-ku ⓣ03/3211-4111,
ⓦ www.takashimaya.co.jp; Nihombashi Station;
see map p.54. Daily 10am–7pm. Like Mitsukoshi,
Takashimaya has a long and
illustrious past and, though it appeals to
decidedly conservative tastes, is a good
place to look for traditional household items.
There's also a huge branch in Shinjuku at
Takashimaya Times Square (5-24-2
Sendagaya, Shibuya-ku ⓣ03/5361-1122).

Tōbu

東武デパト

1-1-25 Nishi-Ikebukuro, Toshima-ku
ⓣ03/3981-2211, ⓦ www.tobu.co.jp; Ikebukuro
Station; see map p.91. Daily 10am–8pm.
Japan's largest department store is mainly
of interest for its excellent basement food
halls on two levels and dozens of restaurants in its Spice and Spice 2 annexes.

Tōkyū

Tōkyū

2-24-1 Dōgenzaka, Shibuya-ku ⓣ03/3477-3111,
ⓦ www.tokyu-dept.co.jp; Shibuya Station; see
map p.115. Daily 11am–7pm. Top dog in the
Shibuya department store stakes, with
branches all over the area, particularly around
the train station. This main branch specializes
in designer fashions and interior goods. They
also run Tōkyū Hands (see p.208).

Wakō

Wakō

4-5-11 Ginza, Chūō-ku ⓣ03/3562-2111; Ginza
Station; see map p.54. Mon–Sat 10.30am–6pm,
open Sun 10.30am–6pm end April to early Aug.
Ginza's most elegant department store, this
century-old establishment (which started as
the home of Seiko – meaning "precision" –
watches) might not have as wide a range of
goods as its rivals, but it does have a
sterling reputation for custom-making
anything its clients desire, including fine
jewellery and watches.

Fashion

The city's epicentre of chic is **Omotesandō**, the tree-lined boulevard
cutting through Harajuku and Aoyama. The roll call of brands here – Gucci,
Louis Vuitton, Armani, Chanel – reads like a who's who of fashion, and you'll
also find top Japanese designers such as Issey Miyake and Comme des Garçons.
The area's backstreets are prime hunting grounds for up-and-coming designers
and streetwear labels including Underground, A Bathing Ape and Hysteric
Glamour.

Daikan'yama, Naka-Meguro and Shimo-Kitazawa are also worth browsing around – the fashion shops in the last two areas are slightly cheaper and less precious. In addition, all Tokyo's big **department stores** have several floors devoted to clothes, from haute couture to more modest wear at affordable prices, albeit rather uninspired.

Finding clothes that fit is becoming easier as young Japanese are, on average, substantially bigger than their parents, and foreign chains tend to carry larger

The comeback of the kimono

Few visitors to Japan will fail to be impressed by the beauty and variety of **kimono** available for both women and men. This most traditional form of Japanese dress is still commonly worn by both sexes for special occasions, such as weddings and festival visits to a shrine (the male kimono is much less florid in design than the female, usually in muted colours such as black, greys and browns). Over the last few years it has also made something of a comeback in the fashion stakes particularly amongst young women, who sometimes wear kimono like a coat over Western clothes or who co-ordinate their kimono with coloured rather than white *tabi* (traditional split toed socks).

The kimono boom has been helped by several kimono makers offering their services over the Internet and fashion designers turning to kimono fabrics and styles for contemporary creations. Every department store has a corner devoted to ready-made or tailored kimono. None is particularly cheap: the ready-made versions can easily cost ¥100,000, while ¥1 million for the best made-to-measure kimono is not uncommon.

There are, however, much more affordable secondhand or antique kimono to be found at tourist shops, flea markets or in the kimono sales held by department stores, usually in spring and autumn. Prices can start as low as ¥1000, but you'll pay more for the sumptuous highly decorated wedding kimono (they make striking wall hangings), as well as the most beautifully patterned **obi**, the broad, silk sash worn with a kimono.

A cheaper, more practical alternative is the light, cotton kimono, **yukata**, which are popular with both sexes as dressing gowns; you'll find them in all department stores and many speciality stores, along with *happi* coats – the loose jackets that just cover the upper body. To complete the outfit, you could pick up a pair of *zōri*, traditional straw **sandals**, or their wooden counterpart, *geta*.

Chicago
Shikago
6-31-21 Jingumae, Shibuya-ku
ⓣ03/3409-5017; Meiji-Jingūmae Station; see map p.106. Daily 11am–8pm. There's a fine selection of kimono, *obi*, and so on at this highly popular thrift store, as well as rack upon rack of good used clothes.

Chidoriya
Chidoriya
2-3-24 Asakusa, Taitō-ku
ⓣ03/3841-1868; Asakusa Station; see map p.76. Daily except Wed 10am–6.30pm. Not the most stylish collection, but a decent range of men's kimono and *yukata* at prices that won't break the bank.

Gallery Kawano
Garuri Kawano
Flats-Omotesandō 102, 4-4-9 Jingūmae, Shibuya-ku ⓣ03/3470-3305; Omotesandō Station; see map p.106. Daily 11am–6pm. Excellent selection of vintage kimono, *yukata* and *obi* with swatches of gorgeous kimono fabric available too.

Hayayashi Kimono
Hayayashi Kimono
International Arcade, 2-1-1 Yurakuchō, Chiyoda-ku ⓣ03/3501-4012; Yūrakuchō Station; see map p.54. Daily 10am–7pm. English-speaking staff can help you find the right size of new or vintage kimono, *yukata* or shorter *happi* coats at this large kimono boutique.

sizes. **Shoes**, however, are more of a problem. Some stores do stock bigger sizes; Washington shoe shops and ABC-Mart are usually a good bet, though the women's selection is pretty limited and you'll be hard-pressed to find anything for average Western-size men. One of the best places to hunt for bargain shoes is Higashi-Shinjuku, especially around the Studio Alta fashion supermarket, and Ueno's Ameyoko-chō market.

ABC-Mart
ABC-Māto
4-5-12 Ueno, Taitō-ku ☎03/5818-3018; Okachimachi Station; see map p.82. Daily 10am–8pm. Shoe and sports-shoe shop on Ameyoko-dōri specializing in imported brands at reasonable prices. There are branches in all the main city areas.

Bapexclusive
Bepu Ekurushibu
5-5-8 Minami-Aoyama, Minato-ku ☎03/3407-2145; Omotesandō Station; see map p.106. Daily 11am–8pm. A Bathing Ape, the streetwear brand that took its inspiration from the *Planet of the Apes* movies, has taken over Aoyama and Harajuku with a string of boutiques of which this is the main showroom. There's a *Bape Cafe!?* down the road and a gallery around the corner. A T-shirt as worn by pop stars will set you back at least ¥6000.

CA4LA
Kashira
6-29-4 Jingūmae, Shibuya-ku ☎03/3406-8271; Meiji-Jingūmae Station; see map p.106. Daily 11am–8pm. Pronounced *Ka-shi-ra*, this is the hat shop to the eternally trendy, with everything from foppish fedoras and swoony sunhats to hip-hop beanies and designer baseball caps.

Comme des Garçons
Komu de Garuson
5-2-1 Minami-Aoyama, Minato-ku ☎03/3409-6006; Omotesandō Station; see map p.106. Daily 11am–8pm. More like an art gallery than a clothes shop, this beautiful store offers a suitable setting for high fashion for men and women by world-famous designer Rei Kawakubo.

Five Foxes' Store
Fuaibu Fokusu Sutoā
3-26-6 Shinjuku, Shinjuku-ku ☎03/5367-5551; Shinjuku Station; see map p.98. Mon–Sat 11am–11pm, Sun 11am–8pm. Stylish showcase for Comme ça de Mode, the bright and affordable fashion brand-of-the-moment– there's also a large section in Seibu's Loft department store in Shibuya

and another branch in Harajaku opposite the station.

Footsoldier
Futosoruja
1F Kinoshita Building, 3-7 Sarugakuchō, Shibuya-ku ☎03/5784-1660; Daikan'yama Station; see map p.118. Daily 11am–8pm. The oh-so-trendy all-black interior helps A Bathing Ape's multicoloured footwear stand out.

Hysteric Glamour
Hisuteriku Guramā
6-23-2 Jingūmae, Shibuya-ku ☎03/3409-7227; Meiji-Jingūmae Station; see map p.115. Daily 11am–8pm. The premier outlet for Hysteric Glamour, the fun, retro-kitsch 60s/70s Americana label which has become Japan's leading youth brand.

Issey Miyake
Miyake Isei
3-18-11 Minami-Aoyama, Minato-ku ☎03/3423-1407, ⓦwww.isseymikaye; Omotesandō Station; see map p.106. Daily 11am–8pm. One of the top names in world fashion, famous for his elegant, eminently wearable designs. There's a new branch, Issey Miyake by Naoki Takizawa (6-12-4 Roppongi, Minato-ku ☎03/5772-2777), in the new Roppongi Hills development on Keyakizaka-dōri, showcasing the designs of Miyake's protégé Takizawa (see map p.71).

Laforet
Rafuore
1-11-6 Jingūmae, Shibuya-ku ☎03/3475-0411; Meiji-Jingūmae Station; see map p.106. Daily 11am–8pm. One of Tokyo's first "fashion buildings", packed with trendy boutiques, many catering to the fickle tastes of Harajuku's teenage shopping mavens. Wander through and catch the *Zeitgeist*.

Love Girls Market
Rabu Garuzu Māketo
2-16-4 Dōgenzaka, Shibuya-ku ☎03/5459-1905; Shibuya Station; see map p.115. Daily 11am–8pm. Can't afford Issey Miyake, Jean-Paul Gaultier or Katherine Hamnett? Then check out the colourful cheap streetwear at this popular store to achieve that funky Tokyo-girl-about-town look. There's another branch in Daikan'yama.

Mannenya
Mannenya

3-8-1 Nishi-Shinjuku, Shinjuku-ku
ⓣ03/3373-1111; Tochōmae Station; see map
p.98. Mon–Sat 8am–9pm, Sat & Sun 9am–7pm.
If you want to achieve the baggy pants,
split-toed pump look of a Japanese construction worker, this work clothes superstore is the place to head. Don't scoff – the
likes of Jean-Paul Gaultier come shopping
here and it's a great place to pick up all
kinds of underwear and outdoors wear at a
fraction of designer-label prices.

Momo
Momo

6-1-6-107 Minami-Aoyama, Minato-ku
ⓣ03/3406-4738; Omotesandō Station; see
map p.106. Tues–Sun noon–7pm. This shop
showcases the designs of Masako Yamada,
who creates lovely original clothes
(including blouses and decorated jeans)
and accessories using vintage kimono.

Parco
Paruko

15-1 Udagawachō, Shibuya-ku ⓣ03/3462-5430;
Shibuya Station; see map p.115. Daily
10.30am–8.30pm. Dozens of boutiques in
Parts 1 and 2 of this store specialize in
trendsetting, youth-oriented fashion. There's
another branch in Ikebukuro.

Pink Dragon
Pinku Doragōn

1-23-23 Shibuya, Shibuya-ku ⓣ03/3498-2577;
Shibuya Station; see map p.115. Daily
11am–8pm. Easily identified by the giant
golden egg outside, this Art Deco building,
just off Meiji-dōri, hosts an amazing array
of kitsch 1950s clothes and ephemera,
with men's clothing upstairs and the
Miracle Woman designer threads downstairs.

Prada
Purada

5-2-6 Minami-Aoyama, Minato-ku
ⓣ03/6418-0400; Omotesandō Station; see map
p.106. Daily 11am–8pm. Even if the fashion
lines of Miuccia Prada don't appeal, you
really should swing by this pure temple to
high fashion to admire the incredible architecture of the Herzog- and de Meuron-
designed building.

Shiseido Cosmetic Garden
Shiseido Kosumeteiku Gāden

Harajuku Piazza Building, 4-26-18 Jingūmae,
Shibuya-ku ⓣ03/5474-7409; Meiji-jingūmae
Station; see map p.106. Tues–Sun

11am–7.30pm, closed every second Tues.
Not a shop as such, but an "immersive
brand space" where you can try Shiseido
products for free and seek advice from
beauty consultants, some of whom speak
English. Japanese-speakers shouldn't
miss the Beauty Navigator, which snaps
your skin-tone and then gives you a
virtual makeover.

Tsumori Chisato
Tsumori Chisato

4-21-25 Minami-Aoyama, Minato-ku
ⓣ03/3423-5170; Omotesandō Station; see map
p.106. Daily 11am–8pm. Girlish streetwear
that captures the Harajuku look but with
better tailoring, quality of materials and
attention to detail.

Undercover
Andākobā

5-3 Minami-Aoyama, Minato-ku
ⓣ03/3407-1232; Omotesandō Station; see map
p.106. Daily 10am–8.30pm. Jun Takahashi's
Undercover brand of clothing isn't so
underground any more, but remains
youthful and eclectic.

UniQlo
Unikuro

6-10-8 Jingūmae, Shibuya-ku, ⓣ03/5468-7313;
Meiji-jingūmae Station; see map p.106. Daily
11am–9pm. The Japanese version of Gap
has proved that cheap can still be cool. The
clothes are simple but good quality –
mostly plain cotton fabrics – and come in a
wide range of colours, if not huge sizes.
There are branches in all Tokyo's main
shopping centres.

Washington
Washinton

5-7-7 Ginza, Chūō-ku ⓣ03/3572-5911; Ginza
Station; see map p.54. Daily 10.30am–8pm. The
main store of an upmarket shoe-shop chain
which carries a reasonable selection of
sizes and styles to fit big Western feet.

Yohji Yamamoto
Yamamoto Yōji

5-3-6 Minami-Aoyama, Shibuya-ku
ⓣ03/3409-6006, ⓦwww.yohjiyamamoto.co.jp;
Omotesandō Station; see map p.106. Daily
11am–8pm. Discreetly hidden behind a
bronze facade, this is the flagship store of
Japanese fashion icon Yamamoto, famed
for his edgy, one-colour designs. For his
more populist line of clothing check out
Y's on Keyakizaka-dōri in Roppongi Hills
(6-12-14 Roppongi, Minato-ku; see
map p.71).

Food and drink

The best one-stop places to find unsual and souvenir food and drink items – such as beautifully boxed biscuits, cakes and traditional sweets (*wagashi*) and sake from across the country – are the department store **food halls** (see p.202). There are also some highly regarded food and drink shops in Tokyo, some of which have been around for centuries.

For a couple of places to buy premium **teas**, try Cha Ginza (p.166) and Yamamotoyama (p.167). For general foodstuffs and snacks you'll seldom be far from a **24-hour convenience store**, of which Tokyo has thousands (often located near subway or train stations). Lawson, Family Mart, AM/PM and Seven-Eleven have the widest geographical coverage.

Food Magazine
Fudo Magashin
6-9 Roppongi, Minato-ku ⊕03/5410-5445; Roppongi Station; see map p.71. Daily 24 hours. Not the cheapest supermarket, but the selection is good, they're open around the clock and are used to dealing with foreigners, so have staff on hand to explain all those unusual food items.

Le Chocolat de H
Re Shokorato De Echi
Keyakizaka-dōri, Roppongi Hills, 6-12-4 Roppongi, Minato-ku ⊕03/5772-0075; Roppongi Station; see map p.71. Daily 11am–8pm. From the moment it opens there's usually a queue in front of this divinely decadent chocolate salon and café that's been one of the consistent hits of Roppongi Hills.

National Azabu
Nashonaru Azabu
4-5-2 Minami-Azabu, Minato-ku ⊕03/3442-3181; Hiro-o Station; see map p.118. Daily 9.30am–8pm. Firmly geared towards the tastes of the local expat community, with a great selection of international food goods and fresh veggies, fruits, meat and fish.

Sakaya Kurihara
Sakaya Kurihara
3-6-17 Moto-Azabu, Minato-ku ⊕03/3408-5378; Hiro-o Station; see map p.71. Mon–Sat 10am–9pm. This small shop stocks a fine selection of sake, including brands and

types rarely found elsewhere, and they're used to dealing with *gaijin*.

Sake Plaza
Sake Puraza
1-1-21 Nishi-Shinbashi, Minato-ku ⊕03/3519-2091; Toranomon Station; see map p.68. Mon–Fri 10am–6pm. The first-floor shop and tasting room has an excellent range of sake from all over the country – you can sample substantial slugs of five different varieties (focusing on a particular region) for ¥525, or three different types for ¥315.

Tensuya Honten
Tensuya Honten
1-9 Tsukuda, Chūō-ku ⊕03/3531-2351; Tsukishima Station; see map p.61. Daily 9am–6pm. This ancient shop specializes in *tsukudani*, delicious morsels of seaweed and fish preserved in a mixture of soy sauce, salt and sugar – a wooden box set of six different types from their selection of eighteen costs ¥2000. The preserves last for three weeks.

Toraya
Toraya
4-9-22 Akasaka, Minato-ku ⊕03/3408-4121; Akasaka-Mitsuke Station; see map p.68. Mon–Fri 8.30am–8pm, Sat & Sun 8.30am–6pm. Makers of *wagashi* (traditional confectionery often used in tea ceremonies) for the imperial family. It's not cheap, but everything is beautifully packaged and products vary with the season.

Homeware

Japan is justly famous for the delicate beauty and practicality of its interior design, particularly the ingenious way it makes the most of limited space.

Agito
Agito
2F West Walk Roppongi Hills, 6-10-3 Roppongi, Minato-ku ⊕03/5570-4411; Roppongi Station; see map p.71. Daily 11am–9pm. This design store within the Roppongi Hills complex exhibits a tasteful collection of contemporary Japanese interior products from silky

lacquerware to modern pottery designs and furniture.

Muji
Muji
3-8-3 Marunouchi, Chiyoda-ku ☎03/5208-8241; Yūrakuchō Station; see map p.54. Daily 10am–9pm. The largest Tokyo branch of this internationally famous "no-brand" homewares, lifestyle and fashion chain has the full range of Muji goods, plus a decent café and even bikes for rent (see "Directory", p.211). There are branches all over the city; the one near Gaienmae Station (2-12-18 Kita-Aoyama, Minato-ku) is stylishly built from salvaged wood and steel.

Nippon Form
Nippon Forumu
6F Living Design Centre Ozone, Shinjuku Park Tower, 3-7-1 Nishi-Shinjuku, Shinjuku-ku ☎03/5322-6620; Tochōmae Station; see map p.98. Daily 10.30am–6.30pm. One-stop shop for the best in Japanese homewear design including products from the Yanagi range (see below) and Isamu Noguchi's paper lanterns, and classic modern furniture such as the spoke chair by Toyoguchi Katsuhei.

Nuno
Nuno
B1 Axis, 5-17-1 Roppongi ☎03/3582-7997; Roppongi Station; see map p.71. Mon–Sat 11am–7pm. In the basement of the Axis Building (which has several other good interior design shops), Nuno stocks its own range of exquisite original fabrics made in Japan, either sold on their own by the metre or made into clothes, cushions and other items.

Three Minute Happiness
Surii Minito Hapinesu

3-5 Udagawachō, Shibuya-ku ☎03/5459-1851; Shibuya Station; see map p.115. Daily 11am–9pm. Part of the Comme Ça fashion chain, with colourful, inexpensive homeware and fashion – look in the window to see what the week's top-selling items are. There's another big branch at the Aqua City mall in Odaiba.

Tōkyū Hands
Tōkyū Hanzu
12-10 Udagawachō, Shibuya-ku ☎03/5489-5111; Shibuya Station; see map p.115. Daily 10am–8pm, except second and third Wed of the month. If you're planning home improvements or have a hobby of practically any type, from rock climbing to crochet, this offshoot of the Tōkyū department store is the place to head. They stock everything that a handy person or an outdoors type could want. It's also a great place to look for quirky souvenirs. Also branches in Ikebukuro (1-28-10 Higashi-Ikebukuro, Toshima-ku; see map p.91) and at Takashimaya Times Square in Shinjuku (see map p.98).

Yanagi
Yanagi
1F Edlehof Building, 8 Honshio-cho, Shinjuku-ku ☎03/3359 9721; Yotsuya Station; see map p.98. Wed–Fri 1–5.30pm. Little more than a tiny office in front of their stockroom, this is the HQ for the homewares of the legendary Yanagi Sori, whose Butterfly Stool – two elegant folds of wood – is exhibited in design museums and hailed as a classic. Yanagi cutlery, crockery and glassware is equally good-looking and reasonably affordable.

Records and CDs

Tokyo's tastes in **CDs and records** are nothing if not eclectic, with a huge range of foreign imports – including world music, jazz and classical recordings – boosting an already mammoth local output of ephemeral pop and rock. In recent years foreign outlets including HMV, Virgin and Tower Records have broken into the market with huge selections, listening stations and lower prices for imported CDs (typically under ¥2000). CDs of foreign artists produced for the Japanese market, with translated lyrics and extra tracks, are more expensive.

Disk Union
Deisuku Union
3-31-4 Shinjuku, Shinjuku-ku ☎03/3352-2691; Shinjuku Station; see map p.98. Mon–Sat 11am–8pm, Sun 11am–7pm. Along with

Recofan (see below), Disk Union has Tokyo's broadest selection of secondhand records and CDs – if not necessarily the cheapest prices. As well as the general Shinjuku branch there are some twenty other branches scattered around Tokyo; some stores specialize, so ask for the genre you're interested in.

HMV

HMV

24-1 Udagawachō, Shibuya-ku; ☎03/5458-3411; see map p.115. Daily 10am–10pm. The main outlet of the British music store has a good selection of discs, videos and DVDs. There are also branches in Laforet in Harajuku, Shinjuku's Takashimaya Times Square, ABAB in Ueno, Ginza, and the Metropolitan Plaza in Ikebukuro.

Recofan

Rekofan

4F Shibuya BEAM, 31 Udagawachō, Shibuya-ku ☎03/3463-0090; Shibuya Station; see map p.115. Daily 11.30am–9pm. A mixed bag of new and used records and CDs, both imported and locally produced, at bargain prices. There are three branches in Shibuya and two in Shimo-Kitazawa, plus other outlets around the city.

Rizumu

Rizumu

6-4-12 Ueno, Bunkyō-ku ☎03/3831-5135; Okachimachi Station; see map p.82. Tues–Sun 11am–7pm. This ancient record shop under a railway arch in the Ameyoko market is *the* place to come for *enka* – traditional Japanese "chanson". Owner Kobayashi-san will help you search for that haunting track you just can't get out your head.

Tony Record

Tonii Rekodo

1-52 Kanda-Jimbōchō, Chiyoda-ku ☎03/3294-3621; Jimbōchō Station; see map p.61. Mon–Sat 11am–8pm, Sun noon–7pm. Classic jazz, swing and pop platters – including all kinds of rarities – are the stock-in-trade of this record store. Mainly specializes in secondhand vinyl, but also stocks CDs.

Tower Records

Tawā Rekodo

1-22-14 Jinnan, Shibuya-ku ☎03/3496-3661; Shibuya Station; see map p.115. Daily 10am–10pm. Currently Tokyo's biggest music store, with six floors of CDs, records and related paraphernalia, including videos and games. There are also branches in Shinjuku and Ikebukuro.

Virgin Megastore

Birujin Megasutoā

3-30-16 Shinjuku, Shinjuku-ku ☎03/3353-0056; Shinjuku-Sanchōme Station; see map p.98. Daily except Wed 11am–10pm. Virgin concentrates its energies in its flagship Shinjuku store, where you'll find a wide selection of discs; there's a smaller outlet in Nishi-Ikebukuro (see map p.91) and free Internet cafés at both.

Toys, games and novelties

The land that gave the world Donkey Kong, Super Mario Brothers, the Tamigotchi and Hello Kitty is forever throwing up new must-have toys, games and novelties. Step into one of Tokyo's major toy stores, such as Kiddyland, and you'll find the range quite amazing. These places are among the best places to hunt for unusual souvenirs and the next big craze before it hits the world market.

Aso Bit City

Aso Bito Shiitei

4-3-3 Akihabara, Chiyoda-ku ☎03/3251-3100, ⓦwww.laox.co.jp; Akihabara Station; see map p.61. Daily 10am–9pm. Multi-level store dedicated to computer games, DVDs, CDs, books and toys – all the latest Japanese hits. You can also try out the latest game consoles here.

Don Quixote

Don Kihotei

1-16-5 Kabuki-chō, Shinjuku-ku ☎03/5291-9211; Shinjuku Station; see map p.98. Daily 24 hours. Piled high and sold cheap, a mind-boggling array of cheap stuff is offered here – everything from liquor to sex toys and gadgets galore. Worth visiting just for the gawp factor. There's another branch in Roppongi (see map p.71) – look for the huge fish tank out the front.

Hakuhinkan Toy Park

Hakuhinkan

8-8-1 Ginza, Chūō-ku ☎03/3571-8008; Shimbashi Station; see map p.54. Daily 11am–8pm. This huge toy shop also houses a theatre staging Japanese-language shows which might entertain junior – or at least distract him from spending up a storm on your behalf.

Automated shopping

A promising source of unusual Japanese souvenirs is **vending machines**; the nation boasts an estimated 5.4 million of them – roughly one for every twenty people. Nearly all essentials, and many non-essentials, can be bought from a machine: pot noodles, drinks, films, batteries, shampoo, razors, CDs, flowers and so on. Some of them are getting pretty crafty, too. Some cold drinks machines, for example, are equipped with wireless modems so that the price can be adjusted according to the prevailing temperature, while Coca-Cola has been experimenting with "intelligent" machines that automatically raise their prices in hot weather.

The prime attraction of vending machines is obviously convenience, but they also allow people in this highly self-conscious society to buy things surreptitiously – condoms, sex aids and alcohol are obvious examples; Japanese law prohibits the sale of alcohol to anyone under 20 years old. But since mid-2000, concern over rising levels of alcoholism and under-age drinking has led to a voluntary restriction by alcohol vendors – it's estimated that around seventy percent of machines have been taken out of action or restocked with soft drinks.

Kiddyland
Kidirando
6-1-9 Jingūmae, Shibuya-ku ☎03/3409-3431; **Meiji-Jingūmae Station; see map p.106. Daily 10am–8pm, closed every third Tues.** If you want to know what the latest toy or novelty craze sweeping Tokyo is, this is the place to head, with six floors of toys, stationery, sweets and other souvenirs.

Pokémon Centre
Pokemon Sentā
3-2-5 Nihonbashi, Chūō-ku ☎03/5200-0707; **Nihonbashi Station; see map p.54. Daily**

10am–7pm. Kids will adore this store, selling a range of cuddly toys and character goods designed around the Japanese anime phenomenon.

Village Vanguard
Bireji Bangādo
B2 Hollywood Plaza, Roppongi Hills, 6-4-1 Roppongi, Minato-ku ☎03/5770-3201; **Roppongi Station; see map p.71. Daily 11am–11pm.** This "exciting book store" stocks all manner of toys, novelties, books, fun CDs ("I was a Yeh Yeh Girl") and accessories.

Directory

Airlines Aeroflot ☎03/3343-9671; Air Canada ☎03/5404-8800; Air China ☎03/5251-0711; Air France ☎03/3475-1511; Air India ☎03/3214-1981; Air New Zealand ☎03/3287-6311; Air Nippon ☎03/5435-0707; Air Pacific ☎03/5208-5171; Alitalia ☎03/3580-2181; All Nippon Airways ☎0120-029333; American Airlines ☎03/3214-2111; Asiana Airlines ☎03/3582-6600; British Airways ☎03/3593-8811; Cathay Pacific ☎03/3504-1531; China Airlines ☎03/3436-1661; Delta Airlines ☎03/5275-7000; Dragonair ☎03/3506-8361; Garuda Indonesia ☎03/3240-6161; Japan Airlines international ☎0120-255931; Japan Air System international ☎0120-711283; KLM ☎03/3216-0771; Korean Air ☎03/5443-3311; Lufthansa ☎03/3699-5551; Malaysian Airlines ☎03/3503-5961; Northwest Airlines ☎03/3533-6000; Philippine Airlines ☎03/3593-2421; Qantas ☎03/3593-7000; Singapore Airlines ☎03/3213-3431; South African Airways ☎03/3470-1901; Thai Airways International ☎03/3503-3311; United Airlines ☎0120-114466; Varig ☎03/3211-6751; Vietnam Airlines ☎03/3508-1481; Virgin Atlantic ☎03/3499-8811.

Airport information Haneda ☎03/5757-8111; Narita ☎0476/34-5000; Tokyo City Air Terminal (TCAT) ☎03/3665-7111.

American Express 4-30-16 Ogikubo, Suginami-ku ☎03/3220-6000; travel service centre (Mon–Fri 9am–7pm).

Bike rental The cheapest place to rent bikes is at the kiosk in Asakusa by the Azuma-bashi in Sumida-kōen (daily 6am–8pm; ¥200 for 24hr; ☎03/5246-1305); Muji in Yūrakuchō (see p.208) rents bikes for ¥500 per day (¥1000 on Sundays and holidays), plus a ¥3000 deposit. Otherwise try Rental Acom, 1-1-8 Shinjuku, Shinjuku-ku (☎03/3350-5081) or 3-11-1 Shimbashi, Minato-ku (☎03/5401-0800), both open daily 10am–7pm – an ordinary bike is ¥2100 per day and a mountain bike ¥4200 (minimum two-day rental). You'll need to present your passport and make an advance booking in Japanese.

Car rental The main rental companies are: Avis ☎0120-311-911; Hertz ☎0120-489-882, 🌐www.hertz-car.co.jp; Nippon ☎03/3469-0919; Nissan ☎03/5424-4111; Orix ☎03/3779-0543; and Toyota ☎0070/8000-10000. All have branches around the city and at Narita and Haneda airports, and English-speaking staff. Prices start at around ¥6500 per day for the smallest car, plus ¥1000 insurance.

Electricity 100 volts AC at 50 cycles in Tokyo. Plugs are generally American-style (two flat pins), and most appliances designed for 117 volts will work perfectly well. Travellers from Britain (240 volts) will need both an adapter and a transformer. Major hotels provide razor sockets at both 110 and 220 volts.

Email and Internet access See p.33.

Embassies Australia, 2-1-14 Mita, Minato-ku ☎03/5232-4111; Canada, 7-3-58 Akasaka, Minato-ku ☎03/5412-6200; China, 3-4-33 Moto-Azabu, Minato-ku ☎03/3403-3380; Ireland, 2-10-7 Kōjimachi, Chiyoda-ku ☎03/3263-0695; New Zealand, 20-40 Kamiyamachō, Shibuya-ku ☎03/3467-2271; Russian Federation, 2-1-1 Azabudai, Minato-ku ☎03/3583-4291; South Africa 2-7-9 Hirakawachō, Chiyoda-ku ☎03/3265-

3366; UK, 1 Ichibanchō, Chiyoda-ku ☎03/5211-1100; US, 1-10-5 Akasaka, Minato-ku ☎03/3224-5000.

Emergencies Police ☎110; fire and ambulance ☎119. Phone the English-language helpline of Tokyo Metropolitan Police on ☎03/3501-0110 (Mon–Fri 8.30am–5.15pm). Tokyo English Life Line (TELL; ☎03/5774-0992, ⓦwww.teljp.com) provides telephone counselling on their helpline (daily 9am–4pm & 7–11pm).

Hospitals and clinics To find an English-speaking doctor and the hospital or clinic best suited to your needs, phone the Tokyo Medical Information Service (Mon–Fri 9am–8pm; ☎03/5285-8181); they can also provide emergency medical translation services. Otherwise, two major hospitals with English-speaking doctors are St Luke's International Hospital, 9-1 Akashichō, Chūō-ku (☎03/3541-5151) and Tokyo Adventist Hospital, 3-17-3 Amanuma, Suginami-ku (☎03/3392-6151); their reception desks are open Monday to Friday 8.30am to 11am for non-emergency cases. Among several private clinics with English-speaking staff, try Tokyo Medical and Surgical Clinic, 32 Mori Building, 3-4-30 Shiba-kōen, Minato-ku (☎03/3436-3028, by appointment only), or the International Clinic, 1-5-9 Azabudai, Minato-ku (☎03/3583-7831).

Immigration To renew your tourist or student visa, apply to the Tokyo Regional Immigration Bureau, ☎5-5-30 Konan, Minato-ku (Mon–Fri 9am–noon & 1–4pm; ☎03/5796-7112, ⓦwww.moj.go.jp/ENGLISH/IB/ib-18.html). To reach it, take the Konan exit from Shinagawa Station and then bus #99 from bus stop 8. Go early in the day since the process takes forever.

Language courses Tokyo has numerous language schools offering intensive and part-time courses. Among the most established are Berlitz, 2F Akasaka Capital Building, 1-7-19 Akasaka, Minato-ku ☎03/3584-4211 and Kokusai Gakuin, 12F, 2-15-1 Dōgenzaka, Shibuya-ku ☎03/3770-5344. For details of other schools, contact the Association of International Education Japan, 4-5-29 Komaba, Meguro-ku ☎03/5454-5216, ⓦwww.aiej.or.jp.

Left luggage Most hotels will keep luggage for a few days. If not, the baggage room at Tokyo Station takes bags for up to fifteen days at a daily rate of ¥410 for the first five days and ¥820 per day thereafter; you'll find it at the far southeast end of the station, beyond the Express Bus ticket office. Note that coin lockers can only be used for a maximum of three days.

Lost property If you've lost something, try the local police box (kōban). Alternatively, ask your hotel to help call the following Japanese-speaking offices to reclaim lost property: taxis ☎03/3648-0300; JR Tokyo Station ☎03/3231-1880; Eidan subways ☎03/3834-5577; Toei buses and subways ☎03/3812-2011. If all else fails, contact the Metropolitan Police Lost and Found Office ☎03/3814-4151.

Pharmacies The American Pharmacy, Marunouchi Building, 2-4-1 Marunouchi, Chiyoda-ku (Mon–Fri 8am–9pm, Sat 10am–9pm; ☎03/5220-7716), has English-speaking pharmacists and a good range of drugs and general medical supplies. Alternatively, try the National Azabu Pharmacy (☎03/3442-3495), above the National Azabu supermarket (nearest subway station Hiro-o). Major hotels usually stock a limited array of common medicines.

Ticket agencies To get tickets for theatre performances, films, concerts and sporting events, it's best, in the first instance, to approach one of the major advance ticket agencies. Ticket Pia (☎03/5237-9999, ⓦhttp://t.pia.co.jp) can be found in the main city areas, such as Ginza, Ikebukuro, Shibuya and Shinjuku, or try phoning Lawson (☎03/3569-9900, ⓦwww2.lawsonticket.com) or CN Playguide (☎03/5802-9999, ⓦhttp://eee.eplus.co.jp). Major events sell out quickly; don't expect to be able to buy tickets at the venue door.

Time zones Tokyo is nine hours ahead of Greenwich Mean Time (so at noon in London, it's 9pm in Tokyo), fourteen hours ahead of New York, seventeen hours ahead of Los Angeles and two hours behind Sydney. There is no daylight saving, so during British Summer Time, for example, the difference drops to eight hours.

Travel agents For international tickets, try one of the following English-speaking agents: No. 1 Travel (7F Don Quixote Building, 1-16 Kabuki-chō, Shinjuku-ku ☎03/3205-6073, ⓦwww.no1-travel.com; other branches in Shibuya and Ikebukuro); A'cross Traveller's Bureau (2F Yamate-Shinjuku Building, 1-19 Nishi-Shinjuku, Shinjuku-ku ☎03/3340-6749, ⓦwww.across-travel.com; other branches in Shibuya and Ikebukuro); and Hit Travel (Ebisu; ☎03/3473-9040). The main domestic travel agents are Japan Travel Bureau (JTB; ☎03/5620-9500, ⓦwww.jtb.co.jp), which has dozens of branches all over Tokyo; Nippon Travel Agency (☎03/3572-8744); and Kinki Nippon Tourist (☎03/3263-5522).

Out of
the City

Out of the City

Nikkō and around

I f you make one trip from Tokyo, it should be to the pilgrim town of **NIKKŌ**, 128km north of the capital, where the World Heritage-listed **Tōshō-gū** shrine complex sits amid splendid mountains crisscrossed by outstanding hiking trails. The antithesis of the usually austere Shinto shrines – and often considered overbearingly gaudy – Tōshō-gū (appropriately enough, the name means "sunlight") attracts masses of Japanese tourists year-round, who tramp dutifully around the shrine and the surrounding holy buildings, which include the **Futarasan-jinja** shrine and the Buddhist temple of **Rinnō-ji**. Also worth investigating are the **Nikkō Tōshō-gū Museum of Art**, in the woods behind Tōshō-gū, and the dramatically named **Ganman-ga-fuchi abyss**, which is in fact a tranquil riverside walk. If it's the great outdoors you're after, don't miss out on the most beautiful part of the Nikkō National Park around **Chūzenji-ko**, some 17km from Nikkō.

Although with an early start it's possible to see both Tōshō-gū and Chūzenji-ko in a long day-trip from Tokyo, it's better to stay overnight in or around Nikkō. Cramming both places into one day during the peak summer and autumn seasons is impossible – it's far better to concentrate on Nikkō alone. A final tip: pack some warm clothes, since Nikkō is cooler than lowland Tokyo, and in winter you can expect plenty of snow.

Some history

Although Nikkō has been a holy place in both the Buddhist and Shinto religions for over a thousand years – a hermitage was built here in the eighth century – its fortunes only took off with the death of **Tokugawa Ieyasu** in 1616. In his will, the shogun requested that a shrine be built here in his honour, which was duly done and finished in 1617. The structure, however, was deemed not nearly impressive enough by Ieyasu's grandson, **Tokugawa Iemitsu**, who ordered work to begin on the elaborate decorative mausoleum seen today.

Iemitsu's dazzling vision was driven by practical as well as aesthetic considerations. The shogun wanted to stop rival lords amassing money of their own, so he ordered the *daimyō* to supply the materials for the shrine, and to pay the thousands of craftsmen. The mausoleum, Tōshō-gū, was completed in 1634 and the jury has been out on its over-the-top design ever since. Whatever you make of it, Tōshō-gū – along with the slightly more restrained Taiyūin-byō mausoleum of Iemitsu – is entirely successful at conveying the immense power and wealth of the Tokugawa dynasty. Every year, on May 18, the **Grand Festival** restages the spectacular interment of Ieyasu at Tōshō-gū, with a cast of over one thousand costumed priests and warriors in a colourful procession through the shrine grounds, topped off with horseback archery. It's well worth attending, as is the smaller-scale festival on October 17 – this doesn't have the archery and only lasts half a day, but does coincide with "Light Up Nikkō" (Oct 16–20), during which the major temple buildings are illuminated at night to great effect.

The Town and around

First impressions of Nikkō as you come out of either train station aren't great – the uphill approach to the shrine is lined with run-down shops and houses. However, frequent buses head towards the main approach to Tōshō-gū and the walk along the town's main street only takes fifteen minutes. At the top of the gently sloping road you'll pass one of Nikkō's most famous landmarks, the red-lacquered **Shin-kyo bridge**. Legend has it that when the Buddhist priest Shōdō Shōnin visited Nikkō in the eighth century he was helped across the Daiya-gawa River at this very spot by the timely appearance of two snakes, which formed a bridge and then vanished. The original arched wooden structure first went up in 1636, but has been reconstructed many times since – the bridge was being completely rebuilt at the time of writing and is due to reopen in March 2005.

Nikkō and around

Nikkō	*Nikkō*	日光
Chūzenji-ko Lake	*Chūzenji-ko*	中禅寺湖
Futarasan-jinja	*Futarasan-jinja*	二荒山神社
Ganman-ga-fuchi abyss	*Ganman-ga-fuchi*	含満ヶ淵
Kegon Falls	*Kegon-no-taki*	華厳の滝
Nikkō Tōshō-gū	*Nikkō Tōshō-gū*	日光東照宮美術館
Museum of Art	*Bijutsukan*	
Rinnō-ji	*Rinnō-ji*	輪王寺
Shin-kyo bridge	*Shin-kyo*	神橋
Taiyūin-byō	*Taiyūin-byō*	大猷院廟
Tōshō-gū	*Tōshō-gū*	東照宮
Accommodation		
Hotori-an	*Hotori-an*	ほとり庵
Narusawa Lodge	*Narusawa Rojji*	鳴沢ロッジ
Nikkō Daiyagawa	*Nikkō Daiyagawa*	日光大谷川ユースホステル
Youth Hostel	*Yūsu Hosuteru*	
Nikkō Kanaya Hotel	*Nikkō Kanaya Hoteru*	日光金谷ホテル
Nikkō-shi Kōryū	*Nikkō-shi Kōryū*	日光市個交流促進センター
Sokushin Centre	*Sokushin Sentā*	
Pension Green Age Inn	*Penshon Guriin Eiji In*	ペンショングリーンエイジイン
Turtle Inn Nikkō	*Tātoru In Nikkō*	タートルイン日光
Eating		
Hippari Dako	*Hippari Dako*	ひっぱり凧
Kikou	*Kikō*	希光
Meiji-no-Yakata	*Meiji-no-Yakata*	明治の館
Milky House	*Mirukii House*	ミルキーハウス
Suzuya	*Suzuya*	鈴家

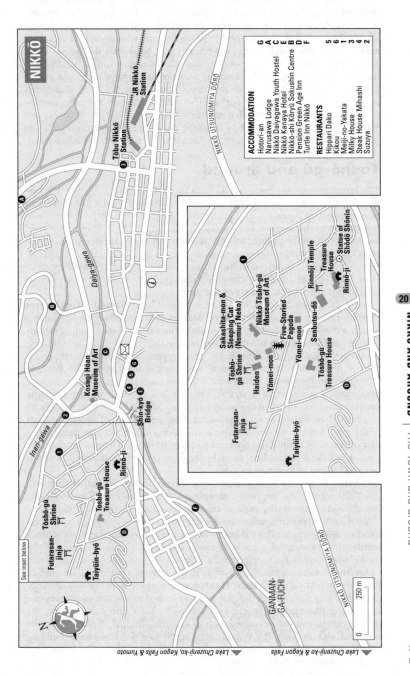

NIKKŌ

JR Nikkō Station

Tōbu Nikkō Station

NIKKŌ UTSUNOMIYA DŌRŌ

Daiya-gawa

Kosugi Hōan Museum of Art

Shin-kyō Bridge

Inari-gawa

ACCOMMODATION
Hotori-an G
Narusawa Lodge A
Nikkō Daiyagawa Youth Hostel C
Nikkō Kanaya Hotel E
Nikkō-shi Kōryū Sokushin Centre B
Pension Green Age Inn D
Turtle Inn Nikkō F

RESTAURANTS
Hippari Dako 5
Kikou 6
Meiji-no-Yakata 1
Milky House 3
Steak House Mihashi 4
Suzuya 2

See inset below

Futarasan-jinja

Tōshō-gū Shrine

Tōshō-gū Treasure House

Rinnō-ji

Taiyūin-byō

Sakashita-mon & Sleeping Cat (Nemuri Neko)

Nikkō Tōshō-gū Museum of Art

Tōshō-gū Shrine

Haiden

Yōmei-mon

Futarasan-jinja

Taiyūin-byō

Five-Storied Pagoda

Yōmei-mon

Tōshō-gū Treasure House

Sanbutsu-dō

Rinnōji Temple

Treasure House

Rinnō-ji

Statue of Shōdō Shōnin

N

0   250 m

GANMAN-GA-FUCHI

NIKKŌ UTSUNOMIYA DŌRŌ

▼ Lake Chuzenji-ko, Kegon Falls & Yumoto

▼ Lake Chuzenji-ko & Kegon Falls

For the main shrine and temple complex take the left-hand path uphill across from the bridge and you'll emerge in front of the main compound of **Rinnō-ji** (daily: April–Oct 8am–4.30pm; Nov–March 8am–3.30pm), a Tendai Buddhist temple founded in 766 by Shōdō Shōnin, whose statue stands on a rock at the entrance. The large, red-painted hall, **Sanbutsu-dō**, houses three giant gilded statues: the thousand-handed Kannon, the Amida Buddha and the fearsome horse-headed Kannon. It's worth paying to view these awe-inspiring figures from directly beneath their lotus-flower perches – entry is included in the combination ticket (see opposite), which you can buy at the booth outside. Rinnō-ji's **Treasure House** (daily 8am–5pm; ¥300), opposite the Sanbutsu-dō, has some interesting items on display, but its nicest feature is the attached Shōyō-en, an elegant garden with a strolling route around a small pond.

Tōshō-gū and around

The broad, tree-lined Omotesan-dō leads up to the main entrance to **Tōshō-gū** (daily: April–Oct 8am–4.30pm; Nov–March 8am–3.30pm), just to the east of Rinnō-ji. You'll pass under a giant stone *torii* gate (one of the few remaining features of the original 1617 shrine), while on the left is an impressive red and green five-storey pagoda, an 1819 reconstruction of a 1650 original, which burned down. Ahead is the Omote-mon gate, the entrance to the main shrine precincts, where you'll need to hand over a section of your combination ticket or Tōshō-gū and sleeping-cat-only ticket (¥1300), either of which can be bought from the booth in front of the gate.

Inside the precincts, turn left to reach the **Three Sacred Storehouses** (*Sanjinko*) on the right and the **Sacred Stables** (*Shinkyūsha*) on the left. There's usually a crowd of amateur photographers in front of the stables jostling to capture one of Tōshō-gū's many famous painted woodcarvings – the "hear no evil, see no evil, speak no evil" **monkeys**, which represent the three major principles of Tendai Buddhism. The route leads to the steps up to the dazzling **Yōmei-mon** (Sun Blaze Gate), with wildly ornate carvings, gilt and intricate decoration. Impressive as it is, the gate has less dramatic impact than the detailed panels on the flanking walls, which are adorned with fantastic flowers and birds. A belfry and drum tower stand alone amid pools of pebbles in front of the gate. Behind the drum tower is the **Honji-dō** (¥50). This small hall is part of Rinnō-ji temple and contains a ceiling painting of a "roaring dragon"; a priest will demonstrate how to make the dragon roar by standing beneath its head and clapping to create an echo.

It's better to pay the small charge to see the roaring dragon rather than fork out ¥520 for the less impressive **sleeping cat** (*Nemuri neko*), just above the Sakashita-mon gate to the right of the inner precinct beyond the Yōmei-mon – you'd easily miss this minute carving if it wasn't for the gawping crowd. Two hundred stone steps lead uphill from the gate to the surprisingly unostentatious **tomb of Ieyasu**, amid a glade of pines, and about the only corner of the shrine where the crowds are generally absent.

Directly in front of the Yōmei-mon is the serene white and gold gate of **Kara-mon**, beyond which is the **Haiden**, or hall of worship. The side entrance to the hall is to the right of the gate and you'll need to remove your shoes and stop taking photographs. Inside, you can walk down into the Honden, the shrine's central hall, still decorated with its beautiful original paintwork. On the way back out through the Yōmei-mon, you'll pass the Jinyōsha, a building where the *mikoshi* (portable shrines) used during Tōshō-gū's spring and autumn festivals are hidden away.

Around the back of the shrine complex, to the left as you walk out of the Omote-mon gate, is the **Nikkō Tōshō-gū Museum of Art** (daily 8am–4pm, April–Oct until 5pm; ¥800). The traditional, impressively simple wooden mansion which the museum is set in dates from 1928 and is the former head office of the shrine. Inside, the sliding doors and screens were decorated by the top Japanese painters of the day and together constitute one of the most beautiful collections of this type of art that you'll see anywhere in the country.

Not far east of here are the grounds of **Meiji-no-Yakata**, the early-twentieth-century holiday home of the American trade representative F.W. Horne. The various houses amid the trees are now fancy restaurants (see p.224), but it's worth wandering around even if you don't eat here to take in the pretty gardens and sylvan setting.

Futarasan-jinja and Taiyūin-byō

A trip around Tōshō-gū is likely to leave you visually (if not physically) exhausted but it's worth pressing on to some of the other temples and shrines in the surrounding woods. At the end of the right-hand path next to Tōshō-gū's pagoda, the simple red colour scheme of the **Futarasan-jinja** comes as a relief to the senses. This shrine, originally established by the priest Shōdō Shōnin in 782, is the main one dedicated to the deity of Nantai-san, the volcano whose eruption created nearby Chūzenji-ko. The middle shrine is beside the lake and the innermost shrine stands on the top of the mountain. There are some good paintings of animals and birds on votive plaques in the shrine's main hall, while the attached garden (¥200) offers a quiet retreat, with a small teahouse serving *matcha* green tea and sweets for ¥350. You can also inspect the *bakemono tōrō*, a "phantom lantern" made of bronze in 1292 and said to be possessed by demons.

Just beyond Futarasan-jinja, and bypassed by the tourist mêlée is the charming **Taiyūin-byō** (¥550), which contains the mausoleum of the third shogun, Tokugawa Iemitsu, who died in 1651. This complex – part of Rinnō-ji and hidden away on a hillside, surrounded by lofty pines – was deliberately designed to be less ostentatious than Tōshō-gū. Look out for the green god of wind and the red god of thunder in the alcoves behind the Niten-mon gate, and the beautiful Kara-mon (Chinese-style gate) and fence surrounding the gold and black lacquer inner precincts.

Ganman-ga-fuchi abyss

If the relative peacefulness of Taiyūin-byō has left you wary of Nikkō's ever-present tourist scrum, make for another nearby tranquil escape. From the temple area, head for the Nishi-sandō main road (where the bus to and from Nikkō's stations stops), cross over and continue down to the Daiya-gawa River – five minutes' walk west is the Ganman-bashi, a small bridge across from which begins the riverside pathway through the **Ganman-ga-fuchi abyss**.

You can save money if you buy the right **ticket** for the temples and shrines in Nikkō. If you intend to see Rinnō-ji, Tōshō-gū and Futarasan-jinja, buy the ¥1000 *nisha-ichiji* **combination ticket**, which includes entrance to the Taiyūin-byō mausoleum and the roaring-dragon hall (*Honji-dō*) in Tōshō-gū, but not the area containing the sleeping cat (*Nemuri neko*) carving and Ieyasu's tomb at Tōshō-gū (these last two can be tacked on to your combination ticket for an additional ¥520). The combination ticket can be bought from booths beside the Sanbutsu-dō hall in Rinnō-ji and outside the Omote-mon gate to Tōshō-gū.

Part of this restful walk, along the attractive and rocky river valley, is lined by the *Narabi-jizō*, some fifty decaying stone statues of Jizō, the Buddhist saint of travellers and children.

Chūzenji-ko and the Kegon Falls

Some 10km west of Nikkō lie **Chūzenji-ko** and the dramatic **Kegon Falls** that flow from it. Local buses (¥1100 each way without a pass) usually take less than an hour to get here, running east along Route 120 and up the twisting, one-way road to reach Chūzenji, the lakeside resort, though travelling times can easily be doubled – or even tripled – during *kōyō* in mid-October, the prime time for viewing the changing autumn leaves, when it's bumper-to-bumper traffic.

Both the lake and waterfalls were created thousands of years ago, when nearby Mount Nantai erupted, its lava plugging the valley. The best way of seeing the evidence of this geological event is to hop off the bus at Akechi-daira, the stop before Chūzenji, where a **cable car** (daily 9am–4pm; ¥390 one way, ¥710 return) will whisk you up to a viewing platform. From here it's a 1.5-kilometre walk uphill and across the Chanoki-daira plateau, where there are sweeping views of Chūzenji-ko, Mount Nantai and the famous waterfalls. An even better view of the falls can be had from the **viewing platform** at their base (daily: May–Sept 7.30am–6pm; Oct 7.30am–5pm; March, April & Nov 8am–5pm; Jan, Feb & Dec 9am–4.30pm; ¥530). The lift to this vantage point lies east across the car park behind the Chūzenji bus station; don't be put off by the queues of tour groups – a shorter line is reserved for independent travellers. The lift drops 100m through the rock to the base of the falls, where you can see over a tonne of water per second cascading from the Ojiri River, which flows from the lake.

Walking west along the shore for around 1km will bring you to the second **Futarasan-jinja** of the Nikkō area. This colourful shrine, which once bore the name Chūzenji now adopted by the town, has a pretty view of the lake, but is nothing extraordinary. There's also a third Futarasan-jinja, on the actual summit of the volcano; to reach it you'll have to pay ¥500 to climb the sacred volcano of Nantai-san, which is owned by the shrine. The hike up to the 2484-metre peak takes around four hours and should only be attempted in good weather.

Practicalities

The cheapest and easiest way of reaching Nikkō is to take a Tōbu-Nikkō **train** from Asakusa in Tokyo (the station is in the basement of the Matsuya department store and connected by tunnel to Asakusa subway station). *Kaisoku* (rapid) trains make the journey in around two hours and twenty minutes and cost ¥1320 one way. The marginally faster "Spacia" *tokkyū* (limited express) takes just under two hours, and costs ¥2740. On some trains you'll need to change at Shimo-Imaichi. Nikkō is also served by JR trains, but this route, which takes longer and costs more than the Tōbu line, only makes sense if you have a JR pass. The fastest route is by Shinkansen from either Tokyo or Ueno stations to Utsunomiya Station, a journey of fifty minutes, where you must change to the JR Nikkō line for a local train taking 45 minutes to reach the Nikkō terminus, a minute's walk east of the Tōbu station.

The Tōbu railway offers various **travel passes**, known as "free passes", for travel to and around the Nikkō area from Tokyo. These tickets, which can only be bought at Tokyo's Tōbu stations, include the train fare from Asakusa to Nikkō (express train surcharges still apply), unlimited use of local buses, and discounts on entrance charges at many of the area's attractions, including the cable cars and boat trips at Chūzenji-ko. If you only intend to visit Tōshō-gū, it's not worth buying the pass, but if you're planning a trip out to Chūzenji-ko the most useful ticket is the Nikkō Mini Free Pass, which is valid for two days and costs ¥4940.

The **Tōbu–Nikkō Station**, designed like a giant Swiss chalet, is fronted by a square surrounded by gift shops; the main road in the western corner runs up to Tōshō-gū. Inside the station there's a cloakroom for left luggage and an **information desk** (daily 8.30am–5pm; ☎0288/53-4511), where the assistant speaks some English and can provide you with maps and leaflets on the area. The town's main **tourist information centre** is the Nikkō Kyōdo Centre (daily 8.30am–5pm; ☎0288/54-2496, ⓦwww.city.nikko.tochigi.jp), on the main road from the station to the Tōshō-gū complex; assistants here can make accommodation bookings. The centre also has an attached **gallery** (daily 8.30am–5pm) showcasing local art and showing short videos – with English commentaries – on local attractions, history and culture. If you're planning on **walking** in the area, pick up copies of the excellent English-language *Guidebook for Walking Trails* (¥150) and the free *Tourist Guide of Nikkō*, both of which feature good maps and pictures of local flora and fauna. The centre also has coin-operated **Internet** access (¥100 per 30min). Note that the post office on the main approach road to Tōshō-gū has an **ATM** which accepts foreign-issued cards; otherwise, it's near impossible to use credit cards in the town.

Accommodation

Nikkō has plenty of **accommodation**, ranging from youth hostels and pensions to plush hotels and ryokan. However, in peak holiday seasons and autumn, advance reservations are essential. Rates at virtually all places are slightly higher from August 21 to November 3, and during major holidays.

Hotori-an 8-28 Takumi-chō ☎0288/53-3663, ⓦwww.turtle-nikko.com. The modern annexe to the *Turtle Inn* (see below) is set in a tranquil location beside the path to the Ganman-ga-fuchi abyss and has good-value en-suite tatami rooms. There's a pottery shop and café, and a bath with forest views. Dinner is served at the *Turtle Inn*. ⑤

Narusawa Lodge 1 Tokorono ☎ & ⓕ0288/54-1630, ⓦwww.nikko-narusawa.com. Delightful *minshuku*, surrounded by flowers and set well away from the tourist throng. The tatami rooms are lovely, the shared bathrooms are spotless and the family who run it are very friendly and speak a little English. Prices drop by ¥300 per person if you stay more than one night. ④

Nikkō Daiyagawa Youth Hostel 1075 Naka-Hatsuishi-machi ☎0288/54-1974, ⓦwww.jyh.or.jp. From either station, take the first left after you've passed the NTT building on the main road and follow the English signposts that

point the way down a narrow back path to this cosy hostel facing the river. Run by a very hospitable family, and deservedly gets rave reviews. Dorms have bunk beds. Dinner (¥840; book ahead) is good. Dorms ¥2730 per person.

Nikkō Kanaya Hotel 1300 Kami-Hatsuishi-machi ☎0288/54-0001, ⓦwww.kanayahotel.co.jp. Nikkō's top Western-style hotel harks back to the glamorous days of early-twentieth-century travel. Most rooms are pricey – and rates skyrocket during peak holiday seasons – though there are some cheaper rooms with en-suite shower or just a toilet (the hotel has a communal bath). They also run the equally salubrious *Chūzenji Kanaya* (☎0288/51-0001, ⓦwww.kanayahotel.co.jp; ⓦ), up beside Chūzenji-ko, which was specially designed to blend in with its woodland surroundings. ⑤–⑦

Nikkō-shi Kōryū Sokushin Centre 2854 Tokorono ☎0288/54-1013, ⓦwww.city.nikko .tochigi.jp/nyh. On the far side of the Daiya-gawa from the town, this hostel/hotel has a secluded location behind the high school. The en-suite tatami rooms are excellent and have lovely views of the town, and there are also Western-style rooms, a laundry and a small kitchen for self-caterers. There's a 10pm curfew. ④

Pension Green Age Inn 10-9 Nishi-sandō ☎0288/53-3636, ⓦwww.nikko-pension.jp. Eccentric decorations (including an organ, stained-glass windows and mock-Tudor facade) enliven this small Western-style hotel close by Tōshō-gū.

The rooms are comfy and excellent value, and there's also French-influenced cooking and an onsen bath. ⑥

Turtle Inn Nikkō 2-16 Takumi-chō ☎0288/53-3168, ⓦwww.turtle-nikko.com. Popular pension run by an English-speaking family in a quiet location next to the Daiya-gawa River, close to the main shrines, with small, plain tatami rooms, common bathrooms and a cosy lounge. The ¥2000 evening meal is a good deal, but breakfast is pricey. ④

Eating

Avoid the bland tourist restaurants clustered around Nikkō's train and bus stations and chances are you'll **eat** pretty well. This area's speciality is *yuba-ryōri* – thin, tasty strips of tofu made from soya beans, usually rolled into tubes and cooked in various stews. You're likely to be served this at your hotel or pension, the best place to eat if you stay overnight, since most restaurants shut around 8pm.

Hippari Dako Inexpensive *yakitori* and noodle café – look for the giant kite outside – popular with just about every *gaijin* who has ever set foot in Nikkō, as the written recommendations and *meishi* that plaster the walls testify. The menu has plenty of vegetarian options, plus beer and sake.

Kikou Just before *Hippari Dako* as you come from the station. A small Korean restaurant with tatami-mat seating and hearty set meals under ¥1000. Open till midnight.

Meiji-no-Yakata ☎0288/53-3751. The smartest restaurant in the collection of eateries beyond the Tōshō-gū car park. It's best to dig into your wallet and sample the exquisite *shojin-ryōri* vegetarian course (¥3500) in the traditional *Gyoshintei*, where the waitresses wear kimono and you can gaze out on a lovely garden. The Art Nouveau *Fujimoto* is very elegant, French-influenced and expensive.

Milky House 2-2-3 Inari-machi. Convivial coffee shop, serving inexpensive snacky meals and beer; also has Internet access (¥300 for 30min). Closed Wed.

Nikkō Kanaya Hotel 1300 Kami-Hatsuishi-machi. A meal in this hotel's elegant second-floor dining room will set you back at least ¥3500 for lunch and ¥6000 for dinner. The first-floor *Maple Leaf* coffee shop is cheaper, but less glamorous. Your best bet is the *Yashio* Japanese restaurant, behind the coffee shop, which has set lunches for under ¥2000. On the approach to the hotel you'll also find the *Steak House Mihashi* with set Western-style meals fairly good value at ¥2800 per person.

Suzuya Stand-alone restaurant just before you cross over the bridge up the slope from the Kosugi Hōan Museum of Art. This is a good place to sample *yuba-ryōri*; the set lunch costs ¥1300 and includes tempura, rice, noodles and rolled tofu. Daily except Thurs 11am–3pm.

Fuji Five Lakes

he best reason for heading 100km west from Tokyo towards the area
known as **FUJI FIVE LAKES** is to climb **Mount Fuji**, Japan's most
sacred volcano and, at 3776m, its highest mountain. Fuji-san, as it's
respectfully known by the Japanese, has long been worshipped for its
latent power (it last erupted in 1707) and near-perfect symmetry; it is most
beautiful from October to May, when the summit is crowned with snow. The
climbing season (see box overleaf) runs from July to September, but even if you
don't fancy making the rather daunting ascent, just getting up close to Japan's
most famous national symbol is a memorable experience.

Apart from Fuji-san, the single most interesting place to head for is the area's
transport hub of **Fuji–Yoshida**, with its wonderfully atmospheric shrine, **Fuji
Sengen-jinja**, and nearby state-of-the-art amusement park. During the summer, the **five lakes** – the large Yamanaka-ko, south of Fuji-Yoshida, touristy
Kawaguchi-ko to the west, and the smaller lakes of Sai-ko, Shōji-ko and
Motosu-ko – are packed with urbanites fleeing the dust and grime of
Tokyo. The best lake to head for is **Kawaguchi-ko**: as well as being a popular
starting point for climbing Mount Fuji, it features a kimono museum and the
easily climbable Mount Tenjō, with its outstanding views of Fuji-san and the
surrounding lakes.

Fuji Five Lakes

Fuji Five Lakes	*Fuji Go-ko*	富士五湖
Fujikyū Highland	*Fujikyū Hairando*	富士急ハイランド
Fuji Sengen-jinja	*Fuji Sengen-jinja*	富士浅間神社
Fuji-Yoshida	*Fuji-Yoshida*	富士吉田
Kawaguchi-ko	*Kawaguchi-ko*	河口湖
Kubota Itchiku	*Kubota Itchiku*	久保田一竹美術館
Art Museum	*Bijutsukan*	
Mount Fuji	*Fuji-san*	富士山
Accommodation and eating		
Fuji-Yoshida	*Fuji-Yoshida*	富士吉田ユースホステル
Youth Hostel	*Yūsu Hosuteru*	
Hanaya	*Hanaya*	花屋
Kawaguchi-ko	*Kawaguchi-ko*	河口湖ユースホステル
Youth Hostel	*Yūsu Hosuteru*	
Petit Hotel Ebisuya	*Puchi Hoteru Ebisuya*	プチホテルエビスヤ
Taikoku-ya	*Taikoku-ya*	大国屋

"A wise man climbs Fuji once. A fool climbs it twice," says the Japanese proverb – don't let the sight of children and grannies trudging up lull you into a false sense of security: this is a tough climb. There are several **routes** up the volcano, with the ascent divided into sections known as **stations**. Most people take a bus to the Kawaguchi-ko fifth station (*go-gōme*), where a Swiss-chalet-style gift shop marks the end of the road about halfway up the volcano. The traditional hike, though, begins at Fuji-Yoshida; walking from here to the fifth station takes around five hours, and it's another six hours before you reach the summit. Many choose to climb at night to reach the summit by dawn; during the season, the lights of climbers' torches resemble a line of fireflies trailing up the volcanic scree.

Essential items to carry include at least one litre of water and some food, a torch and batteries, a raincoat and extra clothes; however hot it might be at the start of the climb, the closer you get to the summit the colder it becomes, with temperatures dropping to well below freezing, and sudden rain and lightning strikes are not uncommon. You can rest en route at any of seventeen **huts**, most of which provide dorm accommodation from around ¥5000 per night for just a bed (no need for a sleeping bag), and ¥7000 with dinner, though it's essential to book in advance (☎0555/22-1948). Once at the summit, it will take you around an hour to make a circuit of the crater. Otherwise you can take part in the time-honoured tradition of making a phone call or mailing a letter from the post office.

Mount Fuji's official **climbing season**, when all the facilities on the mountain are open, including lodging huts and phones at the summit, runs from July 1 to August 27. You can climb outside these dates, but don't expect all, or indeed any, of the facilities to be in operation, and be prepared for snow and extreme cold towards the summit. For more details, pick up a free copy of the *Mt Fuji Climber's Guide Book*, published by the Fuji-Yoshida city hall and available at the local tourist information office (see p.228) and Tokyo TIC (see p.19).

Fuji-Yoshida and around

FUJI-YOSHIDA, some 100km west of Tokyo, lies so close to Mount Fuji that when the dormant volcano eventually blows her top the local residents will be toast. For the time being, however, this small, prosperous town acts as an efficient transport hub for the area, as well as the traditional departure point for journeys up the volcano, with frequent buses leaving for Fuji-san's fifth station (see box above) from outside the train station.

The volcano aside, the town's main attraction is its Shinto shrine. To reach it, head southwest from the station uphill along the main street, Honchō-dōri, which will take you past several ornate **pilgrims' inns** (*oshi-no-ie*). These old lodging houses, where pilgrims used to stay before climbing Mount Fuji, are set back from the road, their entrances marked by narrow stone pillars. Some of the inns still operate as minshuku (family-run lodgings) today. Where the road hits a junction, turn left and after a couple of hundred metres you'll see a giant *torii* and a broad gravel pathway lined with stone lanterns leading to **Fuji Sengen-jinja**, a large, colourful shrine set in a small forest. Sengen shrines, dedicated to the worship of volcanoes, encircle Fuji, but this is the most important, dating right back to 788. The beautiful main shrine (*honden*) was built in 1615. Look around the back for the jolly, brightly painted wooden carvings of the deities Ebisu the fisherman and Daikoku, the god of wealth, good humour and happiness, who appears content to let a rat nibble at the bales of rice he squats upon.

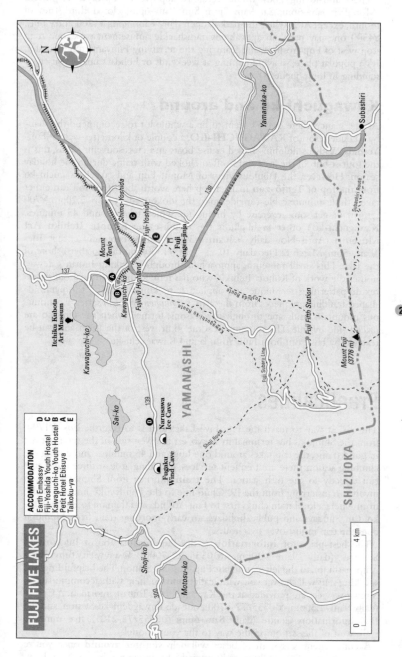

FUJI FIVE LAKES

ACCOMMODATION
Earth Embassy D
Fuji-Yoshida Youth Hostel C
Kawaguchi-ko Youth Hostel B
Petit Hotel Ebisuya A
Taikoku-ya E

N

Yamanaka-ko

Subashiri

Subashiri Route

Chuo Expressway

Shimo-Yoshida

138

Fuji-Yoshida

Mount
Tenjo

Fuji
Sengen-jinja

E

A

B

Fujikyū Highland

Kawaguchi-ko

137

Itchiku Kubota
Art Museum

Kawaguchi-ko

Yoshida Route

Fuji Fifth Station

Kawaguchi-ko Route

Fuji Subaru Line

Mount Fuji
(3776 m)

YAMANASHI

Sai-ko

139

Narusawa
Ice Cave

Shoji Route

D

Fugaku Wind Cave

Shoji-ko

SHIZUOKA

Motosu-ko

300

0   4 km

These fun-loving gods would certainly approve of **Fujikyū Highland** (Mon–Fri 9am–5pm, Sat 9am–7pm, Sun 9am–6pm; closed third Tues of month, except Aug, when the park is open daily 8am–9pm; ¥1200 entry only, ¥4500 one-day pass), an appealingly ramshackle amusement park, one train stop west of Fuji-Yoshida, and featuring the terrifying Fujiyama roller coaster. It's a popular place, so avoid coming at weekends or holidays unless you enjoy standing in long queues.

Kawaguchi-ko and around

At first glance, there doesn't seem to be a whole lot to recommend the shabby lakeside resort of **KAWAGUCHI-KO**, a couple of kilometres west of Fuji-Yoshida. With its dolphin-shaped cruise boats and crass souvenir shops, this is the tourist hub of the area and is often choked with traffic during the holiday season. However, the fabulous view of Mount Fuji and lake Kawaguchi-ko from the top of **Tenjō-zan** make a trip here worth the effort. You can either take a three-minute cable-car ride up to the lookout (daily 9am–5.20pm; ¥700 return) or get some exercise by hiking up, which takes around 45 minutes. Kawaguchi-ko's other highlight is the Gaudí-esque **Kubota Itchiku Art Museum** (April–Nov daily 9.30am–5.30pm; Jan & Feb daily except Tues 10am–5pm; March & Dec daily 10am–5pm; ¥1300), on the northern shore of the lake. This small museum, approached through a striking Indian gateway, houses the work of Kubota Itchiku, who has refined the traditional *tsujigahana* textile-patterning technique and applied it to kimono. Inside the pyramid-shaped building are pieces from the artist's *Symphony of Light* series, a continuous mountain landscape through the seasons, formed when the kimono are placed side by side. The museum is some 4km west of the town and can be reached by bus from both Fuji-Yoshida and Kawaguchi-ko.

Practicalities

The easiest way to reach the Fuji Five Lakes area is to take the **bus** (¥1700) from the Shinjuku bus terminal in Tokyo, on the west side of the train station; in good traffic, the trip takes around one hour and 45 minutes, and during the climbing season there are frequent services, including at least three a day that run directly to the fifth station. The **train** journey from Shinjuku Station involves transferring from the JR Chūō line to the Fuji Kyūkō line at Ōtsuki, from where a local train chugs first to Fuji-Yoshida and then on to Kawaguchi-ko. On Sundays and public holidays, an early-morning train from Shinjuku does the trip in just over two hours.

The best place for **information** is the Fuji-Yoshida Tourist Information Service (daily 9am–5.30pm; ☎0555/22-7000, ⓦwww.city.fujiyoshida .yamanashi.jp), to the left as you exit Fuji-Yoshida Station. The helpful English-speaking staff will shower you with leaflets and can help with accommodation. Similar services are provided at the Kawaguchi-ko Tourist Information Centre (daily 9am–4.30pm; ☎0555/72-6700), outside Kawaguchi-ko Station, and the Fuji Information Centre (daily 8am–6pm; ☎0555/72-2121), five minutes' walk west of the station on the way to the youth hostel.

A comprehensive system of buses will help you **get around** once you've arrived at either Fuji-Yoshida or Kawaguchi-ko. Individual bus fares are high, so if you're going to be touring the area it's worth buying the Yutari Fuji Isshu Free Pass (¥3500) at Shinjuku or as soon as you arrive at Ōtsuki – this is valid for three days and covers all rail travel and buses around the five lakes, plus tickets for the cable car and lake cruise at Kawaguchi-ko.

Accommodation

Fuji-Yoshida and Kawaguchi-ko have plenty of good **places to stay**, including youth hostels and hotels. Fuji climbers could consider overnighting in one of the mountain huts (see p.226), but the claustrophobic should stick to the roomier accommodation at the base of the mountain. There are also several campsites around the lakes.

Earth Embassy and Solar Café Narusawa-mura 8529-74 ☎0555/85-2576, ⓦwww .earthembassy.org. This organic café and farm is run by volunteers who give cooking and farming workshops as well as providing basic dorm accommodation (¥2500 per person) and camping space (¥2000 per person, or ¥1500 per person if you bring your own tent). Reservations strongly advised. Add ¥2000 for a vegetarian dinner and breakfast. Take the local (not express) Motosu-ko bus from Kawaguchi-ko Station (last bus 7.23pm) and get off at the Koyodai Entrance bus stop. The *Embassy* is on Route 139, 300m past the bus stop on the right.
Fuji-Yoshida Youth Hostel 2-339 Shimo Yoshida Hon-chō, Fuji-Yoshida-shi ☎0555/22-0533, ⓦwww.jyh.or.jp. Small, basic hostel in a family home twenty minutes' walk from Fuji-Yoshida Station, or a shorter walk from Shimo-Yoshida, the preceding station. English is spoken and you can also get meals. Dorm beds ¥2700 per person.

Kawaguchi-ko Youth Hostel 2128 Funatsu, Kawaguchi-ko-machi ☎0555/72-1431, ⓦwww.jyh.or.jp. Run by a friendly manager who speaks a little English, this large hostel, a five-minute walk southwest of Kawaguchi-ko Station, has tatami rooms and bunks, and bikes for rent (¥800 per day). Dorm beds ¥2900 per person.
Petit Hotel Ebisuya 3647 Funatsu, Kawaguchi-ko-machi ☎0555/72-0165, ⓕ72-1165. Though it's not much to look at from the outside, this family-run hotel is conveniently located to the right of the concourse as you come out of Kawaguchi-ko Station and has splendid views of Mount Fuji from some of its tatami rooms. The café downstairs serves hearty set meals. ⑥
Taikoku-ya Honchō-dōri, Fuji-Yoshida ☎0555/22-3778. This original pilgrims' inn on the main road still takes guests in its very traditional and beautifully decorated tatami rooms from May to September (though the owner prefers not to accept guests who can't make themselves understood in Japanese). ⑥ including two meals

Eating

The best place to **eat** is Fuji-Yoshida, renowned for its thick *teuchi udon* (handmade) noodles, prepared and served in people's homes at lunchtime only – the tourist information office can provide a list and map of the best places (in Japanese). One of the easiest to locate is the convivial *Hanaya*, towards the top of Honchō-dōri, which serves just three types of dishes: *yumori*, noodles in a soup; *zaru,* cold noodles; and *sara*, warm noodles dipped in hot soup – simple stuff, but manna from heaven compared to the dreary, overpriced tourist cafés in **Kawaguchi-ko**, where the best option is a picnic lunch from the lakeside 7-Eleven convenience store. During the climbing season you can buy snacks and stamina-building dishes, such as curry rice, from the huts on Mount Fuji – but the prices, needless to say, are high.

22

Hakone

S outh of Mount Fuji and 90km west of Tokyo is the lakeland and mountain area known as **HAKONE**. There aren't any must-see sights here, but a visit to the region is enjoyable, especially if you follow the well-established day-trip route, which combines rides on several trains or buses, a funicular, cable car and pirate ship. You can also take in the lake,

Hakone

Hakone	*Hakone*	箱根
Amazake-jaya Teahouse	*Amazake-jaya*	甘酒茶屋
Ashino-ko	*Ashino-ko*	芦の湖
Gōra	*Gōra*	強羅
Hakone Barrier	*Hakone Sekisho*	箱根関所
Hakone Gongen	*Hakone Gongen*	箱根権現
Hakone-machi	*Hakone-machi*	箱根町
Hakone Open-Air Museum	*Chōkoku-no-Mori Bijutsukan*	彫刻の森美術館
Hakone-Yumoto	*Hakone-Yumoto*	箱根湯元
Hatajuku	*Hatajuku*	畑宿
Kappa Tengoku Notemburo	*Kappa Tengoku Notemburo*	かっぱ天国野天風呂
Komaga-take	*Komaga-take*	駒ヶ岳
Miyanoshita	*Miyanoshita*	宮ノ下
Moto-Hakone	*Moto-Hakone*	元箱根
Odawara	*Odawara*	小田原
Ōwakudani	*Ōwakudani*	大湧谷
Ōwakudani Natural History Museum	*Ōwakudani Shizen Kagakukan*	大湧谷自然科学館
Tenzan Notemburo	*Tenzan Notemburo*	天山野天風呂
Accommodation		
Fuji Hakone Guest House	*Fuji Hakone Gesuto Hausu*	富士箱根ゲストハウス
Fujiya Hotel	*Fujiya Hoteru*	富士屋ホテル
Hakone Lake Villa Youth Hostel	*Hakone Reiku Vira Yūsu Hosuteru*	箱根レイクヴィラユースホステル
Hakone Prince Hotel	*Hakone Purinsu Hoteru*	箱根プリンスホテル
Hakone Sengokuhara Youth Hostel	*Hakone Sengokuhara Yūsu Hosteru*	箱根仙石原ユースホステル
Moto-Hakone Guest House	*Moto-Hakone Gesuto Hausu*	元箱根ゲストハウス
Motonamikan	*Motonamikan*	元波館

Ashino-ko, numerous **onsen**, some excellent walks, several art museums, and – weather permitting – great views of nearby Mount Fuji. There's so much to do that it's best to stop overnight, especially if you want to unwind at one of Hakone's top-notch hotels and ryokan, all with their own hot-spring baths. The region is always busy at weekends and holidays, however; if you want to avoid the crowds, come during the week.

The traditional day-trip route through Hakone runs anticlockwise from Hakone-Yumoto, gateway to the Fuji-Hakone-Izu National Park, then over Mount Sōun, across the length of Ashino-ko lake to Moto-Hakone and back to the start. Approaching Hakone from the west, you can follow a similar route clockwise from Hakone-machi on the southern shore of Ashino-ko to Hakone-Yumoto.

If you plan to follow the traditional route, it's well worth buying either the three-day **Hakone Free Pass** (¥5500) or the two-day **Hakone Weekday Pass** (¥4700), valid Monday to Thursday, not including public holidays. Both are available from Odakyū stations and cover a return journey on the Odakyū line from Shinjuku to Odawara, and unlimited use of the Hakone-Tōzan line, Hakone-Tōzan funicular railway, cable car, pirate boat across the lake and most local buses. The passes save you money on the total cost of all these trips and get you discounts at many of Hakone's attractions. For ¥870 extra one way, you can take the more comfortable "Romance Car", which goes directly through to Hakone-Yumoto in ninety minutes, around 25 minutes faster than the regular express train. With a JR pass, the fastest route is to take a Shinkansen to Odawara, from where you can catch an Odakyū train or bus into the national park area (Odakyū transport passes from Odawara cost ¥4130 and ¥3410 respectively; there's also a ¥2000 one-day ticket that doesn't cover the cable car or the boat). If you don't fancy hopping on and off trains, take the Odakyū express **bus** (¥1950) from Shinjuku bus terminal, which will get you to Ashino-ko in a couple of hours.

Hakone-Yumoto

Hakone-Yumoto, the small town nestling in the valley at the gateway to the national park, is marred by scores of concrete-block hotels and *bessō* (vacation lodges for company workers), not to mention the usual cacophony of souvenir shops. It does, however, have some good **onsen** which are ideal for unwinding after a day's sightseeing around the park. You can also pick up a **map** of the area at the Hakone Tourist Information Office (daily 9.30am–5.30pm, Ⓦ www.kankou.hakone.kanagawa.jp/index_e.html), across the street from the Hakone-Yumoto Station, in the buildings at the bus terminal. Up the hill from the station is the **Kappa Tengoku Notemburo** (daily 10am–10pm; ¥750), a small, traditional outdoor onsen, which can get crowded. More stylish is **Tenzan Notemburo** (daily 9am–11pm; ¥900), a luxurious public onsen complex at Oku-Yumoto, 2km southwest of town. The main building has separate male and female outdoor baths, including waterfalls and Jacuzzi in a series of rocky pools. There's also a clay-hut sauna for men, and for ¥200 extra on weekdays (¥900 at weekends) both men and women can use the wooden baths in the building across the car park. A free shuttle bus runs to the baths from the bridge just north of Hakone-Yumoto Station.

Hakone-Yumoto is a good place **to eat**. *Yama Soba*, on the main road between the station and the tourist information office, serves up soba sets from ¥1100. *Chikuzen*, across the road, is the best of the town's *udon* restaurants. There are also three good-value restaurants at the Tenzan Notemburo, serving rice, *shabu-shabu* (sautéed beef) and *yakiniku* (grilled meat) dishes.

HAKONE

▲ Tokyo

Shinjuku ◄

ODAKYŪ LINE

Odawara

Hakone Itabashi

JR TŌKAIDŌ LINE

Nagoya & Ōsaka ►

TŌKAIDŌ SHINKANSEN

Kazamatsuri

Iriuda

HAKONE-TŌZAN LINE

Hakone-Yumoto

Tenzan
Notemburo

Kappa
Tengoku
Notemburo

Tonosawa

Ōhiridai

HAKONE-TŌZAN LINE

Miyanoshita

Hakone-Tōzan Driveway

Kowakudani

Mt Sengen
(804 m) ▲

Hatajuku

Hakone Open-Air Museum

E D

Gōra

C

Hakone Museum of Art

Sōunzan

Ōwakudani

Amazake-jaya
Teahouse

Ōwakudani
Natural Science

Mt Komaga-take
(1357 m) ▲

Stone-paved
section of
Tōkaidō

Ubako

Avenue of
Cryptomeria

H
G

Hakone
Shrine

Hakone Barrier

Moto-Hakone

Hakone-machi

Ashi-no-ko
Camping
Ground

Togendai

Sightseeing Boats

Ashino-ko

Hakone Detached
Palace Garden

FUJI-HAKONE-IZU
NATIONAL PARK

Sengokuhara ◄

F

Atami ►

Hamamatsu & Nagoya ►

Gotemba & Mt Fuji ◄

138

A
B

Gotemba ◄

Ashi-no-ko Skyline Driveway

N

0   2 km

ACCOMMODATION

Chōraku	C
Fuji Hakone Guest House	A
Fujiya	E
Hakone Lake Villa Youth Hostel	G
Hakone Prince	F
Hakone Sengokuhara Youth Hostel	B
Moto-Hakone Guest House	H
Motonamikan	D

Miyanoshita and around

Rising up into the mountains, the Hakone-Tōzan switchback railway zigzags for nearly 9km alongside a ravine from Hakone-Yumoto to the village of Gōra (see below). There are small traditional inns and temples at several of the stations along the way, but the single best place to alight – and even stay overnight – is the village onsen resort of **Miyanoshita**. As well as hot springs, the village has decent antique shops along its main road, and several hiking routes up 804-metre **Mount Sengen** on the eastern flank of the railway – one path begins just beside the station. At the top, you'll get a great view of the gorge below.

Miyanoshita's real draw is its handful of splendid **hotels**. Worth popping into – if only for a peek at the handsome wooden interior – is the *Fujiya Hotel* (☎0460/2-2211, ⓦwww.fujiyahotel.co.jp; ❻–❼), which opened for business in 1878 and is a living monument to a more glamorous era of travel. Despite being the first Western-style hotel in Japan, the *Fujiya* has lots of Japanese touches, including traditional gardens and temple-like decorative gables. The plush, 1950s-style decor is retro-chic and the rooms are good value, especially from Sunday to Friday, when foreign guests qualify for a cheaper rate. There's also the delightful, European-style *Motonamikan* (formerly the *Pension Yamaguchi*; ☎0460/2-3158, ⓔmotonami@jt5.so-net.ne.jp; ❼), a five-minute walk downhill from the train station, and tucked away off the main road behind the post office – the rates here include meals.

As for **eating**, the *Fujiya's Orchid Lounge* is great for afternoon tea, while its ornate French restaurant is an excellent, if pricey, choice for lunch or dinner. The *Picot Bakery* on the main road outside the *Fujiya* is a good place to pick up bread and cakes for breakfast or lunch. Opposite Miyanoshita's singularly unhelpful tourist information centre is *An*, a small, cheerful café with an English menu that features reasonably priced spaghetti and curry-rice dishes.

Moving on, two more stops on the Hakone-Tōzan railway bring you to Chōkoku-no-Mori Station, where the nearby **Hakone Open-Air Museum** (daily 9am–4pm, March–Nov until 5pm; ¥1600) is well worth making time for. This wide-ranging museum is packed with sculptures, with works from Rodin and Giacometti to Michelangelo reproductions and bizarre modern formations scattered across the landscaped grounds, which have lovely views across the mountains to the sea. There's an enclave of 26 pieces by Henry Moore, a "Picasso Pavilion", which houses 230 paintings, lithographs, ceramics and sculptures by the Spanish artist, and four galleries featuring works by Chagall, Miró and Renoir, plus works by modern Japanese artists such as Umehara Ryuzaburo and Takeshi Hayashi. You can rest between galleries at several restaurants or cafés – there's also a traditional Japanese teahouse.

Gōra to Ōwakudani

There's little reason to stop at **Gōra** except to have lunch (see below) or to transfer from the Hakone-Tōzan railway to a funicular tram (¥410), which takes only ten minutes to cover the short but steep distance to **Sōunzan**, the start of the cable car across Mount Sōun.

From Sōunzan, the **cable car** (¥1330 one way) floats like a balloon on its thirty-minute journey high above the mountain to the Tōgendai terminal, beside the lake, Ashino-ko, stopping at a couple of points along the way. The first stop, **Ōwakudani**, is the site of a constantly bubbling and steaming valley formed by a volcanic eruption three thousand years ago. You can learn more about this at the informative **Ōwakudani Natural History Museum** (daily 9am–4pm; ¥400), downhill from the cable-car station, with an entertaining diorama model of a volcano that flashes, rumbles and glows red at the point of eruption. To see the real thing, hike up the valley through the lava formations to the bubbling pools, where eggs are boiled until they are black and scoffed religiously by every Japanese tourist, for no better reason than it's the done thing when visiting Ōwakudani.

There are a couple of good **places to stay** on this side of Hakone. The quiet *Fuji-Hakone Guest House* (T0460/4-6577, W www.remix.ne.jp/~hakone;), in Sengokuhara (best reached by bus #4 from the east exit of Odawara Station), is run by the friendly, English-speaking Takahashi-san, and has tatami rooms and onsen water piped into a communal bath; only breakfast is available. Directly behind, in a lovely wooden building, is the *Hakone Sengokuhara Youth Hostel* (T0460/4-8966, W www.jyh.or.jp; dorms ¥2950 per person, rooms), run by the same family and offering accommodation in dorms or Japanese-style rooms.

You shouldn't miss out on the *Gyōza Centre* (daily except Thurs 11.30am–3pm & 5–8pm) on the main road between Gōra and the Hakone Open-Air Museum. This two-floor **restaurant** usually has a long line of customers waiting to sample the thirteen types of delicious home-made dumplings (*gyōza*), including ones stuffed with prawns (*ebi*) and fermented beans (*nattō*). A set meal with rice and soup costs ¥1155. At Ōwakudani the best eating choice is one of the noodle bars beside the entrance to the volcanic area. Also good for lunch is the café downstairs at the Tōgendai cable-car terminal, which is reasonably priced and has pleasant views across the lake.

Ashino-ko and around

Emerging from the cable car at Tōgendai you'll find yourself at the northern end of the bone-shaped lake, **Ashino-ko**, from where, weather permitting, you'll get fantastic views of **Mount Fuji**. If it's cloudy you'll have to make do with the less impressive 1357-metre **Komaga-take** on the eastern shore. A walk around the shoreline trails along the western side of the lake to the small resort of Hakone-machi, some 8km south, takes around three hours. It's more fun to board one of the colourful, cartoon-like "pirate ships" (¥840) that regularly sail the length of the lake in around thirty minutes. This area of Hakone, part of the *Prince* empire of hotels and resorts, is not covered by the Hakone Free Pass and so is somewhat marginalized from the rest of the national park's attractions – and all the more peaceful for it. Boats run from Tōgendai to the *Prince* hotel resort at Hakone-en, midway down the east side of the lake, where there's also a large outdoor skating rink and a cable car up to Komaga-take's summit, from where there's a fabulous view. The summit can also be reached by bus from the tourist village of Moto-Hakane.

A cluster of upmarket hotels and ryokan can be found at **Hakone-machi**, where the "pirate ships" dock. This is also the location of the **Hakone Barrier** (daily 9am–4.30pm; ¥200) through which all traffic on the Tōkaidō, the ancient road linking Kyoto and Edo, once had to pass (see box opposite). What stands here today is a reproduction, enlivened by waxwork displays which provide the historical background. There's nothing much to keep you here, though; instead, stroll north of the barrier around the wooded promontory, past the bland reconstruction of the Emperor Meiji's Hakone Detached Palace, and take in the views of the lake.

Running for around 1km beside the road leading from the Hakone Barrier to the lakeside village of **Moto-Hakone** is part of the Tōkaidō road, shaded by 420 lofty cryptomeria trees, planted in 1618 and now designated "Natural Treasures". Across the lake, you'll spot a vermilion *torii* gate, standing in the

The Hakone Barrier

In 1618, the second shogun, Tokugawa Hidetada, put up the Hakone Barrier (Sekisho) – actually more of a large compound than a single gate – which stood at Hakone-machi until 1869. The shogun decreed that all his lords' wives and their families live in Edo (now Tokyo) and the lords themselves make expensive formal visits to the capital every other year, a strategy designed to ensure no one attempted a rebellion. The Tōkaidō, on which the barrier stands, was one of the major routes in and out of the capital, and it was here that travellers were carefully checked to see how many guns they were taking into the Edo area and that the lords' hostage families were stopped from escaping. Any man caught trying to dodge the barrier was crucified and then beheaded, while accompanying women had their heads shaved and were, according to contemporary statute, "given to anyone who wants them".

water just north of Moto-Hakone – a scene celebrated in many a *ukiyo-e* print and modern postcard. The gate belongs to the **Hakone Gongen** and is the best thing about this small Shinto shrine, set back in the trees, where samurai once came to pray.

Though it's fairly touristy, you'll find some decent **accommodation** at Moto-Hakone. At the bottom of the price range is the *Hakone Lake Villa Youth Hostel* (☎0460/3-1610, ⓦwww.jyh.or.jp; dorms ¥3300 per person), in a secluded spot above Ashino-ko lake. The hostel has tatami and Western-style dorms, a lounge with a large outdoor deck surrounded by woods, a bath filled with onsen water, and good-value meals. A lot more upmarket is the *Hakone Prince Hotel* (☎0460/3-1111, ⓦwww.princehotels.co.jp/hakone-e/index .html; ❼), with a prime location on the Komaga-take side of Ashino-ko and a multitude of facilities – the nicest rooms are in the Japanese-style annexes. A short bus ride (get off at Ashinokoen-mae) or stiff ten-minute walk uphill from the village lies the *Moto-Hakone Guest House* (☎0460/3-7880, ⓦwww .remix.ne.jp/~hakone; ❺), offering spotless, Japanese-style rooms, with singles at ¥5000, though serving breakfast only (¥800).

Back to Hakone-Yumoto

From either Moto-Hakone or Hakone-machi you can take a **bus** back to Hakone-Yumoto or Odawara. Far more rewarding, however, is the eleven-kilometre **hike** along part of the Tōkaidō road, which after the first couple of kilometres is all downhill and takes around four hours. The route begins five minutes up the hill from the Hakone-Tōzan bus station in Moto-Hakone, where large paving stones are laid through the shady forests. When the path comes out of the trees and hits the main road, you'll see the **Amazake-jaya Teahouse**, where you can rest, just as travellers did hundreds of years ago, and sip a restorative cup of the milky, sweet and alcoholic rice drink *amazake*, with some pickles, for ¥400.

From the teahouse, the path shadows the main road to the small village of **Hatajuku**, where since the ninth century craftsmen have perfected the art of *yose-gi-zaiku*, or marquetry. The wooden boxes, toys and other objects inlaid with elaborate mosaic patterns make great souvenirs and there are workshops throughout the village, including one right where the path emerges onto the main road. Hatajuku is a good place to pick up the bus for the rest of the way to Hakone-Yumoto if you don't fancy hiking any further. From here the path descends to the **Sukumo-gawa** and past several old temples, as well as the Tenzan Notemburo (see p.231), before ending up in the centre of Hakone-Yumoto.

Mt Takao and around

eading west from Shinjuku Station along the Chūō line there are several pleasant day-trip opportunities, the best of which is a visit to **MOUNT TAKAO**, crowned by a picturesque temple, **Yakuo-in**, which hosts a spectacular fire-walking festival annually. The rest of the year, pilgrims are joined by multitudes of hikers who meander along the many trails around the 600-metre mountain; several paths lead further afield to Chichibu-Tama National Park to the northwest.

Heading back towards Tokyo along the Chūō line you could stop off at the **Edo-Tokyo Open Air Architectural Museum**, an annexe of the Edo-Tokyo Museum to view prime examples of vernacular architecture from the mid-nineteenth century onwards saved from the wrecking ball. The museum was the inspiration for the Oscar-winning animated movie *Spirited Away*, one of the many Studio Ghibli films brought to life in the charming **Ghibli Museum, Mitaka**, where you can see the wonderful work of animator Miyazaki Hayao.

Mount Takao

Only an hour west of Shinjuku, **Mount Takao**, also referred to as Takao-san, is a popular hiking area – so much so that you'd be well advised to avoid it at the weekend, when the main trails are clogged with day-trippers and picnic parties cover the slopes of the 600-metre mountain. This said, Takao-san, surrounded by a quasi-national park and also home to the attractive and venerable **Yakuo-in** temple, is a particularly pleasant place midweek for a quick escape from Tokyo, and a starting point for longer trails into the mountains.

The Keiō line from Shinjuku provides the simplest and cheapest way of reaching the terminus of Takao-san-guchi (1hr; ¥370). If you take the slightly slower and more expensive JR Chūō line, you'll need to change to the Keiō line at Takao to go one last stop to Takao-san-guchi. It comes as something of a relief to arrive here, as the unremitting city sprawl is brought to a halt by the verdant slopes of the Takao Quasi National Park.

Mt Takao and around		
Mount Takao	*Takao-san*	高尾山
Mount Kobotoke Shiroyama	*Mount Kobotoke Shiroyama*	小仏城山
Ukai Toriyama	*Ukai Toriyama*	うかい鳥山
Yakuo-in	*Yakuo-in*	薬王院

There are seven marked trails on the mountain of various lengths and difficulty, with the longest three starting from Takao-san-guchi; all are detailed on a map (in Japanese) provided by the Keiō train company, or in English from the TICs in Tokyo (see p.19) or the Takao Visitor Centre at the top of the mountain. To reach the start of these trails turn right outside the station and follow the riverside path for 100m past the noodle restaurants to the **cable car and chairlifts** (both ¥470 one way, ¥900 return). If you take these, you'll save a kilometre or so of slogging up the main no. 1 trail.

Rejoin the no. 1 trail at the top of the cable-car station, pass the undistinguished **Wild Grass and Monkey Park** (daily 9.30am–4.30pm; ¥500), home to scores of Japanese macaques, and continue to the ranks of red-painted lanterns leading up to **Yakuo-in**. This temple was founded in the eighth century and is notable for the ornate polychromatic carvings which decorate its main hall, very reminiscent of those in Nikkō. In front of the hall and dotted around the temple grounds are striking statues of Tengu, the winged, Pinocchio-nosed deity of the mountains. Just before climbing the stairs to the main hall, pause to sample the *okashi* (sweets) and nuts offered at a temple stall – good hiking snacks for later in the day. Yakuo-in also has a small temple beside the Biwataki falls on the no. 6 trail and hosts a spectacular **fire ritual** annually on the second Sunday in March back in Takao-san-guchi, where you can watch priests and pilgrims march across hot coals – and even follow them yourself.

It doesn't take very long from the temple to reach Takao's summit, where you'll find a cluster of soba stalls and the **visitor centre** (Tues–Sun 10am–4pm; ☎0426/64-6157), which has some nature displays, though all the information is in Japanese. On a fine day there are good views back towards the city and, in the opposite direction, if you're really lucky, of Mount Fuji. However, those hoping for a real hiking workout would be forgiven for feeling somewhat short-changed. If you want to continue, take the path down the hill behind the visitor centre and pick up the undulating trail to **Mount Kobotoke Shiroyama** (670m), another 45 minutes away, where the panoramic views of Lake Sagami make up for the ugly telecommunications tower. This route is also part of the seven-stage, 74-kilometre **Kantō Fureai-no-michi** hike from Takao-san-guchi to Kamihinata in the Chichibu-Tama-Kai National Park; pick up a topographical map from the visitor centre if you plan to follow this trail.

Of the several routes back from the visitor centre to Takao-san-guchi, no. 6 trail is particularly attractive, passing through a range of forest habitats and then hugging the side of a stream (and at one point running down its rocky centre). On the way you'll pass the **Biwataki**, a freezing waterfall under which religious ascetics take a shower. This route remains within the trees; if you want some more countryside views, follow the Inariyama trail. Neither route should take more than ninety minutes at a steady pace.

While there are plenty of places to **eat** along the trails and at Takao-san-guchi, with rustic cafés dishing up soba and *udon* noodles, there's little to choose between them and they tend to be overpriced and undistinguished. The exception is the delightful *Ukai Toriyama* (☎0426/61-0739), a traditional restaurant in a sylvan setting specializing in charcoal-broiled chicken and Hida beef; meals are served by kimono-clad waitresses in small tatami rooms. Set course menus start at ¥4500.

Edo-Tokyo Open Air Architectural Museum

A kind of retirement home for old Tokyo buildings which have proved surplus to requirements in modern times, the **Edo-Tokyo Open Air Architectural**

Museum is worth swinging by on your way to or from Takao or Mitaka if you don't have the time to visit similar (and better) museums around the country. The museum (Tues–Sun: April–Sept 9.30am–5.30pm; Oct–March 9.30am–4.30pm; ¥400) was the inspiration for the abandoned theme park in Studio Ghibli's Oscar-winning *Spirited Away* and is set within the parkland of Koganei-kōen, a twenty-minute walk north of Musashi Koganei Station or a five-minute bus ride (¥170). Some 35 buildings of varying degrees of interest are gathered here, plus an exhibition hall with archeological artefacts and folk crafts. You can enter most of the buildings (taking your shoes off first), whose interiors have also been faithfully preserved or recreated. On the west side of the sprawling complex, the most engaging structure is the very grand Mitsue residence, an 1852 mansion moved from Kyoto and furnished with painted screens, lacquered shrines and chandeliers. There are also several thatched farmhouses. On the east side a Shitamachi (Tokyo downtown) street of houses and shops has been reconstructed, including a tailor's shop and stationers, plus kitchenware and flower stores. The highlight is a public bathhouse, a veritable palace of ablutions with magnificent Chinese-style gables and a lakeside view of Fuji painted on the tiled wall inside. Also look out for the House of Uemura, its copper cladding pocked by shrapnel from World War II bombings.

Ghibli Museum, Mitaka

Less than thirty minutes out of Shinjuku along the Chūō line, is **Mitaka**, near where you'll find the charmingly inventive **Ghibli Museum, Mitaka** (daily except Tues 10am–6pm; ¥1000, reductions for children; ☎0570/055777, ⓦwww.ghibli-museum.jp), located at the southwest corner of leafy Inokashira Park. The museum celebrates the work of the Ghibli animation studio, responsible for some of Japan's biggest-ever movies, including *My Neighbour Totoro*, *Princess Mononoke* and the Oscar-winning *Spirited Away*. Beautifully designed throughout, the museum gives visitors an insight not only into Ghibli's films but also the animator's art in general. There's also a small movie theatre where original short animated features, exclusive to the museum, are screened. Kids will love it, and it's a guaranteed fun day out that will probably have you scurrying to the video shop later.

In order to keep the museum free of crowds, only 2400 entry **tickets** are available daily; all must be purchased in advance and are for a specified time. The museum's website lists details in English of how to apply for tickets overseas. This is much easier than applying for tickets in Japan itself, where you'll have first to make a reservation by phone (☎0570/00-0403, if your Japanese is up to it), then go to one of the country's 7600 Lawson convenience stores within three days to pick up your ticket; you'll need to specify the date and time (10am, noon, 2pm or 4pm) you would like to visit. Given the massive popularity of Ghibli's movies the museum can be booked out for weeks at a time, particularly during school holidays and over weekends.

The museum is a short walk or bus ride from the south exit of Mitaka Station on the JR Chūō line. Follow the canal for about fifteen minutes towards Inokashira Park (there are signs) or take the regular bus (¥200). It's a good idea to combine a visit here with a stroll around **Inokashira Park**, which has a pleasant carp-filled lake, tree-shaded walks and a small zoo. Long a favourite haunt of courting couples, during *hanami* season the park is a profusion of pink blossoms.

Kawagoe and around

Saitama-ken, immediately northeast of the capital, comes in for a lot of stick as an achingly dull place. This is a gross generalization and, if anything, the prefecture should be high on your list of places to visit because it's home to the old castle town of **KAWAGOE**, an interesting and highly enjoyable day-trip, only 40km north of Tokyo. Although it doesn't look promising on arrival, Kawagoe's compact area of sights, around 1km north of the main station, is aptly described as a "Little Edo", and can easily be toured in a few hours, although once you've browsed the many traditional craft shops and paused to sample the town's culinary delights you'll probably find the day has flown by. This would certainly be the case on the third Saturday and Sunday of October, when Kawagoe's grand **matsuri** is held, one of the most lively festivals in the Tokyo area, involving some 25 ornate floats (called *dashi*) and hundreds of costumed revellers.

Kawagoe

Kawagoe	*Kawagoe*	川越
Chōki-in	*Chōki-in*	長喜院
Honmaru-goten	*Honmaru-goten*	本丸御殿
John Lennon Museum	*Jon Renon Myūjiamu*	ジョンレノンミュジアム
Kashiya Yokochō	*Kashiya Yokochō*	菓子屋横町
Kita-in	*Kita-in*	喜多院
Kumano-jinja	*Kumano-jinja*	熊野神社
Kurazukuri Shiryōkan	*Kurazukuri Shiryōkan*	蔵造り資料館
Naritasan Betsu-in	*Naritasan Betsu-in*	成田山別院
Saitama Shintoshin	*Saitama Shintoshin*	さいたま新都心
Toki-no-kane	*Toki-no-kane*	時の鐘
Yamazaki Museum of Art	*Yamazaki Bijutsukan*	山崎美術館
Yoju-in	*Yoju-in*	養寿院
Eating		
Kotobukian		寿庵
Ogagiku	*Ogagiku*	小川菊
Ogatō	*Ogatō*	小川藤
Unton	*Unton*	うんとん

Kawagoe's fortunes owe everything to its strategic position on the Shingashi River and Kawagoe-kaidō, the ancient highway to the capital. If you wanted to get goods to Tokyo, then called Edo, they more than likely had to go via Kawagoe, and the town's merchants prospered as a result, accumulating the cash to build fireproof **kurazukuri**, the black, two-storey shophouses the town is now famous for. At one time there were over two hundred of these houses, but their earthenware walls didn't prove quite so effective against fire as hoped (nor were they much use in the face of Japan's headlong rush to modernization). Even so, some thirty still remain, with sixteen prime examples clustered together along Chūō-dōri, around 1km north of the JR and Tōbu stations.

The Town and around

Along Chūō-dōri, around 200m before the main enclave of *kurazukuri*, you'll pass a small shrine, **Kumano-jinja**, beside which is a tall storehouse containing a magnificent *dashi* float; this is your only chance to inspect one up close outside of the annual festival. At the next major crossroads, on the left-hand side, is the old Kameya *okashi* (sweet) shop, warehouse and factory. These buildings now house the **Yamazaki Museum of Art** (daily except Thurs and the last two days of the month; 9.30am–5pm; ¥500), dedicated to the works of Meiji-era artist Gaho Hashimoto. Some of his elegant screen paintings hang in the main gallery, while there are artistic examples of the sugary confections once made here in the converted *kura* (storehouses); entry includes a cup of tea and *okashi*.

Heading up Chūō-dōri, you'll pass several craft shops, including Machikan, which specializes in knives and swords (costing anything from ¥20,000 to ¥800,000), and Sōbiki Atelier, which sells woodwork. On the left, take a moment to duck into **Choki-in**, a temple with a statue of an emaciated, Gandhara-style Buddha in its grounds along with a pretty lily pond and sculpted bushes and trees. Back on the main street, the **Kurazukuri Shiryōkan** museum (Tues–Sun 9am–5pm; ¥100) is housed inside an old tobacco wholesaler's, one of the first *kurazukuri* to be rebuilt after the great fire of 1893. In the living quarters you can squeeze around the tiny twisting staircase that leads from the upper to the ground level, and one of the *kura* contains turn-of-the-century firefighting uniforms and woodblock prints of the fires that ravaged the town. Just north of here on the main road is the new **Kawagoe Festival Museum** (daily except second and fourth Wed of the month; 9.30am–4.30/5pm; ¥500) which houses two magnificent *dashi* floats along with videos of past festivals and various displays, though there are no English descriptions.

Opposite the Kurazukuri Shiryōkan, you won't miss the **Toki-no-Kane**, the wooden bell tower, rebuilt in 1894, that was used to raise the alarm when fires broke out. An electric motor now powers the bell, which is rung four times daily. Take the turning on the left after the bell tower and follow it down until you reach **Yoju-in**, another handsomely wrought temple with pleasant grounds. Just north of here is the **Kashiya Yokochō**, or confectioners alley, a picturesque pedestrian street still lined with several colourful sweet and toy shops – another great place to browse for souvenirs.

It's a 500-metre hike east of the Kurazukuri Shiryōkan, along the main road, to reach the scant remains of **Kawagoe Castle**, now mainly parkland and the

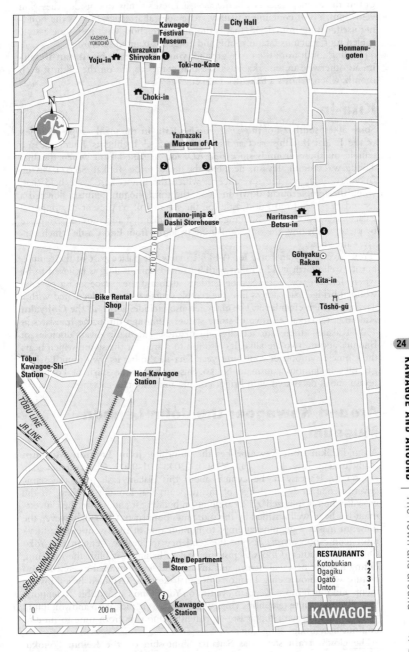

KASHIYA
YOKOCHŌ

Kawagoe
Festival
Museum

City Hall

Honmanu-
goten

Yoju-in

Kurazukuri
Shiryokan ❶

Toki-no-Kane

Choki-in

N

Yamazaki
Museum of Art

❷   ❸

Kumano-jinja &
Dashi Storehouse

Naritasan
Betsu-in

❹

Gōhyaku ⊙
Rakan

Kita-in

CHŪO-DŌRI

Bike Rental
Shop

Tōshō-gū

Tōbu
Kawagoe-Shi
Station

Hon-Kawagoe
Station

TŌBU LINE

JR LINE

SEIBU SHINJUKU LINE

Atre Department
Store

ⓘ

Kawagoe
Station

RESTAURANTS	
Kotobukian	4
Ogagiku	2
Ogatō	3
Unton	1

KAWAGOE

0   200 m

grounds of the senior high school, but still containing the vast **Honmaru-goten**, the former residence of the *daimyō*. There's a museum inside (Tues–Sun 9am–5pm; ¥100) containing mainly archeological artefacts, but it's the building itself, dating from 1848, that is the main attraction, with its Chinese-style gabled roof, spacious tatami rooms and gorgeous painted screens.

Heading south from the castle grounds you'll soon reach **Naritasan Betsuin**, an otherwise unremarkable shrine that comes to life on the 28th of each month, when it hosts a busy flea market.

Kita-in

Some 500m southeast of the *kurazukuri* lies **Kita-in**, the main temple complex of the Tendai Buddhist sect and one of Kawagoe's highlights. There's been a temple on these grounds since 830 AD, and it gained fame when the first Tōkugawa shogun, Ieyasu, declared the head priest Tenkai Sōjō a "living Buddha". Such was the reverence in which the priests here were held that, when the temple burnt down in 1638, the third shogun, Iemitsu, donated a secondary palace from Edo Castle (on the site of Tokyo's present-day Imperial Palace) as a replacement building. This was dismantled and moved here piece by piece, and is now the only remaining structure from Edo Castle which survives anywhere.

You have to pay an entry fee (¥400) to view the palace part of the temple, but it's well worth it. The room with a painted floral ceiling is believed to be where Iemitsu was born. Serene gardens surround the palace and a covered wooden bridge leads across into the temple's inner sanctum, decorated with a dazzling golden chandelier. The entry fee also includes access to the **Gōhyaku Rakan**, a remarkable grove of stone statues. Although the name translates as "500 Rakans", there are actually 540 of these enigmatic dwarf disciples of Buddha, and no two are alike. It's also fun to search for the statue which bears the Chinese symbols of your birth year. Kita-in also has its own mini **Tōshō-gū**. Like its famous cousin in Nikkō, this enshrines the spirit of Tōkugawa Ieyasu and is decorated with bright colours and elaborate carvings.

Around Kawagoe: the John Lennon Museum

Around 23km from Kawagoe lies the absorbing **John Lennon Museum** (daily except Tues 11am–6pm; ¥1500; ☎048-601-0009, ⊛www.taisei.co.jp/museum). It's easy to be cynical about this blatant cash grab: the semi-governmental body in charge of the museum was looking to draw in the crowds when it splurged £12.7 million on building it and, so far, their investment has been well justified by the museum's popularity. Overall, however, the museum makes a genuine attempt to honour one of the twentieth century's most iconic pop artists, despite the tendency to idealize Lennon and Yoko Ono's life together (Ono was instrumental in helping establish the museum, gifting it many personal items), and anyone with even a casual interest in pop culture will enjoy seeing Lennon's original sketches, scribbled lyrics, instruments and much more. Keep an eye too on Yoko Ono's art exhibit "Telephone Peace": if this white telephone rings when you pass it, pick it up and you'll find yourself chatting with the artist – apparently Ono calls from time to time to find out how things are going.

The closest **train** station is Saitama Shintoshin on the Keihin Tōhoku, Utsunomiya and Takasaki train lines from Ueno in Tokyo (around 35min); the museum is a five-minute walk from the station. Kita-yono station, on the Saikyo line from Shinjuku and Ikebukuro, is also close by.

Practicalities

Of the three **train lines** to Kawagoe, the fastest is the express on the Tōbu line from Ikebukuro (32min; ¥450); you can get off either at Kawagoe Station (which is also on the slower JR Saikyō line) or at Tōbu Kawagoe-shi, which is marginally closer to Chūō-dōri. Seibu Shinjuku line trains runs from Shinjuku to Hon-Kawagoe Station (43min; ¥480), which is the most convenient of the lot for the *kurazukuri*. Immediately northwest of the main square in front of the Seibu line terminus is the Shimo bicycle store (closed Wed and second Thurs of the month; some English spoken), where you can rent **bicycles** (¥700 per day) – handy if you plan to see all of Kawagoe's somewhat scattered sights. Note that there's an unrelated bicycle repair shop (which doesn't rent out bikes) confusingly close to the Shimo store. The staff at the **tourist information office** (daily 9am–4.30pm; ℡0492/22-5556, Ⓦwww .sainokuni-kanko.jp/english/index.html) at Kawagoe Station don't speak English but can provide you with a map of the town and an English pamphlet on the sights.

Kawagoe has a fine range of **eating** options. The local speciality is *unagi* (eel); a couple of good rustic places to try this rich dish are *Ogatō* and *Ogagiku*, both a short walk southeast of the *kurazukuri*. *Kotobukian*, beside Kita-in, is renowned for its soba (buckwheat noodles) and eel. For *udon*, try the popular *Unton*, behind the soy-sauce store Kinbue on Chūō-dōri, opposite the Kawagoe Festival Museum.

25

Kamakura and around

An hour's train ride south of Tokyo lies the small, relaxed town of **KAMAKURA**, trapped between the sea and a circle of wooded hills. Kamakura is steeped in history, and many of its 65 temples and 19 shrines date back some eight centuries, when, for a brief and tumultuous period, this was Japan's political and military centre. Its most famous sight is the **Daibutsu**, a glorious bronze Buddha surrounded by trees, but the town's ancient **Zen temples** are equally compelling.

Kamakura's prime sights can be covered on a day-trip from Tokyo, starting with the temples of **Kita-Kamakura**, the town's northern suburb, and then walking south to the sights of **central Kamakura**, before finishing up at the Great Buddha in **Hase** on its western outskirts. If you can only spare a day, make sure you get an early start: most sights close early (generally 4.30pm in winter and only a little later in summer). However, the town more than justifies a two-day visit, allowing you time to explore the enchanting temples of **east Kamakura**, to follow one of the gentle "hiking courses" up into the hills, or to ride the Enoden line west to tiny **Enoshima** island. If at all possible, avoid weekends and national holidays, when both Kamakura and Enoshima are swamped with tourists.

Kamakura's biggest **festivals** take place in early April and mid-September, including displays of horseback archery and costume parades, though the hour-long summer fireworks display (second Tues in Aug) over Sugami Bay is its most spectacular event. The town is also well known for its spring blossoms and autumn colours, while many temple gardens are famous for a particular flower – for example, Japanese apricot at Zuisen-ji and Tōkei-ji (February) and hydrangea at Meigetsu-in (mid-June).

Some history

In 1185 the warlord **Minamoto Yoritomo** became the first permanent shogun and the effective ruler of Japan. Seven years later he established his military government – known as the *Bakufu*, or "tent government" – in Kamakura. Over the next century, dozens of grand monuments were built here, notably the great Zen temples founded by monks fleeing Song-dynasty China. Zen Buddhism flourished under the patronage of a warrior class who shared similar ideals of single-minded devotion to duty and rigorous self-discipline.

Kamakura	*Kamakura*	鎌倉
Daibutsu	*Daibutsu*	大仏
Daibutsu Hiking Course	*Daibutsu Haikingu Kōsu*	大仏ハイキングコース
Engaku-ji	*Engaku-ji*	円覚寺
Ennō-ji	*Ennō-ji*	円応寺
Hase	*Hase*	長谷
Hase-dera	*Hase-dera*	長谷寺
Hōkoku-ji	*Hōkoku-ji*	報国寺
Jōchi-ji	*Jōchi-ji*	浄智寺
Kamakura-gū	*Kamakura-gū*	鎌倉宮
Kamakura National Treasure Hall	*Kamakura Kokuhō-kan*	鎌倉国宝館
Kenchō-ji	*Kenchō-ji*	健長寺
Kita-Kamakura	*Kita-Kamakura*	北鎌倉
Sugimoto-dera	*Sugimoto-dera*	杉本寺
Ten'en Hiking Course	*Ten'en Haikingu Kōsu*	天園ハイキングコース
Tōkei-ji	*Tōkei-ji*	東慶寺
Tsurugaoka Hachiman-gū	*Tsurugaoka Hachiman-gū*	鶴岡八幡宮
Zeniarai Benten	*Zeniarai Benten*	銭洗弁天
Zuisen-ji	*Zuisen-ji*	瑞泉寺
Accommodation		
Kamakura Kagetsuen Youth Hostel	*Kamakura Kagetsuen Yūsu Hosuteru*	鎌倉花月園ユースホステル
Hotel Kamakura Mori	*Hoteru Kamakura Mori*	ホテル鎌倉モリ
Shangrila Tsuruoka	*Shangurira Tsuruoka*	シャングリラ鶴岡
Hotel Tsurugaoka Kaikan	*Hoteru Tsurugaoka Kaikan*	ホテル鶴岡会館
Restaurants		
Chaya-kado	*Chaya-kado*	茶屋かど
Hachi-no-ki Honten	*Hachi-no-ki Honten*	鉢の木本店
Ōishi	*Ōishi*	大石
Raitei	*Raitei*	櫂亭
Sometarō	*Sometarō*	染太郎
Enoshima	*Enoshima*	江の島

The Minamoto rule was brief and violent. Almost immediately, Yoritomo turned against his valiant younger brother, Yoshitsune, who had led the clan's armies, and hounded him until Yoshitsune committed ritual suicide (*seppuku*) – a favourite tale of Kabuki theatre. Both the second and third Minamoto shoguns were murdered, and in 1219 power passed to the Hōjō clan, who ruled as fairly able regents behind puppet shoguns. Their downfall followed the Mongol invasions in the late thirteenth century, and in 1333 Emperor Go-Daigo wrested power back to Kyoto; as the imperial armies approached Kamakura, the last Hōjō regent and an estimated eight hundred retainers committed *seppuku*. Kamakura remained an important military centre before fading into obscurity in the late fifteenth century. Its temples, however, continued to attract religious pilgrims until Kamakura was "rediscovered" in the last century as a tourist destination and a desirable residential area within commuting distance of Tokyo.

Kita-Kamakura

As the Tokyo train nears Kita-Kamakura Station, urban sprawl gradually gives way to gentle, forested hills which provide the backdrop for some of Kamakura's greatest Zen temples. Chief among these are **Kenchō-ji** and the wonderfully atmospheric **Engaku-ji**. It takes over an hour to cover the prime sights, walking south along the main road, the Kamakura-kaidō, to the edge of central Kamakura. With more time, follow the Daibutsu Hiking Course up into the western hills to wash your yen at an alluring temple dedicated to **Zeniarai Benten**.

Engaku-ji

The second most important but most satisfying of Kamakura's major Zen temples, **Engaku-ji** (daily 8am–4/5pm; ¥200) lies buried among ancient cedars just two minutes' walk east of Kita-Kamakura Station. It was founded in 1282 to honour victims (on both sides) of the ultimately unsuccessful Mongolian invasions in 1274 and 1281. The layout follows a traditional Chinese Zen formula – a pond and bridge (now cut off by the train tracks), followed by a succession of somewhat austere buildings – but the encroaching trees and secretive gardens add a gentler touch.

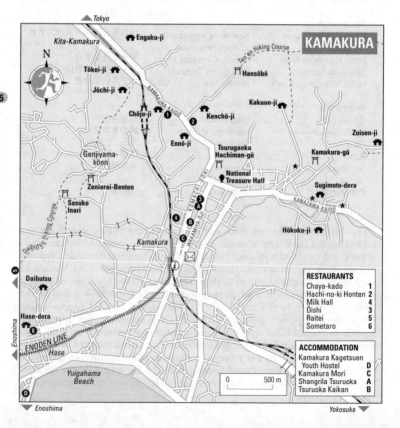

KAMAKURA

RESTAURANTS
Chaya-kado 1
Hachi-no-ki Honten 2
Milk Hall 4
Ōishi 3
Raitei 5
Sometaro 6

ACCOMMODATION
Kamakura Kagetsuen
 Youth Hostel D
Kamakura Mori C
Shangrila Tsuruoka A
Tsuruoka Kaikan B

The first building inside the compound, Engaku-ji's two-storeyed main gate, **San-mon**, rebuilt in 1783, is a magnificent structure, beneath which the well-worn flagstones bear witness to generations of pilgrims. Beyond, the modern **Butsu-den** (Buddha Hall) houses the temple's primary Buddha image, haloed in soft light, while behind it the charming **Shari-den** lies tucked off to the left past an oblong pond. This small reliquary, usually closed to visitors, is said to contain a tooth of the Buddha brought here from China in the early thirteenth century. It's also considered Japan's finest example of Song-dynasty Zen architecture, albeit a sixteenth-century replica. The main path continues gently uphill to another pretty thatched building, **Butsunichi-an** (¥100), where regent Hōjō Tokimune was buried in 1284; in fine weather they serve green tea (¥500 including entrance) in its attractive garden. Finally, tiny **Ōbai-in** enshrines a pale-yellow Kannon statue, but its best attribute is a nicely informal garden with a grove of February-flowering Japanese apricot.

On the way out, follow signs up a steep flight of steps to the left of San-mon to find Kamakura's biggest bell, **Ōgane**, forged in 1301 and an impressive 2.5m tall. From its wooden platform you get a fine view across the valley to Tōkei-ji, the next stop.

Tōkei-ji and Jōchi-ji

Two minutes' walk along the main road from Engaku-ji, **Tōkei-ji** (daily 8.30am–4/5pm; ¥100) was founded as a nunnery in 1285 by the young widow of Hōjō Tokimune. It's an intimate temple, with a pleasing cluster of buildings and a profusion of flowers at almost any time of year: Japanese apricot in February, magnolia and peach in late March, followed by peonies and then irises in early June; September is the season for cascades of bush clover.

Tōkei-ji is more popularly known as the "Divorce Temple". Up until the mid-nineteenth century, when women were given the legal right to seek divorce, this was one of the few places where wives could escape domestic ill-treatment. If they reached the sanctuary, which many didn't, they automatically received a divorce after three years according to traditional temple law. Husbands could be summoned to resolve the dispute or, ultimately, sign the divorce papers. Some of these documents are preserved, along with other temple treasures, in the **Treasure House** (¥300), including two books detailing the women's reasons for seeking sanctuary – unfortunately, not translated. At the back of the temple, take a walk round the peaceful, mossy cemetery hidden among stately cryptomeria trees where many famous and forgotten nuns lie buried.

Further along the main valley almost as far as the train tracks, a sign to the right indicates **Jōchi-ji** (daily 9am–4.30pm; ¥150). The fourth most important of Kamakura's great Zen temples, founded by the nephew of Hōjō Tokimune in 1283, Jōchi-ji was almost completely levelled by the 1923 earthquake. Nevertheless, it's worth walking up the lane to see its beautifully proportioned Chinese-style gate which doubles as a bell tower. The small worship hall contains a trinity of Buddhas while, at the back, there's another graveyard, this time sheltered by a bamboo grove.

Zeniarai Benten and the Daibutsu Hiking Course

Follow the lane running north beside Jōchi-ji and you'll find the steps which mark the start of the **Daibutsu Hiking Course**. This meandering ridge-path

(2.2km) makes an enjoyable approach to Hase's Great Buddha (see p.252), but in any case it's well worth taking a diversion as far as the captivating cave-shrine dedicated to the goddess **Zeniarai Benten** (Money-Washing Benten). From Jōchi-ji, follow signs for Genjiyama-kōen along a trail heading southeast through the park to a road junction, where the main trail turns right. Here, take the steps straight ahead and duck under the shrine's tunnel-entrance to emerge in a natural amphitheatre filled with a forest of *torii* wreathed in incense and candle-smoke.

Despite its being so hidden, a constant stream of hopeful punters come to test the goddess's powers. According to tradition, money washed in the spring, gushing out of a cave on the opposite side from the entrance, is guaranteed to double at the very least, though not immediately. It's worth a shot – your notes won't dissolve, but let the money dry naturally, to retain the beneficial effects.

If you're following the hiking trail **to Hase** (see p.251), rather than retracing your steps, take the path heading south under a tunnel of tightly packed *torii*, zigzagging down to the valley bottom, then turn right at a T-junction to find another avenue of vermilion *torii* leading deep into the cryptomeria forest. At the end lies a simple shrine, **Sasuke Inari**, dating from before the twelfth century, which is dedicated to the god of harvests. His messenger is the fox; as you head up the steep path behind, climbing over tangled roots, you'll find fox statues of all shapes and sizes peering out of the surrounding gloom. At the top, turn right and then left at a white signboard to pick up the hiking course for the final kilometre to the Daibutsu.

South to Kenchō-ji and Ennō-ji

Back at the main road near Jōchi-ji, walk southwest for another five minutes to find the greatest of Kamakura's Zen temples, **Kenchō-ji** (8.30am–4.30pm; ¥300). Headquarters of the Rinzai sect and Japan's oldest Zen training monastery, Kenchō-ji is more formal than Engaku-ji and a lot busier, partly because of the neighbouring high school and some major construction work. It contains several important buildings, most of which have been relocated here from Tokyo and Kyoto to replace those lost since the temple's foundation in 1253. Again, the design of the layout shows a strong Chinese influence; the founding abbot was another Song Chinese émigré, in this case working under the patronage of Hōjō Tokiyori, the devout fifth regent and father of Engaku-ji's Tokumine.

> ### Zazen
>
> **Zazen**, or sitting meditation, is a crucial aspect of Zen Buddhist training, particularly among followers of the Rinzai sect. Several temples in Kamakura hold public *zazen* sessions at various levels, of which the most accessible are those at Engaku-ji and Kenchō-ji, as detailed below. These hour-long sessions are free and no reservations are required, though it's best to check the current schedule with the temple or Kamakura information office (see p.254) before setting out. Though non-Japanese speakers are welcome, you'll get much more out of it if you take an interpreter.
>
> **Engaku-ji** ☏0467/22-0478 (Japanese language only). April–Oct daily 5.30am; Nov–March daily 6am in the Butsu-den; Sat at 5pm & Sun at 10am (year-round) in the Kojirin.
>
> **Kenchō-ji** ☏0467/22-0981 (Japanese language only). Every Fri & Sat 5pm in the Hōjō (year-round).

The main complex begins with the towering, copper-roofed **San-mon**, an eighteenth-century reconstruction, to the right of which hangs the original temple **bell**, cast in 1255 and considered one of Japan's most beautiful. Beyond San-mon, a grove of gnarled and twisted juniper trees hides the dainty, nicely dilapidated **Butsu-den**. The main image is, unusually, of Jizō seated on a lotus throne, his bright, half-closed eyes piercing the gloom. Behind is the **Hattō**, or lecture hall, one of Japan's largest wooden Buddhist buildings. The curvaceous Chinese-style gate, **Kara-mon**, and the **Hōjō** hall beyond are much more attractive structures. Walk round the latter's balcony to find a **pond-garden** generally attributed to a thirteenth-century monk, making it Japan's oldest-surviving Zen garden, though it's recently been spruced up considerably.

Behind the Hōjō, a path head the up steep steps past **Hansōbō**, a shrine guarded by statues of long-nosed, mythical *tengu*. This is the start of the **Ten'en Hiking Course**: it takes roughly two and a half hours to complete the five-kilometre trail from Kenchō-ji, which loops round the town's northeast outskirts to Zuisen-ji (see p.251); for a shorter walk (2.5km), you can cut down earlier to Kamakura-gū (see overleaf).

Sticking to the main road, though, from Kenchō-ji there's one last temple to visit before you hit central Kamakura. **Ennō-ji** (daily 9am–3.30/4pm; ¥200) looks fairly insignificant, but inside its hall reside the red-faced King of Hell, Enma, and his ten cohorts. This ferocious crew are charged with deciding the appropriate level of reincarnation in your next life and their wonderfully realistic expressions are meant to scare you into better ways. The statues are actually reproductions – the originals are in safekeeping in the National Treasure Hall, but usually only one is displayed there, whereas here you get to see the whole gang.

From Ennō-ji it's only another five minutes through the tunnel and downhill to the side entrance of Tsurugaoka Hachiman-gū (see below).

Central Kamakura

Modern Kamakura revolves around its central **train station** and a couple of touristy streets leading to the town's most important shrine, Tsurugaoka Hachiman-gū. The traditional approach to this grand edifice lies along **Wakamiya-ōji** (also known as Dankazura-dōri), at its northern end, which runs straight from the sea to the shrine entrance. Shops here peddle a motley collection of souvenirs and crafts, the most famous of which is *kamakura-bori*, an 800-year-old method of laying lacquer over carved wood. More popular, however, is *hato*, a pigeon-shaped French-style biscuit first made by Toshimaya bakers a century ago – follow the trail of yellow and white bags to find their main shop (daily except Wed 9am–7pm) halfway up Dankazura-dōri. Shadowing Wakamiya-ōji to the west, **Komachi-dōri** is a narrow, pedestrian-only shopping street, packed with more souvenir shops, restaurants and expensive boutiques.

Tsurugaoka Hachiman-gū

A majestic, vermilion-lacquered *torii* marks the front entrance to **Tsurugaoka Hachiman-gū**, the Minamoto clan's guardian shrine since 1063. Hachiman-gē, as it's popularly known, was moved to its present site in 1191, since when it has witnessed some of the more unsavoury episodes of Kamakura history.

Most of the present buildings date from the early nineteenth century, and their striking red paintwork, combined with the parade of souvenir stalls and the constant bustle of people, create a festive atmosphere in sharp contrast to Kamakura's more secluded Zen temples.

Three humpback bridges lead into the shrine compound between two connected ponds known as **Genpei-ike**. These were designed by Minamoto Yoritomo's wife, Hōjō Masako, and are full of heavy, complicated symbolism, anticipating the longed-for victory of her husband's clan over their bitter enemies, the Taira; strangely, the bloodthirsty Masako was of Taira stock. Moving hurriedly on, the **Mai-den**, an open-sided stage at the end of a broad avenue, was the scene of another unhappy event in 1186, when Yoritomo forced his brother's mistress to dance for the assembled samurai. Yoritomo wanted his popular brother, Yoshitsune, killed and was holding Shizuka prisoner in the hope of discovering his whereabouts; instead, she made a defiant declaration of love and only narrowly escaped death herself, though her newborn son was murdered soon after. Her bravery is commemorated with classical dances and Nō plays during the shrine **festival** (Sept 14–16), which also features demonstrations of horseback archery.

Beyond the Mai-den, a long flight of steps leads up beside a knobbly, ancient gingko tree, reputedly one thousand years old and scene of the third shogun's murder by his vengeful nephew, to the **main shrine**. It's an attractive collection of buildings set among trees, though, like all Shinto shrines, you can only peer in. Appropriately, the principal deity, Hachiman, is the God of War.

The **Hōmotsu-den** (daily 8.30am–4.15pm; ¥100), in a corridor immediately left of the shrine, contains a missable exhibition of shrine treasures – although its ticket desk sells informative maps of Hachiman-gē (¥100). Instead, head back down the steps and turn left to find the beautifully restrained, black-lacquered **Shirahata-jinja**, dedicated to the first and third Kamakura shoguns, then take the path south to the modern **Kamakura National Treasure Hall** (Tues–Sun 9am–4pm; ¥300). This one-room museum is noted for its collection of Kamakura- and Muromachi-period art (1192–1573), mostly gathered from local Zen temples. Unfortunately, only a few of the priceless pieces are on display at any one time.

East Kamakura

The eastern side of Kamakura contains a scattering of less visited shrines and temples, including two of the town's most enchanting corners. Though it's possible to cover the area on foot in a half-day, or less if you hop on a bus for the return journey, by far the best way to explore these scattered locations is to rent a bicycle (see p.254 for information on buses and bikes).

From Hachiman-gē work your way eastwards through a quiet suburban area north of the main highway, the Kanazawa-kaidō, until you find signs indicating an optional left turn for **Kamakura-gū**. Mainly of interest for its history and torchlight Nō dramas in early October, this shrine was founded by Emperor Meiji in 1869 to encourage support for his new imperial regime. It is dedicated to Prince Morinaga, a forgotten fourteenth-century hero who helped restore his father, Emperor Go-Daigo, briefly to the throne. The prince was soon denounced, however, by power-hungry rivals and held for nine months in a Kamakura cave before being executed. The small cave and a desultory treasure house (daily 9.30am–4.30pm; ¥300) lie to the rear of the classically styled shrine, but don't really justify the entry fee.

A road heading north from Kamakura-gū marks the beginning – or end – of the short cut to the Ten'en Hiking Course (see p.249), though the main trail starts 900m further east, near **Zuisen-ji** (daily 9am–5pm; ¥100). The temple's fourteenth-century Zen garden, to the rear of the main building, is rather dilapidated, but the quiet, wooded location and luxuriant gardens in front of the temple make it an attractive spot.

From Kamagura-gū you have to join the main road for the last short stretch to Kamakura's oldest temple, **Sugimoto-dera** (daily 8am–4.30pm; ¥200), at the top of a steep, foot-worn staircase lined with fluttering white flags. Standing in a woodland clearing, the small, thatched temple, founded in 734, exudes a real sense of history. Inside its smoke-blackened hall, spattered with pilgrims' prayer stickers, you can slip off your shoes and take a look behind the altar at the three wooden statues of Jūichimen Kannon, the eleven-faced Goddess of Mercy. The images were carved at different times by famous monks, but all three are at least one thousand years old. According to legend, they survived a devastating fire in 1189 by taking shelter – all by themselves – behind a giant tree; since then the temple has been known as *Sugimoto* ("Under the Cedar").

Just a few minutes further east along Kanazawa-kaidō, turn right over a small bridge to reach the entrance to **Hōkoku-ji** (daily 9am–4pm; ¥200), or *Take-dera*, the "Bamboo Temple". The well-tended gardens and simple wooden buildings are attractive in themselves, but the temple is best known for a grove of evergreen bamboo protected by the encircling cliffs. This dappled forest of thick, gently curved stems, where tinkling water spouts and the soft creaking of the wind-rocked canes muffle the outside world, would seem the perfect place for the monks' meditation. Too soon, though, the path emerges beside the manicured rear garden, which was created by the temple's founding priest in the thirteenth century.

To return to central Kamakura, you can catch a bus for the two-kilometre ride from opposite Sugimoto-dera. Alternatively, take the small lane to the left in front of Hōkoku-ji and follow it west through an attractive residential area, which cuts off at least a chunk of the highway.

Hase-dera and the Daibutsu

The west side of Kamakura, an area known as **Hase**, is home to the town's most famous sight, the Daibutsu (Great Buddha), cast in bronze nearly 750 years ago. On the way, it's worth visiting Hase-dera to see an image of Kannon, the Goddess of Mercy, which predates the Daibutsu by at least five hundred years and is said to be Japan's largest wooden statue. Both these sights are within walking distance of Hase Station, three stops from Kamakura Station (¥190) on the private Enoden line.

Hase-dera (daily: March–Sept 8am–5pm; Oct–Feb 8am–4.30pm; ¥300) stands high on the hillside a few minutes' walk north of Hase Station, with good views of Kamakura and across Yuigahama beach to the Miura peninsula beyond. Though the temple's present layout dates from the mid-thirteenth century, according to legend it was founded in 736, when a wooden eleven-faced Kannon was washed ashore nearby. The statue is supposedly one of a pair carved from a single camphor tree in 721 by a monk in the original Hase, near Nara; he placed one Kannon in a local temple and pushed the other out to sea.

Nowadays the **Kamakura Kannon** – just over 9m tall and gleaming with gold leaf (a fourteenth-century embellishment) – resides in an attractive, chocolate-brown and cream building at the top of the temple steps. This central hall is flanked by two smaller buildings: the right hall houses a large Amidha Buddha carved in 1189 for Minamoto Yoritomo's 42nd birthday to ward off the bad luck traditionally associated with that age; while on the left is a small **treasure hall** (daily 9am–4pm), whose most prized exhibits are the original temple bell, cast in 1264, and an early fifteenth-century statue of Daikoku-ten, the cheerful God of Wealth. Beside the viewing platform, the Sutra Repository contains a revolving drum with a complete set of Buddhist scriptures inside – one turn of the wheel is equivalent to reading the whole lot. Ranks of Jizō statues are a common sight in Hase-dera, some clutching sweets or "windmills" and wrapped in tiny, woollen mufflers; these sad little figures commemorate stillborn or aborted children.

From Hase-dera, turn left at the main road and follow the crowds north for a few hundred metres to find the **Daibutsu** (daily 7am–5.30/6pm; ¥200), in the grounds of Kōtoku-in temple. After all the hype, the Great Buddha can seem a little disappointing, but as you approach, and his serene, rather aloof face comes into view, the magic begins to take hold. He sits on a stone pedestal, a broad-shouldered figure lost in deep meditation, with his head slightly bowed, his face and robes streaked grey-green by centuries of sun, wind and rain. The eleven-metre-tall image represents Amida Nyorai, the future Buddha who receives souls into the Western Paradise, and was built under the orders of Minamoto Yoritomo to rival the larger Nara Buddha (near Kyoto). Completed in 1252, the statue is constructed of bronze plates bolted together around a hollow frame – you can climb inside for ¥20 – and evidence suggests that, at some time, it was covered in gold leaf. Amazingly, it has withstood fires, typhoons, tidal waves and even the Great Earthquake of 1923. Its predecessor, however, was less successful: the wooden statue was unveiled in 1243, only to be destroyed in a violent storm just five years later. Various attempts to build a shelter suffered similar fates until, happily, they gave up after 1498 and left the Daibutsu framed by trees and an expanse of sky.

Enoshima

With so much to see in Kamakura, there's little time left for exploring the surrounding area. However, one possibility is the tiny, sacred island of **Enoshima**, twenty minutes west of Kamakura Station on the private Enoden line (¥250). Tied to the mainland by a 600-metre-long bridge, Enoshima has a few sights – some shrines, a botanical garden and a missable cave – but its prime attraction is as a pleasant place to walk away from motor traffic. The island is best appreciated on weekdays in the off-season; during summer and at holiday weekends, it seems liable to sink under the weight of visitors. If you do happen to be here in July or August, there's solace to be had in the funky wooden bars lining the beaches from Kamakura to Enoshima and in the spectacular summer firework displays – Enoshima's (July 25) lasts a staggering ninety minutes. This Shōnan coast, as it's known, is also a favourite spot for windsurfers.

As the Enoden line train rattles into Enoshima Station from Kamakura, look out on the right for the copper-clad roofs of **Ryūkō-ji**. This temple was built on the spot where the monk Nichiren, founder of the eponymous Buddhist sect, was nearly beheaded in 1271 for his persistent criticisms of the government and rival sects. According to legend, as the executioner's sword was about to fall, a fortuitous bolt of lightning split the blade in two, just in time for the shogun's messenger to arrive with a reprieve. Ryūkō-ji was founded a few years later and the main hall, its Buddha image surrounded by a sea of gold, is a good example of the sect's striking decorative style. To the left of the hall there's a statue of Nichiren in the cave where he was imprisoned and a staircase leading up to a smaller temple. Turn right here and follow the path round to where a magnificent five-storey pagoda, erected in 1910, seems part of the surrounding forest.

From Enoshima Station it's roughly fifteen minutes' walk southwest to the island via a bridge constructed over the original sand spit. Enoshima's eastern side shelters a yacht harbour and car parks, but otherwise the knuckle of rock – less than 1km from end to end – is largely covered with woods and a network of well-marked paths. Where the bridge ends, walk straight ahead under the bronze *torii* and uphill past restaurants and souvenir shops (the first on the left stocks informative English maps), to where the steps begin; though the climb's easy enough, there are three escalators tunnelled through the hillside (¥330, or pay for each separately).

Enoshima is mostly famous for a naked **statue of Benten**, the Goddess of Fortune and the Arts, which is housed in an octagonal hall (daily 9am–5pm; ¥150) halfway up the hill. Though the pale-skinned, purple-haired beauty strumming her lute is said to be 600 years old and is ranked among Japan's top three Benten images, it's a little hard to see what all the fuss is about. Continuing uphill you'll pass several other shrine buildings belonging to Enoshima-jinja, founded in the thirteenth century and dedicated to the guardian of sailors and fisherfolk, before emerging beside a nicely laid-out **botanical garden** (daily 9am–5pm; ¥200). If it's clear, you'll get good views south to Ōshima's smoking volcano and west to Fuji from the lighthouse (an extra ¥280) inside the garden. The path then drops down steeply to the island's rocky west shore and two caves known as **Iwaya** (daily 9am–4pm, 5pm in summer; ¥500). Though it's an attractive walk, you might want to give these very artificial grottoes, with their piped music and roaring dragons, a miss.

If you're heading back **to central Tokyo** from Enoshima, the easiest route is the Odakyū-Enoshima line direct to Shinjuku, though note that these trains depart from a different station; from the island causeway, turn left across the river to find Katase-Enoshima Station, with its distinctive Chinese-style facade. Alternatively, walk back to Enoshima Station and take the Enoden line west to its terminal in Fujisawa, where you have to change stations for Tōkaidō-line trains to Tokyo Station via Yokohama and Shinagawa.

Practicalities

The easiest way of **getting to Kamakura** is on the JR Yokosuka line from Tokyo Station (¥890) via Yokohama. Trains stop in Kita-Kamakura before pulling into the main Kamakura Station three minutes later; make sure you board a Yokosuka- or Kurihama-bound train to avoid changing at Ōfuna. On the west side of Kamakura Station you'll find ticket machines and platforms for the private Enoden line to Hase and Enoshima, with trains running from roughly 6am to 11pm. Outside the station's main, eastern exit, and immediately to the right, there's a small **tourist information** window (daily 9am–5/6pm; ℡0467/22-3350, ⓦwww.kcn-net.org/kamakura) with English-speaking staff. There are no free maps here; a simple one costs ¥200 or a small guidebook ¥800 – check with a tourist information centre in Tokyo before heading out here if you want free maps or pamphlets.

Local **buses** depart from the main station concourse. Given the narrow roads and amount of traffic, however, it's usually quicker to use the trains as far as possible and then walk. The only time a bus might come in handy is for the more far-flung restaurants or the eastern sights; in the latter case you want bus #23, #24 or #36 from stand 5 (¥170 minimum fare). A better, but more expensive, option is to rent a **bike** from the outfit (daily 8.30am–5pm; ℡0467/24-2319) up the slope beyond the tourist office; rates are on a sliding scale from ¥500 for the first hour to ¥1500 for a day. Note that prices increase by ¥100 at weekends and national holidays, when you'll need to get there early.

Accommodation

Central Kamakura offers little budget **accommodation**, but a fair choice of mid-range hotels. Many places charge higher rates at weekends and during peak holiday periods – generally over New Year, Golden Week (April 29–May 5) and the summer months of July and August – when it's hard to get a room in any case.

Kamakura Kagetsuen Youth Hostel 27-9 Sakanoshita ℡0467/25-1238. Small hostel with rather aged bunk-bed dormitories in a hotel on the seafront ten minutes' walk from Hase Station. Reception is open from 3.30pm to 8pm, and there's an 11pm curfew. Neither evening meals nor a members' kitchen are available, but there are convenience stores close by and restaurants around Hase Station. ¥3000 per person.

Hotel Kamakura Mori 3F, 1-5-21 Komachi ℡0467/22-5868, ⓦwww1.ocn.ne.jp/~hotelkm/. Round the corner from the station on Dankazura, offering bright, clean decent-sized twin or triple rooms with TV and en-suite bathrooms. Expensive single rates. ❻

Shangrila Tsuruoka 3F, 1-9-29 Yukinoshita ℡0467/25-6363, ⒻF25-6456. If the *Mori* is full, or too expensive, try this small, friendly hotel hidden away on the third floor of a shopping mall. Though a bit fussy, the rooms are light, well kept and perfectly adequate. They're all twins, but single rates are a reasonable ¥8400. ❺

Hotel Tsurugaoka Kaikan 2-12-27 Komachi ℡0467/24-1111, ⒻF24-1115. Big, old-fashioned hotel on Dankazura with glitzy chandeliers and expanses of floral wallpaper. The comfortable rooms are more restrained, with Western beds, a tatami sitting area and en-suite bathroom. ❼

Eating and drinking

Kamakura is famous for its beautifully presented vegetarian cuisine, known as **shōjin ryōri**, though there's plenty more affordable food on offer at local **restaurants**. To eat in a temple and sample the traditional vegetarian food eaten by monks, call **Chōju-ji** (℡0467/22-2149) and make a reservation at least a day in advance. For a **picnic**, Kinokuniya has a good food hall on the west side of Kamakura Station, or try Union Store on Dankazura.

Chaya-kado 1518 Yamanouchi. This homely soba restaurant, on the opposite side of the main road just north of Kenchō-ji, makes a good pit stop on the temple trail. Try *chikara udon* with a couple of

filling *mochi* (steamed rice cakes). Meals from ¥700. Daily 10am–5pm.

Hachi-no-ki Honten 7 Yamanouchi ℡0120/22-8719. Reservations are recommended for this famous *shōjin ryōri* restaurant beside the entrance to Kenchō-ji, though it's easier to get a table at their newer Kita-Kamakura branch (☎0120/23-3722) opposite Tōkei-ji. Whichever you opt for, prices start at around ¥3500 for a set course.

Milk Hall 2-3-8 Komachi. Relaxed, jazz-playing coffee-house-cum-antique-shop buried in the backstreets west of Komachi-dōri. Best for a coffee and cake, or an evening beer, rather than a place to eat.

Ōishi 2F, 1-9-14 Yukinoshita. Locals swear by this small, discreet tempura restaurant; the lunchtime deals offer best value, such as *tendon teishoku* at ¥1400. Closed Wed.

Raitei Takasago ☎0467/32-5656. Atmospheric restaurant in an old farmhouse set in gardens among the hills west of Kamakura, with views to Fuji if you're lucky. Basic soba dishes start at around ¥900 and there's a choice of beautifully presented bentō from ¥3700 up; the garden entry fee (¥500) is discounted from your bill. Though a bit off the beaten track, it's worth the effort; take bus #4 or #6 from stand 6 outside Kamakura Station to the Takasago stop (2–3 hourly; 20min; ¥230). Daily 11am–dusk.

Sometarō 2F, 3-12-11 Hase. Traditional *okonomiyaki* (do-it-yourself savoury pancakes) restaurant in front of Hase-dera. It costs around ¥900 for a bowl of ingredients, or try the more expensive *teppanyaki*.

Yokohama

O n its southern borders Tokyo merges with **YOKOHAMA**, Japan's second most populous city (home to 3.5 million people) and a major international port. It feels far more spacious and airy than the capital thanks to its open harbour-frontage and generally low-rise skyline. Locals are proud of their city's international heritage, and there's definitely a cosmopolitan flavour to the place, with its scattering of Western-style buildings, Chinese temples and world cuisines, and its sizeable foreign community.

Though it can't claim any outstanding sights, Yokohama has enough of interest to justify a day's outing from Tokyo. It might seem strange to come all this way to look at nineteenth-century European-style buildings, but the upmarket suburb of **Yamate** is one of the city's highlights, an area of handsome residences, church spires and bijou teashops. Yamate's "exotic" attractions still draw Japanese tourists in large numbers, as do the vibrant alleys and speciality restaurants of nearby **Chinatown**. There's a clutch of assorted **museums** along the seafront, and north to where **Kannai** boasts a few grand old Western edifices, in complete contrast to **Minato Mirai 21**'s high-tech skyscrapers in the distance. This "harbour-city of the 21st century" forms the focus of Yokohama's ambitious plans to grab some of the initiative away from Tokyo.

A tour of these central sights will easily fill a day, but with a little extra time **Sankei-en**, just south of Yokohama, makes a good half-day excursion. This extensive Japanese garden provides a perfect backdrop for its collection of picturesque temples and other ancient buildings. If modern culture's more your thing, don't miss Shin-Yokohama's **Raumen Museum** on the way back to Tokyo, which celebrates Japan's answer to the hamburger.

Some history

When Commodore Perry sailed his "Black Ships" into Tokyo Bay in 1853 (see p.272), Yokohama was a mere fishing village of some eighty houses on the distant shore. But it was this harbour, well out of harm's way as far as the Japanese were concerned, that the shogun designated one of the five **treaty ports** open to foreign trade in 1858. At first foreign merchants were limited to a small compound in today's Kannai – allegedly for their protection from antiforeign sentiment – but eventually they moved up onto the more favourable southern hills.

From the early 1860s until the first decades of the twentieth century, Yokohama flourished on the back of raw silk exports, a trade dominated by British merchants. During this period the city provided the main conduit for new ideas and inventions into Japan: the first bakery, photographers, ice-cream shop, brewery and – perhaps most importantly – the first railway line, which linked today's Sakuragichō with Shimbashi in central Tokyo in 1872. Soon established as Japan's major international port, Yokohama held pole position until the **Great Earthquake** levelled the city in 1923, killing more than 40,000 people. It was eventually rebuilt, only to be devastated again in air raids at the end of World War II. By this time Kōbe was in the ascendancy and, though Yokohama still figures among the world's largest ports, it never regained its hold over Japanese trade.

Arrival and accommodation

The best way to get to Yokohama **from central Tokyo** is on a Tōkyū-Tōyoko-line **train** from Shibuya Station (every 5min; 40min; ¥270), which calls at Yokohama Station before heading off underground to Minato Mirai and terminating at the Motomachi, Chukagai, Yamashita Kōen station. Coming from Tokyo Station, there's a choice between the Tōkaidō line and Yokosuka line (both every 5–10min; 30min; ¥450) or the Keihin-Tōhoku line (every 5–10min; 40min; ¥450). All three are JR lines; the first two terminate at Yokohama Station, while the latter is more convenient if you're continuing to Sakuragichō, Kannai or beyond.

Yokohama's plethora of "i" **information** centres with English-speaking staff puts Tokyo to shame. You'll find them in the underground concourse outside the east exit of **Yokohama Station** (daily 10am–6pm; ℡045/441-7300); in the booth immediately outside **Sakuragichō Station**'s east entrance (daily 9am–6pm, Aug until 8pm; ℡045/211-0111); and at the harbour-front **Sanbo Centre** east of Kannai Station (Mon–Fri 9am–5pm; ℡045/641-4759). A block west you'll find the **Kanagawa Prefectural Tourist Association** (Mon–Sat 9am–5.30pm, ℡045/681-0077, Ⓦwww.kanagawa-kankou.or.jp/index-e.html). There's also a small office in **Shin-Yokohama Station** under the Shinkansen tracks on the northwest side of the main concourse (daily 10am–1pm & 2–6pm; ℡045/473-2895). All these places provide free **city maps** and brochures and can help with hotel reservations. While there's no official information desk at **YCAT**, some staff there speak English and will help with basic enquiries. The city's website is Ⓦwww.city.yokohama.jp.

Getting around central Yokohama is best done on either the Tōkyū-Tōyoko line or the JR Negishi line (the local name for Keihin-Tōhoku trains); trains on both lines run every five minutes. A single **subway** line connects Kannai and stations north to Shin-Yokohama, but it's more expensive and usually slower than regular trains; services run every five to fifteen minutes and the minimum fare is ¥200. The most enjoyable way of getting about the city and sightseeing at the same time is on one of the *Sea Bass* **ferries** that shuttle between Yokohama Station (from beside Sogō department store) and southerly Yamashita-kōen via Minato Mirai. There are departures every fifteen minutes (10am–7pm), with one-way tickets costing ¥600 for the full fifteen-minute journey, or ¥340 to Minato Mirai. From Yamashita-kōen you can also join the *Marine Shuttle* for a variety of **sightseeing cruises** round the harbour; prices start at ¥900 for forty minutes. In addition, the **Royal Wing** cruise ship (℡045/662-6125, Ⓦwww.royalwing.co.jp) departs from the new Yokohama International Port Terminal for lunch, tea or dinner cruises (1hr 45min). The cost of the cruise is ¥2000 plus anything from ¥2000 to ¥25,000 depending on what you eat.

Accommodation

Yokohama's luxury **hotels**, all located in MM21, are a tourist attraction in their own right. You'll need a reservation at the weekend (when premium rates also usually apply), though weekdays shouldn't be a problem. Lower down the scale, there are a few reasonable business hotels scattered round the city centre, particularly the *Toyoko Inn* chain, but very little in the way of budget accommodation.

YOKOHAMA

RESTAURANTS, CAFÉS & BARS

Alte Liebe	5
Beer Next	2
Chano-ma	2
Enokitei	12
Gas Panic	1
Heichinrou	6
Manchinrou	9
Motion Blue	2
Peking Hanten	4
Pure	8
Rikyuan	13
Shei Shei	11
Suro Saikan	7
Honkan	3
The Tavern	1
Yamate	
Jūbankan	10
Yokohama Curry	
Museum	14

▲ Yokohama Bay Bridge

Harbour View Park

Motomachi-Chūkagai & Yamashita-kōen

Foreigner's Cemetery ✝✝✝

Yamate Museum 10 12

Christ Church

YAMATE

Motomachi-kōen

MOTOMACHI

0   500 m

METROPOLITAN EXPRESSWAY

Sea Bass Pier

Doll Museum

Hikawa-maru

Yamashita-kōen

Marine Tower

Sanbo Centre & Silk Museum

Yokohama Daisekai

CHINATOWN

Kantei-byō

Ishikawachō

Royal Wing Cruise Terminal

Yokohama International Passenger Terminal

Akarenga 2

Yokohama Archives of History

Customs House

Kanagawa Government Offices

NIHON ŌDŌRI

SHINKŌ-CHŌ

World Porters

Bashamichi

Port Opening Memorial Hall

Kanagawa Prefectural Museum

KANNAI ŌDŌRI

MINATO ŌDŌRI

Yokohama Stadium

KANNAI

BASHAMICHI

Kannai

Convention Hall

Minato Mirai Pukari-sanbashi

Pacifico Yokohama Exhibition Hall

MINATO MIRAI 21 (MM21)

Queen's Square

Cosmo Clock 21

Nippon-maru

Yokohama Maritime Museum

Landmark Tower

Landmark Plaza

Minato Mirai

Sakuragichō

METROPOLITAN EXPRESSWAY

ISEZAKICHŌ

Media Tower

Yokohama Museum of Art

Mitsubishi Minato Mirai Industrial Museum

Jackmall Yokohama

Shin-Takashima

JR NEGISHI LINE

Sakuragichō

Sakuragichō

Hinodechō

Tobe

Sea Bass Pier

Sogō Department Store

Luminé Department Store

YCAT

Takashimachō

Takashimachō

▲ Tokyo

◀ Shin-Yokohama & Tokyo

▲ Yokohama

◀ Negishi & Sanker-en

N

ACCOMMODATION

Echigoya Ryokan	F
Kanagawa Youth Hostel	E
Navios Yokohama	A
New Grand	B
Royal Park Nikkō	C
Tōyoko Inn Yokohama	
Sakuragichō	D

Echigoya Ryokan 2F, 1-14 Ishikawachō, Naka-ku ℡ 045/641-4700, Ⓦ wwwny.airnet.ne.jp/i~mall/4-10html. One of the few budget places in central Yokohama, conveniently located on the chic Motomachi shopping street, one minute's walk east of Ishikawachō Station. The tatami rooms are basic and a bit worn, and none is en suite, but it's a relaxed, friendly place and the landlord can speak a little English. Look out for a sign next to Vie de France bakery. No meals are served and there's a mid-night curfew. Ⓞ

Kanagawa Youth Hostel 1 Momijigaoka, Nishi-ku ℡ 045/241-6503, Ⓔ yokohama@xf6.so-net.ne.jp. Aged and overpriced, this isn't the most appealing youth hostel, but its dormitory beds are the cheapest option in town. From the west exit of Sakuragichō Station, walk north along the tracks, beside a graffiti-spattered wall, and take the first left after the Jomo gas stand, over a small bridge and uphill. Reception open 5am–8pm. ¥3000 per person.

Navios Yokohama Sinkō-chō, Naka-ku ℡ 045/633-6000, Ⓦ www.navios-yokohama-com. The light, spacious rooms and reasonable rates make this one of the best-value options in Yokohama. Ask for a room facing Landmark Tower for the best night-time views. Facilities include a restaurant, coffee shop and the International Seamen's Club bar. Ⓞ

Hotel New Grand 10 Yamashitachō, Naka-ku ℡ 045/681-1841, Ⓦ www.hotel-newgrand.co.jp. Built in the late 1920s in European style, the main building retains some of its original elegance, while rooms are slightly cheaper than in the new tower. All come with satellite TV and en-suite bath, and many have harbour views. There's also a choice of three restaurants. Ⓞ

Royal Park Hotel Nikkō 2-2-1-3 Minato Mirai, Nishi-ku ℡ 045/221-1111, Ⓦ www.yrph.com/index-e.html. The gargantuan Landmark Tower houses the *Nikkō's* guest rooms on its 52nd to 67th floors, so spectacular views are guaranteed. The rooms are spacious and elegant, with a separate bath and shower cubicle. As well as a fitness club (¥5000) and swimming pool on the 49th floor, facilities include a tea- ceremony room (¥1100), Sky Lounge bar, and French, Chinese and Japanese restaurants. Ask about special week-day rates. Ⓞ

Tōyoko Inn Yokohama Sakuragichō 6-55 Honchō, Naka-ku ℡ 045/671-1045, Ⓦ www.toyoko-inn.co.jp. One of several Yokohama branches of this Japan-wide chain of budget business hotels, with good-value rooms (including non-smoking rooms), free Internet access and breakfast. Singles are ¥6800. Ⓞ

The City

Though much of Yokohama was destroyed in the 1923 earthquake and again in bombing raids during World War II, it retains a few European-style buildings from its days as a treaty port, some of which lie scattered around **Kannai**, the traditional city centre. For a more evocative atmosphere, climb up to **Yamate** (also known as "the Bluff"), a genteel residential area of clapboard houses, tennis clubs and church spires on the southern hills. **Chinatown**, back down on the levels, makes for a lively contrast, with its hordes of colourful trinket shops and bustling restaurants. From here it's a short stroll down to the **harbour-front** Marine Tower and a couple of nearby museums, or a train ride north to where the aptly named **Landmark Tower**, Japan's tallest building, pinpoints the futuristic **Minato Mirai 21** (MM21) development. There are a couple of specific sights among its gleaming hotels, shopping malls and conference centres, notably a modern art museum and an incongruous four-masted barque, the **Nippon-maru**. All these central sights can be covered in an easy day's outing; the account below starts with Yokohama's southern districts and heads north.

Motomachi and Yamate

Southeast of central Yokohama, the JR Negishi line stops at **Ishikawachō Station** before plunging into a series of tunnels beneath Yamate hill. Take the station's southeastern exit to find **Motomachi**, a fashionable shopping street from prewar days which used to serve the city's expatriate community and still exudes a faint European flavour. Today this narrow lane of small shops, selling foreign brand names and exotic foodstuffs, continues to draw the punters, particularly on Sundays and holidays, when it's turned over to pedestrians; note that many stores close on Monday or Thursday.

At the east end of Motomachi, a wooded promontory marks the beginning of **Harbour View Park**; take any of the paths going uphill to find the lookout point where the British and French barracks once stood – the panoramic view of the harbour and its graceful Bay Bridge is particularly beautiful at night. Turning inland and walking through the park will bring you to the **Foreigners' Cemetery** on the western hillside. Over 4500 people from more than forty countries are buried here, the vast majority either British or American. Wandering among the crosses and sculpted angels, look out for Edward Morel, chief engineer on the Yokohama–Tokyo railway, who died of TB at the age of 30, and Charles Richardson, a British merchant whose murder in 1862 provoked a war between Britain and the Satsuma clan. You'll also find more modern tombstones – an average of twenty foreigners a year are still buried on Yamate.

Heading south along the cemetery's eastern perimeter, you'll pass a handsome row of houses, including the turreted *Yamate Jūbankan* – now a French restaurant (see p.266) – and, next door to it, the city's oldest wooden building. The latter, erected in 1909 for a wealthy Japanese family, now houses the **Yamate Museum** (daily 11am–4pm; ¥200), most interesting for its collection of cartoons from *Japan Punch*, a satirical magazine published in Yokohama for a while in the late nineteenth century. Just beyond, the square tower of **Christ Church**, founded in 1862 but rebuilt most recently in 1947, adds a village-green touch to the neighbourhood, which is still the most popular residential district for Yokohama's wealthy expatriates.

Down to the harbour

From the cemetery, drop down through Motomachi-kōen and cross Motomachi shopping street to find one of the several entrance gates to **Chinatown**. Founded in 1863, Yokohama's Chinatown is the largest in Japan: its streets contain roughly two hundred restaurants and over three hundred shops, while some eighteen million tourists pass through its narrow byways every year to browse among stores peddling Chinese herbs or cooking utensils, and grocers, silk shops and jewellers with windows full of flashy gold. Few leave without tasting what's on offer, from steaming savoury dumplings to a full-blown meal in one of the famous speciality restaurants (see "Eating", p.266).

The fortunes of the Chinese community based here (around two thousand ethnic Chinese) have followed the vagaries of mainland history: during the late nineteenth and early twentieth centuries hundreds of radicals (most famously, Sun Yat-sen and Chiang Kai-shek) sought refuge here, while Communist and Nationalist factions polarized Chinatown in the 1940s and later during the Cultural Revolution. The focus of community life is **Kantei-byō** (daily 10am–8pm; free), a shrine dedicated to Guan Yu, a former warlord and guardian deity of Chinatown. The building is a bit cramped, but impressive nonetheless, with a colourful ornamental gateway and writhing dragons wherever you look. Inside, a long-haired Guan Yu sits on the main altar, gazing over the heads of supplicants petitioning for health and prosperity. The best times to visit are during the major festivities surrounding Chinese New Year (late Jan or early Feb) and Chinese National Day (Oct 1).

A few hundred metres northeast of Kantei-byō at 97 Yamashita-chō is the new **Yokohama Daisekai** (daily: 10am–10pm; ¥500), a Disneyland-esque China museum that aims to recreate Shanghai in the roaring 1920s. About the only thing possibly worth spending the entrance fee on here are Chinese dance shows – the food courts that take up the majority of floors are decidedly passé.

From the eastern edge of Chinatown it's a short hop down to the harbour – aim for the pink-grey **Marine Tower** (daily: Feb–Nov 10am–9pm; Jan & Dec 10am–7pm; ¥700; joint ticket with *Hikawa-maru* ¥1300, or ¥1550 including the Doll Museum). This 106-metre-high tower, built in 1961 to celebrate the port's centenary, is supposedly the world's tallest lighthouse, but it's better to save your money for the Landmark Tower's much higher observation deck (see opposite). In front of the tower, **Yamashita-kōen** is a pleasant seafront park created as a memorial to victims of the Great Earthquake. Here you can pick up a *Sea Bass* ferry (see p.258) or take a harbour cruise from the pier beside the **Hikawa-maru** (mid-June to mid-Sept daily 9.30am–9/9.30pm; mid-Sept to mid-June Mon–Fri 9.30am–7.30pm, Sat & Sun 9.30am–9pm; ¥800), a retired passenger liner. The vessel, also known as the *Queen of the Pacific*, was built in 1930 for the NYK line Yokohama–Seattle service, though it was commandeered as a hospital ship during the war. It now serves as a "floating amusement ship" whose best feature is a small museum full of nostalgic memorabilia from the days of the great ocean-going liners.

At the south end of Yamashita-kōen, the **Doll Museum** (Tues–Sun 10am–5pm, until July & Aug 7pm; ¥300) offers a more diverting display of dolls from around the world. Unfortunately there's little information in English, but the vast collection of Japanese folk and classical dolls is worth a look. Don't miss the exquisite, ceremonial *hina* dolls, traditionally displayed on March 3 during the Hina Matsuri (Doll Festival).

On the southwestern flank of Chinatown outside Kannai Station is **Yokohama International Stadium** (☎045/477-5006, ⓦwww .hamaspo.com/stadium), venue for the 2002 soccer World Cup final. If you wish to relive the drama of that match or just take a look around the 70,000-capacity stadium, one of Japan's largest, there are tours (¥500) four times daily except when there's an event on.

North to Sakuragichō

Yokohama's rapid growth in the late nineteenth century was underpinned by a flourishing export trade in raw silk. You can check out the practical aspects of silk production, from mulberry leaves to gorgeously coloured kimono, at the **Silk Museum**, at the north end of Yamashita-kōen (Tues–Sun 9am–4.30pm; ¥500).

Continuing north across a leafy square, you'll come to a modern, windowless building which houses the **Yokohama Archives of History** (Tues–Sun 9.30am–5pm; ¥200). This is the best of the city's historical museums, thanks to an unusual amount of English translation. The museum itself details the opening of Yokohama (and Japan) after 1853 through an impressive collection of photos, artefacts and documents, including contemporary newspaper reports from London.

You're now in the thick of Yokohama's administrative district, where several European-style facades still survive. Kanagawa government offices occupy the next block north, while the biscuit-coloured **Customs House**, opposite, is a more attractive structure, topped by a distinguished, copper-clad dome. Alternatively, follow the road heading inland, Minato Ōdōri, to find the graceful **Port Opening Memorial Hall**; erected in 1918, this red-brick neo-Renaissance building now serves as public function rooms. In front of the hall, turn north again, onto Honchō-dōri, to reach the last and most ornate of Yokohama's Western-style facades. The building was completed in 1904 as the headquarters of a Yokohama bank, and then later converted into the **Kanagawa Prefectural Museum** (Tues–Sun 9.30am–4.30pm; ¥300). The exhibition itself is missable, dealing primarily with local archeology and natural history.

The museum sits near the junction of Honchō-dōri and **Bashamichi** – this tree-lined shopping street, once the showcase of Yokohama and much vaunted in the tourist literature for its old-fashioned streetlamps and red-brick paving, is somewhat disappointing. Bashamichi heads west across the train tracks near Kannai Station and then continues as a pedestrianized shopping mall called **Isezakichō**. For now, though, follow Honchō-dōri north over a bridge for 500m to **Sakuragichō Station**.

Minato Mirai 21 (MM21)

In a bid to beat Tokyo at its own game, Yokohama now boasts Japan's tallest building and is in the process of creating a nonstop, high-tech international 21st-century city: **Minato Mirai 21** – or **MM21** as the development is better known. This mini-city of hotels, apartment blocks, offices and cultural facilities is rapidly changing the face of Yokohama, and will eventually occupy over two square kilometres of reclaimed land and disused dockyards, with its own subway line and state-of-the-art waste disposal and heating systems. The bulk of the hotels, conference facilities, shopping malls and museums are already in place. Next will come the office blocks, exhibition halls and waterfront parks to fill the empty plots behind.

MM21 can be accessed from either the Minato Mirai station on the Tōkyū-Tōyoko-line or Sakuragichō train and subway station, from where a covered moving walkway whisks you towards the awesome, 296-metre-tall **Landmark Tower**. Inside, take the world's fastest lift for an ear-popping, forty-second ride up to the 69th-floor **Sky Garden** (July & Aug daily and Sat all year 10am–10pm; Sept–June daily 10am–9pm; ¥1000). On clear days, when Fuji is flaunting her beauty, superb views more than justify the observatory's steep entry fee. Alternatively, if you don't mind missing the thrill of the elevator, you can enjoy a coffee for about the same price in the opulent *Sirius Sky Lounge* on the seventieth floor of the *Nikkō Hotel*, or splash out on an early-evening cocktail as the city lights spread their magic. Next door, the **Landmark Plaza** consists of a swanky shopping mall set around a five-storey-high atrium. Here you'll find flash boutiques, the Yurindo bookstore on the fifth floor – with an excellent foreign-language section – and plenty of restaurants, bars and coffee shops, some of which are built into the stone walls of an old dry dock.

Another water-filled dock in front of Landmark Tower is now home to the sleek **Nippon-maru** training sail ship, part of the enjoyable **Yokohama Maritime Museum** (Tues–Sun 10am–4.30/5pm; July & Aug 10am–6.30pm; ¥600). The *Nippon-maru* was built in 1930 and served up until 1984, during which time she sailed the equivalent of 45 times round the world; when her pristine white sails are hoisted twice monthly, it's clear why she's more familiarly known as the *Swan of the Pacific*. You can explore the entire vessel, from the engine room to the captain's wood-panelled cabin. There's copious English labelling and alternating Japanese and English commentary over the loud-speakers. The museum's main exhibition rooms occupy a purpose-built under-ground hall beside the ship. In addition to well-designed coverage of Yokohama's historical development, there's also a lot about the modern port and the technical side of sailing, though little in English. Nevertheless, you can still test your navigational skills at a mock-up bridge with a simulator, or have a bash at unloading a container vessel.

Landmark Tower stands in the extreme southern corner of MM21. Off to the east, the stepped towers of **Queen's Square** – another vast complex of shops, offices, a concert hall and the sail-shaped *Intercontinental Hotel* – fill the skyline. More inviting is the slowly revolving **Cosmo Clock 21** (daily: mid-March to Nov 11am–9/10pm; Dec to mid-March 11am–8/9pm;¥700), standing on the adjacent island of **Shinkō-chō**, which was reclaimed about a hundred years ago as part of Yokohama's then state-of-the-art port facilities. With a capacity of 480 passengers, this 112-metre ferris wheel claims to be the world's largest; one circuit takes around fifteen minutes, allowing plenty of time to admire the view. A short walk east of here past Yokohama World Porters, yet another shop-ping centre, are the **Akarenga**, two handsome red-brick warehouses dating from 1911 which reopened in 2002 as a smart shopping, dining and entertain-ment complex.

MM21's two major museums are to be found in the blocks immediately north of Landmark Tower. Head first for the splendid **Yokohama Museum of Art** (Mon–Wed, Sat & Sun 10am–6pm, Fri 10am–8pm; ¥500; varying prices for special exhibitions) in which mostly twentieth-century Japanese and Western art is set off to fine effect by designer Tange Kenzō's cool, grey space. In fact, the architecture – particularly the magnificent central atrium – grabs your attention as much as the exhibits. The photography galleries are always worth checking out, while the Art Library contains a wealth of international art and design publications.

Kids will be in their element at the **Mitsubishi Minato Mirai Industrial Museum** (Tues–Sun 10am–5.30pm;¥500; ⓦ www.mhi.co.jp/museum) in the neighbouring block. The museum's six well-laid-out zones illustrate techno-logical developments, from today's power generators, oil platforms and deep-sea probes to the space stations of tomorrow. There are plenty of models and interactive displays, with English-speaking staff on hand if needed, but the biggest draw is the "Sky-Walk Adventure" up on the second floor. At one time kids were queuing round the block to have a ride in this helicopter simulator, though it's now usually pretty clear. After a two-minute flying lesson, you get to take the "real" chopper swooping and soaring over Fuji or down into the Grand Canyon for a stomach-wrenching fifteen-minute ride.

Yokohama Station to the Raumen Museum

Apart from one small but important art museum, there's not a great deal to see around **Yokohama Station**. However, this is the city's prime centre for department stores. The east side of the station is home to the city's Central Post Office, the long-distance bus terminal and to Yokohama City Air Terminal (YCAT), while *Sea Bass* ferries for Minato Mirai and Yamashita-kōen depart from a pier behind Sogō (see p.258 for details).

The area's only real attraction is located on Sogō's sixth floor. The two-room **Hiraki Ukiyo-e Museum** (daily except Tues 10am–7/7.30pm;¥500) houses one of Japan's most highly rated collections of woodblock prints. Unfortunately, only a small portion of the museum's 8000 *ukiyo-e* can be displayed during each month-long exhibition. Nevertheless, all the great woodblock artists are represented and there's usually something to capture the imagination of any art enthusiast.

Even if you're not a noodle fan, it's worth making the trek to **Shin-Yokohama** – on the subway or JR Yokohama line – to visit the **Raumen Museum** (daily except Tues 11am–11pm; restaurants open until 9.45pm; ¥300). This well-designed museum-cum-restaurant is devoted to Japan's most popular fast food, in its most basic form a noodle soup garnished with roast pork, bamboo shoots and dried seaweed. It's five minutes' walk northeast of Shin-Yokohama Station; walk straight ahead, to the left of the NTT Building, to the second set of traffic lights, then turn right and first left.

The museum's first-floor hall delves into the roots of ramen, tracing them back to southern China, and then chronicles the moment in 1958 when instant rāmen – chicken-flavoured – was launched on the world, followed in 1971 by cup noodles. There are some mind-boggling statistics: as a taster, in 1993 the world consumed an estimated 22.1 billion bowls of ramen. Once you've digested all of that, head for the basement, where you're transported into 1950s downtown Japan. Below you lies a city square at dusk: lights are coming on in the shops and pachinko parlours, as vendors call out their wares under grimy film posters. Walk round the mezzanine's dingy alley, complete with bars and an old-fashioned sweet shop, before heading down into the courtyard, where each storefront hides a restaurant from Japan's most famous ramen regions. The local variety are available in the Beauty Salon, while other stalls specialize in rāmen from Fukuoka, Sapporo, Kumamoto or Tokyo; buy a ticket (from around ¥900, or ¥500 for a half-portion) at the machine – ask for help, as it's all in Japanese – and then join the slurping throng at tables in the courtyard. Note that there's no smoking except in the bars on the mezzanine floor, and it's best to avoid the crowds at lunchtimes and weekends.

Sankei-en

In the late nineteenth century a wealthy silk merchant, Hara Tomitaro, established his residence in sculptured parkland on Yokohama's southern hills and filled it with rare and beautiful buildings from Kamakura and the Kansai region. Today **Sankei-en** (daily: outer garden 9am–5pm, inner garden 9am–4.30pm; ¥300 each; ⓦwww.sankeien.or.jp) is divided into an outer garden and a smaller inner core, where most of the famous structures are located. To reach Sankei-en, take bus #8 from Yokohama or Sakuragichō stations to Honmoku Sankeien-mae, from where the garden is a three-minute walk, or hop on a JR Negishi-line train to Negishi Station and then a bus as far as the Honmoku stop, 600m north of the main gate.

From the gate, follow the well-marked route to the **inner garden**, where **Rinshunkaku** – an elegant, lakeside mansion built for one of the Tokugawa lords in 1649 – is the only structure of its kind still in existence. Another Tokugawa legacy, dating from 1623, sits beside a picturesque stream a few minutes further on; named **Choshukaku**, it originally served as a tea-ceremony house in the grounds of Kyoto's Nijō Castle. **Tenju-in** may not be as famous, but it's worth walking up beside the stream to see its fine carving. This little seventeenth-century temple dedicated to Jizō, the guardian deity of children, hails from Kamakura.

In the less formal **outer garden**, thatched farm roofs blend with bamboo thickets and groves of twisted plum trees, above which rises a graceful three-tiered pagoda. The most interesting building here is **Old Yanohara House** (¥100), the former home of a wealthy farmer, where you can take a close look at the vast roof built in *gassho* style – no nails but plenty of rope. Don't bother climbing up the hill to Shofukaku: the concrete viewing platform has great views of billowing chimney stacks and industrial dockyards.

Eating, drinking and nightlife

One of Yokohama's highlights is its great choice of cuisines. Most visitors head straight for **Chinatown**, but there's also a huge variety of other options, including plenty of Japanese restaurants, of course. Shopping malls such as Landmark Plaza, Queen's Square and Shinkō-chō's World Porters and Akarenga are the best hunting grounds for other places to eat.

Chinatown

Heichinrou 149 Yamashitachō ℡045/681-3001. Large, popular Cantonese institution with dark, intimate booths. Food includes dim sum from around ¥800 per plate (until 4.30pm), while evening menus start at ¥3500. Get there early or be prepared to queue, especially at weekends.
Manchinrou 153 Yamashitachō ℡045/681-4004. Another famous old name, this time serving Guangdong cuisine. Choose carefully and eating here needn't break the bank, with noodle and fried-rice dishes starting at around ¥1100 and lunch sets at ¥2700, though evening-course menus (from ¥4600) are less affordable. The branch behind serves a full range of dim sum. English spoken. Daily 11am–10pm.
Peking Hanten 79 Yamashitachō. Right beside Chinatown's eastern gate, this highly decorated

Beijing restaurant is unmissable. It's fairly low-key inside, however, and has well-priced lunchtime menus from around ¥1000. Their late opening hours (until 2am) and English menu are also plus points.
Shei Shei 138 Yamashitachō. Casual Szechuan restaurant serving an excellent-value set lunch on weekdays (¥500), or choose from their picture menu. There are only a handful of tables, so at busy times you'll be asked to share. Daily until 8.30pm.
Suro Saikan Honkan 190 Yamashitachō. Decorated with gorgeous mosaics, this place is popular for its reliable Shanghai cuisine. Weekday lunch sets start at under ¥700 and courses from around ¥3000, but count on at least ¥4000 in the evening.

The rest of the city

Alte Liebe 11 Nihon-dōri, Naka-ku ℡045/222-3346. Pretty authentic-looking Viennese-style café-restaurant on the corner of one of Yokohama's grand old buildings.
Chano-ma 3F Akarenga 2, 1-1-2 Shinkō, Naka-ku ℡045/650-8228. Sit back with a cocktail and nibble interesting modern Japanese dishes at this relaxed restaurant with a very contemporary vibe.
Enokitei 89-6 Yamatechō ℡045/623-2288. Set in a venerable Yamate home, this cute English-style café serves dainty sandwiches and home-made cakes, and you can sit in the front garden and watch the world pass by.
Rikyuan 2-17 Masagochō ℡045/662-2857.

Traditional soba joint tucked down a backstreet, two blocks east of JR Kannai Station. The menu includes *donburi* as well as various soba dishes; prices start at around ¥850. Mon–Sat 11am–8.30pm.
Yamate Jūbankan 247 Yamatechō ℡045/621-4466. Pleasant French restaurant in a pretty clap-board house opposite the Foreigners' Cemetery. There's a restaurant upstairs and a less formal dining area on the ground floor, where you can snack on a sandwich or *croque*. Set lunches cost around ¥3000. In July and August they run a popular beer garden.
Yokohama Curry Museum 1-2-3 Isezaki-chō,

Naka-ku ☎045/250-0833. On the seventh and eighth floors above a pachinko parlour and bearing as much relation to a museum as Japanese curry does to Indian. Still, this collection of some eleven different curry outlets is a fun and colourful place to wander around and sample a few regional Japanese specialties, as well as more common items like spicy curry ice cream – just don't expect to discover much about curry.

Bars and nightlife

Though it's generally less boisterous than Tokyo, Yokohama still has no shortage of lively drinking holes. The west side of Yokohama Station comprises the main **nightlife** area, but the area around Chinatown and across to Kannai Station also has a sprinkling of bars.

Beer Next 3F Akarenga 2, 1-1-2 Shinkō, Naka-ku ☎045/226-1961. Stylish beer hall and restaurant in this warehouse conversion. Their own-brew Spring Valley beer (¥480) is refreshing, and they also have Guinness on tap.

Gas Panic Jackmall East, 4-8-1 Minato Mirai ☎045/680-0291. Yokohama branch of Roppongi's grungiest but ever-popular nightclub. The music is the standard, crowd-pleasing mix of techno, hip-hop, pop and good old rock'n'roll. No cover charge; drinks cost ¥300 all night on Thursdays and from 6pm to 9.30pm other nights.

Motion Blue Akarenga 2, 1-1-2 Shinkō, Naka-ku ☎045/226-1919, ⓦwww.motionblue.co.jp. Cool jazz club in the renovated Akarenga buildings attracting top acts – for which you'll pay top prices. There's no cost, though, for parking yourself at the attached Bar Tune's long counter and soaking up the ambience with a drink.

Pure 1 Ōtamachi ☎045/663-8485, ⓦwww.clubpure.com. The happening club of the moment amongst Yokohama's *gaijin*, with all-you-can-drink nights (men/women ¥3500/2500) on Friday and Saturday.

The Tavern B1, 2-14 Minami Saiwai-chō. This British-style pub, popular with local expats, is a good place to kick off an evening in the nightlife district west of Yokohama Station; turn left out of the station to find it opposite the Daiei store. There's live music on Tuesdays, half-price drinks for women on weekdays (6–7pm) and the sort of bar food that will appeal to homesick Brits.

Contexts

Contexts

A brief history of Tokyo

oday's restless metropolis, sprawling round the western shores of Tokyo Bay, began life as a humble fishing village, called Edo, lost among the marshes of the Sumida-gawa. Its rise to become one of the world's largest, most powerful and influential cities has been undercut by a series of natural and man-made cataclysms, giving Tokyo's history a dramatic arc as intriguing as that of a Kabuki drama.

The birth of Edo

Although Tokyo's founding date is usually given as 1457, the year when **Ōta Dōkan**, a minor lord, built his modest castle on a bluff overlooking the river, there have been people living on the Kantō plain for well over two thousand years. The city's first name of **Edo**, meaning "rivergate", was granted in the twelfth century by Edo Shigenaga, a member of the Taira clan who held control of the Kantō district at the time.

The most significant date in the city's early history, however, was 1590, when the ambitious warlord **Tokugawa Ieyasu** established his power-base in this obscure castle town, far from the emperor in Kyoto. For more than a century Japan had been torn apart by political and social unrest, but in little over a decade Ieyasu succeeded in reuniting the country, taking the title of shogun, effectively a military dictator. Though the emperor continued to hold court in Kyoto, Japan's real centre of power would henceforth lie in Edo.

Under the Tokugawa

The **Tokugawa** dynasty set about creating a city befitting their new status, initiating massive construction projects which have continued to the present day. By 1640 Edo Castle was the most imposing in all Japan, complete with a five-storey central keep, a double moat and a complex, spiralling network of canals. Instead of perimeter walls, however, there were simple barrier gates and then a bewildering warren of narrow, tortuous lanes, sudden dead-ends and unbridged canals to snare unwelcome intruders. At the same time drainage work began on the surrounding marshes, where embankments were raised to protect the nascent city against flooding.

The shogun protected himself further by requiring his *daimyō* (feudal lords) to split the year between their provincial holdings and Edo, where their families were kept as virtual hostages. Maintaining two households with two sets of retainers, travelling long distances and observing prescribed ceremonies on the way left them neither the time nor money to raise a serious threat. But the *daimyō* also enjoyed numerous privileges: within Edo they were granted the most favourable land to the west of the castle, in the area known as **Yamanote**. Artisans, merchants and others at the bottom of the established order, meanwhile, were confined to **Shitamachi**, a low-lying, overcrowded region to the east. Mid-eighteenth-century Edo was the world's largest city, with a population well over one million, of whom roughly half were squeezed into Shitamachi at an astonishing 70,000 people per square kilometre. Though growing less distinct, this division between the "high" and "low" city is still apparent today.

During more than two hundred years of peace, the shogunate grew increasingly conservative and sterile, while life down in Shitamachi was buzzing.

Peace had given rise to an increasingly wealthy merchant class and a vigorous, often bawdy subculture where the pursuit of pleasure was taken to new extremes. In Shitamachi, where rank counted for little, the arbiters of fashion were the irrepressible, devil-may-care *Edo-ko*, the "children of Edo", with their earthy humour and delight in practical jokes. Inevitably, there was also a darker side to life and the *Edo-ko* knew their fair share of squalor, poverty and violence. Licensed brothels, euphemistically known as "pleasure quarters", flourished, and child prostitution was common.

Shitamachi's tightly packed streets of thatch and wood dwellings usually suffered worst in the great fires which broke out so frequently that they were dubbed *Edo no hana*, the "flowers of Edo". In January 1657, the **Fire of the Long Sleeves** laid waste to three-quarters of the district's buildings and killed an estimated hundred thousand people. Subsequent precautions included earth firewalls, manned watchtowers and local firefighting teams, who were much revered for their acrobatic skills and bravery. The fires continued, however, and the life expectancy of an Edo building averaged a mere twenty years.

The Meiji Restoration and modernization

Since the early seventeenth century Japan had been a **closed country**. Distrusting the success of earlier Christian missionaries and fearful of colonization by their European backers, the shogun banned virtually all contact with the outside world. Within this vacuum, by the early nineteenth century the highly conservative shogunate had become a weak and inept regime. When it failed to deal effectively with **Commodore Perry**, the American who insolently sailed his "Black Ships" into Edo Bay in 1853 and 1854 to secure trading rights, the shoguns' days were numbered. Opposition forces gradually rallied round the emperor until, after a brief civil war, the fifteenth Tokugawa shogun surrendered in November 1867. A few months later, in what came to be called the **Meiji Restoration**, power was fully restored to the emperor, and in 1869 Emperor Meiji took up permanent residence in the city now known as **Tokyo**, Japan's "eastern capital".

The first years of **Meiji rule** saw another, very different revolution. Determined to modernize, Japan embraced the ideas and technologies of the West with startling enthusiasm. Tokyo stood at the centre of innovation: brick buildings, electric lights, trams, trains and then cars all made their first appearance here. Within a few decades the castle lost its outer gates and most of its grounds, canals were filled in or built over and the commercial focus shifted to Ginza, while Shitamachi's wealthier merchants decamped for the more desirable residential areas of Yamanote, leaving the low city to sink into slow decline.

Beneath its modern veneer, however, Tokyo remained largely a city of wood, still regularly swept by fire and rocked by earthquakes, most disastrously by the **Great Kantō Earthquake**, which struck the city at noon on September 1, 1923. Half of Tokyo – by then a city of some two million – was destroyed, while a hundred thousand people lost their lives in the quake itself and in the blazes sparked by thousands of cooking-fires.

The war and its aftermath

The city rose from its ashes and for a while development continued apace, but nationalism was on the rise and before long Tokyo, like the rest of Japan, was gearing up for war. The first bombs hit the city in April 1942, followed by more frequent raids throughout 1944 as the Allied forces drew closer, reaching a crescendo in March 1945. During three days of sustained **incendiary**

bombing an estimated hundred thousand people died, most of them on the night of March 9, when great swathes of the city burnt to the ground. The physical devastation surpassed even that of the Great Earthquake: Meiji-jingū, Sensō-ji and Edo Castle were all destroyed, Shitamachi all but obliterated, and from Hibiya it was possible to see clear across the eight kilometres to Shinjuku.

From a prewar population of nearly seven million, Tokyo in 1945 was reduced to around three million residents living in a state of near-starvation. This time, however, regeneration was fuelled by an influx of American dollars and food aid under the **Allied Occupation** led by General MacArthur. A **Security Pact** was signed between the two nations allowing the US to keep bases in Japan in exchange for providing military protection. Not surprisingly, the liveliest sector of the economy during this period was the blackmarket, first in Yūrakuchō and later in Ueno and Ikebukuro. In 1950 the **Korean War** broke out, and central Tokyo underwent extensive redevelopment on the back of a manufacturing boom partly fuelled by the war, while immigrants flooded in from the provinces to fill the factories.

With economic recovery well on the way, political tensions surfaced in the late 1950s. Anti-American **demonstrations** occurred sporadically throughout the decade, but in May 1960 more serious rioting broke out over ratification of the revised Security Pact. The crisis passed, though student discontent continued to rumble on for a long time – so much so that in 1968 the authorities closed Tokyo University for a year – and heavily armed riot police became a familiar sight on the streets. But the situation was never allowed to threaten the major event of the postwar period when, on October 10, 1964, Emperor Hirohito opened the eighteenth **Olympic Games**, the first in Asia, which were welcomed by many Japanese as a sign of long-awaited international recognition. Visitors to the games, for their part, were surprised by the previously war-torn country's rapid transformation, epitomized by the stunning Shinkansen trains zipping between Tokyo and Kyoto.

Like the rest of the industrialized world, Japan suffered during the oil price crisis of the 1970s, but by the following decade her economy was the envy of the world. The late-1980s **boom** saw land prices in Tokyo reach dizzying heights, matched by excesses of every conceivable sort, from gold-wrapped sushi to mink toilet-seat covers. The heady optimism was reflected in building projects such as the Metropolitan Government offices in Shinjuku, the Odaiba reclamation and the vast development of Makuhari Messe on the east side of Tokyo Bay.

Recession and the new millennium

By 1992, the bubble had burst. The sudden sobering-up and subsequent loss of confidence was compounded by revelations of deep-seated political corruption and by the **AUM Shinrikyō** terrorist group releasing deadly sarin gas on Tokyo commuter trains in 1995 – a particularly shocking event which left twelve dead and thousands injured.

Recession was officially announced in 1998, and newspaper headlines during the late 1990s announced a seemingly endless stream of financial misdealings, resignations and suicides. By February 1998, a manual on how to commit suicide had sold an incredible 1.1 million copies, and over 30,000 people – the majority middle-aged men facing unemployment – killed themselves that year, followed by a record 33,000 in 1999. Another type of death – the murder of Lucy Blackman, a young British woman working as a hostess in Roppongi – hit the headlines in 2000, alerting the world to the fact that life in Tokyo wasn't quite as safe as had been imagined.

The new millennium has brought glimmerings of economic **recovery** – hardly surprising after trillions of yen have been pumped into it through various government packages – though the unemployment rate continues to hover stubbornly around a previously unthinkable five percent, and the blue-tarpaulin tent compounds of the **homeless** have become commonplace in the capital's parks.

Tokyo put aside its woes during the **2002 World Cup**, an event which saw the city swamped with visitors and everyone go football crazy. There was the inevitable anticlimax after the final had been played at Yokohama, but it hasn't taken Tokyo long to bounce back. In 2003, a rash of huge new architectural developments opened up across the city, the most prominent of them being **Roppongi Hills**. Contemporary Tokyo is now more international in its outlook than ever before, with more foreign companies seeking to do business here as the economy is deregulated and local new-technology companies take off. At the same time, Tokyo's utterly individual style in matters of art, fashion and popular culture – fuelled by an increasingly cosmopolitan youth – continues to attract an admiring global audience, fully justifying its standing as the capital of world cool.

Books

Many of the titles below are published by Kodansha and Charles E. Tuttle both in Japan and abroad. However, if you can, buy your books before your journey, since they're generally more expensive in Japan. Titles marked with a ▣ are particularly recommended.

History

Pat Barr *The Coming of the Barbarians.* Entertaining and very readable tales of how Japan opened up to the West at the beginning of the Meiji Restoration.

▣⭐ **Ian Buruma** *The Wages of Guilt.* Buruma's skilful comparison and explanation of how and why Germany and Japan have come to terms so differently with their roles in World War II. His *Inventing Japan* (Modern Library Chronicles) looks at the country's history between 1853 and 1964, the period which saw the country go from a feudal, isolated state to a powerhouse of the modern world economy.

John Dower *Embracing Defeat: Japan in the Aftermath of World War II.* This accessible Pulitzer Prize winner looks at the impact of the American occupation on Japan and concludes it had a fundamental and long-lasting effect. First-person accounts and snappy writing bring the book alive.

Edward Seidensticker *Low City, High City* and *Tokyo Rising: The City Since the Great Earthquake.* Seidensticker, a top translator of Japanese literature, tackles Tokyo's history from its humble beginnings to the Great Kantō quake of 1923 in the first book and follows up well with a second volume focusing on the capital's postwar experiences.

Richard Storry *A History of Modern Japan.* Ideal primer for basics and themes of Japanese history.

Richard Tames *A Traveller's History of Japan.* This clearly written and succinct volume romps through Japan's history and provides useful cultural descriptions and essays.

▣⭐ **Paul Waley** *Tokyo: City of Stories.* An intimate, anecdotal history of the capital, which delves into Tokyo's neighbourhoods, uncovering some fascinating stories in the process.

Business, economics and politics

Peter Hadfield *Sixty Seconds that Will Change the World.* The main theme – the terrible threat hanging over Tokyo, and the world, of a coming earthquake – allows Hadfield to reveal much about Japanese attitudes, bureaucracy and politics.

Jacob M. Schlesinger *Shadow Shoguns.* Cracking crash course in Japan's political scene, scandals and all, from *Wall Street Journal*

reporter Schlesinger, who spent five years at the newspaper's Tokyo bureau and whose wife was an aide to current top politician Ozawa Ichiro.

▣⭐ **Karel Van Wolferen** *The Enigma of Japanese Power.* Standard text on the triad of Japan's bureaucracy, politicians and business, and the power gulf between them. A weighty, thought-provoking tome, worth wading through.

Arts, culture and society

Ian Buruma *A Japanese Mirror* and *The Missionary and the Libertine* (Faber). The first book is an intelligent, erudite examination of Japan's popular culture, while *The Missionary and the Libertine* collects together a range of the author's essays, including pieces on Japan-bashing, Hiroshima, Pearl Harbor, the authors Mishima Yukio, Tanizaki Junichirō and Yoshimoto Banana and the film director Ōshima Nagisa.

Lisa Dalby *Geisha* (Vintage). The real-life *Memoirs of a Geisha*. In the 1970s, anthropologist Dalby immersed herself in this fast-disappearing world and became a geisha. This is the fascinating account of her experience and those of her teachers and fellow pupils. *Kimono*, her history of the most Japanese of garments, is also worth a look.

Lesley Downer *The Brothers*. The Tsutsumi family are the Kennedys of Japan and their saga of wealth, illegitimacy and the fabled hatred of the two half-brothers is made gripping reading by Downer.

Edward Fowler *San'ya Blues*. Fowler's experiences living and working among the casual labourers of Tokyo's San'ya district makes fascinating reading. He reveals the dark underbelly of Japan's economic miracle and blows apart a few myths and misconceptions on the way.

★ Robin Gerster *Legless in Ginza*. A funny and spot-on account of the writer's two-year residence at Japan's most prestigious university, Tokyo's Todai. Gerster writes with a larrikin Aussie verve and notices things that many other ex-pat commentators ignore.

Gunji Masakatsu *Kabuki*. Excellent, highly readable introduction to Kabuki by one of the leading connoisseurs of Japanese drama. Illustrated with copious annotated photos of the great actors and most dramatic moments in Kabuki theatre.

David Kaplan and Andrew Marshall *The Cult at the End of the World*. Chilling account of the nerve-gas attack on the Tokyo subway by the AUM cult in 1995. The gripping, pulp-fiction-like prose belies formidable research by the authors into the shocking history of this killer cult and their crazed leader Asahara Shoko.

★ Alex Kerr *Lost Japan*. Although it's part of the usually tedious "Japan's not what it once was" school of writing, this book won a prestigious literature prize when first published in Japanese, and the translation is just as worthy of praise. Kerr, the son of a US naval officer, first came to Japan as a child in the 1960s and has been fascinated by it ever since. This beautifully written and thoughtfully observed set of essays covers aspects of his life and passions, including Kabuki, art collecting and cities such as Kyoto and Ōsaka. His follow-up *Dogs and Demons* (Penguin) is a scathing and thought-provoking attack on Japan's economic, environmental and social policies of the past decades.

★ Donald Richie *Public People, Private People, A Lateral View* and *Partial Views*. These three books, all collections of essays by a man whose love affair with Japan began when he arrived with the US occupying forces in 1947, set the standard other expat commentators can only aspire to. *Public People* is a set of sketches of famous and unknown Japanese, including profiles of novelist Mishima and the actor Mifune Toshiro. In *A Lateral View* and *Partial Views*, Richie tackles Tokyo style, avant-garde theatre, pachinko, and the Japanese kiss, among many other things.

Mark Schilling *The Encyclopedia of Japanese Pop Culture*. Forget sumo,

C

samurai and ikebana. Godzilla, pop idols and instant ramen are really where Japan's culture's at. Schilling's book is an indispensable, spot-on guide to late-twentieth-century Japan. Don't leave home without it.

Frederik L. Schodt *Dreamland Japan: Writings on Modern Manga.* In the sequel to his *Manga! Manga! The World of Japanese Comics*, Schodt pens a series of entertaining and informative essays on the art of Japanese comic books, profiling the top publications, artists, animated films and English-language manga.

Joan Stanley-Baker *Japanese Art.* Highly readable introduction to the broad range of Japan's artistic traditions (though excluding theatre and music), tracing their development from prehistoric to modern times.

Robert Twigger *Angry White Pyjamas.* The subtitle "An Oxford poet trains with the Tokyo riot police" gives you the gist, and although Twigger's writing is more prose than poetry, he provides an intense forensic account of the daily trials, humiliations and triumphs of becoming a master of Aikido. Even if you're not into martial arts, it's worth picking up.

Rey Ventura *Underground in Japan.* The non-Caucasian *gaijin* experience in Japan is brilliantly essayed by Ventura, who lived and worked with fellow Filipino illegal immigrants in the dockyards of Yokohama.

Guides and reference books

John Carroll *Trails of Two Cities.* Enjoyable and informative walking guide to Yokohama and Kamakura by a long-time resident. Full of fascinating historical detail and local insights.

Enbutsu Sumiko *Old Tokyo: Walks in the City of the Shogun.* Tokyo's old Shitamachi area is best explored on foot and Enbutsu's guide, illustrated with characterful block prints, helps bring the city's history alive.

Thomas F. Judge and Tomita Hiroyuki *Edo Craftsmen.* Beautifully produced portraits of some of the traditional craftsmen still working in the backstreets of Tokyo. A timely insight into a disappearing world.

★ **John and Phyllis Martin** *Tokyo: A Cultural Guide to Japan's Capital City.* Finely researched and written book designed around walking tours of Tokyo, which goes well beyond the usual sights.

Caroline Pover *Being a Broad in Japan.* The subtitle sums it up: "Everything a Western woman needs to thrive and survive". Pover proves a sassy guide to the various perils and pitfalls of life in Japan from a female perspective, covering everything from finding day care to getting divorced.

Robb Satterwhite *What's What in Japanese Restaurants.* Handy guide to all things culinary you'll encounter during your adventures in Japanese food and drink. Written by a Tokyo-based epicure who also manages the excellent *Tokyo Food Page* on the Web. The menus annotated with Japanese characters are particularly useful.

Tajima Noriyuki *Tokyo: A Guide to Recent Architecture.* A compact, expertly written and nicely illustrated book that's an essential accompaniment on any modern architectural tour of the capital.

Gary D'A. Walters *Day Walks Near Tokyo.* Slim volume of strolls and hikes all within easy reach of the capital to help get you off the beaten tourist path. The maps are clear, as are the practical details and directions.

Diane Wiltshire Kanagawa and Jeanne Huey Erickson *Japan for Kids*. Immensely practical guide covering everything from vocabulary for the labour ward, to where to hire a Santa. Aimed mainly at expat parents living in Tokyo, but also full of practical tips and recommendations for visitors with kids.

Japanese fiction

Alfred Birnbaum ed. *Monkey Brain Sushi*. Eleven often quirky short stories by contemporary Japanese authors. A good introduction to modern prose writers.

Kawabata Yasunari *Snow Country, The Izu Dancer*, and other titles. Japan's first Nobel Prize winner for fiction writes intense tales of passion usually about a sophisticated urban man falling for a simple country girl.

Mishima Yukio *After the Banquet, Confessions of Mask, Forbidden Colours, The Sea of Fertility*. Novelist Mishima sealed his notoriety by committing ritual suicide after leading a failed military coup in 1970. He left behind a highly respectable, if at times melodramatic, body of literature, including some of Japan's finest postwar novels. Themes of tradition, sexuality and militarism run through many of his works.

Miyabe Miyuki *All She Was Worth*. When a young man's fiancée goes missing, a trail of credit-card debts and worse turns up. There's more to this clever whodunnit set in contemporary Tokyo than immediately meets the eye.

Murakami Haruki

One of Japan's most entertaining contemporary writers, Murakami Haruki has been hailed as a postwar successor to the great novelists Mishima, Kawabata and Tanizaki. His books, which are wildly popular in Japan, are about conspiracies, suicidal women, futile love, disappearing elephants and talking sheep. In 21 years he has published over a dozen novels and, recently, *Underground*, a study of the 1995 Tokyo subway gas attack by the AUM Shinrikyo cult. Translated into some thirty languages, Murakami is being talked of as a future Nobel Prize laureate. And yet the 51-year-old writer and marathon runner (he's run one a year for the past eighteen years with a personal best of 3 hours 34 minutes, and is planning a book on the subject) shuns the media spotlight and is happy that few people recognize him.

Many of Murakami's books are set in Tokyo, drawing on his time studying at Waseda University in the early 1970s and running his own jazz bar in Kokubunji, a place that became a haunt for literary types and, no doubt, provided inspiration for his jazz-bar-running hero in the bittersweet novella *South of the Border, West of the Sun*. He's back living in Tokyo now, but has spent large parts of his career abroad, including five years teaching in the US, at both Princeton University and Boston's Tufts University. The contemporary edge to Murakami's writing, which eschews the traditional clichés of Japanese literature, has been fuelled by his work as a translator of books by John Irving, Raymond Carver, Truman Capote and Paul Theroux among others.

A good introduction to Murakami is *Norwegian Wood*, a tender coming-of-age love story between two students, that has sold over five million copies in both of its volumes. The truly bizarre *A Wild Sheep Chase* and its follow-up *Dance Dance Dance* are funny but disturbing modern-day fables, dressed up as detective novels. His best book is considered to be *The Wind-Up Bird Chronicle*, a hefty yet dazzling cocktail of mystery, war reportage and philosophy.

Murakami Ryū *Almost Transparent Blue, Sixty-nine* and *Coin Locker Babies*. Murakami burst onto Japan's literary scene in the mid-1980s with *Almost Transparent Blue*, a hip tale of student life mixing reality and fantasy. *Sixty-nine* is his semi-autobiographical account of a 17-year-old stirred by the rebellious passions of the late 1960s, set in Sasebo, Kyūshū; while *Coin Locker Babies* is his most ambitious work, spinning a revenger's tragedy about the lives of two boys dumped in adjacent coin lockers as babies.

Natsume Sōseki *Botchan, Kokoro* and *I am a Cat*. In his comic novel *Botchan*, Sōseki draws on his own experiences as an English teacher in turn-of-the-twentieth-century Matsuyama. The three volumes of *I am a Cat* see the humorist adopting a wry feline point of view on the world. *Kokoro* – about an ageing *sensei* trying to coming to terms with the modern era – is considered his best book.

Ōe Kenzaburō *Nip the Buds Shoot the Kids*, *A Personal Matter* and *A Healing Family*. Ōe won Japan's second Nobel Prize for literature in 1994. *Nip the Buds*, his first full-length novel published in 1958, is a tale of lost innocence concerning fifteen reformatory school boys evacuated in wartime to a remote mountain village and left to fend for themselves when a threatening plague frightens away the villagers. *A Personal Matter* sees Ōe tackling the trauma of his handicapped son Hikari's birth, while *A Healing Family* catches up with Hikari thirty years later documenting his trials and triumphs. Never an easy read, but always startlingly honest.

Tokyo in foreign fiction

Alan Brown *Audrey Hepburn's Neck*. Beneath this rib-tickling, acutely observed tale of a young guy from the sticks adrift in big-city Tokyo, Brown weaves several important themes, including the continuing impact of World War II and the confused relationships between the Japanese and *gaijin*.

Ian Fleming *You Only Live Twice*. Bondo-san on the trail of arch-enemy Blofeld in trendy mid-Sixties Tokyo and the wilds of Kyūshū, assisted by Tiger Tanaka and Kissy Suzuki.

William Gibson *Idoru* and *Pattern Recognition*. *Idoru* chronicles love in the age of the computer chip. Cyberpunk novelist Gibson's sci-fi vision of Tokyo's high-tech future – a world of non-intrusive DNA checks at airports and computerized pop icons (the *idoru* of the title) – rings disturbingly true. In his more recent *Pattern Recognition* Tokyo plays a memorable walk-on part in the heroine's search for an elusive movie-maker.

Gavin Kramer *Shopping*. British lawyer Kramer's zippy first novel is on the bleak side, but captures the turn-of-millennium *Zeitgeist* of Tokyo, where schoolgirls trade sex for designer labels and *gaijin* flounder in a sea of misunderstanding.

David Mitchell *Ghostwritten* and *number9dream*. The Hiroshima-based British writer made a splash with his debut *Ghostwritten*, a dazzling collection of interlocked short stories, a couple set in Japan. *number9dream*, shortlisted for the Booker Prize in 2001, conjures up a postmodern Tokyo of computer hackers, video games, gangsters and violence. A demanding, dark yet compulsive read.

John David Morley *Pictures from the Water Trade*. The subtitle, *An*

C

Englishman in Japan, says it all as Morley's alter ego, Boon, crashes headlong into an intense relationship with demure, yet sultry Mariko in an oh-so-foreign world. Along the way, some imaginative observations and descriptions are made.

Peter Tasker *Silent Thunder, Buddha Kiss* and *Samurai Boogie*. Tasker, a British financial analyst, has created a trio of fun, throwaway thrillers mainly set in Tokyo, with Bond-like set pieces and lively Japanese characters, especially Mori, his down-at-heel gumshoe.

C

Language

Language

Language

First the good news. Picking up a few words of Japanese, even managing a sentence or two, is not difficult. **Pronunciation** is simple and standard and there are few exceptions to the straightforward **grammar** rules. With a couple of weeks' effort you should be able to read the words spelled out in **hiragana** and **katakana**, Japanese phonetic characters, even if you can't understand them. And any time spent learning Japanese will be amply rewarded by the thrilled response you'll elicit from the locals, who'll always politely comment on your fine linguistic ability.

The bad news is that it takes a very great effort indeed to become halfway proficient in Japanese, let alone master the language. One of the main stumbling blocks is the thousands of **kanji** characters that need to be memorized, most of which have at least two pronunciations, depending on the sentence and their combination with other characters. Another major difference is the multiple levels of **politeness** embodied in Japanese, married with different sets of words used by men and women (although this is less of a problem). Finally, as you move around Japan there are different **dialects** to deal with, such as Ōsaka-ben, the dialect of the Kansai area, involving whole new vocabularies.

Japanese characters

The exact origins of Japanese are a mystery, and until the sixth century it only existed in the spoken form. Once the Japanese imported Chinese characters, known as *kanji*, they began to develop their own forms of written language.

Japanese is now written in a combination of three systems. The most difficult of the three to master is **kanji** (Chinese ideograms), which originally developed as mini-pictures of the word they stand for. To be able to read a newspaper, you'll need to know around two thousand *kanji*, much more difficult than it sounds since what each one means varies with its context.

The easier writing systems to pick up are the phonetic syllabaries, **hiragana** and **katakana**. Both have 45 regular characters (see box, overleaf) and can be learned within a couple of weeks. *Hiragana* is used for Japanese words, while *katakana*, with the squarer characters, is used mainly for loan words from Western languages (especially English) and technical names. Increasingly, **rōmaji** (see p.285), the roman script used to spell out Japanese words, is also used in advertisements and magazines. Good places to practise reading *hiragana* and *katakana* are on the advertisements plastered in train carriages and on restaurant menus.

The first five letters in *hiragana* and *katakana* (**a, i, u, e, o**) are the vowel sounds (see Pronunciation, p.285). The remainder are a combination of a consonant and a vowel (eg **ka, ki, ku, ke, ko**), with the exception of **n**, the only consonant that exists on its own. While *hiragana* provides an exact phonetic reading of all Japanese words, it's a mistake to think that *katakana* does the same for foreign loan words. Often words are shortened, hence television becomes *terebi* and sexual harassment *sekuhara*. Sometimes, they become almost unrecognizable, as with *kakuteru*, which is cocktail.

The Japanese script consists of **hiragana**, **katakana** and ideograms based on Chinese characters (*kanji*). *Hiragana* and *katakana* are two phonetic syllabaries represented by the characters shown below. *Katakana*, the squarer characters in the table immediately below, are used for writing foreign "loan words". The rounder characters in the bottom table, *hiragana*, are used for Japanese words, in combination with, or as substitutes for, *kanji*.

Katakana

a	ア	i	イ	u	ウ	e	エ	o	オ
ka	カ	ki	キ	ku	ク	ke	ケ	ko	コ
sa	サ	shi	シ	su	ス	se	セ	so	ソ
ta	タ	chi	チ	tsu	ツ	te	テ	to	ト
na	ナ	ni	ニ	nu	ヌ	ne	ネ	no	ノ
ha	ハ	hi	ヒ	fu	フ	he	ヘ	ho	ホ
ma	マ	mi	ミ	mu	ム	me	メ	mo	モ
ya	ヤ			yu	ユ			yo	ヨ
ra	ラ	ri	リ	ru	ル	re	レ	ro	ロ
wa	ワ								
n	ン								

Hiragana

a	あ	i	い	u	う	e	え	o	お
ka	か	ki	き	ku	く	ke	け	ko	こ
sa	さ	shi	し	su	す	se	せ	so	そ
ta	た	chi	ち	tsu	つ	te	て	to	と
na	な	ni	に	nu	ぬ	ne	ね	no	の
ha	は	hi	ひ	fu	ふ	he	へ	ho	ほ
ma	ま	mi	み	mu	む	me	め	mo	も
ya	や			yu	ゆ			yo	よ
ra	ら	ri	り	ru	る	re	れ	ro	ろ
wa	わ								
n	ん								

Traditionally, Japanese is written in vertical columns and read right to left. However, the Western way of writing from left to right, horizontally from top to bottom is increasingly being used. In the media and on signs you'll see a mixture of the two ways of writing.

Grammar

There are several significant **grammar** differences between Japanese and European languages. **Verbs** do not change according to the person or number, so that *ikimasu* can mean "I go", "he/she/it goes", or "we/they go". **Pronouns**, such as I and they, are usually omitted, since it's clear from the context who or what the speaker is referring to. There are no **definite articles**, and **nouns** stay the same whether they refer to singular or plural words.

From the point of view of English grammar, Japanese **sentences** are structured back to front. An English-speaker would say "I am going to Tokyo" which in Japanese would translate directly as "Tokyo to going". Placing the sound "ka" at the end of a verb indicates a **question**, hence *Tokyo e ikimasu-ka* means "Are you going to Tokyo?" There are also levels of **politeness** to contend with, which alter the way the verb is conjugated, and sometimes change the word entirely. For the most part, stick to the polite **masu** form of verbs and you'll be fine.

If you want to learn more about the language and have a wider range of expressions and vocabulary at your command than those listed below, invest in a phrasebook or dictionary. *Japanese: A Rough Guide Phrasebook* is user-friendly and combines essential phrases and expressions with a dictionary section and menu reader. The phonetic translations in this phrasebook are rendered slightly differently from the standard way *rōmaji* is written in this book, as an aid to pronunciation. One of the best books for learning Japanese more thoroughly is *Japanese For Busy People* (Kodansha), which comes in three parts and is often used as a set text in Japanese-language classes. A worthy alternative, although more difficult to buy outside of Japan, is *Communicative Japanese for Time Pressed People* (Aratake Publishing).

Pronunciation

Throughout this book, Japanese words have been transliterated into the standard Hepburn system of romanization, called **rōmaji**. Pronunciation is as follows:

a as in rather	ai as in Thai
i as in macaroni, or ee	ei as in weight
u as in put, or oo	ie as in two separate sounds, ee-eh
e as in bed; e is always pronounced, even at the end of a word	ue as in two separate sounds, oo-eh
o as in not	g, a hard sound as in girl
ae as in the two separate sounds, ah-eh	s as in mass (never z)
	y as in yet

A bar over a vowel or "ii" means that the vowel sound is twice as long as a vowel without a bar. Only where words are well known in English, such as Tokyo, Kyoto, judo and shogun, have we not used a bar to indicate long vowel sounds. Sometimes, vowel sounds are shortened or softened; for example, the verb *desu* sounds more like *des* when pronounced, and *sukiyaki* like *skiyaki*. Apart from this, all syllables in Japanese words are evenly stressed and pronounced in full. For example, Nagano is Na-ga-no, not Na-GA-no.

Useful words and phrases

Basics

Yes	*hai*	はい
No	*iie/chigaimasu*	いいえ／違います
OK	*daijōbu/ōkē*	だいじょうぶ／オーケー
Well ... (as in making things less definite)	*chotto*	ちょっと
Please (offering something)	*dōzo*	どうぞ
Please (asking for something)	*onegai shimasu*	お願いします
Excuse me	*sumimasen/shitsurei shimasu*	すみません／失礼します

I'm sorry	gomen nasai/sumimasen	ごめんなさい／すみません
Thanks (informal)	dōmo	どうも
Thank you	dōmo arigatō	どうもありがとう
Thank you very much	dōmo arigatō gozaimasu	どうもありがとうございます
What?	nani?	なに？
When?	itsu?	いつ？
Where?	doko?	どこ？
Who?	dare?	だれ？
This	kore	これ
That	sore	それ
That (over there)	are	あれ
How many?	ikutsu?	いくつ？
How much?	ikura?	いくら？
I want (x)	Watashi wa (x) ga hoshii desu	私は（x）がほしいです
I don't want (x)	Watashi wa (x) ga irimasen	私は（x）がいりません
Is it possible . . . ?	. . . koto ga dekimasu ka	。。。ことができますか
It is not possible	. . . koto ga dekimasen	。。。ことができません
Is it . . . ?	. . . desu ka	。。。ですか
Can you please help me	Tetsudatte kuremasen ka	手伝ってくれませんか
I don't speak Japanese	Nihongo wa hanashimasen	日本語は話しません
I don't read Japanese	Nihongo wa yomimasen	日本語は読みません
Can you speak English?	Eigo ga dekimasu ka	英語ができますか？
Is there someone who can interpret?	Tsūyaku wa imasu ka	通訳はいますか？
Could you please speak slowly	Motto yukkuri hanashite kuremasen ka	もっとゆっくり話してくれませんか？
Please say that again	Mō ichido itte kuremasen ka	もう一度言ってくれませんか
I understand/I see	Wakarimasu/Naruhodo	わかります／なるほど
I don't understand	Wakarimasen	わかりません
What does this mean?	Imi wa nan desu ka	意味は何ですか？
How do you say (x) in Japanese?	Nihongo de (x) o nan-te iimasu ka	日本語で（x）を何て言いますか？
What's this called?	Kore wa nan-to iimasu ka	これは何と言いますか？
How do you pronounce this character?	Kono kanji wa nan-te iimasu ka	この漢字は何て言いますか？
Please write in English/Japanese	Eigo/Nihongo de kaite kudasai	英語／日本語で書いてください
Clean/dirty	kirei/kitanai	きれい／きたない
Hot/cold	atsui/samui	あつい／さむい
Fast/slow	hayai/osoi	はやい／おそい
Pretty/ugly	kirei/minikui	きれい／みにくい
Interesting/boring	omoshiroi/tsumaranai	おもしろい／つまらない

Greetings and basic courtesies

Hello/Good day	Konnichiwa	こんにちは
Good morning	Ohayō gozaimasu	おはようございます
Good evening	Konbanwa	こんばんは
Good night (when leaving)	Osaki ni	お先に

Good night (when going to bed)	Oyasuminasai	おやすみなさい
How are you?	O-genki desu ka	お元気ですか
I'm fine (informal)	Genki desu	元気です
I'm fine, thanks	Okagesama de	おかげさまで
How do you do/Nice to meet you	Hajimemashite	はじめまして
Don't mention it /you're welcome	Dō itashimashite	どういたしまして
I'm sorry	Gomen nasai	ごめんなさい
Just a minute please	Chotto matte kudasai	ちょっと待ってください
Goodbye	Sayonara	さよなら
Goodbye (informal)	Dewa mata/Jā ne	では又／じゃあね

Chitchat

What's your name?	Shitsurei desu ga o-namae wa	失礼ですがお名前は？
My name is (x)	Watashi no namae wa (x) desu	私の名前は（x）です
Where are you from?	O-kuni wa doko desu ka	おくにはどこですか？
Britain	Eikoku/Igirisu	英国／イギリス
Ireland	Airurando	アイルランド
America	Amerika	アメリカ
Australia	Ōsutoraria	オーストラリア
Canada	Kanada	カナダ
Japan	Nihon	日本
Outside Japan	Gaikoku	外国
New Zealand	Nyū Jiirando	ニュージーランド
How old are you?	Ikutsu desu ka	いくつですか？
I am (age)	(age) sai desu	（ａｇｅ）才です
Are you married?	Kekkon shite imasu ka	結婚していますか？
I am married/not married	Kekkon shite imasu/imasen	結婚しています／いません
Do you like . . . ?	. . . suki desu ka	。。。好きですか？
I do like	. . . suki desu	。。。好きです
I don't like	. . . suki dewa arimasen	。。。好きではありません
What's your job?	O-shigoto wa nan desu ka	お仕事は何ですか？
I work for a company	Kaishain desu	会社員です
I'm a tourist	Kankō kyaku desu	観光客です
Really?	hontō	本当？
That's a shame	Zannen desu	残念です
It can't be helped	Shikata ga nai/shō ga nai (informal)	仕方がない／しょうがない

Numbers, time and dates

There are special ways of **counting** different things in Japanese. The safest option is to stick to the most common first translation, used when counting time and quantities and measurements, with added qualifiers such as minutes (*pun/fun*) or yen (*en*). The second translations are sometimes used for counting objects, as in *biiru futatsu, onegai shimasu* (two beers, please). From ten, there is only one set of numbers. For four, seven and nine alternatives to the first translation are used in some circumstances.

English	romaji	romaji	kanji	kana
Zero	zero		ゼロ	
One	ichi	hitotsu	一	ひとつ
Two	ni	futatsu	二	ふたつ
Three	san	mittsu	三	みっつ
Four	yon/shi	yottsu	四	よっつ
Five	go	itsutsu	五	いつつ
Six	roku	muttsu	六	むっつ
Seven	shichi/nana	nanatsu	七	ななつ
Eight	hachi	yattsu	八	やっつ
Nine	ku/kyū	kokonotsu	九	ここのつ
Ten	jū	tō	十	とう
Eleven	jū-ichi		十一	
Twelve	jū-ni		十二	
Twenty	ni-jū		二十	
Twenty-one	ni-jū-ichi		二十一	
Thirty	san-jū		三十	
One hundred	hyaku		百	
Two hundred	ni-hyaku		二百	
Thousand	sen		千	
Ten thousand	ichi-man		一万	
One hundred thousand	jū-man		十万	
One million	hyaku-man		百万	
One hundred million	ichi-oku		一億	

English	romaji	kanji
Now	ima	今
Today	kyō	今日
Morning	asa	朝
Evening	yūgata	夕方
Night	yoru	夜
Tomorrow	ashita	明日
The day after tomorrow	asatte	あさって
Yesterday	kinō	昨日
Week	shūkan	週間
Month	gatsu	月
Year	nen/toshi	年
Monday	Getsuyōbi	月曜日
Tuesday	Kayōbi	火曜日
Wednesday	Suiyōbi	水曜日
Thursday	Mokuyōbi	木曜日
Friday	Kin'yōbi	金曜日
Saturday	Doyōbi	土曜日
Sunday	Nichiyōbi	日曜日

English	romaji	kanji
What time is it?	Ima nan-ji desu ka	今何時ですか
It's 10 o'clock	Jū-ji desu	十時です
10.20	Jū-ji ni-juppun	十時二十分
10.30	Jū-ji han	十時半

10.50	*Jū-ichi-ji juppun mae*	十一時十分前
AM	*gozen*	午前
PM	*gogo*	午後

Getting around

Aeroplane	*hikōki*	飛行機
Airport	*kūkō*	空港
Bus	*basu*	バス
Bus stop	*basu tei*	バス亭
Train	*densha*	電車
Station	*eki*	駅
Subway	*chikatetsu*	地下鉄
Ferry	*ferii*	フェリー
Left-luggage office	*ichiji azukarijo*	一時預かり所
Coin locker	*koin rokkā*	コインロッカー
Ticket office	*kippu uriba*	切符売り場
Ticket	*kippu*	切符
One-way	*kata-michi*	片道
Return	*ōfuku*	往復
Bicycle	*jitensha*	自転車
Taxi	*takushii*	タクシー
Map	*chizu*	地図
Where is (x)?	*(x) wa doko desu ka*	(x) はどこですか
Straight ahead	*massugu*	まっすぐ
In front of	*mae*	前
Right	*migi*	右
Left	*hidari*	左
North	*kita*	北
South	*minami*	南
East	*higashi*	東
West	*nishi*	西

Places

Temple	*otera/odera/-ji/-in*	お寺／一寺／一院
Shrine	*jinja/jingū/-gū/-taisha*	神社／神宮／一宮／一大社
Castle	*-jō*	一城
Park	*kōen*	公園
River	*kawa/gawa*	川
Street	*tōri/dōri/michi*	通り／道
Bridge	*hashi/bashi*	橋
Museum	*hakubutsukan*	博物館
Art gallery	*bijutsukan*	美術館
Garden	*niwa/teien/-en*	庭／庭園／一園
Island	*shima/jima/tō*	島
Slope	*saka/zaka*	坂
Hill	*oka*	岡

LANGUAGE | Useful words and phrases

Mountain	yama/-san/-take	山／岳
Hot spring spa	onsen	温泉
Lake	-ko	一湖
Bay	-wan	一湾

Accommodation

Hotel	hoteru	ホテル
Traditional-style inn	ryokan	旅館
Guesthouse	minshuku	民宿
Youth hostel	yūsu hosuteru	ユースホステル
Single room	shinguru rūmu	シングルルーム
Double room	daburu rūmu	ダブルルーム
Twin room	tsuin rūmu	ツインルーム
Dormitory	kyōdō/ōbeya	共同／大部屋
Japanese-style room	washitsu	和室
Western-style room	yōshitsu	洋室
Western-style bed	beddo	ベッド
Bath	o-furo	お風呂

Do you have any vacancies?	Aita heya wa arimasu ka	空いた部屋はありますか
I'd like to make a reservation	Yoyaku o shitai no desu ga	予約をしたいのですが
I have a reservation	Yoyaku shimashita	予約しました
I don't have a reservation	Yoyaku shimasen deshita	予約しませんでした
How much is it per person?	Hitori ikura desu ka	一人いくらですか
Does that include meals?	Shokuji wa tsuite imasu ka	食事はついていますか
I would like to stay one night/two nights	Hitoban/futaban tomarimasu	一晩／二晩泊まります
I would like to see the room	Heya o misete kudasaimasen ka	部屋を見せてくださいませんか
Key	kagi	鍵
Passport	pasupōto	パスポート

Shopping, money and banks

Shop	mise/-ten/-ya	店／屋
How much is it?	Kore wa ikura desu ka	これはいくらですか
It's too expensive	Taka-sugimasu	高すぎます
Is there anything cheaper?	Mō sukoshi yasui mono wa arimasu ka	もう少し安いものはありますか
Do you accept credit cards?	Kurejitto kādo wa tsukaemasu ka	クレジットカードは使えますか
I'm just looking	Miru dake desu	見るだけです
Yen	Yen/-en	円
UK pounds	pondo	ポンド
Dollars	doru	ドル
Foreign exchange	gaikoku-kawase	外国為替
Bank	ginkō	銀行
Travellers' cheque	toraberāzu chekku	トラベラーズチェック

Post and telephones

Post office	*yūbinkyoku*	郵便局
Letter	*tegami*	手紙
Postcard	*hagaki*	葉書
Stamp	*kitte*	切手
Airmail	*kōkūbin*	航空便
Poste restante	*tomeoki*	留置
Telephone	*denwa*	電話
International telephone call	*kokusai-denwa*	国際電話
Reverse charge/collect call	*korekuto-kōru*	コレクトコール
Telephone card	*terefon kādo*	テレフォンカード
I would like to call (place)	*(place) e denwa o kaketai no desu*	へ電話をかけたいのです
I would like to send a fax to (place)	*(place) e fakkusu shitai no desu*	へファックスしたいのです

Health

Hospital	*byōin*	病院
Pharmacy	*yakkyoku*	薬局
Medicine	*kusuri*	薬
Doctor	*isha*	医者
Dentist	*haisha*	歯医者
I'm ill	*byōki desu*	病気です

Food and drink

Basics

Bar	*nomiya*	飲み屋
Café/coffee shop	*kissaten*	喫茶店
Cafeteria	*shokudō*	食堂
Pub	*pabu*	パブ
Pub-style restaurant	*izakaya*	居酒屋
Restaurant	*resutoran*	レストラン
Restaurant specializing in charcoal-grilled foods	*robatayaki*	炉端焼
Breakfast	*asa-gohan*	朝ご飯
Lunch	*hiru-gohan*	昼ご飯
Dinner	*ban-gohan*	晩ご飯
Boxed meal	*bentō*	弁当
Set meal	*teishoku*	定食
Daily special set meal	*higawari-teishoku*	日変わり定食
Menu	*menyū*	メニュー
How much is that?	*ikura desu ka*	いくらですか？
I would like (a) ...	*(a) ... o onegai shimasu*	（a）をお願いします
May I have the bill?	*okanjō o onegai shimasu*	お勘定をお願いします

Staple foods

Bean curd tofu	tōfu	豆腐
Butter	batā	バター
Bread	pan	パン
Dried seaweed	nori	のり
Egg	tamago	卵
Fermented soyabean paste	miso	味噌
Garlic	ninniku	にんにく
Oil	abura	油
Pepper	koshō	こしょう
Rice	gohan	ご飯
Salt	shio	塩
Soy sauce	shōyu	しょうゆ
Sugar	satō	砂糖

Fruit, vegetables and salads

Fruit	kudamono	果物
Apple	ringo	りんご
Banana	banana	バナナ
Grapefruit	gurēpufurūtsu	グレープフルーツ
Grapes	budō	ぶどう
Japanese plum	ume	うめ
Lemon	remon	レモン
Melon	meron	メロン
Orange	orenji	オレンジ
Peach	momo	桃
Pear	nashi	なし
Persimmon	kaki	柿
Pineapple	painappuru	パイナップル
Strawberry	ichigo	いちご
Tangerine	mikan	みかん
Watermelon	suika	すいか

Vegetables	yasai	野菜
Salad	sarada	サラダ
Aubergine	nasu	なす
Beans	mame	豆
Beansprouts	moyashi	もやし
Carrot	ninjin	にんじん
Cauliflower	karifurawā	カリフラワー
Green pepper	piiman	ピーマン
Green horseradish	wasabi	わさび
Leek	negi	ねぎ
Mushroom	kinoko	きのこ
Onion	tamanegi	たまねぎ
Potato	poteto	ポテト

Radish	daikon	だいこん
Sweetcorn	kōn	コーン
Tomato	tomato	トマト

Fish and seafood dishes

Fish	sakana	魚
Shellfish	kai	貝
Raw fish	sashimi	さしみ
Sushi	sushi	寿司
Sushi mixed selection	nigiri-zushi	にぎり寿司
Sushi rolled in crisp seaweed	maki-zushi	まき寿司
Sushi topped with fish, egg and vegetables	chirashi-zushi	ちらし寿司
Abalone	awabi	あわび
Blowfish	fugu	ふぐ
Cod	tara	たら
Crab	kani	かに
Eel	unagi	うなぎ
Herring	nishin	にしん
Horse mackerel	aji	あじ
Lobster	ise-ebi	伊勢海老
Octopus	tako	たこ
Oyster	kaki	かき
Prawn	ebi	えび
Sea bream	tai	たい
Sea urchin	uni	うに
Squid	ika	いか
Sweet smelt	ayu	あゆ
Tuna	maguro	まぐろ
Yellowtail	buri	ぶり

Meat and meat dishes

Meat	niku	肉
Beef	gyūniku	牛肉
Chicken	toriniku	鳥肉
Lamb	ramu	ラム
Pork	butaniku	豚肉
Breaded, deep-fried slice of pork	tonkatsu	とんかつ
Chicken, other meat and vegetables grilled on skewers	yakitori	焼き鳥
Skewers of food dipped in breadcrumbs and deep-fried	kushiage	串揚げ
Stew including meat (or seafood), vegetables and noodles	nabe	鍋
Thin beef slices cooked in broth	shabu-shabu	しゃぶしゃぶ
Thin beef slices braised in a sauce	sukiyaki	すきやき

Other dishes

Buddhist-style vegetarian cuisine	*shōjin-ryōri*	精進料理
Chinese-style noodles	*rāmen*	ラーメン
Chinese-style dumplings	*gyōza*	ぎょうざ
Fried noodles	*yakisoba/udon*	焼そば／うどん
Stewed chunks of tofu, vegetables and fish on skewers	*oden*	おでん
Thin buckwheat noodles	*soba*	そば
Soba in a hot soup	*kake-soba*	かけそば
Cold soba for dipping in a sauce	*zaru-soba/mori-soba*	ざるそば／もりそば
Thick wheat noodles	*udon*	うどん
Fried rice	*chāhan*	チャーハン
Lightly battered seafood and vegetables	*tempura*	天ぷら
Meat, vegetable and fish cooked in soy sauce and sweet sake	*teriyaki*	照り焼き
Mild curry served with rice	*karē raisu*	カレーライス
Octopus in balls of batter	*takoyaki*	たこやき
Pounded rice cakes	*mocihi*	もち
Rice topped with fish, meat or vegetable	*donburi*	どんぶり
Rice triangles wrapped in crisp seaweed	*onigiri*	おにぎり
Savoury pancakes	*okonomiyaki*	お好み焼
Chinese food	*Chūka-/Chūgoku-ryōri*	中華／中国料理
French food	*Furansu-ryōri*	フランス料理
Italian food	*Itaria-ryōri*	イタリア料理
Japanese-style food	*washoku*	和食
Japanese haute cuisine	*kaiseki-ryōri*	懐石料理
Korean food	*Kankoku-ryōri*	韓国料理
"No-nationality" food	*mukokuseki-ryōri*	無国籍料理
Thai food	*Tai-ryōri*	タイ料理
Western-style food	*yōshoku*	洋食

Drinks

Beer	*biiru*	ビール
Black tea	*kōcha*	紅茶
Coffee	*kōhii*	コーヒー
Fruit juice	*jūsu*	ジュース
Green tea	*sencha*	煎茶
Milk	*miruku*	ミルク
Oolong tea	*ūron-cha*	ウーロン茶
Powdered green tea	*matcha*	抹茶
Water	*mizu*	水
Whisky	*uisukii*	ウイスキー
Whisky and water	*mizu-wari*	水割り
Sake (rice wine)	*sake/nihon-shu*	酒／日本酒
Wine	*wain*	ワイン

Glossary

banzai Traditional Japanese cheer, meaning "10,000 years".

bashi Bridge.

basho Sumo tournament.

bodhisattva Buddhist who has forsaken *nirvana* to work for the salvation of all humanity.

-chō, or **machi** Subdivision of the city, smaller than a *ku*.

-chōme Area of the city consisting of a few blocks.

dai Big or great.

daimyō Feudal lords.

-dōri Main road.

Edo Pre-1868 name for Tokyo.

gaijin Foreigner.

gawa River.

geisha Traditional female entertainer accomplished in the arts.

geta Wooden sandals.

higashi East.

-ji Buddhist temple.

-jingū, or **-jinja** Shinto shrine.

Jizō Buddhist protector of children, travellers and the dead.

-jō Castle.

kampai "Cheers" when drinking.

kanji Japanese script derived from Chinese characters.

Kannon Buddhist Goddess of Mercy.

katakana Phonetic script used mainly for writing foreign words in Japanese.

kimono Literally "clothes" but usually referring to women's traditional dress.

kita North.

koban Local police box.

-kōen/gyoen Public park.

-ku Principal administrative division of the city, usually translated as "ward".

matsuri Festival.

Meiji Period named after the Emperor Meiji (1868–1912).

mikoshi Portable shrine used in festivals.

minami South.

minshuku Family-run lodge, similar to a bed-and-breakfast, cheaper than a *ryokan*.

mon Gate.

netsuke Small, intricately carved toggles for fastening the cords of cloth bags.

nishi West.

noren Split curtain hanging in shop and restaurant doorways.

obi Wide sash worn with kimono.

okanshi Japanese sweets.

onsen Hot spring, generally developed for bathing.

pachinko Vertical pinball machines.

rōnin Masterless samurai.

ryokan Traditional Japanese inn.

samurai Warrior class who were retainers of the *daimyō*.

sentō Neighbourhood public bath.

Shinkansen Bullet train.

Shinto Japan's indigenous religion, based on the premise that gods inhabit all natural things, both animate and inanimate.

Shitamachi Low-lying, working-class districts of east Tokyo, nowadays usually referring to Asakusa and Ueno.

shogun The military rulers of Japan before 1868.

shōji Paper-covered sliding screens used to divide rooms or cover windows.

soaplands Brothel.

sumi-e Ink paintings.

sumo Japan's national sport, a form of heavyweight wrestling which evolved from ancient Shinto divination rites.

tatami Rice-straw matting, the traditional covering for floors.

-tera/-dera Buddhist temple.

torii Gate to a Shinto shrine.

ukiyo-e "Pictures of the floating world", colourful woodblock prints which became particularly popular in the late eighteenth century.

washi Japanese paper.

yakuza Professional criminal gangs.

yukata Loose cotton robe worn as a dressing gown in a ryokan.

Rough
Guides

advertiser

Rough Guides travel...

298

Rough Guides are available from good bookstores worldwide. New titles are
published every month. Check www.roughguides.com for the latest news.

...music & reference

Also! More than 120 Rough Guide music CDs are available from all good book
and record stores. Listen in at www.worldmusic.net

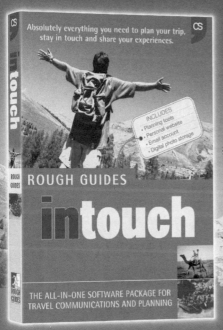

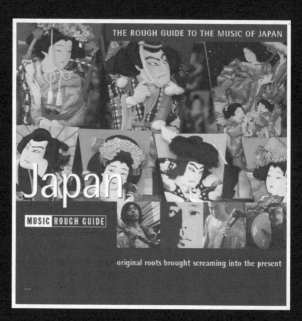

small print +

Index

A Rough Guide to Rough Guides

In the summer of 1981, Mark Ellingham, a recent graduate from Bristol University, was travelling round Greece and couldn't find a guidebook that really met his needs. On the one hand there were the student guides, insistent on saving every last cent, and on the other the heavyweight cultural tomes whose authors seemed to have spent more time in a research library than lounging away the afternoon at a taverna or on the beach.

In a bid to avoid getting a job, Mark and a small group of writers set about creating their own guidebook. It was a guide to Greece that aimed to combine a journalistic approach to description with a thoroughly practical approach to travellers' needs – a guide that would incorporate culture, history and contemporary insights with a critical edge, together with up-to-date, value-for-money listings. Back in London, Mark and the team finished their Rough Guide, as they called it, and talked Routledge into publishing the book.

That first *Rough Guide to Greece*, published in 1982, was a student scheme that became a publishing phenomenon. The immediate success of the book – with numerous reprints and a Thomas Cook Prize shortlisting – spawned a series that rapidly covered dozens of destinations. Rough Guides had a ready market among low-budget backpackers, but soon also acquired a much broader and older readership that relished Rough Guides' wit and inquisitiveness as much as their enthusiastic, critical approach. Everyone wants value for money, but not at any price.

Rough Guides soon began supplementing the "rougher" information about hostels and low-budget listings with the kind of detail on restaurants and quality hotels that independent-minded visitors on any budget might expect, whether on business in New York or trekking in Thailand.

These days the guides – distributed worldwide by the Penguin Group – offer recommendations from shoestring to luxury and cover more than 200 destinations around the globe, including almost every country in the Americas and Europe, more than half of Africa and most of Asia and Australasia. Our ever-growing team of authors and photographers is spread all over the world, particularly in Europe, the USA and Australia.

In 1994, we published the *Rough Guide to World Music* and the *Rough Guide to Classical Music*, and a year later the *Rough Guide to the Internet*. All three books have become benchmark titles in their fields – which encouraged us to expand into other areas of publishing, mainly around popular culture. Rough Guides now publish:

- Travel guides to more than 200 worldwide destinations
- Dictionary phrasebooks to 22 major languages
- History guides ranging from Ireland to Islam
- Maps printed on rip-proof and waterproof Polyart™ paper
- Music guides running the gamut from Opera to Elvis
- Restaurant guides to London, New York and San Francisco
- Reference books on topics as diverse as the Weather and Shakespeare
- Sports guides from Formula 1 to Man Utd
- Pop culture books from *Lord of the Rings* to Cult TV
- World Music CDs in association with World Music Network

Visit **www.roughguides.com** to see our latest publications.

Rough Guide credits

Text editor: Gavin Thomas
Layout: Umesh Aggarwal, Ajay Verma
Cartography: Rajesh Mishra, Ashutosh
Bharti, Karobi Gogoi
Picture research: Harriet Mills
Proofreader: Derek Wilde
Editorial: **London** Martin Dunford, Kate
Berens, Helena Smith, Claire Saunders, Geoff
Howard, Gavin Thomas, Ruth Blackmore,
Polly Thomas, Richard Lim, Lucy Ratcliffe,
Clifton Wilkinson, Alison Murchie, Fran
Sandham, Sally Schafer, Alexander Mark
Rogers, Karoline Densley, Andy Turner, Ella
O'Donnell, Keith Drew, Edward Aves, Andrew
Lockett, Joe Staines, Duncan Clark, Peter
Buckley, Matthew Milton; **New York** Andrew
Rosenberg, Richard Koss, Hunter Slaton,
Chris Barsanti, Steven Horak
Design & Pictures: **London** Simon Bracken,
Dan May, Diana Jarvis, Mark Thomas, Jj
Luck, Harriet Mills; **Delhi** Madhulita
Mohapatra, Umesh Aggarwal, Ajay Verma,
Jessica Subramanian

Production: Julia Bovis, John McKay,
Sophie Hewat
Cartography: **London** Maxine Repath, Ed
Wright, Katie Lloyd-Jones, Miles Irving; **Delhi**
Manish Chandra, Rajesh Chhibber, Jai
Prakash Mishra, Ashutosh Bharti, Rajesh
Mishra, Animesh Pathak, Jasbir Sandhu,
Karobi Gogoi
Cover art direction: Louise Boulton
Online: **New York** Jennifer Gold, Cree
Lawson, Suzanne Welles, Benjamin Ross;
Delhi Manik Chauhan, Narender Kumar,
Shekhar Jha, Rakesh Kumar
Marketing & Publicity: **London** Richard
Trillo, Niki Smith, David Wearn, Chloë
Roberts, Demelza Dallow, Kristina Pentland;
New York Geoff Colquitt, Megan Kennedy
Finance: Gary Singh
Manager Delhi: Punita Singh
Series editor: Mark Ellingham
PA to Managing Director: Julie Sanderson
Managing Director: Kevin Fitzgerald

Publishing information

This third edition published February 2005 by
Rough Guides Ltd,
80 Strand, London WC2R 0RL
345 Hudson St, 4th Floor,
New York, NY 10014, USA
Distributed by the Penguin Group
Penguin Books Ltd,
80 Strand, London WC2R 0RL
Penguin Putnam, Inc.
375 Hudson Street, NY 10014, USA
Penguin Group (Australia)
250 Camberwell Road
Camberwell, Victoria 3124
Penguin Books Canada Ltd,
10 Alcorn Avenue, Toronto,
ON M4V 1E4, Canada
Penguin Group (New Zealand)
Cnr Rosedale and Airborne Roads, Albany,
Auckland, New Zealand
Typeset in Bembo and Helvetica to an original
design by Henry Iles.

Printed and bound in China

320pp includes index
A catalogue record for this book is available from
the British Library.
ISBN 1-84353-277-8
ISBN 13: 9-78184-353-277-4

The publishers and authors have done their best
to ensure the accuracy and currency of all the
information in **The Rough Guide to Tokyo**;
however, they can accept no responsibility for any
loss, injury or inconvenience sustained by any
traveller as a result of information or advice
contained in the guide.

3   5   7   9   8   6   4

Help us update

We've gone to a lot of effort to ensure that
the second edition of **The Rough Guide to
Tokyo** is accurate and up to date. However,
things change – places get "discovered",
opening hours are notoriously fickle,
restaurants and rooms raise prices or lower
standards. If you feel we've got it wrong or
left something out, we'd like to know, and if
you can remember the address, the price, the
time, the phone number, so much the better.

We'll credit all contributions, and send a
copy of the next edition (or any other Rough

Guide if you prefer) for the best letters.
Everyone who writes to us and isn't already a
subscriber will receive a copy of our full-
colour, thrice-yearly newsletter. Please mark
letters: "**Rough Guide Tokyo Update**" and
send to: Rough Guides, 80 Strand, London
WC2R 0RL, or Rough Guides, 4th Floor, 345
Hudson St, New York, NY 10014. Or send an
email to **mail@roughguides.com**.

Have your questions answered and tell
others about your trip at
www.roughguides.atinfopop.com.

Acknowledgements

Simon: Thanks to our diligent editor Gavin Thomas and kanji-supremo Sophie Branscombe back at base, and to Mark Sariban for his work on some of the day-trip sections of this book. Thanks also to the very helpful folks at JNTO in London. Much appreciated were the support of Sophie Hemmel, who arranged my stay at the Four Seasons Marunouchi, Nico Jayawardena for doing the same at the New Ōtani, and Mark Kobayashi for the Grand Hyatt. A huge thanks goes to Toshiko Kiyama, who showed me great hospitality, friendship and some wonderful places to eat. Cheers to Laura Holland, Robb Satterwhite, Gardner Robinson, Dan Riney and Gia Payne for fun nights out in Tokyo. As always Tada Taku did a fine job on fact checking and feeding us incredibly useful information. Finally, this book is lovingly dedicated to Tonny as a memory of our time in the city together.

Readers' letters

Thanks to the readers who wrote in with comments and suggestions: K. Behr, Fabrizio Bosco, Sachiyo Dinmore, Robin Hurford, Adriana Kulczak, Nurul & Petros Leksmono, Kazuhiro Takabatake, Harry Teale, Alison Tudor.

SMALL PRINT

Photo credits

NOTES

Index

Map entries are in colour

INDEX

INDEX

INDEX

315

Map symbols

maps are listed in the full index using coloured text

━━━ ··	Provincial boundary
━━━━	Motorway
═══	Major road
═══	Minor road
━━━	Pedestrianised street
:::::::::	Road under construction
- - - -	Path
────	River
— —	Ferry route
●- - -●	Cable car and stations
━■━	JR line
━━━	Shinkensen line
┼┼┼┼┼┼┼	Private rail line
··········	Funicular railway
– – –	Subway line
- - - -	Tram line
)·········(	Railway tunnel
■ ■ ■ ■	Wall
▲	Peak
◠	Cave
⚱	Waterfall
◆	Place of interest

@	Internet
ⓘ	Tourist office
Ⓔ	Embassy
Ⓢ	Subway station
★	Bus stop
⊠	Gate
⊞	Hospital
⊠	Post office
✈	Airport
‿	Bridge
⊙	Statue
●	Museum
Δ	Campsite
♨	Pagoda
⌵	Shrine
♠	Buddhist temple
▬	Building
⊞	Church
⬭	Stadium
⁺⁺⁺	Cemetery
▦	Park

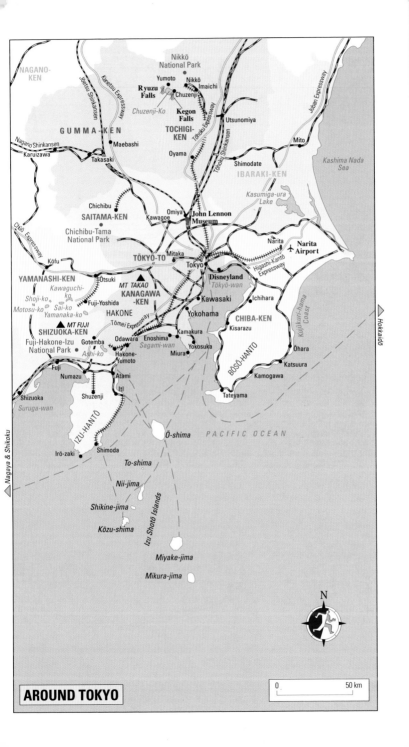

AROUND TOKYO

0   50 km

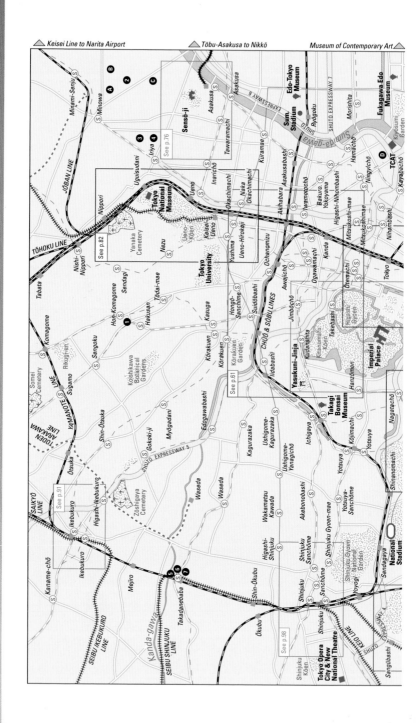

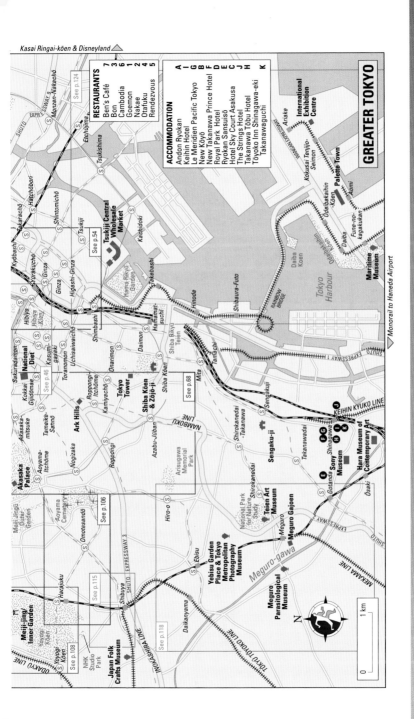

Kasai Ringai-kōen & Disneyland △

GREATER TOKYO

RESTAURANTS
Ben's Café	7
Bon	3
Cambodia	6
Goemon	1
Nakae	2
Otafuku	4
Rendezvous	5

ACCOMMODATION
Andon Ryokan	A
Keihin Hotel	I
Le Meridien Pacific Tokyo	G
New Kōyō	B
New Takanawa Prince Hotel	F
Royal Park Hotel	D
Ryokan Sansuisō	E
The Strings Hotel	C
Hotel Sky Court Asakusa	J
Takanawa Tōbu Hotel	H
Tōyoko Inn Shinagawa-eki Takanawaguchi	K

International Exhibition Centre

▷ Monorail to Haneda Airport

Monzen-Nakachō
See p.124

Etchūjima
Tsukishima

Kyōbashi
Sakaechō
Hatchōbori
Shintomichō

Ginza
Yūrakuchō
Hibiya
Ginza
Higashi-Ginza
Tsukiji
See p.54

Tsukiji Central Wholesale Market

Kachidoki

Hama Rikyū Garden

Takebashi

Hibiya-kōen
Shimbashi
Hamarikyū Teien
Hinode

Shibaura-Futo

RAINBOW BRIDGE

Tokyo Harbour

Daiba Kōen

Kokusai Tenjijo-Seimon
Odaibakaihin-kōen

Fune-no-kagakukan

Daiba

Aomi

Maritime Museum

Ariake

Palette Town

SHUTO EXPRESSWAY 1

KAGAN EXPRESSWAY

Sakuradamon
National Diet
Kasumi-gaseki

Kokkai Gijidōmae
See p.46

Toranomon
Uchisaiwaichō

Onarimon
Daimon
Hamamatsuchō

Shiba Rikyū Teien

Shiba Kōen

Tamachi

Roppongi-Itchōme
Kamiyachō

Tokyo Tower

Shiba Kōen & Zōjō-ji

Mita

See p.68

Sengakuji

KEIHIN KYUKO LINE

Akasaka-mitsuke
Tameike-Sannō

Ark Hills

Akasaka-Itchōme
Aoyama-Itchōme
Nogizaka

Roppongi

Azabu-Jūban

NAMBOKU LINE

Shirokanedai-Takanawa

Shirokanedai

Takanawadai

Sengaku-ji

Takanawa

F G
H J

Alasaka Palace

Arisugawa Memorial Park

Hiro-o

National Park for Nature Study

Shirokanedai

Teien Art Museum

Meguro

Gotanda

Shinagawa

E

Sony Museum

Hara Museum of Contemporary Art

Osaki

SHUTO EXPRESSWAY 3

Aoyama Cemetery
See p.106

Meiji-jingū Outer Garden

Omotesandō

Harajuku
See p.115

Shibuya
SHUTO EXPRESSWAY 3

Ebisu

Yebisu Garden Place & Tokyo Metropolitan Photography Museum

Daikanyama

Meguro-gawa

Meguro Gajoen

Meguro Parasitological Museum

MEKAMA LINE

SHUTO EXPRESSWAY

See p.108

Meiji-jingū/ Inner Garden

Yoyogi-Kōen

NHK Studio Park

Yoyogi Kōen

Japan Folk Crafts Museum

ODAKYU LINE

See p.118

INOKASHIRA LINE

TOKYO-TOYOKO LINE

N

0 1 km

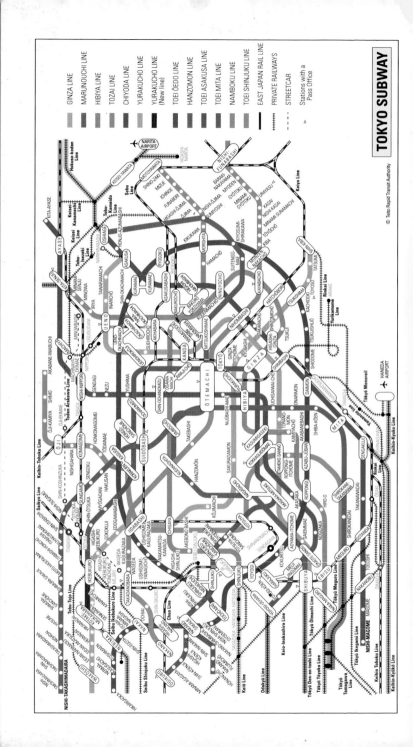

TOKYO SUBWAY

GINZA LINE
MARUNOUCHI LINE
HIBIYA LINE
TOZAI LINE
CHIYODA LINE
YURAKUCHO LINE
YURAKUCHO LINE (New line)
TOEI OEDO LINE
HANZOMON LINE
TOEI ASAKUSA LINE
TOEI MITA LINE
NAMBOKU LINE
TOEI SHINJUKU LINE
EAST JAPAN RAIL LINE
PRIVATE RAILWAYS
STREETCAR
Stations with a Pass Office

© Teito Rapid Transit Authority